Memory, Reconciliation, and Reunions in South Korea

For Maya Stiller 선생님,

with gratitude,

Namhee

2024. 03. 17

Asia World
Series Editor: Mark Selden

This series charts the frontiers of Asia in global perspective. Central to its concerns are Asian interactions—political, economic, social, cultural, and historical—that are transnational and global, that cross and redefine borders and networks, including those of nation, region, ethnicity, gender, technology, and demography. It looks to multiple methodologies to chart the dynamics of a region that has been the home to major civilizations and is central to global processes of war, peace, and development in the new millennium.

Titles in the Series

Water: The Looming Crisis in India, by Binayak Ray
Windows on the Chinese World: Reflections by Five Historians, by Clara Wing-chung Ho
Tommy's Sunset, by Hisako Tsurushima
Lake of Heaven: An Original Translation of the Japanese Novel by Ishimure Michiko, by Bruce Allen
Imperial Subjects as Global Citizens: Nationalism, Internationalism, and Education in Japan, by Mark Lincicome
Japan in the World: Shidehara Kijūrō, Pacifism, and the Abolition of War, Volumes I and II, by Klaus Schlichtmann
Filling the Hole in the Nuclear Future: Art and Popular Culture Respond to the Bomb, edited by Robert Jacobs
Radicalism, Revolution, and Reform in Modern China: Essays in Honor of Maurice Meisner, edited by Catherine Lynch, Robert B. Marks, and Paul G. Pickowicz
The "Other" Karen in Myanmar: Ethnic Minorities and the Struggle without Arms, by Ardeth Thawnghmung
A Localized Culture of Welfare: Entitlements, Stratification, and Identity in a Chinese Lineage Village, by Kwok-shing Chan
Malay Kingship in Kedah: Religion, Trade, and Society, by Maziar Mozaffari Falarti
Refining Nature in Modern Japanese Literature: The Life and Art of Shiga Naoya, by Nanyan Guo
Heritage Politics: Shuri Castle and Okinawa's Incorporation into Modern Japan, 1879-2000, by Tze May Loo
Yokohama Street Life: The Precarious Career of a Japanese Day Laborer, by Tom Gill
Memory, Reconciliation, and Reunions in South Korea: Crossing the Divide, by Nan Kim

Memory, Reconciliation, and Reunions in South Korea

Crossing the Divide

Nan Kim

LEXINGTON BOOKS
Lanham • Boulder • New York • London

Published by Lexington Books
An imprint of The Rowman & Littlefield Publishing Group, Inc.
4501 Forbes Boulevard, Suite 200, Lanham, Maryland 20706
www.rowman.com

Unit A, Whitacre Mews, 26-34 Stannary Street, London SE11 4AB

British Library Cataloguing in Publication Information Available

Library of Congress Cataloging-in-Publication Data

Kim, Nan, 1969-
Memory, reconciliation, and reunions in South Korea : crossing the divide / Nan Kim.
pages cm. -- (Asiaworld)
Includes bibliographical references and index.
ISBN 978-0-7391-8471-4 (cloth : alk. paper) -- ISBN 978-1-4985-2503-9 (pbk.: alk. paper)
ISBN 978-0-7391-8472-1 (electronic)
1. Family reunification--Korea (South) 2. Korean reunification question (1945-)--Social aspects. 3.
Korea (South)--Relations--Korea (North) 4. Korea (North)--Relations--Korea (South) I. Title.
HQ682.5.K5489 2015
951.9'04--dc23
                                    2015022311

Printed in the United States of America

For my parents

Table of Contents

List of Illustrations   ix

Acknowledgments   xi

Notes on Methodology, Translation, and Transliteration   xvii

Introduction   1

Part I: Unsettling the Past
1   Historicizing Korea's Geopolitical Liminality   39
2   Fateful Passages, In-Between States   67

Part II: Centering the Margin
3   Anti-Commemorations   95
4   Threshold Rituals, Fragility, and National Intimacy   113

Part III: Crossing Over
5   Impossible Returns   143
6   Ethical Traversals   161
Conclusion: Meeting with the Past   187
Epilogue: The Afterlife of Division   215

Bibliography   225

Index   243

About the Author   255

List of Illustrations

Fig. 0.1   Site of the first post-Summit reunions of
            North–South Korean separated families, COEX
            Convention Center, Seoul, August 15, 2000.   3

Fig. 0.2   Handmade signs, listing identifying details for
            persons missing since 1950–1953, were posted
            throughout KBS Plaza in Seoul during a special
            live telethon, "Finding Dispersed Families,"
            which lasted for nearly twenty weeks in 1983
            and resulted in over 10,000 successful reunions.   7

Fig. 0.3   Civilians flee from combat during the Second
            Battle of Seoul, September 1950.   13

Fig. 1.1   The Korean peninsula and the four stages of war.   54

Fig. 3.1   "Mother, the Road to the North Is Finally
            Open." Full-color print advertisement published
            in *Screen* magazine, a monthly South Korean
            general-interest periodical, May 2000.   99

Fig. 4.1   An image from the initial moments of the inter-
            Korean family meetings at the COEX
            Convention Center in Seoul, August 15, 2000.   119

Fig. 4.2   This photograph of an elderly South Korean
            mother wiping away the tears of her North
            Korean son became widely circulated as one of
            the iconic images from the August 2000
            reunions.   120

Fig. 5.1   Family members and journalists converged on
                the Seoul headquarters of the Korean Red Cross
                after news broke that a detailed list of candidates
                for the first post-Summit reunions had been
                transmitted from North Korea.   149

Fig. 6.1   In the film *Tae Guk Gi: The Brotherhood of War*
                (*T'aegŭkki hwinallimyŏ*), protagonists Jin-seok
                (Won Bin) and Jin-tae (Jang Dong-gun) are
                brothers conscripted into the army and
                forcefully separated from their family.   188

Fig. 6.2   At the meetings of war-separated families, it
                was common for par- ticipants to bring portraits
                of deceased parents who passed away prior to
                having the chance for reunion, despite having
                waited for several decades in anticipation of any
                news about a son or daughter missing since
                1950–1953.   220

Acknowledgments

Over the long duration of the project that yielded this book, I have been most beholden to those who spoke with me about their lives and shared their stories. At various junctures over several years, I would return to the challenge of attempting to do justice to their narratives and to the convergence of historical events that became this book's central focus, amid complexities that arose in life as well as shifting political conditions on the ground. If I succeeded at all in this endeavor, it was only with the guidance, encouragement, and remarkable support of many individuals, to whom I wish to convey my gratitude. The shortcomings that remain in the book are solely my own.

At Berkeley, where this project got its start, I am most indebted to Aihwa Ong as my doctoral advisor for her vital support and crucial intellectual guidance, as this project grew out of and repeatedly returned to lines of inquiry that had been inspired by her acute insights. I am greatly obliged also to Stefania Pandolfo, Paul Rabinow, and Andrew Barshay for their erudite counsel and encouragement as my dissertation committee members. I am very grateful to Kay Warren, who first got me into anthropology and showed me a path into my training; to Gi-Wook Shin, Edwin Wilmsen, Henry Em, and Eric Stover, for their thoughtful research guidance during my graduate studies in California; and to Katharine Moon, Laura Nelson, Michael Shin, Kyeyoung Park, Madeline Hsu, and David Eng, for sharing their wise advice and support as friends and colleagues at pivotal times when I had reached a crossroads.

While staying in Korea, initially for fieldwork and later for follow-up research and writing, I was honored to have worked with a group of remarkable colleagues. I am deeply thankful to my field advisors, Seong-nae Kim and Dongno Kim, and to Heonik Kwon and Byung-Ho Chung as informal advisors, for how they each shared their discerning wisdom to help me through all manner of intellectual quandaries and practical issues, and for how they thoughtfully brought me into contact with wider communities. It is hard to imagine how I would have undertaken this research without the friendship of Soo-Jung Lee, Gwi-Ok Kim, and Soomin Seo, whose respective keen insights and camaraderie brightened fieldwork from its outset and whose continued support over the years helped me reach the book's completion. I also learned so much from the time I spent in conversation with Eunshil Kim, Hyun Mee Kim, Sojin Park, Son Key-young, and Cho Uhn, and I am grateful for their intellectual engagement as well as their fortifying warmth of spirit. At various stages of research, writing, and revisions, I received judicious feedback as well as support and advice that proved pivotal, and in this regard I sincerely thank Chung Yong-Wook, Kim Dong-Choon, Mikyoung Kim, Cho Han Hae-Joang, Park Myung-Lim, Kwang Kyu Lee, Kwang-ok Kim, Cho Hyong, Dae-Sook Suh, Paik Hak Soon, Lee Sang-man, Kim Jae-yong, Jung Hyang-jin, Lee Woo-young, Jung Kyung-Lan, Kim Soyoung, Jin Heon Jung, Yoon Young Kim, Younsil Huh, and Gwisook Gwon. I am also indebted to Paik Nak-chung for helping me grasp how to reach the book's conclusion.

At Lexington Books, I wish to convey my gratitude to my editor Brian Hill, whose expert guidance saw me through the main stages of revising and preparing the manuscript for publication, and whose patient steadfast support was crucial for getting the book to its final stage. The project evolved past critical thresholds toward fruition thanks to my series editor Mark Selden, who offered salutary advice and extensive early feedback that would set the course for the manuscript's revisions. The book benefitted greatly from the careful attention of an anonymous reviewer and Steven Hugh Lee, who kindly came forward after the fact and revealed that he had been a reviewer of the manuscript. I am thankful also that my editor Sabah Ghulamali provided encouraging reassurance and guidance during initial phases of the editorial process, as did Justin Race in his preliminary feedback as acquisitions editor. I also thank Brighid Stone, who thoughtfully and adeptly handled various editorial issues that came up while wrapping up the final stages.

The book project came into its own while I was working as a faculty member in the Department of History at the University of Wisconsin–Milwaukee. For the time she generously dedicated as a mentor and dear friend, I owe a formidable debt of gratitude to Amanda Seligman. I am deeply thankful also for the sage advice and guidance I received from my chair, Merry Wiesner-Hanks, and for the encouraging support of my department colleagues. The process of publishing a time-sensitive piece in the *Journal of Asian Studies* proved pivotal for moving the book project forward, and in connection with that experience, I wish to express my wholehearted appreciation to Jeffrey Wasserstrom, Robert Oppenheim, Jennifer Munger, and Miri Kim.

Several friends and colleagues generously helped me make this book better by taking the time to read parts of the manuscript and to provide invaluable suggestions. Nancy Abelmann, Christine Hong, and Monica Kim each gave meticulous feedback on the project's framing and introduction, and I am thoroughly indebted, as their careful consideration yielded intellectual guideposts that became beacons throughout the revisions process. For their comments and suggestions on earlier versions of book chapters and other parts of the manuscript, I extend my very appreciative respects to Jae-Jung Suh, Erica Bornstein, Yuson Jung, Michael Herzfeld, Ellen Schattschneider, Jesook Song, Elise Prebin, Adam Bohnet, Christina Klein, Douglas Howland, Shuang Shen, Luc Walhain, Taeyon Kim, Tae Yang Kwak, Michael Robinson, Geetha Govindasamy, Craig Smith, Kim Mi-deok, Donald Nonini, David Price, Eric B. Ross, Susan Diduk, Erin Koch, Sarah Son, Manu Sobti, Jennifer Johung, Deborah Wilk, Jason Puskar, David Allen, Bruce Charlesworth, Paul Brodwin, Tracey Heatherington, Anna Mansson McGinty, Carolyn Seymour-Jorn, Ellen Amster, Shelleen Green, Tami Williams, Anika Wilson, and Molly Doane.

For their advice, encouragement, and collegial support regarding the book's research and its related projects, I also convey my sincere thanks and appreciation to Bruce Cumings, Namhee Lee, Theodore Jun Yoo, Alexis Dudden, Charles K. Armstrong, Laurel Kendall, Valérie Gelézeau, Ramsay Liem, Suzy Kim, Anne Hansen, Mark Bradley, Albert Park, Martin Hart-Landsberg, Sonia Ryang, John Lie, Young-a Park, Eleana Kim, Youngju Ryu, J. T. Takagi, Karin Lee, John Feffer, Richard Grinker, Judy Ju Hui Han, Ji-Yeon Yuh, Kyeong-Hee Choi, Andre Schmid, John Duncan, Jennifer Jung-Kim, Clark Sorenson, Jinhee Josephine Lee, Caren Freeman, June Hee Kwon, Kyoim Yun, Amy Levine, Hosu Kim, Shinee Han, Edward Reed, Charles Kim, Cristine Ahn, Thomas Malaby, Hyejin Yoon, DeAnn Borshay-Liem, Keum Hwi Lee, Soonja Lee, Jane Jin Kaisen, and KilSangYoon.

A number of grants and fellowships made this project possible, and I gratefully acknowledge that generous support: the Andrew W. Mellon Fellowship in Humanistic Studies from the Woodrow Wilson National Fellowship Foundation; the Fulbright Research grant from the Institute for International Education; a Korea Foundation grant administered through the Center for Korean Studies at UC–Berkeley; the University of California's Chancellor's Opportunity Fellowship; the Summer Institute fellowship at the Columbia University Oral History Institute; Foreign Language Area Studies fellowships from the U.S. Department of Education; and, at UW–Milwaukee, the Center for 21st Century Studies fellowship, the Graduate School Research Committee Award, and a faculty travel grant from the Center for International Education. Research for this book was also supported through resident-scholar affiliations with Yonsei University's Institute for Social Development Studies, the Korea Development Institute (KDI) School of Public Policy and Management, and UW–Milwaukee's Center for International Education. I also benefitted from opportunities to present my work in a variety of settings, and in this regard I thank the Korea Workshop at the University of Illinois at Urbana-Champaign, the Edmund A. Walsh School of Foreign Service at Georgetown University, the Sigur Center for Asian Studies at George Washington University, the Department of Sociology/Anthropology at Denison University, the Department of Anthropology and the Institute for Cross-Cultural Studies at Seoul National University, and the Yeongwol-Yonsei International Forum. I also wish to express my appreciation for pivotal support from the Beyond the Korean War project, which is sponsored by the Academy of Korean Studies and hosted within the Division of Social Anthropology at Cambridge University.

The final draft of the book was completed during a semester at Korea University as a Visiting Scholar at the International Center for Korean Studies at the Research Institute of Korean Studies; I am indebted to RIKS Director Choe Yong Chul, ICKS Research Professor Seungyoun Choi, and the ICKS staff, as that period of dedicated writing was indispensable. I was fortunate to work with wonderful research assistants at different stages of the project: Ayun Yoo and Sungmi Cho in Korea, and JaYoung Oh, J. J. Choi, and Seon Joo So in the United States. I greatly appreciate the kindness of We Jung Yi and particularly Saehee Chang, who generously stepped in to help out with further research assistance as friends and colleagues.

I also wish to acknowledge my appreciation to the National Archives of Korea for permitting me to use several images from its photography holdings in Seongnam. I am grateful to David Douglas Duncan for personally granting permission to publish his photograph, *Seoul Staircase, Korean War 1950*; to Linda Briscoe Meyers for facilitating that communication through the Harry Ransom Center at UT–Austin; and to Kyleigh Heggie for arranging permission from the Australian Department of Veterans' Affairs for the use of its Korean War map illustration. In Milwaukee, graphic artist Trevor G. Berman did excellent work adapting that map and refining the digitization of photographic images in the book.

I am thankful to several individuals for their friendship, valuable feedback, and kind support in many forms. In addition to those named above, they include Milwaukee-area friends and colleagues Patrice Petro, Kris Ruggiero, Neal Pease, Tasha Oren, Stewart Ikeda, Jasmine Alinder, Aims McGuinness, Marc Levine, Margo Anderson, David Buck, Sally and Ihab Hassan, Aneesh Aneesh, Sandra Braman, Rachel Buff, Robert Smith, Jeffrey Merrick, Carla Bagnoli, Michelle and Michael McCoy, Rachel Young-Binter, Mark McDonough, Margaret Keehn, Alma Regalia, Sunwoong Kim, Yong-Cheol Kim, Aparna Datey, Unchu Ko, Sam Knox, Hyunjoo Han, Gwi-

Seok Peggy Hong, Bill Sell, Jean Dow, Rob Ater, Deborah Block, Johanna and John Allen, and Lauren Beckmann; friends from Bay Area days Ebba Segerburg, Amy Lonetree, Annette Kim, Dorothy Wang, Damani Partridge, Frédéric Keck, Rashmi Sadana, Grace Lee, Jaeyoun Won, Minkoo Kim, Jennifer Chun, Geon Soo Han, Sunny Vergara, Diana Blank, Jody Ranck, Sara Dorow, and Hildi and S. W. Kang; and long-time friends Aiyoung Choi, Winnie Hu, Dusty Clayton, Jamie Lew, Helen Song, Evelyn and Ben Gilbert-Bair, Aimée Gilbert-Loinaz, Terry Hong, and Kristina Chew. To my co-working community of academic writers, Karen, Kate, Kirsten, Cheryl, and Tobia, I send big cheers and my warm appreciation.

This book is dedicated in memory of Gloria Emerson and Jonathan Schell, for it was their teaching, prescient advice, and humane convictions as former war correspondents that altered my path as an undergraduate, re-directing me from pursuing very different aspirations toward eventually studying divided Korea. My appreciation extends also to Micah Sifry, Joanne Wypijewski, Roane Carey, and Victor Navasky, in sheepish recognition that it was while fact-checking as a young intern at *The Nation* that I learned how little I knew about the Korean War. I am greatly indebted also to John McPhee, Thomas Keenan, LynNell Hancock, Diana Fuss, and Eduardo Cadava, for their dedicated engagement as writers, scholars, educators, and mentors, which left a deep impression that would stay with me many years later.

To our dearly cherished Lee Young-ja *halmŏni*, and in memory of three other remarkable elders, Lee Hak-seon, Gill-Chin Lim, and Reverend Syngman Rhee, I offer my tribute of appreciation for how they shared through their lives the lessons of personal courage, gentle fortitude, and grounded wisdom. To Sara Sherman, Kim Kyoung-hui, Soo-Na's family, and Julia and Sunny's family, with my heartfelt thanks I salute your re-sourceful ingenuity, gracious hospitality, and many benevolent influences.

Behind the completion of this book was a lengthy and uncertain journey that was profoundly enriched by the companionship of Peter Yoonsuk Paik and immeasurably brightened by the presence of our son, Seung-joon. I am tremendously thankful for the members of my immediate and extended fami-ly for their love and support, which sustained me along the way. It is my hope that this book, at long last, will stand as a memento of gratitude to my given and chosen families for their forbearance and faith, particularly to my parents for the inspiration they provided again and again through their perse-verance, their discernment, and their devotion.

Notes on Methodology, Translation, and Transliteration

I came to this research out of an interest in the contemporary ramifications of Korean division, particularly its impact on the everyday lives of ordinary people. I was formally trained as a cultural anthropologist, and my current research and teaching take an interdisciplinary approach toward contemporary history. I carried out the initial fieldwork in South Korea for a total of eighteen months from September 1999 until December 2000 and again in February–March 2001. The fieldwork during the first three rounds of reunions in Seoul (August 15–18, 2000; November 30–December 2, 2000; February 26–28, 2001) was particularly significant, given that those rounds of family meetings were the only ones held in both Seoul and Pyongyang. Such circumstances contrasted with the subsequent iterations of inter-Korean reunions, which were held only in North Korea under more restricted circumstances, as I explain in chapter 4. My fieldwork in South Korea was largely conducted in the Seoul metropolitan region—including at the Korean Red Cross headquarters and at the venues where the inter-Korean family meetings were held. I also traveled to several other locations throughout South Korea during 1999–2001, and I returned to South Korea for brief follow-up visits in 2009, 2010, and 2011, as well as a longer stay in Seoul for several months during 2014.

My fieldwork was comprised of formal and informal interviews, archival research, conversations in various social settings, observations of daily life and organized events, and participation in study groups, conferences, and organizational meetings. My sources would eventually include interviews with reunion participants and their families; analyses of political speeches, briefing materials, news articles, and commentaries; video footage of live and recorded media coverage, film, and television programs; and conversations with relatives, personal friends, and professional colleagues. I also spoke with representatives from organizations of separated families, government officials, NGO workers, academics, activists, writers, and journalists. At some events and interviews, I also conducted research in tandem with my colleague Soo-Jung Lee, a Korean anthropologist then pursuing her PhD at the University of Illinois at Urbana-Champaign, who shared invaluable insights into the history and implications of Korean family separation. While undertaking fieldwork in 2000, I also received research assistance from Sungmi Cho, then a master's student in sociology at Ewha Women's University, who accompanied me on a number of formal interviews and transcribed several of my interviews with research participants which I had audio-recorded in Korean. Most of the interviews and conversations were carried out in Korean, but among bilingual research participants the language often alternated between Korean and English.

IDIOMS OF IDENTIFICATION

Regarding a key term in this study, *isan'gajok*, I choose to translate it as "separated families," in contrast to alternative terms, "divided," "dispersed," or "sundered" families.[1] The salient modifer, "*isan*" is derived from the Korean verb meaning "to scatter," so "dispersed families" or "scattered families" would be the most literal translation. However, such an interpretation tends to place more weight on a kin group's physical dispersion and arguably lacks the key emphasis on the experience of separation undergone by those displaced by the upheaval of war. "Sundered families" suggests that the family members were forcibly rent apart, when in most cases the family separation was only realized after the fact, when it became apparent that national division would endure well beyond 1953. "Divided families" is more neutral, but it carries the nuance that a separation occurred among a relatively comparable number of members on either side of the border. In reality, as discussed in chapters 2 and 6, separated families were affected and rendered vulnerable by the condition of separation even when it involved loss of contact with a single family member.

Beyond its literal meaning, the "family," or "*gajok*," is a ubiquitous metaphor in Korea, one that anchors a normalizing discourse with overriding patriarchal and heteronormative presumptions. In an essay published in 2000, anthropologist Cho Han Hae-Joang analyzes how, during South Korea's decades of compressed growth, human beings were regarded as highly instrumentalized, which left little space for individual subjectivities or an engaged civil society. Instead, the exigencies of mass mobilization meant individuals were to be subsumed within patriarch-led families, and the subject-position otherwise accorded to the citizen was instead designated as "*kukmin*," or "member of the nation." As Cho writes, "The period of compressed growth produced a society with only grand state power and patriarchal families, but no citizens or autonomous individuals."[2] South Korea's democratization would later give rise to the proliferation of civic organizations in the late 1980s and 1990s, but Cho observes how the circumstances of the 1997–1998 Asian financial crisis belied public attitudes that too easily reverted to an enduring regressive bias toward the patriarchal family and the default identity of "*kukmin*" in the face of recurring national emergencies.

Truly, the family remains a predominant organizing concept of social life in South Korea, but it is one that can also represent a double-edged sword. That is, its moral politics are available for appropriation by *both* conservative multinational corporations and progressive social activists. For example, the conglomerates that dominate the South Korean economy, the *chaebol*, are family-controlled businesses. In 2006, the largest of these conglomerates, Samsung, adopted the slogan, "Another Family," in an attempt to highlight its corporate responsibility and community relations programs.[3] The firm's products are so omnipresent in South Korean everyday life that the slogan has been more commonly perceived to imply that its consumers are encouraged to rely upon the company as if it were a second family beyond their own consanguineous kin. Taking the well-known Samsung slogan as its original title in 2014, the independent feature film *Another Family* dramatized the real-life legal battles of leukemia patients who had worked at Samsung's factory in Suwon, located just south of Seoul. The film was based on the true story of a working-class father who set out to prove his daughter's leukemia death resulted from her exposure to hazardous chemicals while employed at the plant. As the first South Korean film to have been produced entirely with private donations and crowdfunding, it became a sleeper box-office success despite having a limited release.[4] Then, in May 2014, three months after the film premiered at the Busan International Film Festival, Samsung unexpectedly issued an official apology for the first time and offered to compensate the families of factory workers who suffered from leukemia and other illnesses that may have resulted from working conditions at the company's plant. Although the film's producers had decided to change the title to *Another Promise* after the Busan premiere in order to avoid possible legal action, among South Koreans the impact of this documentary would still go on to resonate with the irony of how the potent invocation of familial ties as "Another Family" could be used as both a shill for, and an effective bludgeon against, the nation's most powerful company.

Reinforcing the pervasiveness of the family as an idiom of belonging, fictive-kin relationships are constantly invoked and reinforced by colloquial language, as the terminology of kinship is used to address relatives, friends, and strangers alike. For example, rather than calling someone "mister" to catch the attention of a passerby, one would instead say "*ajŏshi*," or "uncle."

Similarly, the word "*ŏnni*," or "big sister," is used among both girls and grown women, and a younger woman might refer to an older one as "*ŏnni*" in a wide range of contexts from intimate to superficial, whether the latter is an actual sister, a female cousin, a close friend, a new acquaintance, or a favorite K-pop star.

In this study, I refer to my research participants with the Korean honorifics that are considered appropriate to my respective relationship with each of them, which takes into account aspects such as age, gender, and degree of formality or closeness. For those who were educators or intellectuals, regardless of gender, I refer to them by *Sŏnsengnim*, which means "teacher," but that can also be used more loosely as a polite term of respect for addressing someone older. In using the Korean vernacular, I still struggle with the fact that, to an extent far greater than among men, older women are generally not referred to by their given names, but rather indirectly through their relationships; for example, a polite form of referring to a woman who has children would be identifying her as the mother of her first-born. I still feel chagrined by this gendered discrepancy in naming and, at the risk of sounding rude in Korean, sometimes eschew these linguistic conventions, out of a reflexive resistance to the patriarchal implications of relying more heavily upon such role-centric forms of address for women.[5] However, during my fieldwork and interviews, I generally followed Korean convention since I had asked research participants what they would feel comfortable being called, and I did my best to comply. In the book, in order to distinguish research participants from each other, I combine the pseudonym for a woman's family name and the fictive-kin term that I would have used in person, such as "*Halmŏni*" or "*Ajumŏni*," meaning "grandmother" or "aunt," respectively. In cases regarding a woman with whom I had a closer personal relationship, I may refer to her by teknonym, (e.g., "Su-yeon's Mother"), which would carry the nuance in colloquial Korean of conveying greater intimacy as well as courtesy through indirection. In some cases, research participants asked me to follow the American convention, using the generic honorific "Mr." (*misŭt'a*) or "Mrs." (*misŏsŭ*) combined with their family name. This partly reflects how South Koreans have readily appropriated English loan words into the contemporary Korean vernacular, and they may have also anticipated that it would be more comfortable or familiar for me to do so as someone from the United States. But I also took it as another reminder that some had likely agreed to speak with me because they knew I was from abroad and therefore at more of a distance from their own social world.

Indeed, at various points while working on this project, I had to come to terms with my own liminality both as a foreign researcher and a Korean American in South Korea. When I did my initial field research as a graduate student, I initially went about my interviews identifying myself as a PhD candidate from the United States doing my dissertation research. I later realized how tone-deaf such a self-description must have sounded when a Korean graduate student suggested that I instead describe myself as "*gongbu hanŭn haksaeng*"—that is, as "a student who studies." The phrase initially struck me as child-like and disarming, as this phrase could just as easily be used to describe a grade-schooler. Yet that versatility later proved helpful, given that an overseas graduate-student identity would potentially be alienating or intimidating to many of my potential informants. This was particularly true for the Korean War generation, as many were unable to pursue their educations beyond middle school and only the elites of that age-cohort had the opportunity to enter university. In contrast, the benign familiarity of a generic student identification might have served to allay some anxieties for these families about the fact that my research was delving into subjects that until recently had been regarded as taboo.

At the same time, as I describe in chapter 3, a new atmosphere of openness beginning in mid-July 2000 broke the silence around certain Koreans for whom speaking of their family backgrounds had once been verboten. Although I am not myself a member of a North–South separated family, most Korean Americans and other overseas Koreans can identify with the diasporic condition of family separation and the haunting tension of having unknown or unaccounted-for relatives.[6] Many of my research participants were surprisingly forthcoming, and a few were genuinely enthusiastic to talk about their lives, explaining that they welcomed the opportunity given the fact that their children or grandchildren were uninterested in their old stories. I too can relate to this communication gap among generations, as I rarely have the occasion to talk about war memories with my own extended family members. Subsequently, it has struck me as ironic that it was often far easier to interview these strangers in my role as an ethnographer who at the time was dutifully completing my fieldwork as part of my studies than it would have been to pose the same questions to my own relatives or family members.

By informally volunteering at the Red Cross headquarters to help applicants fill out forms, I came into contact with scores of separated family members. I would speak briefly with those who visited the Red Cross offices, helping them with their applications or sharing information that I had gleaned about the process. If they seemed open to conversing further, I would request to speak with them at greater length either at their homes or another place of their choosing. In that way, I conducted follow-up interviews with nearly two dozen families, and I carried out multiple, in-depth interviews with ten individuals whose families participated in the reunions. In general, among those I approached at the Red Cross headquarters in Seoul, most said they were puzzled as to whether they could say anything about their families that would be of value to an academic study, but offered to meet anyway in case there was something they could do to help. I received half a dozen interviews from people who said that they were avoiding the press at all costs, but they were willing to speak with a student. Over and over during my fieldstay, I benefited from such personal generosity as well as from the special regard that education holds in Korean society.

After receiving contact information, generally I was the one to follow through by phone in order to set up an interview. So I was surprised when I received a call one day from a woman who had actually declined to share her own contact details but had nevertheless taken my business card. She said that she decided to contact me only after seeing a small article about my research in *Kyunghyang Shinmun*, one of the daily South Korean newspapers. She explained that, though she did not wish to speak with any reporters, what moved her to reach out was the fact that I was a student from the United States, where she has relatives. As it happened, when we went through the initial interview-formalities of exchanging information about our respective families, we fairly quickly discovered that not only did her brother's family live in the same area as my childhood home in the New Jersey, but my parents and her relatives knew each other as part of the same large Korean American community in that area. Her nephews were around my own age, and though it had been many years, I remembered them by name. One cannot always so readily collapse the degrees of separation between given members of the Korean diaspora, as in this case of remarkable serendipity, but the possibility of such connections was another aspect of being an insider-outsider during this field research.

Among those families with whom I was able to secure a follow-up interview, I met them either at their home, an office, or at a café or restaurant. At the start of an interview, often the first fifteen to twenty minutes or more were taken up by questions about my own background and family, often including several questions about my parents. Research participants would inquire into their line of work, which schools they had attended, and their respective hometowns. Among older Koreans especially, making such inquiries into one's family background, not to mention one's age and marital status, is not only socially acceptable but is considered polite. When I mentioned to Korean friends that Westerners might find such questions nosy or intrusive, they explained that it was a way of showing interest in another person and also was important to establishing a relationship. Because of the sensitive nature of my research, being able to participate in this common Korean ritual of making each other's acquaintance was crucial for establishing rapport and afforded a measure of balance when it came my turn to pose questions.

Yet, as a non-native speaker of Korean, I worried that my research participants would assume I knew more than I actually did, and I invariably missed much. But several Korean colleagues also reassured me that those I encounter would likely feel less self-conscious to speak with someone like myself—someone with whom they could identify as a person of Korean descent but who was raised abroad—because that meant I had not grown up heavily exposed to anticommunist education and therefore may not have the prejudices that might have made them wary to speak about their families among other South Koreans. On the other hand, I also encountered suspicion for doing this study as a researcher from the United States. In the course of my field research, a few people flatly challenged me, asking whether I was working for the U.S. government or the South Korean government. I took such suspicion as one of the particular constraints of doing research in a context still very much shaped by the global Cold War.[7] I also recognized that the wariness of these individuals was understandable and warranted, given the past experiences of surveillance and harassment that they had once had to endure.

Nevertheless, in the few cases where the question arose, I still felt terribly awkward trying to explain that I was not a spy or government agent. One research participant started our interview by gently but doggedly grilling me with a set of pointed questions about my graduate program and the sources of my research funding. When I explained that I was being supported at the time by a Fulbright grant, he pressed further to find out the program's sponsor. I mentioned that it was administered through an international educational agency in New York and sponsored by the U.S. Department of Education. At the mention of a government connection, he sat back and seemed satisfied. He made a point of saying that, although I may not be aware of it, I would be naïve to deny that my research would someday be used by the U.S. government. He confidently predicted that, once I finished my study, "They're going to send one copy straight to the headquarters of the CIA." He punctuated that sentence by stabbing his finger into the air, pointing over my shoulder, as if to gesture in the direction of McLean, Virginia. By then, I had become accustomed to suspicions about my research, but his resolute certainty about how my work would eventually be used for intelligence purposes was sobering. As much as I might protest such use of my work, how could I say whether this was untrue? It was yet another reminder, among many during the course of my field research, about the risks and sensitivities—as well as the attendant ethical obligations—surrounding ethnographic research about a place like divided Korea, even if my book's focus was on South Korea rather than North Korea.

ETHNOGRAPHIC CONTINGENCY

When I first undertook field research in the fall of 1999, inter-Korean family reunions seemed at best an unlikely prospect. At the time, the separated-families issue had long been at an impasse, and it was hard to imagine how, and if ever, the problem of separated families could be resolved, short of eventual Korean reunification. One separated family member, a university administrator in her mid-fifties, told me in November 1999, "Our hands are tied until the leaders of the two Koreas are able to negotiate, but that gives me little hope." Another woman, a community health worker in her late twenties whom I had met through friends, offered the explanation of compassion fatigue. She believed that Koreans genuinely feel sympathy for the separated families but also feel helpless, and after so many decades without real progress on the issue, such frustration eventually turns into indifference.

During the first part of my field-stay in South Korea, I encountered a pattern of refusal regarding the topic of separated families. When I would mention my research interest to friends, relatives and acquaintances, I heard the appraisal, time and again, that not many Koreans were interested in separated families, and that the separated families themselves represented a very small minority. A colleague leveled with me, saying that *Korean Americans* were more interested in separated families than South Koreans were; she recommended that I turn around and do fieldwork in Los Angeles instead of Seoul. This professed lack of interest toward separated families baffled me, especially in light of polls at the time that showed an overwhelming majority of South Koreans favored prioritizing separated-family reunions as a pressing task for their government and the primary reason to improve inter-Korean relations.[8]

Yet, even among intellectuals who had written about the social aspects of Korean division, I encountered an uneasiness about the subject of separated families. I had assumed that they would have a strong opinion about this issue, but instead often the first response I received was that they actually knew little about separated families or, frankly, were not terribly interested in the topic. A Korean sociologist colleague explained to me that he was hardly surprised by this wariness among his fellow political progressives. He took it as a reflection of how deeply coded the term "*isan'gajok*" was as a cipher of Cold War anticommunist ideology in South Korea. It was indicative, he explained, of the way that the issue of wartime family separation had been so opportunistically appropriated by past military-authoritarian governments that it left a strong sense of cynicism among those who would otherwise be sympathetic toward those victimized by local manifestations of the Cold War.

As I continued to search for research leads, I kept running into this question of what happened to the "other" group of separated families, those with a family member who went missing in wartime and who likely ended up on the northern side of the border after the war. Early on during my field stay, I spoke with a family friend, Yang *Sŏnsaengnim*, who wrote down the Sino-Korean characters for the term, *yŏnjwaje*, noting that the word shares the first character with *yŏn'gyŏl*, or "connection." *Yŏnjwa* means "implication, involvement, or complicity." *Yŏnjwaje* signifies a system of laws and surveillance by which the government had investigated and discriminated against those related to communists and leftist sympathizers. She confided a story about a relative in her family who reportedly went to the North during the war. She said, "He left because of ideology and because he had a very strong will," describing him as idealistic and very patriotic. It was the son of her father's elder brother, and when he disappeared during the war, the family assumed he had left voluntarily because he had mentioned his desire to go to the North. "The time was really unsettled, and we were all uncertain about what the future would be. There was much debate among intellectuals about what was best for Korea, capitalism or communism," she said. Many years later, a relatively distant cousin applied for a government position and was denied. She said: "Up to second cousins!" In other words, not just immediate family members but also one's extended kin group encountered discrimination. Yet Yang *Sŏnsaengnim* said her immediate family was "lucky" given that so far none of them seemed to have been affected by having a relative who "crossed over" to the North during the war. I was intrigued by the contrast of fates she had described within the same extended kin group, which suggested the existence of a far-reaching network of surveillance, but one that was hidden and inconsistently enforced.

All the same, several well-meaning colleagues advised me that I would be wise to reconsider my research topic altogether. They explained that this area was still too sensitive to handle. One colleague in sociology brought up the ethical dilemma of approaching people who may have been affected by this taboo. She cautioned that in the process of seeking research participants, even the very act of identifying and attempting to contact these family members could be perceived as potentially threatening to them if they had long strived to escape a persecuted past. A seasoned expert on North Korean politics told me that he felt that the topic certainly warranted study but that securing enough interviews to write a dissertation would be all but impossible. He leveled with me in English: "You can try to find these people, but trust me, you will run into a stone wall."

I agonized over these ethical roadblocks and bleak prospects, and I prepared to abandon the project if I failed to find any promising research leads by winter's end. In retrospect, the difficulties I encountered in fieldwork during that time, as discouraging as they were, would prove to afford an important diagnostic. They offered a gauge to the severity of taboo surrounding these families and suggested the depth of silence enshrouding their personal and family histories. It was a silence that would soon be broken when, only months later, scores of such families would essentially become national media celebrities as iconic symbols at the time representing the promise of Korean reconciliation. At the start of my field research, however, it would have been impossible to predict the dramatic transformations in inter-Korean relations that would arise on the Korean peninsula in the months and years to come.

Korean words in this book are transliterated using the McCune-Reischauer system, except in cases of place names (e.g., Seoul) and well-known proper names (e.g., Syngman Rhee). Also, where I refer to a published author, I follow the transliteration used by that individual. Throughout the text, I have followed the Korean convention in which the family name precedes the given or personal name. However, this rule is reversed in cases where doing so is consistent with the format chosen by authors for their publications in English. In case of confusion, all names in the bibliography and index appear in alphabetical order by family name.

Because of the sensitivity of some topics addressed, it was necessary to handle matters of confidentiality carefully. I use actual proper names when relaying accounts that appeared on television, in newspaper articles, or elsewhere in the public domain. Otherwise, the names of research participants included in this book are pseudonyms, and I altered identifying details to protect their privacy. However, in changing the details about some individuals, they may have inadvertently come to resemble that of others in comparable circumstances; to borrow the disclaimer that appears in movie credits: Regarding research participants identified by pseudonyms, any such resemblance is purely coincidental.

NOTES

1. Choong Soon Kim, *Faithful Endurance: An Ethnography of Korean Family Dispersal* (Tucson: University of Arizona Press, 1988); James Foley, *Korea's Divided Families: Fifty Years of Separation* (London and New York: Routledge, 2004).

2. Cho Han Hae-Joang, "'You Are Entrapped in an Imaginary Well': The Formation of Subjectivity Within Compressed Development—A Feminist Critique of Modernity and Korean Culture," *Inter-Asia Cultural Studies* 1, no. 1 (2000): 57. See also Eunshil Kim, "The Cultural Logic of the Korean Modernization Project and Its Gender Politics," *Asian Journal of Women's Studies* 6, no. 2 (2000): 50–77; and Hyun Mee Kim, "Work, Nation and Hypermasculinity: The 'Woman' Question in the Economic Miracle and Crisis in South Korea," *Inter-Asia Cultural Studies* 2, no. 1 (2001): 53–68.

3. "Samsung Corporate Profile," September 2007, http://www.samsung.com/cn/aboutsamsung/corporateprofile/download/2007_9_corporate%20citizenship-coprosperity-greenmanagement.pdf.

4. Catherine Shu, "Samsung Reportedly Tried to Suppress a Film Critical of Its Safety Record," *Tech Crunch*, February 25, 2014, http://techcrunch.com/2014/02/25/samsung-another-family/.

5. In contrast, linguist Ho-min Sohn refers to such indirect forms of address as strategies to compensate for a "rather pervasive taboo in Korean culture against using personal names when speaking to or about adults." See Ho-min Sohn, *Korean Language in Culture and Society* (Honolulu: University of Hawaii Press, 2006).

6. See, for example, *Memory of Forgotten War*, directed by Deann Borshay Liem and Ramsay Liem (Berkeley, CA: Mu Films, 2012), DVD; Eleana J. Kim, *Adopted Territory: Transnational Korean Adoptees and the Politics of Belonging* (Durham, NC: Duke University Press, 2010).

7. It was a question that also shouldn't have surprised me, given the historical and contemporary connections between American anthropologists and various military and intelligence agencies. See Laura A. McNamara and Robert Rubinstein, eds., *Dangerous Liaisons: Anthropologists and the National Security State* (Santa Fe: School for Advanced Research Press, 2011); David Price, *Anthropological Intelligence: The Deployment and Neglect of American Anthropology in the Second World War* (Durham, NC: Duke University Press, 2008); and Robert Oppenheim, "On the Locations of Korean War and Cold War Anthropology," *Histories of Anthropology Annual* 4 (2008): 220–59.

8. In a national poll of 1500 people conducted by the Ministry of Unification between February 26–27, 2000, for example, over 90 percent of the respondents chose "reunion of separated families" to be the primary task facing the government that year. See "Gov't to Raise Financial Support for Separated Families," *Korea Times*, March 2, 2000.

Introduction

Borders take on many forms to assert their power. Some appear as delineations on official and unofficial maps. Others take material form by way of barricades, electrified fences, and coiled double helices of concertina razor wire. Sensitive border regions may be further reinforced by armed patrols and surveillance from military guard posts. All of these characteristics apply to the line dividing North Korea and South Korea along the 38th parallel, so it may be surprising to many that the inter-Korean divide is merely a de facto border, not a true one. What began in 1945 as a temporary partition of the Korean peninsula following the end of the Second World War took on more conventional characteristics as a border with the establishment of separate republics in 1948. It was soon afterward, during the bloody military conflicts of the Korean War, that an enduring political and territorial condition of national division would become firmly entrenched. Although the Armistice Line established in 1953 would continue to serve as an inter-Korean demarcation for over six decades into the present, no international treaty or agreement has ever settled an official border to divide the two Korean states. In accordance with the 1953 truce agreement, the Geneva Conference was held the following year, and central to its agenda was "the purpose of reaching a peaceful settlement of the Korean question."[1] However, amid the rising tensions of the Cold War, that conference would end without proposals or an agreement regarding the situation on the Korean peninsula. To this day, a peace treaty has never been signed to bring the Korean War to an end, thus leaving the matter of a formal inter-Korean boundary unresolved.

Amid this lack of resolution regarding the Korean War and its outcome, perhaps the most profound form in which a dividing boundary has been reproduced on the peninsula is not on land or on paper, but within the intimate spaces of families.[2] Strict prohibitions against communication or en-

1

counters between the two Korean populations meant that, despite the end of the 1950–1953 period of major Korean War hostilities, ordinary people on opposite sides had virtually no means of contact for several decades. Unable to ascertain whether or not their missing relatives had survived the war's catastrophic destruction, Koreans were thus denied the ability to sort the living from the dead, a crucial post-conflict process arrested by national division. Indeed, the North–South separated family (*nambuk isan'gajok*) has long served as an icon of the nation's ongoing division. While an estimated 1.7 million Koreans remained on the opposite side of the dividing line from their respective regions of origin when the Armistice was signed in 1953, it has been difficult to ascertain an accurate statistic of wartime family separation. Notably, the colloquial referent for separated families in South Korea is "*ch'ŏnman isan'gajok*," or "ten million separated families," though the widespread citation of this figure as an actual statistic suggests how a metaphor can be taken too literally. Rather than denoting a calculated estimate, "ten million" in Korean rhetorically connotes a quantity of such great magnitude as to be virtually countless. Indeed, if one were to include the extended kin group and descendants of those separated by war, one could invoke the power of numbers by claiming an exponentially large demographic constituency. But in truth, there are a rapidly diminishing number of those old enough to have formed strong attachments with relatives they had lost contact with during the 1950–1953 period of the Korean War.[3]

Instead, rather than for the sake of sheer demographic scale, the crisis of kinship facing Korean separated families has retained a haunting cultural resonance for the ways it so clearly figures the human costs of unended war and division on the peninsula. Within the last decade, images from the periodic reunions of Korean separated families have circulated globally as emblematic figures of social suffering at the mercy of the residual Cold War, appearing at once timeless and anachronistic.

These reunions are most often represented by tearful embraces among anguished family members, as the protagonists of events steeped in human pathos and shadowed by vexing politics. Sensationalized by the international press and domestic Korean news media, such meetings arguably occupy a key site of what anthropologist Joseph Masco has elsewhere called the "emotional ruins of the Cold War."[4] Yet these Korean separated family members appear as ciphers of unspoken grief, with often little or no articulation for what is being grieved. What did these reunions mean for the participating individuals who would meet their relatives after having had no contact for over fifty years on opposite sides of the territorial divide? Why did the two Korean states hold these temporary meetings among traumatized war-separated family members, at a time on the Korea peninsula characterized by extraordinary moments of social, political, and economic change, driven in part by neoliberal globalization? Given the pendulum swings between inter-

Figure 0.1. Site of the first post-Summit reunions of North–South Korean separated families, COEX Convention Center, Seoul, August 15, 2000. Reproduced with permission from the National Archives of Korea.

Korean engagement and confrontation in recent decades, how has the significance of these family meetings been evoked and contested amid the changing contexts of reconciliation and collective war memory?

UNSETTLING DIVIDES

This book examines the reunions of long-separated family members as part of a complex process of national reconciliation undertaken between the two states of divided Korea at the cusp of the twenty-first century, when ordinary people came to grips with the continuing everyday consequences of events that occurred in wartime a half-century earlier. Although high-level talks between the two Koreas have been held at multiple junctures since the early 1970s, the family meetings that took place in August 2000 were arguably the most prominent inter-Korean events focused on civilians, a particularly significant development in light of the unusually large number of North Koreans visiting Seoul. As negotiated and arranged by official representatives on both sides, these "North–South separated-family exchange visits" (*nambuk isan'gajok kyohwan pangmun*)—or "reunions," as they are simply called in most English-language sources—were a simultaneous exchange in which one hundred North Koreans came to Seoul and one hundred South Koreans went to Pyongyang; each individual participant was to meet with a small handful of family members over the course of four days. In other words, delegations of elderly Korean War survivors were flown across the de facto border in opposite directions so that they could meet briefly with family members who in most cases had long given them up for dead, given the lack of all contact for over half a century.

Indeed, the impact of these events was heightened because the reunions precipitated the unexpected resurfacing and temporary return of hundreds of those presumed to have died in the mid-1950s during the Korean War. To prepare for the reunions, the respective Red Cross societies on the two sides each sent a list of two hundred names in advance to ascertain whether the family members of these "reunions candidates" were still alive and traceable. Among those confirmed out of that initial pool, a delegation of one hundred from each side would be selected to participate in the August family meetings. With less than a month to prepare for the reunions,[5] officials were pressed to locate the prospective reunion participants quickly, and in South Korea they did so by publicizing the names sent from North Korea via mass media outlets. While the entire list would be published the following day in South Korean major newspapers, the names first appeared in special television broadcasts that temporarily interrupted normal programming. Through breaking news reports, it quickly became apparent that the names sent from North Korea represented those who had gone missing during episodes of wartime chaos in late 1950 and early 1951, and in many cases these were names of formerly missing persons who had been presumed dead and mourned for decades as losses of a brutally destructive and catastrophic war.

As scores upon scores of such people began resurfacing in mid-July of 2000, the very meaning of war death in Korea became unsettled. Prior to 2000, the dilemma of inter-Korean separated families had been perceived as an important but relatively marginal issue. That is, Koreans widely acknowledged the legacies of wartime family separation as significant in an abstract sense, but those who directly identified with matters affecting separated families represented a small fraction of the overall Korean population.[6] Yet virtually every Korean lost a relative or family member during the upheaval and devastation of the Korean War, including countless deaths in which bodies could not be reclaimed. It was a shocking development to learn that North Korean officials sent information about so many of those who had been formerly presumed dead, including several individuals who were later revealed to be prominent cultural figures and high-ranking Party members in North Korean society. As one separated family member put it when I met him at the Korean Red Cross headquarters in Seoul during the summer of that year, "If even *these* people can come forward to find their family [in the South], then things must finally be changing, aren't they?" Preparations surrounding the reunions therefore made apparent a compelling aspect of what was at stake for ordinary people in the breakthroughs of the North–South peace process. Given the seemingly impossible returns of those who had been mourned as dead for fifty years, there arose the possibility that nearly any Korean could prove to be a member of a North–South separated family, with the potential to shake basic assumptions about family history, personal identity, and selfhood.

When later reflecting upon the dramatic events that unfolded that summer, I was struck by how deeply their impact resonated with one of the most well-worn plot twists employed in melodramatic South Korean television dramas: namely, the sudden revelation that upends a character's entire lifeworld by disclosing a long-concealed and scandalous kin relation. Indeed, the shocking reappearance of one who had been presumed dead—or more generally, the discovery of complicated kin relations that were previously unknown—often emerges as a deus ex machina in these popular serial dramas. Consider, for example, a coincidence that suggests how commonly this plot device recurs in the genre: the same actor, Jeon In-taek, played roles in two different highly successful dramas where his character had been presumed to be dead for years until, in a momentous and bewildering disclosure, he was revealed to have been alive all along. In this example, what is striking is that this trope appeared both in the landmark South Korean epic drama, *Dae Jang Geum* (*Jewel in the Palace*)—a period biopic, set in the sixteenth century during the Chosŏn dynasty, that broke viewership records in South Korea when it first aired in 2003—and another successful television drama, *Ch'allanhan Yusan* (*Brilliant Legacy*), set in contemporary Seoul, which was itself a top-rated South Korean series in 2009. In other words, the two serial narratives are otherwise vastly different from each other in their premise and settings, and like most South Korean dramas, neither of them involves any North–South theme whatsoever.

While an underlying anxiety may persist in South Korean popular culture about missing persons and the havoc they could unleash for their unwitting relatives, emotional scenes of reunion in real life among long-separated families have been a staple of South Korean media culture since the early 1980s. In 1983, a special program on KBS, the state-owned broadcaster, unexpectedly turned into a marathon broadcast and captivated a national audience as a media sensation that extended for nearly five months. Originally begun as part of a commemorative special program intended to shed light on the ongoing suffering of war-separated families, ordinary people were invited to appear briefly during a featured segment, where they would hold up signs bearing information about their relatives to make an appeal for help in locating them. The broadcast was originally planned to last only ninety-five minutes in duration, but it generated such a tremendous response that KBS was left with no choice but to extend the live broadcast as a special television marathon that would come to be known as "Finding Dispersed Families" (*isan'gajok ch'atgi*). The KBS telethon continued for a total of 138 days, from June 30 to November 14, eventually resulting in 10,189 successful reunions. Among the 100,952 applicants for reunion, 53,536 participants appeared on air, either briefly to make their appeals, or for longer attempts to confirm whether a possible match was indeed a lost family member.[7]

With its interactive use of the television medium and the real-time unfolding of highly emotional personal dramas, the KBS telethon is regarded by international media scholars as a landmark event no less than the global forerunner of reality television.[8] While it would become a precursor of that now-ubiquitous genre internationally, for Koreans it served as a painful reminder of how the enduring effects of the 1950–1953 war had continued for decades afterward as repetitions of a foundational trauma underpinning modern Korean identity. Within South Korea at the time, the KBS telethon would in fact become by far the most popular television program broadcast then to date, drawing more than a 78 percent share of ratings at its peak.[9] In a sense, the wrenching and melodramatic encounters of mass-mediated reunion elicited a collective gaze among an "intimate public"[10] presumed to share a bond of communal longing as survivors of the war. In this way, the KBS telethon quickly became the object of binge-watching among riveted South Korean audiences and its public memory would endure in later decades as a cultural touchstone of family separation as national tragedy.

The KBS telethon is also the event in South Korean media history that established television as the representative technology for reconnecting those separated during wartime, while it also demonstrated television's efficacy as a medium for the transmission of intense affect. On the first night of the broadcast, thousands of people descended upon KBS Plaza, the location of the station headquarters, in their attempts to appear on camera to appeal for information about lost family members.

This forced KBS to cancel its regular programming and continue the broadcast without commercial interruption into the night. That groundswell was touched off in part by the use of split-screen technology, as viewers could watch in real time while two individuals from different provinces asked each other questions and tried to compare memories in order to confirm whether they were indeed related to each other. In some cases the family resemblance was obvious, and the kin tie was readily confirmed. In others, the suspenseful process of trying to match recollections ended in frustration or a burst of recognition. Among the most emotionally fraught moments were those scenes in which one sibling informed another that a parent had already died, as both could be seen sharing this most intimate of tragic personal moments unfolding in real time on live national television.[11]

It should be noted that the families reunited through the 1983 KBS telethon were *not* North–South Korean separated families whose members had lived on opposite sides of the 38th parallel. Rather, the family members reunited via the 1983 KBS telethon had all lived within South Korea for

Figure 0.2. Handmade signs, listing identifying details for persons missing since 1950–1953, were posted throughout KBS Plaza in Seoul during a special live telethon, "Finding Dispersed Families," which lasted for nearly twenty weeks in 1983 and resulted in over 10,000 successful reunions. Reproduced with permission from the National Archives of Korea.

those thirty years of separation, and in some cases they unknowingly resided in close proximity to each other. Even though these were not inter-Korean cases, their stories of family separation nevertheless developed within the complex political field of one half of a divided nation. Indeed, an underlying reason why many did not seek to inquire about lost family members in South Korea was because of the severe social risk posed by the possibility that those relatives may have ended up in North Korea. Moreover, the KBS producers would at times deliberately frame the program as a vehicle for broadcasting anticommunist sentiments. In his ethnography of the KBS telethon, anthropologist Choong Soon Kim writes, "For the one-thousandth family reunion, KBS appeared to have carefully selected a particular family who could propagandize the accomplishments of the South Korean government, including the telethon and its strong anticommunist stand, and condemn the North Korean communists."[12] Notwithstanding the explicitly anti-North orientation projected by the program's producers, anthropologist Soo-Jung Lee argues that, by focusing public attention upon the real-life implications of the unresolved situation facing war-separated families, the emotional impact of scenes from the 1983 KBS telethon could hardly be contained by solely an anticommunist political agenda.[13]

While narratives of reuniting lost family members remain a common motif in Korean popular culture, the issue of North–South separated families had long been among the most intractable dilemmas in inter-Korean relations. Prior to 2000, the only official exchange of families between the two Koreas occurred in September 1985, when delegations of fifty separated family members were sent from each side to meet relatives in Seoul and Pyongyang. Held at the height of the Cold War, those events were marred by ideological grandstanding on both sides, and the reunions program would not continue past a single exchange meeting.[14] Despite recurring diplomatic negotiations dedicated to the issue, another fifteen years would pass without concrete progress. Finally, a breakthrough occurred at the historic inter-Korean summit meeting in June 2000, a watershed event when the leaders of North Korea and South Korea met for the first time since the two republics were established in 1948. By the conclusion of the three-day summit, South Korean president Kim Dae-jung and North Korean leader Kim Jong-il had signed the June 15th North–South Joint Declaration, which included the agreement to "exchange visits by separated family members and relatives on the occasion of the August 15 National Liberation Day."[15]

In South Korea, that Joint Declaration became the hallmark of Kim Dae-jung's "Policy of Reconciliation and Cooperation," or what is more commonly known as the "Sunshine Policy," which marked a fundamental departure from the prior official position that had long regarded North Korea as an enemy and a rival for political and diplomatic legitimacy. Instead, after Kim Dae-jung assumed the presidency in 1998, the Sunshine Policy pursued an inter-Korean approach based not on hostile confrontation or anticipation of the North's imminent collapse, but rather one that aimed for gradual change in North Korea, with China and Vietnam as precedents.[16] The Sunshine Policy therefore pursued engagement with the North to an unprecedented degree, emphasizing diplomatic dialogue, mutual recognition, economic cooperation, and peaceful reconciliation. While earlier South Korean administrations had sought to engage North Korea, international relations scholar Key-young Son argues that prior attempts at engagement with North Korea were at best "limited engagement" where "economic incentives are bargaining chips, which can be withdrawn if an enemy state does not take due steps in an envisioned dyad of incentives and punishments." In contrast, the Kim Dae-jung administration pursued what Son calls "comprehensive engagement," an approach that sought to resolve the underlying threat of war and to address the condition of inter-state enmity as the root problem of recurring instability. Son writes that, in pursuing comprehensive engagement, "economic exchange and cooperation amount to steps for tension reduction, trust building and, most of all, integration of previously separate economies."[17] As discussed further below, in order to spearhead this far-reaching agenda of establishing cooperative North–South relations and finally bringing an end to the Korean War, the Kim Dae-jung government regarded among the highest priorities the issue of war-separated families.

Notably, these South Korean overtures began in 1998, during the same year as the first-ever change in North Korea's top leadership. After a four-year period of transition following Kim Il-sung's death in 1994, an ammendment to the DPRK Constitution established the late leader as "Eternal President of the Republic," while Kim Jong-il assumed full power under the bureaucratic title of "Chairman of the National Defense Commission." Following this transition, it became apparent that, within the North Korean political elite, the tide was shifting toward those who favored overcoming the state's isolation and who sought to revitalize its economy in part by establishing diplomatic ties with several countries in Western Europe and the Middle East, as well as with Canada, Brazil, South Africa, and the Phillippines.[18] In South Korea, the Sunshine Policy would later continue under Kim Dae-jung's liberal successor Roh Moo-hyun (2003–2008) as the "Peace and Prosperity Policy." Roh would also visit Pyongyan for the second inter-Korean summit in October 2007, when he and Kim Jong-il signed the October 4th Declaration that called for peace and co-prosperity while committing both sides to concrete measures toward developing inter-Korean relations.[19] However, the following presidential election saw a change in power to the conservative Lee Myung-bak (2008–2013), who reversed course in inter-Korean relations when he came to office. Capitalizing on frustration generated by the difficult work of reconciliation, Lee abandoned engagement with North Korea and returned to a harder line.

Unlike his pro-engagement predecessors, Lee instead pursued a reunification agenda that aimed to hasten North Korea's collapse, with the ambition of reunifying the Koreas by force or of triggering a crisis that would lead to the South's absorption of the North. At around that time, the North Korean leadership was also preoccupied with uncertainties regarding its own transition, given Kim Jong-il's poor health after suffering a stroke in August 2008.

In *De-Bordering Korea: Tangible and Intangible Legacies of the Sunshine Policy*, Valérie Gelézeau, Koen De Ceuster, and Alain Delissen point out that, as North Korea anticipated its leadership transition, it retreated to survival mode in an effort to avoid further destabilizing effects stemming from the inter-Korean rapprochement during the 1998–2008 period. They argue that, while the dramatic changes during the Sunshine Policy Era could be understood as a "de-bordering" between the Koreas—that is, the breaking down of borders not only physical but also cultural, social, and psychological in nature—the political changes that took place on both sides after 2008 effectively amounted to a process of "re-bordering."[20] During subsequent years, relations between North and South again fluctuated between a taut uneasiness and highly volatile flare-ups. A low point came in 2010, the year of two military crises. Either months after the sinking of the South Korean *Cheonan*, the North Korean shelling of *Yŏnp'yŏng* Island raised worldwide alarm over the risk of a "second Korean War."[21]

Although those 2010 military crises would eventually pass without triggering a wider conflict, the renewed global awareness of dangers posed by tensions between the two Koreas begged the question of how one can properly assess the dramatic developments toward reconciliation that took place during the previous decade of active inter-Korean engagement.

Despite a rapid deterioration of relations on the peninsula signified by the 2010 crisis, it should be recalled that, in its aftermath, there remained among South Koreans a general consensus that nevertheless favored peaceful engagement over hostile confrontation and regarded inter-Korean cooperation as advantageous to both Koreas.[22] To grasp an illustration of this point, consider the South Korean presidential election campaign of 2012, during which both of the major candidates—one liberal and the other conservative—differed little in their policies regarding North Korea. Indeed, both Park Geun-hye, a political conservative and the eventual winner, and her opponent Moon Jae-in, a progressive lawyer who had served as chief of staff for the Roh Moo-hyun administration, promised to calm the volatility that had characterized the then-incumbent President Lee's hardline policy, which had become extremely unpopular among the South Korean electorate.[23] As a result, it was striking at the time that, unlike in previous South Korean elections, North Korea did not figure significantly into presidential politics. Indeed, in 2012 it barely registered as a campaign issue, except to signal the agreement of both sides to a return to engagement with the North. This broad sentiment favoring peaceable relations on the peninsula would therefore endure as a legacy of South Korea's decade of center-left government, and the impact of breakthroughs toward North–South Korean reconciliation undertaken in the early 2000s would continue in spite of the reversion to inter-state animosity on the Korean peninsula amid the political changes since 2008.

The resilience of a consensus among South Koreans favoring inter-Korean reconciliation rather than hostile confrontation—despite deep divisions among the South Korean citizenry in other respects—indicates why the pivotal months at the start of the engagement period during the Kim Dae-jung presidency warrant greater attention and deeper understanding. This book revisits that period at the start of the millennium, which saw the most rapid change ever to take place in relations between North and South Korea.

Contrary to the characterization of the Sunshine Era as a "lost decade" by its detractors, political scientist Moon Chung-In asserts that the window of time for truly implementing the engagement policy's initiatives was far shorter, as they were only in effect for six months, from mid-June 2000 to mid-January 2000, before being fundamentally hampered by a reversal in U.S. foreign policy toward Korea when the White House transitioned from Bill Clinton to George W. Bush.[24] That relatively brief period following the June Summit is therefore a crucial interval for assessing the significance of the Sunshine Policy at its outset. While discussing implications of inter-Korean developments, this analysis focuses on South Korea, the context where the Sunshine Policy had its widest immediate social impact. Indeed, a criticism of the Sunshine Policy in the initial months following the Summit was that its efficacy was questioned since there was little apparent change within North Korea.[25] However, one should not underestimate how pivotal and meaningful were the social developments that occurred *within South Korea* during that incipient period of inter-Korean engagement, the legacies of which bore implications more long-lasting than generally acknowledged. Contrary to the belief that Korean separated-family meetings amounted to little more than fleeting emotion-filled spectacles or intermittent gestures of diplomatic goodwill, these events should be recognized both as a political threshold ritual with enduring repercussions for South Korea's era of liberal engagement with North Korea and as a cultural prism that revealed multiple dimensions of traumatic war memory and its contemporary legacies in a nation that had been riven by civil and international war.

In studies of inter-Korean engagement, the impact of rapprochement in South Korea under the Kim and Roh administrations is largely examined by way of their agreements, policies, and crises vis-à-vis North Korea.[26] In this literature, the reunions of separated families generally receive only token recognition, if any mention at all. Yet, as the first important concrete outcome of that summit, these family meetings carried profound political and diplomatic significance. South Korean officials described the successful accomplishment of the reunions as a sign that other aspects of the June 15th Joint Declaration could be taken in good faith, commonly referring to these family meetings as a prerequisite to continuing on with the agenda of inter-Korean economic cooperation. Regarding the broader level of public interest, television ratings in South Korea actually proved to be higher for the August 2000 family meetings than for the June Summit coverage itself,[27] reflecting widespread curiosity over how the relatives from the two sides would interact. Despite popular speculation in the run-up to the reunions broadcast that the North Koreans might appear as stereotypical apparatchiks and use these events primarily as a vehicle for pro-DPRK propaganda,[28] the meetings would instead generate searing images of raw human emotion and intimate expressions of affection, in scenes where mutual resemblances among the participating families were unmistakable.[29] Rather than the June Summit, it was the August 2000 reunions that saw the peak of South Korean public opinion favoring engagement. Although the elevated level of public interest would fall off during later rounds of such family meetings, the period coinciding with the reunions broadcasts in mid-August of 2000 marked the highest point of support among South Koreans for the Sunshine Policy. Approval ratings reached nearly 88 percent in favor of engagement with North Korea in August 2000, compared to 49 percent in February of that year and approximately 75 percent at the time of the June Summit itself.[30] Sociologist Cho Uhn aptly describes this first set of inter-Korean reunions held in the wake of the June Summit as the social and cultural counterpart to the diplomatic and political breakthroughs of the period.[31]

Regarding the wider atmosphere surrounding these breakthroughs, pundits and observers have described a "post-Summit euphoria" in South Korea, implying that it was a phase of irrational exuberance that would soon pass.[32] Yet the months following the Summit marked a significant cultural shift, whose wider implications would outlive that temporary boost in popular interest. Indeed, the positive public mood toward the summit was itself a notable development, which did not materialize immediately. As sociologist Gi-Wook Shin observes, "Although most South Koreans eventually embraced the historic summit with enthusiasm, their initial reaction was one of shock and confusion because their suspicion and fear of the communist regime runs so deep."[33] Regarding those months following the June Summit and culminating in the August reunions, this book considers what occurred on the level of popular memory and cultural practice that contributed toward making reconciliation possible to imagine, thus facilitating the political agency for concrete changes in South Korea's inter-Korean policy that set the course for the ensuing decade of engagement. In part, the events surrounding the August 2000 reunions contributed toward making kinship a mode of recognition and legibility vis-à-vis North Koreans by displacing the demonized anticommunist caricatures that had still been prevalent.[34] This familial framework suggests why these events, with their normative appeal, have been largely overlooked in political and academic commentaries, which instead focus on inter-Korean meetings between heads of state. Yet, as this book seeks to capture, wartime family separation remains deeply resonant in the Korean cultural imaginary, not only as a evocative metaphor for national division, but also as the embodied experience of the ongoing losses brought about by unended war.

CRITICAL EVENTS AND THE MOBILIZATION OF MEMORY

Family separation during the Korean War can be traced to the fragmenting of kin groups and communities caused by the practice of forced conscription and the precipitous flight of civilians amid the oscillation of battle lines down and up the peninsula.

During the fiercely embattled period from June 1950 until July 1951, Seoul changed hands four times, as did nearly all of the territory on the peninsula at least once during the war.[35] Amid such volatility, there were countless instances in which the bodies of the dead could not be found or reclaimed and were never given proper burial, and this was true of both soldiers and civilians caught in the crossfire. Among Koreans displaced while fleeing from the fighting or while pressed into taking up arms, what they had thought to be temporary emergency departures later became a fate of indefinite exile and displacement when they found themselves unable to return to their homes after the active hostilities came to an end. In the weeks leading up to the reunions in August 2000, one woman recalled the shock of

Figure 0.3. Civilians flee from combat during the Second Battle of Seoul, September 1950. Photograph by David Douglas Duncan, *Seoul Staircase, Korean War* 1950 © David Douglas Duncan, reproduced with permission from the artist and the Photography Collection at the Harry Ransom Center, University of Texas at Austin.

discovering her lost brother to be alive while also conveying her sense of guilt that her family had long mourned him among the casualties of the war; as she put it, "We searched for days, months, then waited for years. How long could we wait? When so many others died in the war?"[36] Given the devastation wreaked by warfare, the hardships of the postwar period, and the discrimination endured by those with relatives believed to be on the other side of the territorial and ideological divide, it is not surprising that so many separated family members said they eventually gave up searching for their relatives who went missing during the war. The occasion of the separated families' reunions thereby prompted a sudden foregrounding of the Korean War's traumatic memory, as these meetings revived the haunting unknowns left behind by the war's catastrophic toll of mass death.

Concurrent with these dramatic new openings in Korea, the public history of the Korean War was also undergoing transformation on an international scale. In April 2000 the Pulitzer Prize for investigative journalism was awarded to three Associated Press correspondants for their reporting on a massacre of unarmed Korean civilians committed by U.S. soldiers during late July 1950, at a railroad bridge in South Korea's North Chungchŏng province near the village of No Gun Ri.[37] The prestigious honor instantly brought widespread attention among the global media to previously marginalized testimonies of surviving witnesses. The massacre had also been covered in the South Korean alternative press during prior years; most notably, the progressive news monthly *Mal* published a groundbreaking story in July 1994.[38] While it took five to six years for contemporary accounts of the No Gun Ri massacre to receive greater attention outside of Korea following the AP's investigations, even the initial 1994 article in the South Korean progressive media represented a lapse of more than four decades for it to appear as part of a "First Testimony" series. In other words, such deferral itself indicates the tenacity of silences that had persisted about controversial aspects of the war and reflected the chilling effect of the dominant anticommunist social milieu in South Korea.[39] Sociologist George Katsiaficas similarly registers the irony revealed by the fact that the No Gun Ri massacre became known in the U.S. media as a "Korean My Lai," even though those civilian killings in Korea took place nearly twenty years *before* the far more widely known 1968 massacre of Vietnamese villagers.[40]

On a regional scale, such breaking of taboos about memories of the Korean War occurred within a broader context in East Asia where contemporary testimonies of World War II survivors had brought new attention to traumatic war memory throughout the 1990s.[41] Amid the epochal historical developments in former Cold War configurations globally, previously suppressed memories about World War II also began to resurface, and in East Asia these included the testimonies of those who had been victimized fifty years earlier by Japanese aggression and militarism.[42] This in turn triggered new waves of transnational political activity and, most notably during this period, momentum gathered internationally around the movement on behalf of the survivors of the Japanese military's system of "comfort stations" during the Asia Pacific War/Second World War. In Japanese-occupied territories, the "comfort women" were those who had been kidnapped, defrauded, or otherwise coerced into a system that subjected them to horrifying conditions of sexual slavery. In an attempt to curtail the kind of wanton violence and rapes of local women that had been committed by its soldiers during the 1937 Nanjing Massacre, Japanese authorities had developed this system of military "comfort stations" as a means to avoid inciting hostility and resistance among the local populations.[43] However, the military "comfort system" did not prevent rape; it instead created an infrastructure of systemic mass rape based on human trafficking and the brutalizing enslavement of an estimated two hundred thousand young women and girls, some as young as thirteen years old, who had been relocated from elsewhere. The women and girls victimized by this system were predominantly those brought from Korea, who comprised an estimated 80 percent, with other women brought from China, the Philippines, the Dutch East Indies, Taiwan, Malaya, and Burma. Beginning in the late twentieth century, advocates for survivors have demanded reparations and an official state apology from the Japanese government, in a movement that had been initially led by local and national organizations of women from South Korea. They worked in coalition with counterparts in Japan, the Philippines, and other Asian nations, and their advocacy inspired the involvement of scholars and activists elsewhere in the international community.[44]

Historian Laura Hein analyzes the proliferation of scholarship and sudden prominence of advocacy about the comfort women issue in the 1990s, arguing that it was propelled in considerable part by two developments increasingly salient at the time: the burgeoning influence of global feminism and the mobilization of Asian diasporic identities. The military comfort women, as Hein writes, thereby became "the site for several different battles over the future" whose narratives have galvanized "an array of contemporary and competing visions of citizenship, race, gender and human rights throughout the world."[45] Moreover, the breaking of such silences would have tremendous stakes, particularly in East Asia amid the emergence of new forms of nationalism. As Hein puts it, "The comfort women's placement at the vortex of the global battle known as World War II means that remembrance of their plight forces a reassessment of all the symbolic meanings already assigned to that conflict."[46] The extraordinary stakes of this controversy help to explain its recurring intensity well after the 1990s and into the present, with ongoing clashes in the realms of international diplomacy, transnational activism, and public memory.

If the politics of memory regarding legacies of World War II have been bound up in various battles over the future, so have such intense struggles similarly arisen over implications of the production and reproduction of memories about the Korean War, a war that never formally ended. As literary critic Jeon Seung-Hee observes in a 2010 article on artistic representations of Korean War memory, "a more comprehensive memory of the [Korean] War never entered into the global consciousness" in the same way as World War II or the Vietnam War. Indeed, during a period otherwise regarded globally as "post–Cold War," the persistance of the global Cold War in Northeast Asia is perhaps most evident in divided Korea. The continued dominance of Cold War memory on the peninsula not only characterizes official discourse in North Korea but is also an ongoing dynamic in South Korean memory politics. Jeon writes, "In South Korea, until very recently, the state allowed only one kind of war-related memory, one based on the Manichean scheme of good versus evil, South Korea and its allies representing the former and North Korea and its ally representing the latter."[47] Significantly, it was as an extension of democratization in South Korea, a process ongoing since the 1980s, that controversies over historical memory roiled public debate during the last decade of the twentieth century. "If the 1980s was the period of political struggle [over democratization], the 1990s was the period of 'struggle for memory' in interpreting contemporary history in Korean society," writes historian Chung Yong-Wook in his guest editor's introduction to a 2004 special issue on war and memory in Korean history. "These phenomena meant that the 'official view' [of] contemporary Korean history was weakened by post–Cold War Korean society and its democratization, and thus, social powers competed over historical interpretation and historical vision at the level of civil society."[48]

The summer of 2000 therefore represented the historical conjunction of factors that yielded the June Summit meeting, at a time when South Korea's turbulent "history wars" of the 1990s would be profoundly altered by a sudden and unprecedented degree of global attention to 1950s-era wartime atrocities in Korea. That is, for the Pulitzer Prize committee to recognize the AP team's journalistic coverage, which drew heavily upon accounts by survivors of the No Gun Ri massacre, meant that those narratives of abiding war trauma would reach a new and greatly expanded audience beyond Korea. This suddenly shifted the cultural terrain for the public memory of such contested Korean War narratives to expand beyond a domestic scale to a broadly international one. As issues formerly proscribed as unspeakable in South Korea entered into wider public discussion there and beyond, that brought new momentum to oral history as a means of bringing greater attention to these previously repressed discursive spaces about social suffering caused by the Korean War. Furthermore, in the 1990s in South Korea, clashes over historical interpretations arose not only with respect to the

1950–1953 Korean War but also regarding two other highly controversial topics: the period under Japanese colonial rule, and the Park Chung Hee era. These confrontations between official and unofficial histories suggest why, for Koreans, it has been so difficult to honor the loss of those who died or were never recovered in the Korean War without playing into divisive ideological conflicts.

At the same time, the stakes surrounding such contested politics of war memory are tremendous, particularly given the disturbingly high proportion of civilian casualties in the Korean War. Although statistics are difficult to verify, Korean War deaths are estimated to exceed four million, and more than half of those who died were civilians.[49] As noted by anthropologist Heonik Kwon, recent academic research into the war's historical traumas has illuminated how the Korean War was "not primarily a violent struggle between contending armed forces" but rather "the struggle for survival by unarmed civilians against the generalized, indiscriminate violence perpetrated by the armed political forces of all sides."[50] Even so, the bitter reality of what Kwon calls "the Korean War's war against civilians" became off-limits as a taboo subject through a suppression of ordinary people's narratives by dominant Cold War interpretations on both sides. Given that it has only been in recent years that an emphasis on traumatic memory has emerged in Korean War historiography,[51] the conciliatory invocation of shared social suffering at the heart of reunions in August 2000 cannot be taken for granted.

Truly, through the experiences of separated families, the enduring costs of unresolved war are evident as liabilities not only in diplomatic and military terms, but also in the subtle dimensions of everyday life, kinship, and personhood.[52] It is in these intimate realms where Koreans have internalized the dynamics of two opposing national security states buttressed by an unending war, and separated families are among those most painfully conscious of that internalization. The ongoing separation of families across the 38th parallel therefore reflects how national division has been *lived*—as quotidian reality, as a persistent reminder of the losses incurred during a prior era, and as the site of unanswered questions and family secrets engendered by the Korean War and its lack of resolution. In the months following the June Summit and at a transformative moment in the history of inter-Korean reconciliation, the reunions of separated families in August 2000 effectively served as an unprecedented joint North–South Korean commemoration of the Korean War, one which centered on ordinary people as the war's victims.

This book argues that, prior to the two states' proceeding with the terms of inter-Korean economic cooperation, the reunions opened a liminal space to recognize the war's staggering human devastation, invoking a sense of bereavement to which both sides could lay claim.

This study therefore analyzes these reunions and their surrounding developments as means to explore the broader questions: What makes reconciliation possible to imagine? If local instantiations of the Cold War had long been sustained largely by fear, suspicion, and animosity,[53] what affective transformations are required to bring one of the last conflicts of the global Cold War to an end? Regarding the social construction of history and the role of popular memory in envisioning alternatives for the future, anthropologist Allen Feldman writes, "Perhaps the most powerful insight to emerge from cultural anthropology in the last decade is that history does not constitute a neutral milieu within which people act, but that it is the constructed object of social action, situated performances, and symbolic mediation. The vernacular depiction of history and the mobilization of popular memory inform and structure political agency."[54] This insight builds upon Paul Connerton's model of cultural memory as mediated through deliberate interventions by social actors who work to disrupt or alter dominant systems of meaning with intentional performances that often take the form of ritual.[55] Connerton theorizes that cultural memory is reproduced through what he calls "legitimized agents of memory, collective recollection practices, and formal spaces for the articulation and public depiction of memory."[56] Popular cultural memory is thereby generated under conditions shaped in no small part by events, which in turn have political effects.

Arguing for a form of ethnography that plumbs the transformative potential of events, anthropologist Veena Das has explored the implications of "critical events" whose catalytic impact resonates simultaneously across multiple spaces and diverse institutions.[57] Following Das, anthropologist Emma Tarlo describes such moments of intense dynamism as those which are productive of "new modes of action and encourage new social and political formations as people are propelled into unpredicted terrains."[58] The Korean family reunions that took place in 2000 provide classic examples of the convergence of such historical and cultural processes. This study therefore approaches the reunions in August 2000 as critical events that provide an analytical prism through which to consider the mobilization of popular cultural memory at the onset of the decade of inter-Korean engagement.

This book also seeks to complicate historian John Bodnar's distinction between official and vernacular memory. In a widely cited discussion on public memory and commemoration, Bodnar argues that official memory serves to stabilize the status quo for the interests of elites, while vernacular memory addresses the concerns of ordinary people and involves events of most immediate impact to the multitude.[59] However, such a conceptual opposition presumes overly straightforward notions of the power of the state. In the case of the Kim Dae-jung administration, the South Korean state actually held a politically weak position as a minority government facing domestic skepticism with respect to its policy toward North Korea. Such doubts stemmed partly from a general ambivalence among South Koreans toward reunification, and also from the strong opposition among elites and political conservatives who remained both distrustful of North Korea and also invested in the status quo of national division.[60] Kim Dae-jung himself was a long-time opposition candidate who had been imprisoned and narrowly escaped assassination during South Korea's period of military authoritarian rule. Kim Dae-jung assumed the presidency in 1998 in South Korea's first democratic transfer of power to the opposition party, but that was only after eking out a razor-thin victory over his conservative rival, Lee Hoi-chang.[61] Though Kim's election victory had profound resonance among the generation of Koreans who had participated in the democratization movement in the 1980s, his government would face the formidable challenge of navigating a wholesale bureaucratic turnover while also managing the fallout of the Asian Financial Crisis amid a divided electorate. Kim therefore came into office with a bold inter-Korean reconciliation agenda, but also an unquestionably attenuated political base.[62]

If inter-Korean rapprochement meant a departure from patterns of hostile recriminations, it further entailed unsettling the hegemonic Cold War interpretation of the Korean War. The dominant orthodox view in South Korea had placed blame for the war entirely on North Korea for launching a general invasion along the 38th parallel on June 25, 1950, which marked the beginning of all-out combat in Korea. Yet reconciliatory activities in the early twenty-first century were predicated on a broader understanding of the conditions leading to war rather than strictly the circumstances surrounding the North Korean invasion, instead tracing the origins of the Korean War as a civil war back to Korea's division in 1945 at the end of World War II.[63] Liberated from thirty-five years of Japanese colonial rule following Japan's surrender, Korea did not become an independent nation, but rather was partitioned by the Allied Forces into two zones: one occupied by the United States south of the 38th parallel, and the other by the Soviet Union north of that dividing line. Koreans on both sides, after enduring the hardships particularly during the harsh wartime mobilization and brutal repression of the colonial period's final decade, opposed partition and divided occupation as unacceptable. The international community also regarded this arrangement as provisional, but the deterioration of U.S.–Soviet relations and the growing rivalry of the early Cold War jeopardized international negotiations intended to resolve Korea's temporary division. The conditions for enduring national division soon thereafter took root when separate elections were held in the two halves of the peninsula in 1948, leading to the establishment of the Republic of Korea in the South and the Democratic People's Republic of Korea in the North. As both Korean states laid claim to sovereignty over the entire peninsula, each denounced the other as a traitorous puppet of foreign powers, and the competition for legitimacy grew more heated as armed skirmishes broke out along the border.

Historian Park Myung-Lim has argued that the post-1945 partition produced a driving imperative to restore the lost unitary nation on both the
opposing sides, which gave rise to the tension and conflict on the peninsula
that culminated in the Korean War.[64] As the North Korean premier Kim Il-
sung in North Korea called for the destruction of the Southern regime, so did
the South Korean president Syngman Rhee vigorously push for an ROK
strategy of unification by force. Amid anxieties among the Communists over
the prospect of a rearmed Japan allied with both the United States and the
nascent South Korean Rhee regime, Kim Il-sung lobbied the Soviet leader
Joseph Stalin to back a plan for invasion.[65] Full-scale war broke out when
North Korean forces, supplied with Soviet weapons, invaded the South in
June 1950. The resulting Korean War would draw the United States and
China into a grim and bitter conflict alongside South Koreans and North
Koreans, while the threat of thermonuclear warfare and the possibility of a
third World War loomed ominously. The major hostilities would eventually
end in a stalemate that returned the line of Korea's division roughly to the
same location as it had been prior to the fighting. Although combat was
suspended with the signing of a temporary armistice on July 27, 1953, a
breakdown in further negotiations the following year meant that a peace
treaty was never signed. With Korea's national division deeply entrenched
following the brutal warfare, the two Korean states would remain in a technical state of war that endures until the present.

Korea's war-separated families have therefore faced exceedingly formidable obstacles to family reunification. In contrast to comparable historical
circumstances of post-conflict partition in Germany, China/Taiwan, and
Vietnam, what distinguishes the case of Korea is the extremity of conditions
surrounding its enduring national division. As historian Charles K. Armstrong has written, "Nowhere else on earth has national division been so
acute, antagonism so bitter, cross-boundary contact so limited, or mutual
suspicion so high as on the Korean peninsula."[66] Although the term "reunions" is used widely in English to refer to these series of family meetings, the
word is misleading, for they were not reunions in the same sense as the
family meetings held between family members divided between East and
West Germany or family members separated from each other between China
and Taiwan or Hong Kong.[67] In these other instances, telephone communication or letter exchanges had already long been possible before reunions took
place. However, for ordinary citizens in either Korean state to attempt making private contact with anyone on the other side was an offense punishable
by imprisonment and potentially other social risks that could affect one's
entire kin network.[68] Even for those families who refused to consider their
relative dead until they had irrefutable proof, the formidable risks attached to
being related to someone across the divide meant that the missing family
member underwent a social death. Regarding the North–South Korean separ-

ated family members who participated in the reunions, they had not only been physically separated from each other, but were essentially lost to each other for five decades.

The long-term separation of families between the two Koreas has therefore persisted at the intersection between the territorial and subjective dimensions of the peninsula's national division. On the one hand, the sheer logistical reality of Korea as a divided territory has imposed daunting impediments to even the possibility of imagining family reunification. These include, among others, legal prohibitions against unauthorized contact through telephone calls or postal exchanges, the absence of infrastructure for regular civilian inter-Korean contact or communication, and a de facto border that has been all but impassable to ordinary citizens.[69] On the other hand, the experiences of living amid the conditions of national division in the wake of civil war would take a particularly exacting toll on North–South separated families. In divided Korea, war survivors traumatized by the loss of missing family members and other loved ones were often left to cope with the insecurity of displacement by physical uprooting and social marginalization. They were also haunted by not being able to determine the fates of those who were presumed to have died in the war, but who could have conceivably survived and may still be alive on the other side of the 38th parallel. Separated families are therefore comprised of individuals who have been inescapably entangled in the historic enmity between two states, through a kin member who is known or believed to be on the other side of the divide. However, the lack of all contact or communication among ordinary people across the 38th parallel meant that their absent kin would remain indefinitely suspended between life and death, leaving their families also in an indefinite state of uncertainty.

LIMINALITIES OF KOREAN DIVISION

The boundaries of life and death have historically been a rich site of anthropological inquiry. The formation of such boundaries express how personhood is attributed, asserted, and attenuated through processes of social recognition. In this literature, what figures highly, alongside themes of memory and identity, is the concept of liminality.[70] Throughout this book, I explore implications of liminality, the state of between-ness or that of being on a threshold in space or in time, which aptly captures Korea's historical and political circumstances at the start of the new millennium. I regard North–South separated families, through their liminal subjectivity, among those who most clearly embody both the material consequences and phenomenological experiences surrounding Korean division.

Liminality, a concept with a long genealogy in anthropology, was first theorized by French ethnographer and folklorist Arnold Van Gennep in his classic study, *The Rites of Passage*, published in 1909. Van Gennep analyzed the transitions between key stages in life, such as puberty, marriage, parenthood, and advancement to a higher-status position, by mapping the dynamics of ritual action that separates the initiates and the uninitiated by an intermediary domain, the *"limen,"* Latin for "threshold." Describing how the change of status achieved in ritual is accomplished only after the initiate passes through the threshold represented by this in-between space, Van Gennep also observed that the passage from one social position to another is often identified as a territorial passage.[71] With a focus on how the liminal stage provides the basis for ritual's wider transformative capacity, Max Gluckman and Victor Turner took up Van Gennep's concept to analyze conflict processes in their respective studies of African societies in the 1950s and 1960s.[72] Ritual makes this transformation possible by bringing about the condition of liminality, whereby participants are separated from the demands and obligations of everyday social existence and take on an ambiguous status. In Turner's theorization, by allowing ritual subjects to experiment with and reconfigure social norms, liminality constitutes a "realm of pure possibility," and the potentiality inherent to ritual pertains not only to ritual subjects themselves but extends to wider society, generating the possibility of "standing aside not only from one's own social position but from all social positions and of formulating a potentially unlimited series of alternative social arrangements."[73] Taking his analysis beyond formal ritual, Turner argues that Van Gennep's model of ritual passage could be adapted to interpret more broadly those societal crises that can arise during epochal periods of transition.

Liminality thus provides a theoretical entrée into the unfolding inchoate state of affairs that characterizes periods of enormous social change, such as those that occur in contexts of post-conflict reconciliation on a national or regional scale. Recent anthropological studies of social and political transformations have furthermore analyzed the ways that literal and figurative boundaries may be crossed, confounded, or reconfigured during liminal periods. In fact, this common thematic thread is shared by ethnographic analyses whose subjects are otherwise highly divergent, and these include: ritual initiations into Thai arch-nationalist communities; borderland identities in the wake of East Germany's collapsed political systems; and the mixing of legal, political, and religious institutions in South Africa's Truth and Reconciliation Commissions.[74] Other studies render liminality a versatile heuristic through which to regard a yet wider range of ongoing contemporary phenomena, including visual ritualization through mass-mediated events, and the formation and contestation of identities among refugees and displaced peoples.[75] Mindful of these disparate traditions of previous work, I undertake this study of the post-Summit reunions of North–South Korean war-separated families while presenting an alternative composite of liminality's many dimensions, posing new questions about their implications and positing new theorizations.

In this book, I consider how these separated-family reunions were initially held as political rituals intended to foster new forms of national intimacy, in keeping with a wider state strategy of facilitating inter-Korean reconciliation and economic cooperation as a response to increased neoliberal pressures following the Asian financial crisis. At the same time, these North–South family meetings held during the immediate post-Summit period would yield unintended and more enduring outcomes in the ways that they unsettled notions of war death and occasioned the reframing of Korean War memory. At the turn of the new millennium, these reunions would create liminal spaces in which Koreans from both sides of the divide could reckon with the traumas of family separation and the unresolved Korean War.

Yet, as the August 2000 reunions made it possible for both South Koreans and North Koreans to participate in a moving public acknowledgment of shared war losses, attempting to account for that acknowledgment's belatedness after a half-century interval is more complicated than strictly pointing to the preceding decades of enmity across the 38th parallel. Take, for example, the 1998 study *Korea and Its Futures: Unification and the Unfinished War* by anthropologist Roy Richard Grinker, who also raised questions about the undertow of thwarted bereavement in modern Korean cultural formations and subjectivities. Characterizing Korea's post–WWII division as a death of the unitary nation, Grinker argues—with an analytical focus on the South Korean side—that the facile presumption that unification would amount to the South's assimilation of the North evinces an "inability to mourn" the losses bound up in national division. According to Grinker, South Koreans' then-widespread misrecognition of the Korean nation as an undiversified "people" split solely by the confrontation of opposing states, led to the false assumption that a homogeneous nation could be restored upon unification. Because "south Koreans cannot mourn the loss of the homogenous nation," he contended at the time, they are also obstructed from fully confronting the past and reconciling with the North.[76]

It should be noted that Grinker's premise of assumed homogeneity would no longer hold true today of South Koreans, who generally recognize that the multiculturalism of their society will only continue to grow and have few illusions about an idealized, ethnically homogenous, post-unification society.[77] Nevertheless, revisiting Grinker's analysis is warranted here particularly for the way that it casts the liminality of Korea's ongoing division, through a striking metaphor of a "death without death." As Grinker writes:

> National division is temporary—it is a death without death—and so south
> Korean responses to national division and north–south differences contain

elements of both grief and outright denial. Koreans cannot mourn the sunder-
ing of their nation because they also persistently maintain a vision and hope
that the symbolic living and dead will be one again, that the homogeneous will
be resuscitated from the heterogeneous. *Representing north Korea and division in the south is a form of bereavement in which loss is denied* (emphasis
added).[78]

For Grinker to assert the denial of loss in bereavement is to invoke Sigmund
Freud's "Mourning and Melancholia." In that influential essay, which dates
to 1915 but was published two years later, Freud seeks to distinguish mourning from melancholia, noting that they share virtually the same traits: "a
profoundly painful dejection, cessation of interest in the outside world, loss
of the capacity to love, inhibition of all activity."[79] Freud recognizes both
mourning and melancholia as reactions to profound loss, whether the death
of a loved one or the loss of a cherished abstraction such as one's country.
However, of the two conditions, mourning is readily understandable and
expected to pass after a given lapse of time; melancholia, in contrast, remains
open ended and is therefore regarded as pathological. In the case of melancholia, Freud writes, "one cannot see clearly what it is that has been lost."
This restricted perception may also be true of the melancholic subject her- or
himself, who "cannot consciously perceive what [he] has lost either" and
who may be "aware of the loss which has given rise to melancholia, but only
in the sense that he knows *whom* he has lost but not *what* he has lost in
him."[80] Freud's discussion suggests that both outside observers and the melancholic subject struggle with understanding the nature of loss as well as the
meaning of that loss. Elusive to both may be the initial cause of the bereavement, and also lacking may be a conscious understanding of *what* was lost in
the state of being bereft. Hence, if the loss that gives rise to melancholia may
well be unconscious, melancholia would indeed correspond with Grinker's
evocation, as bereavement in which loss is denied.

With this in mind, it is significant to weigh the nuanced reading of
"Mourning and Melancholia" offered by literary critics David L. Eng and
David Kazanjian in their introduction to the edited volume *Loss: The Politics
of Mourning*. They note how Freud suggests that melancholia might not be
seen as pathological if only the nature and causes of this condition were more
fully understood. Eng and Kazanjian write, "a better understanding of melancholic attachments to loss might depathologize those attachments, making
visible not only their social bases but also their creative, unpredictable, political aspects."[81] They perceive melancholia or sustained mourning, therefore,
not as pathology but rather as a challenge to comprehension. Drawing upon
their interpretation of Walter Benjamin's *Theses on the Philosophy of History*, they write, "Unlike mourning, in which the past is declared resolved,
finished, and dead, in melancholia the past remains steadfastly alive in the

present. By engaging in 'countless separate struggles' with loss, melancholia might be said to constitute, as Benjamin would describe it, an ongoing and open relationship with the past." Testifying to the intellectual, mnemonic, and creative potential that stand to be leveraged through a "new collective politics of mourning," Eng and Kazanjian write, "This engagement generates sites for memory and history, for the rewriting of the past as well as the reimagining of the future." With regard to the melancholia in divided Korea starkly laid bare by the family reunions, then, rather than simply reading them as a negative incapacity to let go of the widespread losses of war and division, such forms of sustained mourning may instead be understood as a continuous and open engagement with the past, which allows for new perspectives on what the future makes possible.

In the context of divided Korea, Grinker also sees transformative potential in melancholia, which he compares to the concept of *han*. Although the Korean word *han* is often translated as "unresolved bitterness," Grinker turns to a 1993 analysis by literary critic Ch'ŏn Yi-du for a comprehensive exploration of the concept's multiple variants. Significantly, Ch'ŏn does not focus solely on the aggrieved manifestation of *han* as unresolvable unhappiness and longing (or *hant'an*)—which is the definition often circulated in Western travel writing and popular narratives as the clichéd explanation to encapsulate the supposed "essence" of a Korean national psyche. Instead, Ch'ŏn also considers "bright" or positive forms of *han*, that which can evoke a sensitive or delicate response, or alternatively can incite determined action. In explaining the precondition to this manifold concept, Grinker demonstrates how he filters his reading of Ch'ŏn's analysis through an explicitly psychoanalytic lens: "*Han* refers to a consciousness of ongoing trauma and a lack of resolution and reconciliation."[82] *Han*'s lack of resolution echoes how melancholia is similarly taken to represent an indefinitely liminal state, suspended within the experience of loss and unable to reach what is presumed to be a healthy and normal resolution in the eventual acceptance of that loss. Thus, whether interpreted as melancholia or *han*, the continuous engagement with past losses and their legacies in the present again underscores how the liminal itself often occupies a stigmatized or pathologized position of marginality. However, following Eng and Kazanjian as well as Ch'ŏn and Grinker, I argue that liminality—like melancholia—should in fact be reclaimed for the ways that it can imbue a position of efficacy, as the generative and transformative space that gives rise to new possibilities.

In bringing attention back to divided Korea through the metaphor of liminality, it should be acknowledged, so readily can such a parallel be drawn, that the condition of Korea's "in-betweenness" risks being taken for granted. Nevertheless, as chapter 1 makes clear, Korea's liminality should not be misrecognized as a timeless condition. Rather, the very perception of the peninsula's "strategic location" at the convergence of interests among continental and maritime powers in Northeast Asia should be itself properly historicized as an outcome of transformed notions of space and power that can be traced to the late nineteenth century, particularly the rise of Japan as a regional hegemon.[83] As detailed in chapter 1, primary documents from 1950 further reveal how references to Korea's geopolitical liminality were explicitly cited in the run-up to the two major turning points of international escalation during the Korean War, the legacies of which have left the peninsula in an ongoing limbo between war and peace. With its focus on the reunions of war-separated families, this book therefore attests to the striking conjuncture of circumstances that enables a multi-scalar investigation of divided Korea's liminality, whose implications range from wider geopolitical horizons, to peripheral social margins, to the most intimate of familial and personal spaces.

This book's analysis is not the first to weigh the salience of liminality to the cultural dimensions of Korean division. In *Korea and Its Futures*, Grinker similarly refers to North–South separated families as "betwixt and between," and he questions the notion of whether Koreans should in fact be regarded as remaining in a liminal stage, particularly when it is often assumed that an increasing percentage of contemporary South Koreans are ambivalent toward reunification.[84] Theater-arts scholar Suk-Young Kim interprets a 2001 production of *Kang Tek-koo*, a play by John Hoon, about the unexpected reunion of two half-brothers—one from North Korea and the other from South Korea—who meet in post–Soviet Russia. As the production builds upon references to liminal spaces and identities on multiple levels, Kim argues that "liminality effectively points to the middle zone which this production creates in between binary oppositions" including that between North and South, past and present, tragedy and comedy, and Cold War narrative and an overly naïve post–Cold War romantic narrative.[85] Compared to the play *Kang Tek-koo*, the 2005 South Korean film *A Bold Family*, directed by Jo Myeong-Nam, gives a more comical take on disenchanted youths' perceptions of reunification as an older generation's national aspiration.[86] That film revolves around an aging South Korean man who left behind a wife and daughter in North Korea during the war before relocating to the South where he remarried and started a new family. When the ailing father decides to stipulate that his South Korean children would only receive their sizeable inheritance if the two Koreas reunify before his death, his two sons scheme to create an elaborate charade in an effort to convince the father that reunification has already happened. If we consider these sardonic recent treatments of reunification and wartime separation in theater and popular culture, they suggest how, to South Korea's younger generations, the national past can loom as tiresome and oppressive when regarded as simply the inherited burden of historical tragedy. Yet, whether one stands inside or outside the South Korean cultural milieu, the historical amnesia that has surrounded the catastrophic losses of the Korean War elicits an ethical imperative to apprehend the war's un-ironic dimensions of tragedy, which must also be given their due. This book therefore considers whether liminality may offer an interpretive heuristic that captures the multiple dimensions of traumatic memory in Korea's modern history, but one tempered with a mitigating hope for the transition to something new.

In this vein, the reunions of Korean separated families during the early post-Summit period provoke what Homi Bhabha calls the "interstitial perspective," which illuminates the condition of cultural liminality *within* the nation. Bhabha refutes the linear narratives of the nation that are imposed upon Third World constituencies in order to naturalize and subordinate them. At the same time, he recognizes such essentialist narratives are invoked and contested *within* the discursive space of the nation. In the *Location of Culture*, Bhabha writes, "The liminal figure of the nation-space would ensure that no political ideologies could claim transcendent or metaphysical authority for themselves. This is because the subject of cultural discourse—the agency of a people—is split in the discursive ambivalence that emerges in the contest of narrative authority between the pedagogical and the performative."[87] In other words, there is an oscillation between the people's status as "historical 'objects' of a nationalist pedagogy" and as subjects of a process whereby they contribute toward bringing a nation into being. In considering the role of liminal subjects in the nation-space, however, I contend that it is valuable to bring the analysis of liminality back to an engagement with ritual theory. This is not only to benefit from an appreciation of political ritual as a national discursive space, but more importantly to take into account critiques that recognize the pitfalls of overly romantic or overly redemptive conceptualizations of liminality.

Keeping in mind Bhabha's theorization of the nation-space itself as a liminal figure, an unexpected dimension of these reunions in South Korea was how they also gave rise to a more inclusive understanding of the sympathetic nationalist category of "separated families" (*isan'gajok*). With the extensive media exposure of the Seoul reunions in August 2000, this category would be widened to incorporate individuals who had been previously marginalized and stigmatized during the Cold War period for having a family member believed or suspected to have gone to the North in wartime.[88] Such was the context for the unexpected resurfacing of hundreds of people discovered to have been alive in North Korea, after they had been presumed dead for several decades. A half-century after they had gone missing during the war, the sudden re-emergence of this sizeable group of unlikely survivors came amid the anticipation of their imminent visit from North Korea, making for sensational news. At the same time, these developments would touch off heady reverberations for their South Korean families and relatives. Since the 1950s, such individuals from kin groups with relatives possibly in the North were subject to harsh interrogations and police surveillance or spent decades scrupulously hiding those family ties. Then, during the summer of 2000, they unexpectedly found themselves pulled from marginalized obscurity and thrust onto a hyper-exposed national stage in a way that foregrounded the same kinship identity that they had previously worked so hard to conceal. [89]

Indeed, the August 2000 reunions in Seoul would give a newly privileged place to those who had long been excluded from anticommunist state idioms of national belonging in South Korea. To hide the taboo of being related to a missing person or someone known to have gone to the North in wartime, families commonly formalized the death of the absent family member by submitting a death report and performing ancestral rites (*chesa*) to memorialize the ostensible death. That is, such family members would report their unaccounted-for kin as dead with the understanding that this could help them avoid discrimination and stigmatization in the context of overarching state anticommunism that prevailed in the years following the Korean War and intensified under the Park Chung Hee era. Given this fraught historical background, the landmark occasion of the family meetings in August 2000 would signify among Koreans a breakthrough that went well beyond mere politically coded events. Resembling instead something akin to a ritual passage from death to life, [90] the events suggested an overturning and suspension of the natural order, while gesturing toward the magnitude of change that all Koreans would also have to undergo in order to overturn the existing political order of national division as well. Thus, at a time of heightened domestic and international media attention and at the peak of popular interest in the separated-families issue, the most widely circulated representations of the August 2000 reunions would reveal and underscore a co-constitutive relationship between, on the one hand, inter-Korean reconciliation on the peninsula, and on the other, a more localized process of reconciliation within South Korea regarding legacies of its past history of state anticommunism under military authoritarian rule.

With intersecting lines of inquiry based upon interpretations of ethnographic field research, archival documents, and academic secondary sources, this book weaves together threads of cultural, social, and historiographical analyses, while its various parts also indulge a bias for storytelling. In broad strokes, the body chapters of this study are divided into three parts: (I) The first part unfolds a chronological historical narrative that traces the origins of war and ideological conflict in modern Korea in order to frame (II) the second part, an analysis of the cultural turning points precipitated by political breakthroughs in inter-Korean reconciliation at the turn of the millennium. Then (III) the third part is more closely based on my ethnographic interviews and field research exploring the liminal subjectivities of separated family members who had participated in the post-Summit reunions in Seoul; their stories and commentaries reflect upon the experiences of living within the long shadow of the Korean War, which for them had meant coping for decades with the risk and uncertainty surrounding the question of whether or not their relatives were in fact among the war's survivors, albeit on the other side of the divide. Finally, as a counterpoint to this introduction, the book concludes by exploring a series of interpretive reflections on the meaning of the August 2000 reunions in light of more recent developments within and beyond Korean memory politics.

Although an analysis of the North–South Korean separated-family meetings is central to this study, the book is not strictly about the reunions per se. Rather, I approach the reunions as a key site in order to examine the unexpected *coming into perceptibility* of that which had been previously hidden for decades: the embodied practices of obscurity and silence in South Korea to which individuals resorted under conditions of division and the national-security state, which only became readily apparent at a crucial juncture in the process of reconciliation and rapprochement with the North. It considers significant instances in which the formerly invisible became highly visible, and the formerly unspeakable could become openly spoken and acknowledged. I do so in order to explore the phenomenological dimensions of reconciliation during this breakthrough period in South Korea—in particular, the simultaneity of the inter-state reconciliation with the North, and the process of reconciliation *within* South Korean society as its members contended with legacies of the anticommunist state under past authoritarian rule. No other individuals so clearly embodied these overlapping processes of reconciliation in South Korea than the family members who participated in the August 2000 reunions, particularly those which occurred in Seoul.[91] Those family meetings thereby offer a lens for approaching the cultural process of moving from a disposition of enmity to one of recognition and engagement amid the complex legacies of a civil war shaped by the exigencies of the global Cold War on the Korean peninsula.

NOTES

1. U.S. Department of State, *The Korea Problem at the Geneva Conference, April 26–June 16, 1954,* Publication 5609 (Washington, DC: U.S. Government Printing Office, 1954).

2. Vazira Fazila-Yacoobali Zamindar makes a similar observation about families divided by the partition of India and Pakistan in *The Long Partition and the Making of Modern South Asia: Refugees, Boundaries, Histories* (New York: Columbia University Press, 2007).

3. For example, see "More than 60,000 S. Koreans likely died before meeting separated family in North," Yonhap News Agency, September 7, 2014. For further discussion on the estimated number of separated families, see the discussion below in this chapter and footnote 8; also James Foley, "'Ten Million Families': Statistic or Metaphor?" *Korean Studies* 25, no. 1 (2001): 96–110.

4. Joseph Masco, "Engineering the Future as Nuclear Ruin," in *Imperial Debris: On Ruins and Ruination,* ed. Ann Laura Stoler (Durham, NC: Duke University Press, 2013), 278.

5. After the leaders of the two Koreas agreed upon the family exchange meetings at the June Summit, the candidate lists were not exchanged until mid-July, leaving only a month's

time to finalize preparations for the reunions on August 15th to coincide with Korea's Liberation Day.

6. As of 2000, there were 127,375 South Koreans registered with the Divided Families Information Center, but that figure does not include all separated families. If we consider the dynamics of wartime migration, border-crossings occurred in both directions during the war—but the far larger number of migrants was that of people moving south, whether to relocate by choice or simply to flee the fighting and bombing campaigns. During the period 1945–1953, that group totaled approximately 1,390,000. It is estimated that approximately 286,000 Koreans went from the South to the North during the post-Liberation and Korean War periods. That total number therefore adds up to 1,676,000 border-crossers who may likely have been separated from family members after 1953. In comparison, South Korea's current overall population is roughly 50 million, and North Korea's population is approximately 24.8 million. See Foley, "'Ten Million Families'"; Tai Hwan Kwon, *Demography of Korea: Population Change and Its Components 1925–66* (Seoul: Seoul National University Press, 1977); and further discussion in chapter 2.

7. Choong Soon Kim, *Faithful Endurance: An Ethnography of Korean Family Dispersal* (Tucson: University of Arizona Press, 1988); James Foley, *Korea's Divided Families: Fifty Years of Separation* (New York: Routledge, 2003).

8. Suk-ho Jun and Daniel Dayan, "An Interactive Media Event: South Korea's Televised 'Family Reunion,'" *Journal of Communication* 36, no. 2 (1986): 73–82. To gain an understanding of the continued impact of this program in South Korean cultural life even decades after the telethon aired, consider recent analyses of the popular television program *Ach'im Madang*, which would run regular segments initially inspired by the KBS telethon but which featured reunions among various kinds of separated families, including adoptees meeting with their birth parents. See Elise Prébin, *Meeting Once More: The Korean Side of Transnational Adoption* (New York: NYU Press, 2013); and Hosu Kim, "Korean Birthmothers Lost and Found in the Search-and-Reunion Narratives," *Cultural Studies Critical Methodologies* 12, no. 5 (2012): 438–449.

9. Kim, *Faithful Endurance*, 112.

10. Lauren Berlant, *The Female Complaint: The Unfinished Business of Sentimentality in American Culture* (Durham, NC: Duke University Press, 2008).

11. Kim, *Faithful Endurance*, 110.

12. Ibid., 113–14; for further discussion of anti-North Korean rhetoric, see also Lee, "Making and Unmaking the Korean National Division: Separated Families in the Cold War and Post–Cold War Eras," PhD dissertation (Urbana-Champaign: University of Illinois, 2006), 55–56.

13. Lee, "Making and Unmaking," 52.

14. Meetings would continue in the unsuccessful attempt to hold further rounds of family meetings; for example, during 1988–1992, Red Cross representatives held at least eighteen meetings to discuss visits of separated family members. See Kongdan Oh, "The Problem and Promise of Inter-Korean Economic Cooperation," in *Korea Briefing: Toward Reunification*, ed. David R. McCann (Armonk, NY: M. E. Sharpe, 1996), 28.

15. Jong-woo Han and Tae-hern Jung, eds., *Understanding North Korea: Indigenous Perspectives* (Lanham, MD: Lexington Books, 2013), 378.

16. In his 2012 memoir Lim Dong-won, the Sunshine Policy's architect and the Minister of Unification during the Kim Dae-jung administration, writes, "The goal of the Sunshine policy was to induce incremental change in the North for opening and reform towards a market economy, and to establish peace on the peninsula to create a state of *de facto* unification first." Lim, *Peacemaker: Twenty Years of Inter-Korean Relations and the North Korean Nuclear Issue* (Stanford, CA: Stanford University Asia-Pacific Research Center, 2012), 165.

17. Key-young Son, *South Korean Engagement Policies and North Korea: Identities, Norms and the Sunshine Policy* (New York: Routledge, 2006).

18. North Korea established diplomatic ties with thirteen countries (including the United Kingdom, Germany, and Bahrain) as well as the EU in 2000–2001, compared with only one (Bosnia and Herzegovina) during the transitional period between 1994 and 1998. See "DPRK Diplomatic Relations," The National Committee on North Korea, http://www.ncnk.org

/resources/briefing-papers/all-briefing-papers/dprk-diplomatic-relations.

19. In comparing this agreement with its precursor signed at the first inter-Korean summit in 2000, political scientist Chung-in Moon has noted that the "June 15 Declaration is largely symbolic and general, whereas the 2007 document is concrete and specific." See Moon, "From Symbols to Substance: Comparing the 2000 and 2007 Inter-Korean Summits," *Global Asia* 2, no. 3 (2007).

20. Gelézeau et al., eds., *De-Bordering Korea: Tangible and Intangible Legacies of the Sunshine Policy* (New York and London: Routledge, 2013), 2.

21. Nan Kim, "Korea on the Brink: Reading the *Yŏnp'yŏng* Shelling and Its Aftermath," *The Journal of Asian Studies* 70, no. 2 (2011): 337–38, 346–351.

22. Charles K. Armstrong, "Contesting the Peninsula," *New Left Review* 51 (2008): 115–36; Jong Kun Choi, "Sunshine Over Barren Soil: The Domestic Politics of Engagement Identity Formation in South Korea," *Asian Perspective* 34, no. 4 (2010): 134.

23. Yul Sohn and Kang Won-taek, "South Korea in 2012: An Election Year under Rebalancing Challenges," *Asian Survey* 53, no. 1 (2013): 201.

24. Moon Chung-in, *The Sunshine Policy: In Defense of Engagement as a Path to Peace in Korea* (Seoul: Yonsei University Press, 2012).

25. Robert Winstanley-Chesters and Christopher Green, "A Bifurcated Review of *De-Bordering Korea: Tangible and Intangible Legacies of the Sunshine Policy*," *Sino-NK* (May 12, 2014). http://sinonk.com/2014/05/12/a-bifurcated-review-of-de-bordering-korea-tangible-and-intangible-legacies-of-the-sunshine-policy/.

26. See, for example, Moon Chung-in, *The Sunshine Policy: In Defense of Engagement as a Path to Peace in Korea* (Seoul: Yonsei University Press, 2012); Sung Chull Kim and David C. Kang, *Engagement with North Korea: A Viable Alternative* (Albany: State University of New York Press, 2009); Key-young Son, *South Korean Engagement Policies and North Korea: Identities, Norms and the Sunshine Policy* (London: Routledge, 2006).

27. Cho Uhn, "Ch'immukkwa kiŏkŭi yŏksahwa: yŏsŏng, munhwa, ideologi" [Historicizing Silence and Memory: Women, Culture, Ideology]. *Ch'angjakkwa bip'yŏng [Creation and Criticism]* 112 (Summer 2001): 76–90.

28. The only official exchange of families between the two Koreas prior to 2000 occurred in September 1985, when delegations of fifty separated family members were sent from each side to meet relatives in Seoul and Pyongyang. Out of the one hundred people involved in the exchange, only sixty-five family members were able to meet their relatives. Furthermore, those events were marred by ideological grandstanding on both sides, including North Korean denunciations of the South Korean government and of the United States. See James Foley, *Korea's Divided Families: Fifty Years of Separation* (London and New York: Routledge, 2004).

29. In later years such emotionally fraught images would have relatively little political impact, seen as sad but clichéd representations, regarded by South Korean audiences with cynicism due in part to the overexposure and sensationalist media coverage of inter-Korean family meetings. But at the time of the August reunions, the intensity of these encounters was not widely expected by South Korean media audiences.

30. Choi, "Sunshine Over Barren Soil," 134.

31. Cho Uhn, "Historicizing Silence and Memory," 76–78.

32. For example, see Institute for Foreign Policy Analysis, *Northeast Asian Security after Korean Reconciliation or Reunification: Preparing the U.S.–Japan Alliance* (Cambridge, MA and Washington, DC: February 2002), 1.

33. Gi-Wook Shin, *Ethnic Nationalism in Korea: Genealogy, Politics, and Legacy* (Stanford: Stanford University Press, 2006), 151.

34. For a discussion of anticommunist slogans and other ongoing deployments of securitized discourse in South Korean everyday life during the period prior to the June Summit, see Kwon Hyuk-bum, "*Pan'gongjuŭi hoerop'an ilgi*" [Reading the Mentality of Anticommunism], in *T'albundan sidae rŭl yŏlmyŏ* [Opening an Era of Post-Division], ed. Cho Han Hae-Joang and Lee Woo-young (Seoul: Samin, 2000), 29–65.

35. In "Korean War Traumas," Kwon writes, "South Koreans were not able to recall this reality publicly until recently, while living in a self-consciously anticommunist political society; the story of this war remains untold among North Koreans who, living in a self-consciously

revolutionary political society, are obliged to follow the singular official narrative of war, a victorious war of liberation against American imperialism." Heonik Kwon, "Korean War Traumas," *The Asia Pacific Journal: Japan Focus* 38, no. 2 (2010). http://japanfocus.org/-heonik-kwon/3413.

36. Field interview with the author at the headquarters of the South Korean Red Cross in Seoul, July 19, 2000.

37. Sang-Hun Choe, Charles J. Hanley, and Martha Mendoza, "War's Hidden Chapter: Ex-GIs Tell of Killing Korean Refugees," *Associated Press* (September 29, 1999), http://www.pulitzer.org/archives/6350 (accessed March 2, 2010); Charles J. Hanley, Sang-Hun Choe, and Martha Mendoza, *The Bridge at No Gun Ri: A Hidden Nightmare From the Korean War* (New York: Henry Holt, 2001); Marilyn Young, "An Incident at No Gun Ri," in *Crimes of War: Guilt and Denial in the Twentieth Century*, ed. Omar Bartov, Atina Grossman, and Mary Nolan, 242–258 (New York: The New Press, 2002).

38. See Oh Yeon-Ho, "Ch'oech'ochŭngŏn Ch'amchŏn Mikun ŭi Ch'ungbuk Yŏngdong Yangmin 3-paek Yŏmyŏng Haksal Sakŏn" [First Testimony: Massacre of 300 Villagers by American Soldiers During the Korean War in Yŏng-dong Ch'ungbuk], *Monthly Mal* (July 1994): 36–45. I am thankful to Soomin Seo for advising me on this earlier coverage by Oh and other South Korean journalists. For a comprehensive listing of academic and journalistic publications on No Gun Ri, see the online archive compiled by Donghee Sinn at the University of Albany, http://www.albany.edu/nogunrimemory/publication.html.

39. Dong-Choon Kim, *The Unending Korean War: A Social History*, trans. Sung-ok Kim (Larkspur, CA: Tamal Vista, 2009), viii.

40. George Katsiafacas, *Asia's Unknown Uprisings: South Korean Social Movements in the 20th Century* (Oakland, CA: PM Press, 2012), 12.

41. See Tessa Morris-Suzuki, Morris Low, Leonid Petrov, and Timothy Tsu, *East Asia Beyond the History Wars: Confronting the Ghosts of Violence* (New York and London: Routledge, 2013); Mikyoung Kim and Barry Schwartz, eds., *Northeast Asia's Difficult Past: Essays in Collective Memory* (New York: Palgrave Macmillan, 2010); Alexis Dudden, *Troubled Apologies Among Japan, Korea, and the United States* (New York: Columbia University Press, 2008); Gi-Wook Shin, Soon-Won Park, and Daqing Yang, *Rethinking Historical Injustice and Reconciliation in Northeast Asia: The Korean Experience* (London and New York: Routledge, 2007); T. Fujitani et al., eds., *Perilous Memories: The Asia Pacific War(s)* (Durham, NC: Duke University Press, 2001).

42. Another important factor was the death of Hirohito in 1989, which brought to an end the longstanding "Chrysanthemum taboo" against criticism of the Japanese Emperor.

43. C. Sarah Soh, *The Comfort Women: Sexual Violence and Postcolonial Memory in Korea and Japan* (Chicago: University of Chicago Press, 2008), 135.

44. Among the extensive literature on the comfort-women issue and related activism, the landmark study, which first appeared in Japanese in 1991, is Yoshimi Yoshiaki, *Comfort Women: Sexual Slavery in the Japanese Military During World War II*, trans. Suzanne O'Brien (New York: Columbia University Press, 2000). See also C. Sarah Soh, *The Comfort Women: Sexual Violence and Postcolonial Memory in Korea and Japan* (Chicago: University of Chicago Press, 2008); Katharine H. S. Moon, "South Korean Movements Against Militarized Sexual Labor," *Asian Survey* (1999): 310–27; and a special issue of *positions: east asia cultures critique* 5 (1997) on "The Comfort Women: Colonialism, War, and Sex."

45. Laura Hein, "Savage Irony: The Imaginative Power of the 'Military Comfort Women' in the 1990s," *Gender & History* 11, no. 2 (July 1999): 364.

46. Hein, "Savage Irony," 338.

47. Seung-Hee Jeon, "War Trauma, Memories, and Truths: Representations of the Korean War in Pak Wan-So's Writings and in 'Still Present Pasts,'" *Critical Asian Studies* 42, no. 4 (2010): 624.

48. Chung Yong-Wook, "War and Memory in Korean History," *The Review of Korean Studies* 7, no. 3 (2004): 3.

49. Bruce Cumings, *The Korean War: A History* (New York: Random House, 2010), 35. For a fuller discussion of the dilemmas surrounding the calculation of Korean War deaths, see chapter 2.

50. Kwon, "Korean War Traumas." *The Asia Pacific Journal: Japan Focus* 38, no. 2 (2010). http://japanfocus.org/-heonik-kwon/3413.

51. Examples of such academic research about the war's historical traumas include Park Chan-sung's *The Korean War That Went into the Village: The Korean War's Small Village Wars* (Paju, Korea: Dolbege, 2010); and Kim Dong-Choon's *Chŏnjaeng kwa sahoe: Uri ege Han'guk chŏnjaeng ŭn muŏt iŏnna?* [War and Society: What is the Korean War to Us?], which was published in English as *The Unending Korean War: A Social History*, trans. Sung-ok Kim (Larkspur, CA: Tamal Vista, 2009). In addition, for a recent South Korean research project based on oral histories of the Korean War, see Han'guk Kusulsa Hakhoe, *Kusulsa ro ingnun Han'guk Chŏnjaeng: Sŏul t'obagi wa mint'ongsŏn saramdŭl, chŏnjaeng mimangin kwa wŏlbuk kajok, kŭdŭl i mal hanŭn arae robut'oŭi Han'guk Chŏnjaeng* (Seoul: Humanist, 2011).

52. Cf. Christopher Nelson's exploration of the will to memory as evident in the fabric of everyday life in Okinawa through storytelling, which keeps layers of the traumatic past alive in the present and in resistance to ongoing militarism. See *Dancing With the Dead: Memory, Performance, and Everyday Life in Postwar Okinawa* (Durham and London: Duke University Press, 2008).

53. Joseph Masco, *The Nuclear Borderlands: The Manhattan Project in Post–Cold War New Mexico* (Princeton, NJ: Princeton University Press, 2006).

54. Allen Feldman, "Securocratic Wars of Public Safety: Globalized Policing as Scopic Regime," *Interventions* 6, no. 3 (2004), 62.

55. Paul Connerton, *How Societies Remember* (Cambridge and New York: Cambridge University Press, 1989), 38.

56. Feldman, "Securocratic Wars of Public Safety," 62.

57. Veena Das, *Critical Events: An Anthropological Perspective on Contemporary India* (Oxford: Oxford University Press, 1995).

58. Emma Tarlo, *Unsettling Memories: Narratives of the Emergency in Delhi* (Berkeley: University of California Press, 2003), 7.

59. John Bodnar, *Remaking America: Public Memory, Commemoration, and Patriotism in the Twentieth Century* (Princeton, NJ: Princeton University Press, 1994), 14–22.

60. See Nak-chung Paik, *The Division System in Crisis: Essays on Contemporary Korea* (Berkeley: University of California Press, 2011).

61. Procedural democracy in South Korea began in 1987, in the sense that direct elections were held that year after a national popular uprising for democratization pressured the military authoritarian government under General Chun Doo Hwan to hold direct elections. However, because the opposition vote was split between Kim Dae-jung and Kim Young-sam, the ruling party candidate Roh Tae-woo was able to win the election that year. After a decade of democratic transition, Kim Dae-jung's electoral victory in December 1997 was the first time in South Korea's history that a handover of power to a new political regime occurred by election. For a discussion of the challenges continuing to face South Korean democratic consolidation, see Hyug Baeg Im, "Faltering Democratic Consolidation in South Korea," *Democratization* 11, no. 5 (2004): 179–198; Jae-Jung Suh, Sunwon Park, and Hahn Y. Kim, "Democratic Consolidation and Its Limits in Korea: Dilemmas of Cooptation," *Asian Survey* 52, no. 5 (2012): 822–44.

62. See Son, *South Korean Engagement Policies and North Korea*, 40, 94.

63. See chapter 1 for a fuller discussion.

64. Myung-Lim Park, *Han'guk chŏnjaengŭi palbal kwa kiwon* [*The Outbreak and Origins of the Korean War*] (Seoul: Nanam Press, 1996).

65. See chapter 1 for further discussion.

66. Charles K. Armstrong, *The Koreas* (London and New York: Routledge, 2007), 131.

67. Cf. John Borneman, *Belonging in the Two Berlins: Kin, State, Nation* (Cambridge: Cambridge University Press, 1992); Daphne Berdahl, *Where the World Ended: Re-Unification and Identity in the German Borderland* (Berkeley: University of California Press, 1999); Charles Stafford, *Separation and Reunion in Modern China* (Cambridge: Cambridge University Press, 2000); Nicole Newendorp, *Uneasy Reunions: Immigration, Citizenship, and Family Life in Post-1997 Hong Kong* (Stanford, CA: Stanford University Press, 2008).

68. This was the case in South Korea since December 1948 when the National Security Law was passed; however, since 1990, changes in both Koreas allowed greater possibilities for private reunions of separated families to occur in third countries and also in North Korea. See chapter 2 for further discussion.

69. As I explain in chapter 2, this was true until the late 1990s, and since that point, South Koreans could travel to North Korea under highly limited circumstances without the ability to meet or contact people there freely. See, for example, Christian J. Park, "Crossing the Border: South Korean Tourism to Mount Kŭmgang," in *De-Bordering Korea: Tangible and Intangible Legacies of the Sunshine Policy*, ed. Valérie Gelézeau et al. (New York and London: Routledge, 2013).

70. Liminality!

71. Arnold Van Gennep, *The Rites of Passage* (Chicago: University of Chicago Press, 1909).

72. Max Gluckman, *Politics, Law and Ritual in Tribal Society* (Oxford, U.K.: Basil Blackwell, 1971); Victor Turner, *The Forest of Symbols: Aspects of Ndembu Ritual* (Ithaca, NY: Cornell University Press, 1967).

73. Victor Turner, *Dramas, Fields and Metaphors: Symbolic Action in Human Society* (Ithaca, NY: Cornell University Press, 1975), 13–14.

74. Katherine A. Bowie, *Rituals of National Loyalty: An Anthropology of the State and the Village Scout Movement in Thailand* (New York: Columbia University Press, 1997); Daphne Berdahl, *Where the World Ended: Re-Unification and Identity in the German Borderland* (Berkeley: University of California Press, 1999); Richard Wilson, *The Politics of Truth and Reconciliation in South Africa: Legitimizing the Post-Apartheid State* (Cambridge: Cambridge University Press, 2001.

75. Bent Steeg Larsen and Thomas Tufte, "Rituals in the Modern World: Applying the Concept of Ritual in Media Ethnography," in *Global Media Studies—Ethnographic Perspectives*, ed. Patrick D. Murphy and Marwan M. Krady (New York and London: Routledge, 2003); Liisa Malkki, *Purity and Exile: Violence, Memory, and National Cosmology Among Hutu Refugees in Tanzania* (Chicago: University of Chicago Press, 1995). See also Jun Uchida, *Brokers of Empire: Japanese Settler Colonialism in Korea, 1876–1945* (Cambridge, MA: Harvard University Asia Center/Harvard University Press, 2011).

76. Roy Richard Grinker, *Korea and Its Futures: Unification and the Unfinished War* (New York: St. Martin's Press, 1998), 10.

77. Jee Sun E. Lee, "Post-Unification Korean National Identity," Working Paper 09/03, Asiatic Research Center, Korea University, Washington, DC: U.S. Korea Institute at SAIS, 2009.

78. Grinker, *Korea and Its Futures*, 10.

79. "Mourning and Melancholia," in *Standard Edition of the Complete Psychological Works of Sigmund Freud*, vol. 14, ed. James Strachey (London: Hogarth Press, 1917), 244.

80. Ibid., 245.

81. Eng and Kazanjian, "Introduction: Mourning Remains," in *Loss: The Politics of Mourning* (Berkeley: University of California Press, 2003), 3.

82. Grinker, *Korea and Its Futures*, 78. In immediately subsequent sections (79–89), Grinker discusses in detail Ch'ŏn Yi du's *Hanŭi kujo yŏngu* [Research on the structure of *han*] (Seoul: Munhakkhwa Chisŏngsa).

83. Notably, while not addressing division, a recent book also uses liminality to examine an earlier historical period on the Korean peninsula. Jun Uchida's study of Japanese colonial settlers in Korea during the 1876–1945 period analyzes the "liminal space" between the imperial metropole and the peninsular colony to gain insight into a group of historical subjects who bridged these two spaces while fully belonging to neither. See Jun Uchida, *Brokers of Empire: Japanese Settler Colonialism in Korea, 1876–1945* (Cambridge, MA: Harvard University Asia Center/Harvard University Press, 2011).

84. Grinker, *Korea and Its Futures*, 22. Recent survey data from South Korea actually indicate a discrepancy among analyses regarding the question of to what extent such ambivalence is actually borne out by public opinion. At a time when there remained a widespread perception that younger people were losing interest in unification, the Center for Deliberative

Democracy of Stanford University conducted a formal survey in conjunction with KBS during August 2011, and their poll findings demonstrated a surprisingly high percentage across age groups in favor of unification: "Overall, South Koreans showed overwhelming support for unification. Before deliberation [in small groups], 71.6% of South Koreans thought unification [was] 'necessary.' This already high number increased to an astounding 91.2% post-deliberation." However, there were considerable differences regarding the timing and the means to pay for unification. See "First Deliberative Polling in Korea: Issue of Korean Unification, Seoul, South Korea," Center for Deliberative Democracy of Stanford University (January 25, 2012), http://cdd.stanford.edu/polls/korea/2012/kr-results-summary.pdf.

85. Suk-Young Kim, "Can We Live as One Family? Rethinking the Two Koreas' Kinship in John Hoon's Kang Tek-koo," *Theatre Research International* 3 (2004): 267–83.

86. The orientation toward comedy should also be understood in these works' artistic context, as a contemporary response to and departure from a long tradition of South Korean artistic work that explored the bitter memories and maddening consequences caused by division. Notably, the theme of liminality also figures highly in representative works of this "division literature" subgenre, such as the novels *The Rainy Spell* by Yun Heung-gil (1972), *Evening Glow* by Kim Won-il (1978), and *The Square* by Choi In-hun (1960).

87. Homi Bhabha, *The Location of Culture* (New York: Routledge, 1994), 148.

88. Soo-Jung Lee, "Making and Unmaking," observes that, after those who had gone to the North during wartime were long vilified for decades, these events served to bring about the first positive representations of *Wŏlbukcha* ever to appear in the South Korean media.

89. For other scholarly analyses of the August 2000 reunions of separated families, see Lee, *Making and Unmaking*; Gwi-Ok Kim, *Isan'gajok, "pan'gongjŏnsa" to "ppalgaengi" to anin* [Separated Families, Neither "Anticommunist Warriors" nor "Reds"] (Seoul: *Yŏksa pip'yŏngsa*, 2004); Foley, *Korea's Divided Families*; and Soo-Jung Lee, "'T'alnaengjŏn minjok spekt'ŏk'ŭl': 2000-nyŏn yŏrŭm nambuk isan'gajok sangbong" ["Post–Cold War National Spectacle": Reunions of Separated Families in the Summer, 2000], *Minjok munhwa yŏngu* 59 (2013): 95–122. Further discussion of this literature appears in chapter 2.

90. This analysis differs somewhat from that put forth by Prébin, *Meeting Once More*, where Prébin emphasizes the parallels between the partition on the peninsula and the binary world separating the living and the dead. She writes, "Impassable for most, the frontier inspires various ritualized practices that all have the same objectives: to ensure the forgiveness of the departed and lost relatives, and to find peace. The performance of these rituals for the dead is the main purpose of these family meetings" (172). While the relationship between the living and the dead is unquestionably significant and also figures into considerations undergirding *Memory, Reconciliation, and Reunions in South Korea*, a key difference in comparison with Prébin's study is that, in the sections where she addresses the 2000–2001 reunions, her focus is the meetings that occurred in Pyongyang. For a discussion of why this book instead primarily addresses the Seoul reunions, see chapter 4.

91. In chapter 4, I further discuss the rationale for focusing this analysis on the reunions in Seoul, rather than on those in Pyongyang.

Part I

Unsettling the Past

Chapter One

Historicizing Korea's Geopolitical Liminality

Geopolitical liminality is central to understanding both the wider context of wartime family separation, as well as why the North–South separated-family reunions—with their acute overtones of social suffering and ethnic national-ism—would become emblematic of Korea's historical condition. However, rather than take for granted Korea's presumed state of physical "between-ness" at the crossroads of Northeast Asia, this chapter explores the historical processes that put the penninsula at the nexus of competing interests among the region's major rival powers in the modern period, namely China, Japan, the United States, and Russia (during 1922–1991, the Soviet Union). Indeed, the continuation of long-term family separation on a mass scale in Korea is the outcome of both the peninsular division and the lack of resolution of the Korean War, and that unresolved situation is itself symptomatic of Korea's geopolitical liminality as a modern construction.

Understanding the Korean peninsula in terms of liminality must therefore take into account what anthropologist Fernando Coronil describes as the fetishization of both history and geography. As Coronil writes, "the prevail-ing understanding of history as fluid, intangible, and dynamic and of geogra-phy as fixed, tangible, and static suggests that modernity is constituted by an asymmetrical integration of space and time." This yields a paradox in which "the territorialization of histories takes place through the obscuring of their history; territories are largely assumed as the fixed natural ground of local histories. The territorialization of histories, in turn, occurs through their fixa-tion in nonhistorical, naturalized territories."[1] In this way, the residue of the colonial past becomes obscured or hidden in what Coronil elsewhere calls "implicit maps of empire."[2] Ironically, territorialization of histories can also serve nationalist interests insofar as it contributes to the belief that identities emerge out of independent histories taking place in bounded spaces, rather than through the dynamics among interrelated peoples, institutions, and ideas that transcend national borders.

The analysis of this chapter therefore does not presume a strategically sensitive geography to be Korea's timeless condition. Rather, it seeks to historicize the peninsula's liminal geography as an outcome of dynamic relations among diverse social actors—Korean, Japanese, Soviet, Chinese, and American—during the modern period.[3] In particular, it reflects the impact of stark changes in configurations of geographical space and geopolitical power after the late nineteenth century. This goes against a popular understanding of Korean history that assumes Korea's vulnerability, by virtue of its geography, extends back in time to the ancient past. Historian John Duncan has described this assumption as "a master narrative, central to the modern Korean nationalist project, of Korean history as a story of foreign aggression and nationalist resistance" as part of a "history of suffering" (*sunan ŭi yŏksa*), which presumes that the peninsula had been subject to incessant invasions over several centuries.[4] Such primordial ethnic nationalism would uncritically trace the roots of an ethnic nation back to antiquity without accounting for the temporal incongruity of claiming a pre-modern national history when the nation itself is a modern institution.[5] Historian Charles K. Armstrong similarly refutes the assumption that the penninsula's geography inevitably reduced its inhabitants to perennial victims. He argues instead that Korea's premodern history is most notable not for a presumed vulnerability to "invasion," but rather for its exceedingly long tradition of geographical continuity with a durable centralized bureaucracy. Indeed, had national division not been imposed after World War II, Korea could claim one of the longest histories in the world among modern nations as a unified political entity within mostly stable territorial boundaries.[6] The development of a unified state in Korea dates to at least the tenth century during the Koryŏ dynasty (918–1392). Under the succeeding Chosŏn dynasty (1392–1910), by the fifteenth century, the central state administered a territorial area whose reach aligned very much with the current boundaries of the Korean peninsula. The Chosŏn dynasty was thus remarkable for its longevity, outlasting its dynastic counterparts in China and Japan.

To understand why Korea was underprepared to meet the new challenges of the modern era, it would be misleading to imagine a premodern history of calamity in which Korean states were always beleaguered by invasion. Such an interpretation risks obscuring the practices and diplomatic disposition that had long allowed Korean states to maintain political integrity and relative stability, which were no longer viable after the late nineteenth century. Throughout the Chosŏn dynasty, successive Korean kings had sent regular tribute missions to the Chinese court, which in turn would send regular envoys to Korea as gestures of reciprocal alliance. During the Imjin War

(1592–1598), Ming China went to great expense to help defend Chosŏn Korea, thereby strengthening the ties between them.[7] The Japanese warlord Hideoyoshi Toyotomi had launched attacks against Korea in a failed attempt to take over the peninsula, control over which would be necessary to conquer Ming China, but the combined forces from China and Korea prevented Japan from fulfilling that ambition. A few decades later, the Manchus also set out to conquer Ming China and attacked Korea as its close ally. The Manchus eventually succeeded at both toppling the Ming and bringing about the capitulation of Korea in 1636. Although Chosŏn was forced to become a tributary to the new Qing court, Korea's political independence remained largely intact.

It should be noted that these earlier opportunistic invasions would seem to undermine the argument that Korea's geographic liminality is inherently a modern nineteenth-century phenomenon. While the invasions led by Hideoyoshi during the Imjin War are indeed often cited as a precedent demonstrating a history of Japanese designs on the peninsula, it would be wrong to assume there was a sense prior to the late Chosŏn period that Korean territory occupied a vulnerable spot between two greater powers.[8] Prior to the late nineteenth century, the Chosŏn court instead regarded its own monarchy as a peer of China and relegated Japan to the margins of the civilized world. This was an assessment not exclusive to Chosŏn Korea, and it would influence notions of race in both China and Korea. In historian Vladimir Tikhonov's discussion of the influential Chinese book of maritime geography, *Haiguo tuzhi* (*Illustrated Gazetteer of the Maritime Countries*, 1852), he describes how perceptions of race in many ways reflected "the hierarchy implicit in the traditional Sinocentric view of the *œcumene* divided into the 'civilized' core (China and the Confucian 'tributary' monarchies around it: Korea, Vietnam, and so forth), 'semicivilized' semiperiphery (Japan, Burma, Thailand), and 'barbarian' periphery."[9] Notably, for Confucian elites, this hierarchical taxonomy of civilized peoples still persisted during this period even after reformist intellectuals embraced "new" Western classificatory schemes of race.[10]

Furthermore, the Chosŏn court worked both within and outside of the Sinocentric tributary system, as Kenneth R. Robinson has detailed. Before the breakdown of the imperial dynastic system in the late nineteenth century, a finely calibrated set of hierarchical diplomatic relationships dictated the parameters for ritual protocol, political recognition, and maritime trade privileges in East Asia. The King of Chosŏn maintained status-parity with rulers of Ryukyu and Japan, all three of whom were subordinate to the Emperor of Ming China in their respective bilateral tributary relationships. Yet the King of Chosŏn also interacted with other Japanese and Ryukyuan elites who were denied tributary relationships with Ming China. As Robinson writes, "[B]y incorporating elites forbidden direct participation in the Ming tribute system, the Korean tribute system placed the King atop a structure for maritime diplomacy more intricate than that designed for the Ming emperor."[11] Thus, far from being a weak state dominated by its neighbors, Chosŏn Korea actively participated in a Sinocentric system while concurrently creating a separate order of tributary interaction and maritime diplomacy centered on itself.

In the seventeenth century the regional ascendance to power by the Manchus, whom Koreans had included among the "barbarians," therefore set off heated debates among educated elites in Korea over the question of whether China could still be regarded the center of the civilized world. After several decades characterized by vehement disputes over the meaning of civilization and the place of Korea within it, there emerged in the eighteenth century a new self-confidence rooted in the resilience of the Chosŏn dynasty. Through classical studies and ritual practice, Korean elites appointed themselves as custodians of the Confucian cultural heritage and as rightful inheritors of the Ming mantle, while presuming Korea to be the last bastion of that civilizational tradition.[12]

With the stabilization of internal discord, however, arose a milieu of complacency regarding relations with foreign powers. After the ascendance of the Manchus, Korea continued its tributary relationship with China and maintained diplomatic relations with Japan, securing peace with its immediate neighbors. Given the Chosŏn dynasty's success at diplomacy with China and Japan, both Korean military technology and preparedness deteriorated. By the end of the nineteenth century, Korea had not developed an adequate force for self-defense, but it could also no longer rely on the protection of its centuries-old tributary relationship with its larger ally, as the Qing Imperial government was itself beset by a crippling combination of internal corruption, domestic unrest, and incursions from Western imperialist powers.[13]

During this period, Japan and Russia became the two main powers that vied for influence over Korea and competed to replace China as the regional hegemon. During the revolutionary modernizing reforms of the Meiji period (1868–1912), Japan's leaders became embroiled during the early 1870s in the *seikan-ron* debate over the question of whether to conquer Korea. For Meiji leaders, the peninsula was newly regarded as a mortal threat to Japan's security were it to fall into the hands of a Western imperialist power, thus rendering Korea a "dagger pointing at the heart of Japan."[14] Despite these anxieties, Japan deferred its policy of military expansionism in favor of first consolidating domestic reforms under the Meiji leadership. Regarding Korea, Japan instead imposed the Kanghwa Treaty in 1876, which resembled the unequal treaties of Western countries and opened three ports to Japanese control. The Kanghwa Treaty placed new financial burdens on the Chosŏn court in order to accommodate the expansion of foreign commercial and diplomatic relationships, and those liabilities were offset through the extraction of additional revenue from the peasantry, who were already straining under high tax levies.[15] Rural class resentment and resistance to foreign intrusion fueled the spread of Tonghak ("Eastern Learning"), a syncretic religion that combined Confucianism, Buddhism, Taoism, and shamanism. The Tonghak Movement challenged orthodox Confucianism and culminated in a major agrarian revolt in 1895.[16] When King Kojong of Korea appealed to China for additional troops to suppress the Tonghak Rebellion, the Chinese complied, and this intervention became the pretext for Japan to provoke a war with China over their conflicting interests in Korea. Following China's defeat in the First Sino–Japanese War (1894–1895), the Chinese imperial court was forced to renounce its historic claim to influence over Korea.

As Japan increased its control over Korea, victory in the Sino–Japanese War removed the obstacle of Chinese interference, eventually clearing the way for Japan to impose a protectorate treaty on Korea in 1905 before annexing the peninsula outright in 1910.[17] Yet, during the decade following 1895, Koreans were generally unaware that they were so close to losing their national sovereignty, or that the risk posed by Japan was any greater than that of Russia.[18] With the collapse of the Sinocentric tributary system and the decline of Confucian monarchies in China and Korea, early Korean nationalists such as Yu Kiljun embraced an agenda of modernizing reform under the banner of *munmyŏng kaehwa* ("civilization and enlightenment"), heavily influenced by Japanese reformist thinkers. Pan-Asianism attracted Korean reformers who championed the notion that collective racial and regional solidarity would allow Asia to resist the increasingly threatening incursions of the West.[19] It was only after Japan prevailed in the Russo–Japanese War (1904–1905) and imposed the protectorate on Korea that these reformers were disabused of their illusions about Japan's benevolent intentions and began to identify with other colonized countries.

TRACING MODERN IDEOLOGICAL CONFLICT IN KOREA

Since the early twentieth century, Korea has undergone two periods of foreign occupation, first by Japan (1910–1945) and then under divided authority by the United States and the Soviet Union (1945–1948). These two occupations are contingently interrelated, as Korea's loss of sovereignty to Japan later left it vulnerable to partition and division—against the wishes of the vast majority of the Korean people—after its liberation from colonial rule. The division of Korea occurred virtually concurrently with its liberation from occupation after thirty-five years as a Japanese colony. Liberation Day is recognized in both North Korea and South Korea as August 15, 1945, the day marking the end of World War II when Japan surrendered to the Allies. As historian Bruce Cumings writes, "A Korean War was inconceivable before the division of Korea in August 1945. But because of that division, it has been conceivable ever since—right down to the volatile present."[20] Social divisions had worsened under Japanese colonial policies, while the divergent post-Liberation experiences of a divided occupation—which set the conditions for the formation of two separate regimes—intensified the class and ideological antagonisms between them. Both of these periods of foreign occupation thus contributed to establishing the conditions that eventually led to war in Korea.

What transpired during these two periods of foreign occupation would transform Chosŏn's agrarian society utterly, but the impact and significance of these changes were not solely determined by the Japanese colonizing agenda or the nascent Cold War opposition of the American and Soviet occupation authorities after the defeat of Japan in the Second World War. Rather, the dynamics of foreign occupation were so deeply divisive because they exploited social cleavages and exacerbated socioeconomic conflicts that had already existed within Korean society. In a seminal article of South Korean progressive historiography, which first appeared in 1971, Kim Yong-sŏp traces these cleavages to the conflicts between landlords and peasants arising from the breakdown of feudal society at the end of the Chosŏn period.[21] During that time, economic changes encouraged the accumulation of property into large estates by wealthy landlords and *yangban* elites, while advances in agricultural technology allowed landlords to benefit from dramatic increases in yields with less labor, leaving tenants at an increasing disadvantage. The resulting inequalities were further magnified by an irrational taxation system based on social status, which disproportionately burdened poorer peasants. The discontent of the peasant class took the form of rural uprisings and other forms of social unrest, but the opening of ports after the Kanghwa Treaty brought new external pressures. For both tenants and elites in Korea during this period, the question of how to reform the feudal agrarian economy in response to modernizing pressures became an increasingly urgent concern.[22]

Kim analyzes two separate reform proposals for agricultural modernization which reflect a confrontation of class interests: the "landlord course" of reform, targeting strictly the tax system while maintaining landlord-based large-scale agriculture; and the "peasant course" of reform, which favored not only a more egalitarian tax system but also extensive land reform that would allow small-scale peasant-based agriculture. Historian Michael Shin observes that the clash between these two opposing courses offers insight into the tensions that have defined modern Korean history. He writes, "The aggressions of the foreign powers in the late nineteenth century obstructed the process of historical resolution between these two courses, and the Japanese occupation only contained the conflict and continued to prevent a resolution. In the end, of course, the landlord course culminated in the formation of the South Korean state, and the peasant course in the North Korean

state."[23] While the recurring importance of Korea's strategic importance informed the challenges that prevented Koreans from resolving internal conflicts on their own terms, the consequences of geopolitical liminality also led
to an intensification of internal rivalries that continue to be expressed by
South Korea and North Korea as the ideological descendants of historically
opposing reformist positions.

RIVAL NATIONALISMS AND BLOODLINE POLITICS
UNDER COLONIAL RULE

Characteristics particular to Japanese imperialism also influenced its approach to colonial rule, including the imposition of highly racialized policies.
As a latecomer to imperialist ambitions, Japan was not in a position to acquire colonies on distant continents like the older European empires, and
instead annexed "near-at-hand territories," beginning with Taiwan in 1895
and Korea in 1910.[24] The Japanese colonizers encountered particularly
strong resistance in Korea. Within the first year after Korea's annexation,
Japanese colonial authorities set up a repressive police state, dissolving political organizations, outlawing all public gatherings, and suspending the publication of Korean newspapers. The colonial restructuring of local civil administration soon brought an unprecedented level of state scrutiny and control to
the everyday lives of Koreans, institutionalized through a powerful police
force and bureaucratic administration. Beginning in 1919, the Government-
General ostensibly eased its dictatorial grip on the Korean population and
initiated a so-called "cultural policy." This change resulted from a chain of
events initiated by the emergence of an independence movement that caught
the colonial authorities by surprise with the breadth of its support. The mass
pro-independence demonstrations of the March First Movement of 1919,
which occurred throughout the colony, are said to have marked the beginning
of Korean nationalism on a popular scale. As the unrest continued for weeks,
colonial police cracked down with violence, which then touched off broader
rioting. In the ensuing months, the Japanese crackdown resulted in the deaths
and arrests of thousands of Koreans, the confiscation of printing presses, the
closure of schools, home searches, and later an increased military presence in
the colony. Meanwhile, the pressure mounted by Korean protests was further
compounded by foreign criticism, which denounced the colonial repression
as outmoded and discredited.

The vehemence of protests within the colony and the negative image
abroad soon led Japanese leaders to reappraise the strategy of the military
policy and to make fundamental changes in its practices of governing the
colony. Under the banner of the new cultural policy, these changes created a
conciliatory aura of moderation, which eventually yielded the colonizers a

more effective means of long-term control. The cultural policy allowed for the publication of vernacular newspapers and lifted the ban on freedom of association, provided the groups posed no threat to Japanese rule, resulting in a proliferation of social, labor, youth, religious, education, and academic organizations after 1920. The colonial authorities also allowed greater economic activity and facilitated the consolidation of landholdings, which afforded them the opportunity to coopt Korean commercial elites and wealthy landlords.

Despite the nationalist aspirations stirred by the March First Movement, the ensuing period saw a deepening ideological divide among Koreans between moderate "cultural nationalists" and militant radical nationalists.[25] The cultural nationalists subscribed to a gradualist vision of independence along the lines of Western liberal democracies. They continued the endeavors of earlier progressive elites, emphasizing education, national consciousness-raising, and economic development to prepare Koreans for independence within the limits of colonial rule. They also took advantage of the new freedoms permitted by the Japanese colonial authorities in the realm of journalism and literature, and became engaged in the efforts to expand and systematize the use of the Korean vernacular.[26] In contrast, Korean radical nationalism grew out of disillusionment with Western liberal democracies after the destruction of the First World War and the lack of official Allied support for Korean independence during the peace negotiations at Versailles. The greater openness under the cultural policy toward freedom of association and freedom of the press enabled filtering of communist ideas into Korea.[27] Influenced by the Bolshevik revolution, socialist texts and ideas spread quickly among Korean intellectuals in the colony as well as those in exile, particularly because they offered an explanation for the colonial situation and were oriented toward national liberation.[28] However, early attempts at political mobilization by communist organizers eventually foundered as a result of factionalism, external pressures, and aggressive suppression by Japanese colonial authorities. The communists therefore were largely driven into exile or forced underground until after liberation.[29]

A significant generation gap also separated the radicals and gradualist reformers, with the most prominent reformers superannuating the leading communist figures by two decades or more. Virtually all the reformers who signed the March First Declaration were also leaders of religious groups, but no communists were signatories. For their part, the Korean Communists would condemn the co-optation of the March First Movement by the more relaxed colonial policy. Although the impact of repression and co-optation of the Japanese colonial government cannot go underestimated, the ideological conflicts among a divided nationalist leadership also created a fundamental obstacle, preventing either of the two main nationalist groups from successfully parlaying the momentum of indigenous nationalism expressed in the March First Movement into a serious challenge to colonial rule.

What is striking is that, despite these polarizing oppositions, both sides shared a common understanding of primordial ethnic nationalism. In his research on Korean ethnic nationalism, historical sociologist Gi-Wook Shin traces its roots to the Japanese colonial period: "By the end of colonial rule, the Korean nation was racialized through belief in a common origin in pre-history, producing an intensely felt sense of collectivity. . . . Koreans defined their identity as 'immutable' or 'primordial' through an imagined conception of Korean blood, regarding themselves as belonging to a unitary nation, an ethnically homogenous and racially distinct collectivity."[30] Indeed, blood-based nationalism became the primary source of Korean identity across the ideological spectrum, but not because it is the "natural" outcome of people whose shared fate is inevitably determined by race or biology. Rather, as Shin has argued, ethnic nationalism won out over other rival ideologies—namely pan-Asianism, colonial racism, international socialism, and capitalist modernization—in a political struggle between the proponents of these divergent forms of collective identification as they vied for influence in colonial Korea during the early twentieth century.[31]

Here I would emphasize the concept of "blood-based nationalism," which I use alongside the far more widely circulated term, "ethnic nationalism." Although the two are generally invoked interchangeably, the additional stress on "blood-based nationalism" in this analysis is to distinguish relevant phenomena in Korea from what ethnic nationalism often implies in more demographically diverse multiethnic contexts. That is, ethnic nationalism is commonly understood to mean the consciousness, ideologies, and practices of one ethnic group in making nationalist claims that conflict with the competing claims of a rival group or groups of different ethnic origin.[32] Yet Korea represents a very rare example where *ethnie* and nation have closely overlapped, given that the population on the peninsula exhibits a strikingly high degree of ethnic homogeneity.[33] The intense conflicts that arose in the name of different forms of Korean blood-based nationalism in the twentieth century therefore occurred among those who lay claim to the same ethnic group. Their conflicting claims are rooted not in inter-ethnic struggle, but rather stem from clashes over who may legitimately represent the Korean nation, the ideal of which has been widely figured to be unitary and consanguineous.

Characterized by the valorization of a common bloodline, the rise of blood-based nationalism in Korea during the colonial period also reveals the persistent influence of a Korean Confucian tradition, even after Confucianism had become the target of acrimonious criticism among reformers. Korean nationalists and Japanese colonialists, despite their opposite goals, similarly condemned the Korean aristocratic *yangban* class as the main obstacle to modernizing Korea.[34] Both groups impugned so-called "corrupt Confucians" for embodying anti-modern traits of conservatism, backwardness, and laziness. Korean nationalists also sought to de-center China as the Middle Kingdom by drawing upon folk traditions and symbols, particularly the foundational myth of Tan'gun as the progenitor of the Korean people.[35]

However, Confucianism was so influential in the ways that Koreans understood the past that it would not be entirely discredited by these attacks. Sin Ch'ae-ho's work is a good case in point, if one considers his pioneering history of Korea focused on the *minjok*, or ethnic nation,[36] a work that defied Confucian court-centered historical conventions. Celebrated by early nationalists for authoring Korea's first truly modern history, Sin ultimately did so by assuming the mode of the *chokpo*, the genealogical clan records that had been used for centuries by Confucians to demonstrate their patrilineal *yangban* status.[37] At the time that Korea was being thrust into the Western international system, the development of Korean nationalism therefore revealed a tension between, on the one hand, the rejection of Confucianism as no longer relevant to the new challenges facing the nation and, on the other, the lingering remainder of Confucian principles and forms, which offered a universalizing moral language in which arguments for reform could be made intelligible and persuasive. Furthermore, the *chokpo* and notion of a nation related by direct descent were appropriated as ways for people to grasp and identify with the new concept of *minjok* as a form of subjectivity that was literally familiar. As Sin wrote in a 1908 editorial that drew parallels between national history and family records, "four thousand years of recorded history is the genealogy of Tan'gun."[38]

In *Ethnic Nationalism in Korea*, Gi-Wook Shin argues that ethnic nationalism was also a response to the racialized policies of the Japanese colonial administration, particularly during the final and harshest decade under colonial rule.[39] During that time, Japan used the colony for labor and resources to wage the Second Sino–Japanese War (1937–1945), imposing a policy of wartime mobilization and forced assimilation. Hundreds of thousands of Koreans were conscripted to work in factories and mines in Korea, Manchuria, Japan, or elsewhere in Japanese-controlled territory[40]—often under harsh surveillance and inhumane conditions. Beginning in 1938, Koreans were drafted as military recruits to offset the war's drain on Japanese soldiers, and tens of thousands of young Korean women and girls were forced into sexual slavery as so-called "comfort women," who were dispatched to military outposts throughout the Japanese empire.[41] After a restructuring of land ownership and the collapse of rice prices in the late 1920s and early 1930s had driven many peasants out of farming, the displaced peasants were coerced into serving as wartime labor during the final throes of the Pacific War.

By the time of the Japanese surrender, roughly 40 percent of the Korean adult population had been uprooted, either living abroad or in provinces other than those in which they had been born, with 20 percent of the entire Korean population or five million Koreans living outside the peninsula.[42] According to Cumings, those who survived became radicalized during the colonial period after enduring an exile under appalling circumstances, and their numbers contributed significantly to the striking degree of popular political participation in Korea after Liberation. He argues that the colonial period's last phase of wartime mobilization effectively laid the ground for widespread political mobilization in the period that followed Liberation.[43] In contrast, Gi-Wook Shin explains the extent of post-Liberation political mobilization through the phenomena of colonial era peasant protests.[44] He contends that, in most analyses of why socialism was espoused by a radicalized peasantry in Korea, there has been an overstatement of the roles played by both radical nationalist intellectuals and post-exilic returnees. Instead, he stresses the importance of the political activism coordinated by tenant unions. From 1920 until the early 1940s, the tenant unions were among the organizations that were allowed to develop under the cultural policy, and they engaged in large-scale, well-organized disputes with landlords, giving rise to networks of social organization that demonstrated to the peasants the efficacy of collective action. While these early tenancy disputes were reformist in nature and not revolutionary, the precipitous drop of agricultural prices due to the global depression in the late 1920s and early 1930s resulted in widening rural poverty, and later protests were characterized by increasing peasant radicalism and the rise of the Red Peasant Union. Despite repression of radical activity by Japanese colonial authorities, particularly during the last period of wartime mobilization, Shin draws upon James Scott to argue that peasant protests continued in the form of "everyday forms of resistance." Diverse precedents of political engagement and protest were therefore available to the Korean populace when colonial rule abruptly came to an end.

POST-LIBERATION DIVERGENCE

The question of the fate of Korea was addressed in the Allied Conferences that would determine the shape of postwar Asia. At the Cairo Conference in 1943, after the war had turned in their favor, Franklin D. Roosevelt, Winston Churchill, and Chiang Kai-shek agreed that Japan would lose control over the territories it had occupied and discussed what would become of these colonies. The United States, Great Britain, and China agreed to Korea's eventual independence, stating that the Allies, "mindful of the enslavement of the people of Korea, are determined that in due course Korea shall become free and independent." The Cairo Declaration drew upon Roosevelt's broader idea of establishing trusteeships as a post-colonial period of tutelage in preparation for independence. Stalin, notably, was not consulted regarding this declaration, but the three leaders anticipated the possibility of Soviet participation in the proposed trusteeship of Korea. The ambiguous timeframe conveyed by the phrase "in due course" denied immediate independence following Japan's defeat, creating uncertainty that would later allow room for manipulation by countries with an interest in Korea.[45]

Korea also came up briefly in Allied negotiations at Yalta in 1945, although that conference was concerned chiefly with the settlement of postwar Europe. Whatever Allied commitment there existed to Korean independence remained vague at best, and no formal mention of Korea was included in the resulting agreement. The United States and Soviet Union discussed a trusteeship that was expected to last between ten and thirty years, and the dismissal of Korea's immediate capacity for sovereignty revealed that both the Americans and Soviets had taken for granted the imperialist attitudes of the Japanese toward the Koreans.[46] It also reflected a disregard toward Korean nationalist claims and aspirations for self-rule while privileging respective U.S. and Soviet strategic interests, which were already taking shape in the region before the beginning of the Cold War. Indeed, the main significance of the Yalta conference for Korea was that it secured the Soviets' entry into the Pacific War, which set down the parameters for what would prove to be a prominent role for the Soviets in the administration of postwar Korea.

Korea's liberation at the end of World War II created a power vacuum with the dismantling of the Japanese Government-General on the peninsula and the wider collapse of Japanese imperialism in the region. While the U.S. military largely disregarded advance studies that would have bolstered preparations to occupy Korea,[47] it put more concerted effort into planning the occupation of Japan with the objective of reviving the economy and setting up a parliamentary democracy beholden to the United States. However, after the Soviet Union entered the war as agreed at Yalta, Soviet troops dispatched a supply-depleted Japanese Kwantung Army with unexpected speed and advanced rapidly through Manchuria toward the Sino-Korean border. At the time, the United States had troops in Okinawa positioned for the Japanese occupation, but they still had to wait for transport to the main islands, therefore raising the possibility that the Soviets would be in a position to occupy not only all of Korea but even part of Japan before the arrival of the Americans.[48] To avert the prospect of a shared occupation of Japan, U.S. officials hastily drafted a proposal for a joint trusteeship of Korea, which divided the peninsula into two zones at the 38th parallel so that the Soviets and Americans would receive the Japanese surrender in the North and South respectively. That would begin with a period of divided military occupation, with the expectation that sovereignty would eventually be restored to Koreans "in due course" after an unspecified length of time. The Soviets accepted the plan, and Korea, without regard to historical administrative boundaries or topographical features, thus became divided into North and South.

Nearly a month before the U.S. forces were transported from Okinawa, the Soviet forces entered the northern zone and advanced to the 38th parallel, reaching the dividing line on August 24, 1945, only nine days after Japan's surrender. The Soviet forces proceeded to set in motion the logistical aspects of the peninsular division. This included a closing of the border to all civilian crossings and transportation of goods, along with the cessation of travel and transport by rail. By the time U.S. occupation forces arrived in South Korea on September 6th, the Soviet troops had two days before already terminated wireless exchanges and suspended telephone communications.[49]

Korea's liberation from colonial rule propelled a spontaneous decentralization of political power, expressed in renewed peasant radicalism and peasant union activism alongside the emergence of people's committees throughout Korea after liberation. This groundswell of Korean political activity was met by vastly different responses from the Soviets and the Americans, and their contrasting approaches to occupation would ultimately set the course for the formation of separate and opposing Korean regimes.[50] In the South, American authorities aimed above all to create an anticommunist regime favorable to U.S. interests, and this imperative led them to rely on the judgment of the defeated enemies, the Japanese, rather than the Koreans whom they were ostensibly liberating. Outgoing Japanese colonizers characterized Korean nationalists as communists, and the American occupiers accepted this assessment, treating popular Korean resistance to foreign occupation and attempts at self-government as manifestations of communist insurgency. Within three weeks after the collapse of Japanese colonialism, an assembly of Korean representatives from the southern provinces met in Seoul, and the nascent modern state reflected a spectrum of political orientations although the popular sentiment was favorably disposed toward revolutionary change. When U.S. occupying authorities arrived in Korea led by Lt. General John Hodge, however, they did not recognize the fledgling Korean Provisional Government and instead set up the U.S. Military Government in Korea (USAMGIK). As part of their efforts, Hodge and his advisors disbanded the people's committees, overturned the land reforms they had initiated, and chose to ally with the small elite of landlords who had collaborated with the Japanese colonizers.[51] The USAMGIK also effectively reconstructed colonial structures of domination in order to suppress political resistance by restoring power to Korean police officials who had worked for the colonial police, a move that alienated the majority of Koreans who had suffered bitterly during the colonial period. The United States eventually supported rightwing political leader Syngman Rhee, whose regime set about eliminating communists and leftists, working in conjunction with a network of rightwing youth groups.[52]

Although the Soviets took an entirely different approach to occupation in the North, their position in 1945 resembled that of the United States in some respects. Like the United States, the Soviet Union sought to foster a friendly regime in its Korean occupied zone, and the Soviets too had not made extensive arrangements in advance. However, the Soviets were at an advantage over the Americans because Korean popular initiatives of land reform and governance by people's committees coincided with their own communist objectives. In their respective historical monographs based on analyses of captured North Korean documents in the National Archives at College Park, Maryland, historians Suzy Kim and Charles K. Armstrong each refute the State Department consensus of the time, which characterized the Soviet occupation as a calculated takeover. Instead, Kim and Armstrong respectively detail how the Soviet occupation of the North was shaped very much by the Korean Communists themselves, compared to the understaffed and ad hoc administration by the Soviets.[53] The early North Korean Communists were comprised of members from various groups: those driven underground by Japanese colonial authorities on the peninsula; those who had fought in the Chinese Civil War; those who had constructed the Korean Provisional Government (KPG) in exile in Shanghai; and others returning from exile in China, the United States, and the Soviet Union. Members of post-Liberation North Korean society carried out revolutionary changes that transformed their social, economic, and political milieu in a remarkably short time, nationalizing major industries and completing by 1946 the confiscation and redistribution of land held by landlords, other collaborators, and the Japanese Government-General. The new government also established control over the press and religious groups to suppress dissent. Strikingly, Korean Communists were mainly behind the drive for social revolution, while Stalin himself ordered restraint toward pro-Japanese elements so as not to provoke the Americans.[54] Landlords and collaborators, as well as Christians and other religious leaders, were therefore pressured to go to the South, though with little bloodshed. The effect of this exodus purged the North of many of those opposed to the regime, and this phenomenon of internal migration contributed toward mapping Korea's ideological polarization onto respective geographical centers of gravity in the north and south.

The policies adopted by the occupying powers and the manner in which they were enforced during these two periods unquestionably deepened Korea's internal conflicts. Led by the U.S.–educated former exile Syngman Rhee, the Republic of Korea was established on August 15, 1948, after the United States had worked through the United Nations to hold elections in May of that year, but only in the southern zone. Nationwide elections in both zones were supposed to have been negotiated between the two occupying powers after 1945, but those talks became deadlocked amid the deterioration of relations between the United States and Soviet Union. With the establishment of the South Korean regime, the North Koreans denounced the separate election as illegitimate. They invoked the need to defend against foreign encroachment by the United Nations and the United States in formalizing their own regime as the DPRK on September 9th under the leadership of Kim Il-sung. By the time of the formation of separate republics in 1948, the rival states already had very different and ideologically opposed societies. As Stewart Lone and Gavan McCormack describe the zero-sum nature of ideological struggle between the two Korean regimes, "The merging of a revolutionary and a counterrevolutionary regime could only be achieved by the surrender of one or other side, or by war."[55]

CATASTROPHE: THE KOREAN WAR

The Korean War stands as the formative catastrophe of Korea's modern history. It ensured the perpetuation of its national division for the next several decades. The war ravaged the peninsula and resulted in horrendous slaughter, taking the lives of more than an estimated four million people, most of whom were civilians. In the years prior to the war there had been vigorous public support for national unification and still enough diversity of political views among Korean leaders to arouse hopes for negotiations toward that objective. However, the war brutally accelerated the process of political and ideological polarization in Korea by strengthening hardliners and embittering survivors bereft by the carnage and destruction. The Korean War also proved to be a watershed event as the Cold War's first "hot" conflict, which expedited the militarization of the ideological divide that soon spanned the globe. A brief overview of the war's course during the period of large-scale military hostilities (June 1950–July 1953) can be divided into four main phases:

(i.) *The War for the South*: After several months of civil conflict and border skirmishes that intensified since late 1949, the North Korean army launched a pre-dawn military offensive across the 38th parallel on June 25, 1950, that overwhelmed the defenses of the lightly armed ROK forces. Equipped with Soviet weapons and heavy armor, the North Korean People's Army (KPA) was further strengthened by the inclusion of roughly forty thousand ethnic Koreans, recently released by Mao from China's People's Liberation Army (PLA), who brought combat experience from having fought in the Chinese civil war. That combination far outmatched the underprepared ROK army, which was initially reinforced by only a small number of U.S. combat troops.[56] The KPA made swift progress, capturing Seoul and driving the ROK and U.S. troops to the southeastern corner of the peninsula in the vicinity of South Korea's largest port city of Pusan. Although it seemed that the North Koreans might realize their goal of unifying the peninsula, U.S. intervention brought additional troops and air power to help ROK forces in defending their last stronghold, an area that would be known as the Pusan Perimeter.

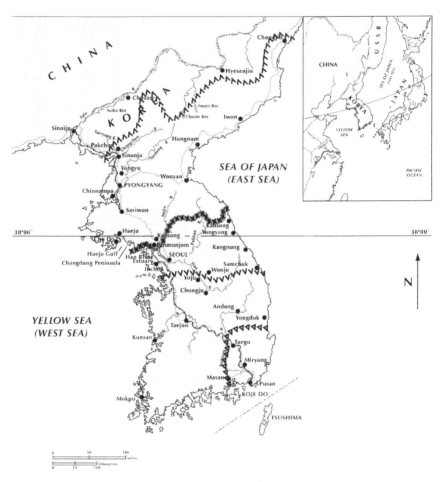

The Korean peninsula and the four stages of the war

▼▼▼▼ i. Pusan Perimeter – limit of the North Korean   ▽▽▽▽ iii. Limit of Chinese advance to
     advance to September 1950   end January 1951

ΛΛΛΛ ii. Furthest advance of UN forces to   ✕✕✕✕ iv. Battle front June 1951 – July 1953
     end October 1950   and eventual demarcation line

Figure 1.1.   The Korean peninsula and the four stages of war. Reproduced from
W. K. Harrex, K. W. Horsley, P. Jelfs, R. van der Hoek, and E. J. Wilson, *Mortality
of Korean War Veterans: The Veteran Cohort Study, A Report of the 2002
Retrospective Cohort Study of Australian Veterans of the Korean War* (Canberra,
Australia: Department of Veterans' Affairs, 2003); map adapted by Trevor G. Ber-
man, with permission from the Australian Department of Veterans' Affairs.

(ii.) *The War for Rollback*: The amphibious landing of more than seventy thousand troops at the port of Inchŏn beginning in mid-September spearheaded a counterattack by UN troops behind KPA lines. The operation planned by General Douglas MacArthur reversed the early course of the war. By that point the North Koreans had already overextended their supply lines, and the massive UN assault following the Inchŏn Landing forced the KPA to retreat north. After UN forces recaptured Seoul in late September 28th, ROK troops continued their advance northward up the east coast. In a bid to "roll back" Communism, American forces received authorization by Washington to cross the 38th parallel northward in early October 1950. Meeting relatively little resistance, they overtook Pyongyang within three weeks and swept up the peninsula toward the Yalu River at the Sino-DPRK border.

(iii.) *Chinese Intervention*: Chinese forces—designated not as regular troops but rather as "Chinese People's Volunteers" (CPV)—began crossing the Yalu River into North Korea in mid-October. By late November, thirty-three Chinese divisions—a force numbering 450,000—had entered combat, launching the massive offensive that would send the UN forces reeling southward in a panicked retreat. In early January 1951, the CPV would take control of Seoul, as they pushed the UN forces past the 38th parallel. However, the situation differed from their vulnerability near the Yalu River, where the CPV had routed sectors of the ROK Army and U.S. Eighth Army and where the U.S. X Corps had been widely dispersed over barren mountain terrain. South of the divide, the Chinese would face a better-equipped and more securely entrenched enemy. By winter, the CPV also contended with worsening difficulties, including shortages of food and ammunition, fatigued troops, and delayed reinforcements.

(iv.) *Stalemate and Armistice Talks*: Seoul would change hands for a fourth and final time when the UN forces launched a counterattack on January 25, 1951. After the failed spring offensives of that year by Chinese and North Korean troops, it became clear that the war had reached a stalemate. The risks and costs of escalating the war significantly were greater than either the Americans or the Chinese were willing to accept. Truce talks began on July 10, 1951, between military commanders from the United Nations Command (UNC) and their counterparts from the Chinese People's Volunteer Army and the Korean People's Army of the DPRK.[57] After more than five months of contentious negotiations, the two sides reached agreement regarding the location of the Military Demarcation Line (MDL) along the line of contact at that time. They also agreed on the terms of the Demilitarized Zone (DMZ), which required both sides to draw back their troops two kilometers from the MDL. By the time the Communists and the UN Command signed the armistice on July 27, 1953, the MDL remained largely unchanged, despite the air assaults and ground combat that had continued during the period of negotiations.

CATALYSTS OF ESCALATION

Given this brief overview of the war's military phases, it is notable that two interrelated factors escalated the Korean War at pivotal junctures: (1) the nationalist drive toward achieving a unified state, which fueled the mutually exclusive ambitions of the two newly formed opposing Korean republics in north and south; and (2) involvement by foreign powers on both sides, which provided the crucial military and logistical support that greatly expanded the war's scale and destructiveness. Insofar as the rise of Korean blood-based nationalisms emerged during the period under Japanese colonial rule, the social and political phenomenon of competitive nationalisms in Korea was intertwined with the condition of Korea's geopolitical liminality.[58] While it may seem a truism that Korea's strategic location was furthermore a key motivation for the involvement of particularly China and the Soviet Union in the Korean War, an examination of the archival record bears out this reasoning in ways, as I explain below, which highlight the ironic resonance of geopolitical liminality in Korea's modern political history.

Regarding the role of nationalism in the origins of the war, Korean nationalists anticipated independence immediately after liberation from colonial rule in 1945. With the formation of separate regimes in 1948, the two states vied for legitimacy, each laying claim to a single nation. The leaders on both sides, Rhee and Kim, became determined to unify the country by military means, which translated to an uncompromising zero-sum rivalry. Historian Myung-Lim Park has argued that the post-1945 partition generated a driving imperative on both sides to restore the lost unitary nation, which gave rise to the tensions and violent conflicts on the Korean peninsula that culminated in the Korean War.[59] In August 1948, Kim Il-sung put unification at the center of his fledgling government's political agenda, calling it the "most urgent condition to guarantee the completion of national territory and the unification of the fatherland." As Kim in the North called for the destruction of the Southern regime, so did South Korean President Syngman Rhee vigorously advocate a ROK strategy of unification by force, adopting the militaristic slogan "Advance North, Unify the Nation" (*pukchin t'ongil*).[60] Thus, it was an intensifying rivalry between mutually exclusive nationalist agendas during the late 1940s that eventually triggered an all-out confrontation on the peninsula. The war's origins therefore arose in a wider social and historical context than simply the narrow circumstances leading up to the outbreak of large-scale military hostilities on June 25, 1950.

Regarding the role of outside intervention, the prevailing interpretation in Western countries for decades after 1950 held that the North Korean attack must have been surely masterminded by Stalin as part of a strategy of communist expansionism, following the victory of the Chinese Communists in 1949. However, with the release of formerly unavailable Soviet and Chinese documents in the 1990s, archival documents depicted a far more complex set of relationships among Stalin, Kim Il-sung, and Mao Zedong than had been previously supposed. Regarding the Korean peninsula, ciphered telegrams between Soviet officials indicate that rather than the North Koreans acting as puppets carrying out Stalin's orders, the North Korean premier Kim Il-sung and his foreign minister Pak Hŏn-yŏng vigorously pressed a reluctant and cautious Stalin for more than a year to gain his support for an invasion plan. In the escalation of conflict from domestic border skirmishes to an international war, Stalin's decision in early 1950 to agree to support the North Koreans' invasion plan, which went against his prior caution, would prove fateful. Stalin had previously rebuffed Kim's proposal out of his determination to avoid the risk of a war between the Soviet Union and the United States. That stance was further confirmed when the Politburo of the CPSU Central Committee voted on September 24, 1945, to reject the North Koreans' invasion plan. The view of the Politburo members was that "if military actions begin at the initiative of the North and acquire a prolonged character, then this can give to the Americans cause of any kind of intervention in Korean affairs."[61] The Politburo assessed that the North Koreans were not sufficiently prepared politically or militarily to launch a general invasion and advised them to augment their guerrilla capabilities in the South instead.

However, two developments dramatically altered the global strategic landscape in the latter part of 1949: (1) the Soviet atomic test in August, and (2) the defeat of the U.S.–backed Nationalists by the Chinese Communists, who proclaimed the establishment of the People's Republic of China in October. In the United States, State Department officials had been unaware of the extent to which Soviet espionage had compromised the atomic program, so when evidence emerged in September 1949 confirming an underground nuclear test in the Soviet Union, the end of the U.S. nuclear monopoly came years ahead of American intelligence estimates. Truman responded by ordering an intensive reassessment of U.S. national security policies. The resulting report, NSC-68, conveyed grave warnings of intensifying ideological struggle with Soviet Communism and argued for a rapid U.S. military buildup financed by a tripling of the defense budget. The NSC-68 authors justified this unprecedented defense outlay in peacetime by insisting upon the capacity to "have the military power to deter, if possible, Soviet expansion, and to defeat, if necessary, aggressive Soviet or Soviet-directed actions."[62] Although the National Security Council issued NSC-68 on April 14, 1950, its proposals did not get implemented right away, but instead were stalled by the process of budgetary review for months. NSC-68 finally received approval in September, and political scientist Robert Jervis stresses that, had it not been for the North Korean invasion in June, it is unlikely that the enormous new outlay would have been approved. In Dean Acheson's words, "Korea came along and saved us."[63]

Compared to the delays surrounding NSC-68, the more immediate U.S. response to the unfolding revolution in China came during the fall of 1948, when all of Manchuria was already under control of the Chinese People's Liberation Army. With the outlook in China increasingly dire, the United States implemented NSC 13/2 in October 1948 to change the agenda for Occupation policy in Japan. NSC 13/2 would give top priority to accelerated economic rehabilitation, shifting the priority of the Occupation government away from its initial emphasis on democratization.[64] This change was in line with a pivot that had been already underway toward focusing on the evolving Cold War and moving away from the democratizing "New Deal" roots of the Occupation as initially planned.[65] In perhaps the clearest example of this shift, the Americans had originally intended to dismantle the *zaibatsu*, the industrial conglomerates which were perceived by many of the Allied forces to have been complicit with Japan's militarist expansionism. However, beginning in the spring of 1948, the U.S. Occupation would opt against the "destabilizing reforms" of an economic purge and instead conform with those in Washington who saw the conglomerates as central to Japan's reconstruction and future economic success.

As historians Mark Caprio and Yoneyuki Sugita observe, the shift away from democratization was not as surprising as the U.S. decision during the same period to reverse course toward rearming Japan. They write: "A more startling policy reversal transpired from 1948, when the United States began to pressure the Japanese government to remilitarize. This represented a direct violation not only of Japan's surrender terms, but also its constitution."[66] After the Japanese surrender in 1945, the Occupation authorities oversaw the disarmament of Japan, including the complete demobilization of its armed forces and a purge of military leaders from positions of influence. The 1947 constitution, written by MacArthur and his staff, included the renunciation of war under Article 9, which declared that Japan would never again maintain "land, sea, or air forces or other war potential."[67] In fact, Japanese Prime Minister Yoshida refused U.S. overtures in 1948 to have Japan reconstitute its armed forces, citing the drag that military expenses would have on the still struggling postwar economy. According to Caprio and Sugita, American pressures on the Japanese to rebuild its military capacity "intensified with communist successes in Northeast Asia and civil unrest in Japan, climaxing just days prior to the outbreak of the Korean War when John Foster Dulles rushed from a tense situation at the 38th parallel to Tokyo, to press Japanese rearmament."[68] Following the post-1945 measures that effected a wholesale demilitarization, Japan was then left virtually defenseless in 1950 after most Occupation troops were deployed to the Korean peninsula following the North Korean invasion. In July 1950, Yoshida finally agreed to authorizing the establishment of the National Police Reserve, comprised of seventy thousand servicemen equipped with light infantry weapons. The National Police

Reserve was put under civilian control and given the administrative status of only an agency, rather than a ministry, and in 1951, these security personnel would be renamed the Self-Defense Forces (SDF). While these measures had been undertaken to avoid charges of the revival of Japanese militarism, other circumstances indicated that the SDF were not simply an extension agency of the civilian police. For example, in the early 1950s, the Occupation forces would move out of the building that had been formerly used as the headquarters of the Japanese Imperial Army; that building, where imperial soldiers had been mobilized to fight the Asia-Pacific War, would be "returned" to the Japanese to use as the base for the Self-Defense Forces. [69]

For the Soviet Union, the two geostrategic breakthroughs in 1949—the Chinese Communist victory and the successful Soviet atomic test—served to offset a series of daunting setbacks they had faced in Europe. Among the challenges and humiliations that the Soviets weathered the prior year were the institution of the Marshall Plan, the failed Berlin Blockade in 1948–1949, and the formation of the North Atlantic Treaty Organization (NATO) in April 1949. The outcome of the Chinese civil war therefore changed the momentum of the global Cold War by taking the United States by surprise and setting off a series of internal recriminations in the State Department and a furious debate over who was to blame for the "loss" of China. For the Communists, Mao's victory on the mainland accordingly recast the situation in Korea as an opportunity to build upon that success in Asia. [70] Yet, it also set off a new competition between Mao and Stalin for the leadership of revolutionary movements in Asia. [71] Hence, both Stalin and Mao felt pressured to aid Korean Communists after the Chinese Communist victory in 1949.

Secretary of State Dean Acheson's National Press Club speech on January 12, 1950, in which he was understood to have left Korea outside of a U.S. defense-perimeter in the Pacific, may have given Stalin the assurance to wager that the Americans would not intervene militarily in Korea. Alternatively, he may have been convinced by Kim Il-sung's overconfident prediction of a swift victory that could be secured before the United States had time to mount an intervention. Still, Stalin gambled on the potential for the invasion's gains over its relative risks, and among those anticipated gains was a stronger Soviet position in the region. Stalin was well aware of the rival nationalist ambitions in Korea, and given the Southern suppression of communist guerrillas, it was evident that a Korean unification favorable to the Soviets was not likely by means other than a full-scale military offensive.

Significantly, by June of 1950, both the Soviets and the North Koreans had become increasingly anxious over the prospect that Japanese militarism would be revived under the aegis of U.S. occupation. For example, when developing plans in 1947 to expand its patrols along the Soviet Pacific border, the U.S. military considered rearming Japan in order to increase available forces in the region; but those plans would later be rescinded in the face of strenuous opposition from the Soviet representative to the Far Eastern Commission.[72] Regarding the North Koreans, Bruce Cumings argues that the clearest motive for the timing of the KPA all-out attack on June 25, 1950, was their growing concerns over the threat posed by a rearmed Japan allied with both the United States and South Korea. More than a generic reaction against what it perceived as recolonization of the South under American occupation, the North Koreans particularly feared the rapid revival of Japan's formidable heavy-industrial economic base through the windfall of a U.S.–sponsored reconstruction, which also promoted Japan's reintegration with South Korea under Rhee.[73] In the political-education materials used among KPA political officers that June, the transcripts of lectures opened with an accusation that North Koreans had already levied in past briefings, stating "the basic policy of the American imperialists is newly to militarize Japan."[74] However, Cumings observes that the lectures held in June placed a new emphasis on a wider interpretation, "suggesting that American plans for remilitarizing Japan were intimately connected with plans for making Korea a bridgehead for attacking China and the Soviet Union."[75]

Notably, when Stalin later sought to pressure Mao to enter the war in the fall of 1950, the Soviet leader similarly underscored the imperative to preempt the threat posed by the prospect of a resurgent Japan allied with their American rivals and the Rhee regime. Stalin makes this connection explicitly in a telegram to Mao, but first it is worth weighing what a consequential communication this was. The crossing of the 38th parallel by UNC troops in October and their headlong rush toward the Sino-Korean border at the Yalu River are often assumed to have provoked the Chinese to enter the war; and the demarcation line was indeed regarded by both Stalin and Mao as an important condition for China's entry into the war. Yet the PRC leadership was initially prepared to intervene even earlier. Judging from the scale of U.S. military reinforcements during the fiercely fought Battle of the Naktong River, Chinese military leaders realized the U.S. was far more committed to the South Korean government than they had previously estimated. As that battle dragged on, Mao made several offers to send Chinese troops, proposals that Stalin declined in favor of waiting for more strategic timing.[76]

However, following the Inchŏn landing in mid-September, it was the collapse of North Korean forces that deepened a division of opinion among the Chinese military leadership, who debated over whether to *reconsider*, rather than immediately reconfirm, the decision to intervene militarily.[77] In a move that reportedly stunned the Soviets, Mao initially expressed reservations in response to Stalin's urgent request to mobilize several divisions to rescue Kim Il-sung. In a message to Stalin sent through Soviet ambassador to China N. V. Roshchin, Mao suggested that the Chinese forces were under-strength, and his overall tone was unmistakably wary, writing: "Many comrades in the CC CPC judge that it is necessary to show caution here." He argued that, if China's troops entered the war but were ultimately driven to retreat by U.S. forces, the PRC's newly established government would be faced with domestic resentment among a war-weary populace, which would ruin the Chinese Communist Party's plans for a rapid reconstruction and modernization of the country.[78]

At a critical juncture in early October, Stalin thus had to press a reluctant Mao to enter the war, as the Soviet leader was determined to avoid a U.S.–Soviet confrontation at all costs. In a carefully worded telegram to Mao, Stalin conveyed his assessment that the United States was unready to fight a major war but could be drawn into one for reasons of national prestige. Should that be the case, he reassured Mao that the Soviet Union would also enter the war to fulfill its commitments to the Mutual Assistance Pact between the two communist powers. Warning that the United States, given time, would eventually provoke a conflict, Stalin wrote, "let it take place now, rather than a few years later, when Japanese militarism will be restored as an American ally, and when the United States and Japan will possess a military springboard on the continent in the form of Rhee's Korea."[79] Just as the North Korean political education materials argued four months earlier in June, Stalin described how a reunified Korean peninsula under Syngman Rhee could serve the United States and Japan as a launching point to attack the continental Communist powers or at least to thwart their objectives, including China's determination to finish off the Nationalists and recover Taiwan. Stalin therefore made a point to reframe the possibility of such a conflict as a way to avert a far worse geopolitical scenario for the Communists.

When Mao resolved to send the Chinese troops across the Yalu, it was not without agonizing over the decision for several days in October. When he finally held an emergency meeting to convey his decision to the Politburo Standing Committee, the members vigorously opposed, making the same arguments that Mao had earlier used to justify his initial refusal of Stalin's troop request. As Sheila Miyoshi Jager describes the deciding factor for the Chinese Communist leader, "Mao's response echoed Stalin's, that if the Chinese did not fight the Americans now, they might be forced to do so at a later date. Since America's plan to occupy North Korea was part of a grand strategy to dominate the whole of East Asia, the task of defending China would be that much harder if the Americans gained a foothold on the Korean peninsula."[80] Considering MacArthur's determination to overturn the outcome of the Chinese civil war and Truman's deployment of the U.S. Seventh Fleet to the Taiwan Straits, Mao believed that a Sino–American confrontation was inevitable. Ultimately, Mao mobilized Chinese forces for intervention in Korea, while invoking the logic that the Chinese would compensate for what they lacked in terms of a modern arsenal by leveraging their strategic advantages of timing and terrain. Mao gauged that it would be favorable for them to fight the Americans on the Korean peninsula, rather than risk having to do so on their own soil.

It is therefore striking that, at two momentous junctures that would profoundly shape the scope of the Korean War, the overriding rationale adopted in Pyongyang, Moscow, and eventually Beijing for expanding the conflict would in fact duplicate the geopolitical reasoning of the Meiji leadership during the late nineteenth century, albeit in reverse direction. That is, the Korean peninsula was singled out for its vital and immediate strategic importance, given its location between Japan and the Eurasian continent. With the specter of "Rhee's Korea" threatening to furnish a springboard for invasion, what was at stake for the leadership of the Soviet Union and China, as well as for North Korea, was therefore not simply to gain control of the peninsula; nor was it primarily to pursue the far-reaching symbolic victory that would result from attaining "total victory" there over the Americans. Rather, the broader and explicitly stated objective that they each weighed above all was to preempt the threat that the United States and a rearmed Japan would take advantage of a reunified Korea to assert their power against the Asian Communists.

As revealed in the historical sources discussed above, specific and literal references to Korea's in-between location figured highly into key strategic considerations that eventually determined the motives for both the North Korean invasion and the Chinese entry into the Korean War. This reflected not only the military situation in the mid-twentieth century but also the historical evolution of regional alliances that had rendered Korea's location strategically sensitive, which can be traced to key developments of the late nineteenth century: namely, the impact of Western imperialist incursions in East Asia, and Japan's rise as a regional hegemonic power. While the geographical position of the peninsula in the modern era would inexorably determine the conditions that led to Korea's colonial annexation, national division, and later war, those conditions would in turn factor significantly into another key factor in the war's escalation: the rise and intensification of rival Korean nationalisms, constructed through notions of inclusion and exclusion imagined in relation to blood lineages.

NOTES

1. Fernando Coronil, "Beyond Occidentalism: Towards Non-Imperial Geohistorical Categories," *Cultural Anthropology* 11, no. 1 (1996): 77.
2. Coronil, "Beyond Occidentalism," 76.
3. Charles K. Armstrong, *The Koreas* (London and New York: Routledge, 2007), 6–13.
4. John B. Duncan, "Uses of Confucianism in Modern Korea," in *Rethinking Confucianism: Past and Present in China, Japan, Korea, and Vietnam,* eds. Benjamin A. Elman, John B. Duncan, and Herman Ooms (Los Angeles: University of California, 2002), 433.

5. Henry H. Em, "Nationalism, Post-Nationalism, and Shin Ch'ae-ho," *Korea Journal* 39, no. 2 (1999): 283–317.

6. Gregory Henderson, *Korea: The Politics of the Vortex* (Cambridge, MA: Harvard University Press, 1968), 15.

7. See Samuel Hawley, *The Imjin War: Japan's Sixteenth-Century Invasion of Korea and Attempt to Conquer China* (Seoul: Royal Asiatic Society, 2005).

8. The initial framing of this chapter was inspired by Charles Armstrong's concise discussion of precisely this point in *The Koreas* (8): "[T]o read Korea's history as a history of victimization due to the peninsula's unfortunate location . . . ignores the historically contingent nature of geographical significance. Geography is never a 'given,' as spatial conceptions change with time. Locations only become 'strategic' at certain conjunctures of power, knowledge, and technology. For most of their history, Koreans did not at all see themselves as inhabiting a small peninsula strategically situated between rival Great Powers." Armstrong points to a Korean map of the world dated 1402 AD, which features both China and Korea prominently while Japan appears as a peripheral archipelago. He writes, "This exemplifies the 'classical' Korean view of Korea's place in the world for over a millennium: China as the central civilization, Korea nearly co-equal with China, and Japan small and insignificant."

9. Vladimir Tikhonov, "The Race and Racism Discourses in Modern Korea, 1890s–1910s," *Korean Studies* 36 (2012): 34.

10. Frank Dikötter, *The Discourse of Race in Modern China* (Stanford: Stanford University Press, 1992).

11. Kenneth R. Robinson, "Centering the King of Chosŏn: Aspects of Korean Maritime Diplomacy, 1392–1592," *The Journal of Asian Studies* 59, no. 1 (2000): 122.

12. JaHyun Kim Haboush, *A Heritage of Kings: One Man's Monarchy in the Confucian World* (New York: Columbia University Press, 1988). Martina Deuchler argues that Korean Confucians set out to transform Korea into a model Confucian society at the outset of the Chosŏn dynasty while John Duncan contends that these changes were already underway during late Koryo. See Deuchler, *The Confucian Transformation of Korea* (Cambridge, MA: Harvard University Press, 1992); and Duncan, *The Origins of the Chosŏn Dynasty* (Seattle: University of Washington Press, 2000).

13. See Kim Key-Hiuk, *The Last Phase of the East Asian World Order: Korea, Japan, and the Chinese Empire, 1860–1882* (Berkeley and Los Angeles: University of California Press, 1980).

14. See Donald Calman, *Nature and Origins of Japanese Imperialism: A Re-interpretation of the 1873 Crisis* (London and New York: Routledge, 1992); Peter Duus, *The Abacus and the Sword: The Japanese Penetration of Korea, 1895–1910* (Berkeley: University of California Press, 1998).

15. Kim, Yong-sŏp, "The Landlord System and the Agricultural Economy during the Japanese Occupation Period," in *Landlords, Peasants, and Intellectuals in Modern Korea*, eds. Kijung Pang and Michael D. Shin. (Ithaca, NY: Cornell University Press, 2005), 135.

16. See George Kallander, *Salvation through Dissent: Tonghak Heterodoxy and Early Modern Korea* (Honolulu: University of Hawaii Press, 2013).

17. Alexis Dudden traces the methodical appropriation of international legal norms and discourse by the Japanese empire during this period in order both to pursue a stepwise colonization of Korea and more broadly to legitimize its status as a colonial power. See *Japan's Colonization of Korea: Discourse and Power* (Honolulu: University of Hawaii Press, 2005).

18. Andre Schmid, *Korea Between Empires: 1895–1919* (New York: Columbia University Press, 2002), 31.

19. Gi-Wook Shin, *Ethnic Nationalism in Korea* (Stanford, CA: Stanford University Press, 2006), 25–40.

20. Cumings, *Korea's Place in the Sun* (New York: Norton, 2005), 238.

21. Kim, Yong-sŏp, "Landlord System," in *Landlords, Peasants*, 100–130.

22. Ibid., 100.

23. Michael D. Shin, *Landlords, Peasants*, 6.

24. Mark R. Peattie, "Introduction," in *The Japanese Colonial Empire: 1895–1945*, ed. Ramon Hawley Myers and Mark Robert Peattie (Princeton, NJ: Princeton University Press, 1984), 7–9.

25. Michael E. Robinson, *Cultural Nationalism in Colonial Korea, 1920–1925* (Seattle: University of Washington Press, 1988).

26. Michael E. Robinson, "Colonial Publication Policy and the Korean Nationalist Movement," in *The Japanese Colonial Empire: 1895–1945*, ed. Ramon Hawley Myers and Mark Robert Peattie (Princeton, NJ: Princeton University Press, 1984), 135.

27. Dae-Sook Suh, *The Korean Communist Movement, 1918–1948* (Princeton: Princeton University Press, 1967).

28. Michael E. Robinson, *Korea's Twentieth-Century Odyssey* (Honolulu: University of Hawaii Press, 2007), 69.

29. See Suh, *The Korean Communist Movement, 1918–1948*.

30. Gi-Wook Shin, "Nationalism and the Korean War," in *Korea and the Korean War*, eds. Chae-Jin Lee and Young Ick Lew (Seoul: Yonsei University Press, 2002), 426.

31. Shin, *Ethnic Nationalism*, 21–110.

32. Anthony D. Smith, *The Ethnic Origins of Nations* (New York: Basil Blackwell, 1986).

33. Eric Hobsbawm, *Nations and Nationalism Since 1780* (Cambridge: Cambridge University Press, 1990), 66. Hobsbawm states in a footnote that the two Koreas and Japan are "99% homogeneous."

34. Schmid, *Korea Between Empires*, 122–29.

35. Ibid., 188–98.

36. Henry H. Em, *The Great Enterprise: Sovereignty and Historiography in Modern Korea* (Durham, NC: Duke University Press, 2013), 79.

37. Schmid, *Korea Between Empires*, 184–85.

38. Ibid., 187.

39. Shin, *Ethnic Nationalism*.

40. Janice C. H. Kim, *To Live to Work: Factory Women in Colonial Korea, 1910–1945* (Stanford, CA: Stanford University Press, 2009); Soon Won Park, *Colonial Industrialization and Labor in Korea: the Onoda Cement Factory*, vol. 181 (Cambridge, MA: Harvard University Press, 1999).

41. Hyun Sook Kim, "History and Memory: The 'Comfort Women' Controversy," *positions* 5, no. 1 (1997), 73–108; Katharine H. S. Moon, "South Korean Movements Against Militarized Sexual Labor," *Asian Survey* (1999), 310–27; C. Sarah Soh, *The Comfort Women: Sexual Violence and Postcolonial Memory in Korea and Japan* (Chicago: University of Chicago Press, 2008); Hyunah Yang, "Re-membering the Korean Military Comfort Women: Nationalism, Sexuality, and Silencing," in *Dangerous Women: Gender and Korean Nationalism*, eds. Elaine Kim and Chungmoo Choi (London and New York: Routledge, 1998).

42. Cumings, *Korea's Place*.

43. Bruce Cumings, *The Origins of the Korean War. Volume 1. Liberation and the Emergence of Separate Regimes, 1945–1947* (Princeton, NJ: Princeton University Press, 1981).

44. Gi-Wook Shin, *Peasant Protest and Social Change in Colonial Korea* (Seattle: University of Washington Press, 1996).

45. Jongsoo James Lee, *The Partition of Korea After World War II: A Global History* (New York: Palgrave Macmillan, 2007).

46. Stewart Lone and Gavan McCormack, *Korea Since 1850* (New York: St. Martin's Press, 1993), 95.

47. Mark E. Caprio, "Silent Voices: The Wartime Views of George McCune and Andrew Grajdanzev for Post-Liberation Korea," paper presented at the Center for Korean Studies Colloquium, University of Hawaii, Honolulu, HI, March 4, 2014. See also Yong-Wook Chung, "The Emergence of 'North Korea' in Cold War United States," Working Paper No. 03/05, The Mario Einaudi Center for International Studies, Cornell University, 2005, http://einaudi.cornell.edu/system/files/03-2005.pdf (accessed April 24, 2011).

48. Gregory Henderson, *Korea: The Politics of the Vortex* (Cambridge, MA: Harvard University Press, 1968), 123; Donald N. Clark, *Living Dangerously in Korea: The Western Experience, 1900–1950* (Norwalk, CT: EastBridge, 2003), 282.

49. Kathryn Weathersby, "Soviet Aims in Korea and the Origins of the Korean War, 1945–1950: New Evidence From Russian Archives." Working Paper 8. Woodrow Wilson International Center for Scholars (1993). http://www.wilsoncenter.org/sites/default/files/Working_Paper_8.pdf (accessed August 28, 2008): 13.

50. See Bruce Cumings, *The Origins of the Korean War.*

51. Steven Hugh Lee, *The Korean War* (New York: Longman, 2001).

52. Bruce Cumings, *The Korean War: A History* (New York: Random House, 2010); Namhee Lee, "Anticommunism, North Korea, and Human Rights in South Korea: 'Orientalist' Discourse and Construction of South Korean Identity," in *Truth Claims: Representation and Human Rights*, ed. Mark Philip Bradley and Patrice Petro (New Brunswick, NJ: Rutgers University Press, 2002).

53. Suzy Kim, *Everyday Life in the North Korean Revolution, 1945–1950* (Ithaca, NY: Cornell University Press, 2013); Charles K. Armstrong, *The North Korean Revolution: 1945–1950* (Ithaca, NY: Cornell University Press, 2004).

54. Charles K. Armstrong, "The Cultural Cold War in Korea, 1945–1950," *Journal of Asian Studies* 62, no. 1 (2003).

55. Lone and McCormack, *Korea Since 1850*, 100.

56. The U.S. military did not fulfill Syngman Rhee's requests for heavier munitions because of fears in the State Department that Rhee would follow through on his own threat to invade the North unilaterally.

57. No representative from the Republic of Korea was a signatory because South Korean president Syngman Rhee had earlier protested the truce negotiations and withdrawn his side's delegates from the talks, believing instead that the ROK military should have continued fighting until Korea was reunified.

58. Already discussed above was the pivotal strategic importance placed on the Korean peninsula's location as the motivating rationale for Japan's colonization.

59. Myung Lim Park, *Han'guk chŏnjaeng ŭi palbal kwa kiwon* [*The Outbreak and Origins of the Korean War*] (Seoul: Nanam Press, 1996).

60. Wada Haruki, *The Korean War: An International History* (Lanham, MD: Rowman & Littlefield, 2013), 8.

61. "Politburo Decision to Confirm the Following Directive to the Soviet Ambassador in Korea," September 24, 1949, History and Public Policy Program Digital Archive, AVP RF, Fond 059a, Opis 5a, Delo 3, Papka 11, listy 75–77. http://digitalarchive.wilsoncenter.org/document/112133.

62. United States Department of State, "United States National Security Policy: Estimates of Threats to the National Security; The Extension of Military Assistance to Foreign Nations; The Preparation of NSC 68, 'United States Objectives and Programs for National Security,'" In *Foreign Relations of the United States, 1950, National Security Affairs; Foreign Economic Policy, Volume I*, 126–49 (Washington, DC: U.S. Government Printing Office, 1950). Accessed at http://digicoll.library.wisc.edu/cgi-bin/FRUS/FRUS-idx?id=FRUS.FRUS1950v01.

63. Robert Jervis, "The Impact of the Korean War on the Cold War," *Journal of Conflict Resolution* 24, no. 4 (1980): 585.

64. Haruki Wada, "The Korean War, Stalin's Policy, and Japan," *Social Science Japan Journal* 1, no. 1 (1998): 11.

65. Mark E. Caprio and Yoneyuki Sugita, *Democracy in Occupied Japan: The U.S. Occupation and Japanese Politics and Society* (New York and London: Routledge, 2007), 16.

66. Ibid., 16; see also Axel Berkofsky, *A Pacifist Constitution for an Armed Empire: Past and Present of the Japanese Security and Defense Policies* (Milan: FrancoAngeli, 2012), 118–30.

67. Berkofsky, *A Pacifist Constitution*, 101–17.

68. Caprio and Sugita, *Democracy in Occupied Japan*, 16–17.

69. Sabine Frühstück, *Uneasy Warriors: Gender, Memory, and Popular Culture in the Japanese Army* (Berkeley and Los Angeles: University of California Press, 2007), 40–41.

70. Mark O'Neill, "Soviet Involvement in the Korean War: A New View from the Soviet-Era Archives," *OAH Magazine of History* 14, no. 3 (2000): 20.

71. Wada, "The Korean War, Stalin's Policy, and Japan," 16.

72. Kathryn Weathersby, "New Russian Documents on the Korean War." *Cold War International History Project Bulletin* (Winter 1995): 32. http://www.wilsoncenter.org/sites/default/files/ACF1A6.pdf (accessed August 28, 2008).

73. Bruce Cumings, *The Origins of the Korean War, Volume II: The Roaring of the Cataract, 1947–1950* (Princeton, NJ: Princeton University Press, 1990), 458.

74. Ibid., 462.

75. Cumings writes that the lectures "referred to, among other things, the revival of *zaibatsu* groups like Mitsubishi, which previously owned many factories in northern Korea, American protection for biological warfare criminal Gernal Ishii . . . and American plans to keep bases at Yokusuka and Sasebo. This [reference to the situation beyond their domestic partisan struggle with the Rhee regime] was, of course, linked to the continuance of colonial social formations and bureaucracies, and pro-Japanese elements in the South." Ibid., 462.

76. Shen Zhihua and Yafeng Xia, "Mao Zedong's Erroneous Decision During the Korean War: China's Rejection of the UN Cease-fire Resolution in Early 1951," *Asian Perspective* 35, no. 2 (2011): 188.

77. Shen Zhihua persuasively interprets the striking divergence between Chinese and Russian versions of Mao's message to Stalin dated October 2, 1950. Although a strongly worded Chinese version has been used for decades to support the claim that Mao had already committed by that point to sending troops to Korea, Shen notes that, while this message was written in Mao's own hand, it was actually left unpublished. Far more likely as the actual transmission to Stalin was the version that was uncovered in Russian archives. In that message, Shen argues, Mao's cautious tone both accurately reflected the considerable reservations among his military leaders and also served to put more pressure on Stalin to provide Soviet military support. See Shen, "The Discrepancy Between the Russian and Chinese Versions of Mao's 2 October 1950 Message to Stalin on Chinese Entry into the Korean War: A Chinese Scholar's Reply," *CWIHP Bulletin*, nos. 8–9 (Winter 1996/1997): 238; Sheila Miyoshi Jager, *Brothers at War: The Unending Conflict in Korea* (New York: W. W. Norton & Company, 2013), 121, fn25.

78. Alexandre Y. Mansourov, "Stalin, Mao, Kim, and China's Decision to Enter the Korean War, September 16–October 15, 1950: New Evidence from the Russian Archives," *Cold War International History Project Bulletin* (Winter 1995), 100; Chen Jian, *China's Road to the Korean War* (New York: Columbia University Press, 1996), 185.

79. Ibid., 101. Conversely, Sergei Goncharov, John Lewis, and Xue Litai have speculated that Stalin may have himself been motivated to support the North Korean proposal for the June 1950 invasion out of his own ambitions to use Korea as a springboard for attacking Japan in the event of a future regional conflict; however, while they repeat that hypothesis numerous times, nowhere do they corroborate their speculation with evidence from primary documents. See *Uncertain Partners: Stalin, Mao, and the Korean War* (Stanford, CA: Stanford University Press, 1994), 139, 152, 213–14.

80. Jager, *Brothers at War*, 122.

Chapter Two

Fateful Passages, In-Between States

Regarding the number of people killed in the Korean War, estimates are notoriously divergent and uncertain. In *The Deaths of Others*—a compelling comparative study of civilian deaths in the Second World War, the Korean War, the Vietnam War, Iraq, and Afghanistan—political scientist John Tirman sorts through what he calls the "chaos of estimates," the inevitable guesswork that factors into attempts to calculate deaths in large-scale military conflicts. He writes, "The Korean War presents the clearest example of *guessing* how many people died as a result of a major war"[1] (emphasis added). Tirman cites the most widely circulated figure as three million deaths, of which civilians are believed to comprise roughly half of those who died in the Korean War. Yet, he also singles out as notably thoughtful a 2003 comprehensive study by arms control analyst Milton Leitenberg, who estimates 4.5 million people died during the Korean War; that includes 2,828,000 civilians and 1,672,000 combatants, which corresponds with the figures published by Jon Halliday and Bruce Cumings in 1988.[2] If there is a point of consensus regarding these vastly divergent estimates, it is that civilian deaths represent without question a disturbingly high proportion of those killed during the Korean War.

Tirman explains that the challenge of approximating an overall mortality figure for Korean War deaths stems in part from the difficulty of compiling a statistic for the North Korean side "from a distance." He writes, "The nature of the war, with heavy bombardment of the North over many months, makes it nearly impossible to estimate war deaths from the US and South Korean standpoint."[3] The lethality of the war's fighting was exacerbated by the heavy use of aerial bombing as a tactic, which indiscriminately killed civilians alongside combatants. The UNC relied on aerial raids as a military tactic in Korea's mountainous terrain earlier in the war, but the bombing of the

North actually reached its most intensive point once the war entered its stalemate phase, when most of the combat was confined to the area surrounding the 38th parallel. It should be noted that, on the communist side, the Soviets also provided air support for the Chinese and North Koreans but did so in a highly limited manner, reflecting their priority not to draw the Soviet Union into a war against the United States.[4] Meanwhile, the UNC's domination of the air war meant that its carpet-bombing campaign from 1950–1953 would represent more bombs dropped in Korea—a total of 635,000 tons— than in the entire Pacific theater during World War II.[5] During the two years of peace talks beginning in 1951, UNC saturation bombing decimated cities and towns in the central and northern parts of the peninsula. At the time, the head of the United Nations Korean Reconstruction Agency, J. Donald Kingsley, described Korea as "the most devastated land and its people the most destitute in the history of modern warfare."[6] Given American public apathy by that point toward the war in Korea, these human costs would incur no accountability from U.S. leaders, and much of the brutal war remained unknown to Americans beyond its presentation as a battle between good and evil.[7]

There were nevertheless reports in the press at the time. Walter Sullivan, former *New York Times* correspondent in Korea, wrote in *The Nation*: "The countless ruined villages are the most terrible and universal mark of the war on the Korean landscape. To wipe out cover for North Korean vehicles and personnel, hundreds of thatch-roofed houses were burned by air-dropped jellied gasoline or artillery fire."[8] Although napalm became notorious as an incendiary weapon during the Vietnam War, more napalm was dropped by UNC aircraft on Korea—32,557 tons, or approximately 250,000 pounds per day—than was used in Vietnam.[9] The Hungarian writer Tibor Meray, who had been a correspondent during the war, recalled how the ravaged North Korean landscape in 1953 nearly resembled the surface of the moon, so thorough was the decimation.[10] Meray described how the incessant bombings obliterated the built environment of entire cities and left in their wake hauntingly incongruous ruins. For example, he recounted how, in a city known to have had two hundred thousand inhabitants, all that remained somehow were thousands of chimneys. Their battered brick columns stood out as remnants of what had once been an urban landscape, though now bereft of the homes and buildings to which the chimneys had once been attached.

THE PHENOMENON OF MASSACRES

Beyond the formidable lethality of such bombing raids, and in addition to the internecine military campaigns on the ground, what also made the Korean

War such a brutal conflict was the widespread phenomenon of civilian massacres. The three-year report published in 2009 by the Truth and Reconciliation Commission, Republic of Korea (TRCK) documents evidence of these
wartime atrocities, giving the bleak assessment: "before, during and after the
Korean War, massacres were a general phenomenon with differences only in
the perpetrators and pattern."[11] In *The Unending Korean War,* historical
sociologist and TRCK High Commissioner Kim Dong-Choon traces the patterns of wartime atrocities, distinguishing different categories while recognizing that the lines between them are often blurred: (1) massacres by the
military and police; (2) unofficial or haphazard military operations that were
retaliatory in nature; (3) executions of those known or suspected to have
colluded with the enemy; and (4) personal retaliations between civilians.

Kim's analysis underscores how civilian mass killings that occurred after
June 25th during the Korean War must be understood in relation to the
escalation of polarizing political violence in the late 1940s.[12] The most dead-
ly among the civilian massacres of the era is known as Cheju *Sasam,* or
"Cheju April Third," to indicate the starting date of an uprising on Cheju
Island in 1948. The violent suppression of that uprising gave impetus to a
cycle of resistance and repression that spiraled out of control, culminating in
a brutal crackdown by police and right-wing paramilitary forces that killed
tens of thousands of island residents. Cheju *Sasam* therefore represents not
the single day of April 3rd, but rather a period of massacre that began during
the time of the American occupation of the South under the United States
Army Military Government in Korea (USMGIK, 1945–1948).

It should be noted that Cheju had been peaceably and effectively administered for nearly two years after Korea's liberation from Japanese colonization, led by indigenous institutions of populist self-rule in the form of people's committees that began in August 1945. This stability contrasted with
the unrest in the southern provinces on the mainland, where massive protests
eventually broke out in autumn of 1946, resulting in the deaths of several
hundred police and demonstrators. That turmoil shifted the stance of the
military government sharply against the Left, which resulted in the loss of
power by people's committees throughout the zone administered by U.S.
occupation. This mandate extended even to Cheju Island where not only had
the people's committee become firmly established in its political leadership,
as widely recognized by island residents, but committee members had also
maintained a close working relationship with representatives of the military
government.[13]

The sudden ouster of their successful local government therefore fueled
islanders' resentment over interference by mainland authorities. That year,
commemorations of Korea's March First independence movement against
the Japanese grew into massive protests against the formation of an interim
South Korean government. After Korean police along with American troops

were sent to break up the protests, an escalation of more serious violence was largely averted, but six people were shot and killed, including a child. Those deaths triggered further protests and led to a general strike on the island. To reinforce the local police, the military government dispatched police forces as well as members of the extreme right-wing Northwest Youth Group, a paramilitary organization comprised of staunchly anticommunist refugees from the North. As John Merrill writes, "A cycle of terror and counterterror soon developed. Police and rightists brutalized the islanders who retaliated as best they could. . . . While the police were temporarily successful in intimidating the population with such tactics, their indiscriminate use of force embittered the islanders and further alienated them from the government."[14]

On April 3, 1948, local armed guerrillas on Cheju raided more than half of the twenty-four police stations mostly in the northern part of the island, resulting in fifteen deaths and many wounded. The military government again sent reinforcements, this time dispatching another 1,700 police from the mainland, and an exchange of attacks ensued between several hundred guerrillas and their supporters and the police and right-wing paramilitary organizations on the island.[15]

The decision to take up arms by the Cheju protestors reflected their move to disrupt the general elections that were scheduled to be held the following month on May 10, 1948. Although on its face, obstructing an election would appear antidemocratic, protestors opposed the May 1948 vote because they regarded those elections as jeopardizing the process for unification, which was clearly favored by the majority of Koreans. Earlier in 1946, the Joint U.S.–Soviet Commission had reached a deadlock in negotiations that were intended to prepare for the unification of the peninsula. As a means to break the impasse, the United States eventually proposed general elections under supervision by the United Nations, but that meant elections would only take place in the area to which the UN Temporary Commission on Korea had access, which was south of the 38th parallel. The Cheju uprising therefore posed a challenge to leadership under the U.S.–backed South Korean president Syngman Rhee, who came to power following the May elections when the Republic of Korea was established in August 1948. Two months later, the Rhee regime launched a violent suppression campaign in Cheju. An intense anticommunist "Red hunt" multiplied the number of those targeted, which included not only those who had engaged in guerrilla warfare but also their families and whole villages, as the entire interior of the island was regarded as enemy territory. A devastating scorched-earth campaign from October 1948 to March 1949 killed an estimated thirty thousand to eighty thousand people, representing a death toll between 10 percent to more than a quarter of Cheju Island's population.[16]

The Cheju massacre would prove to be a watershed in the course of events that heightened oppositional pressures and exacerbated the brutality of fighting when tensions exploded in all-out war on the peninsula. After the new government violently suppressed the Cheju uprising, Rhee instituted the National Security Law in December 1948 and declared martial law less than a year later. Historian Su-kyoung Hwang writes, "While the suppression of the Cheju Uprising marked the beginning of political violence that spilled over to the Korean War, it ended up being directed to an indeterminate enemy," which effectively legalized the use of state-sanctioned violence not only against dissidents but also people at large.[17] Furthermore, the brutality unleashed in the suppression campaign on Cheju in 1948–1949 would radicalize the North Korean regime. When the North Korean military occupied much of the South in the early weeks of the war, they set about punishing those identified as class enemies, with the Northern regime setting up people's courts to authorize the execution of rightists and landlords. In their punitive violence, the North Koreans were further radicalized by the atrocities that had been committed by U.S. and ROK troops, who at times indiscriminately fired on groups of civilians, presumably out of fear of possible guerrillas or peasant irregulars but also influenced by racism on the part of the Americans and exclusionary ethnic nationalism on the part of the South Koreans. When the North Korean forces themselves retreated after a brief occupation lasting roughly fifty days, they acted as the South Korean forces had done before them, continuing the vicious cycle of preemptive violence against those judged to be potential collaborators with the enemy regime, along with members of their families.[18]

Providing insight into why such massacres were both prevalent and ruthless, Kim Dong-Choon contends that mutually exclusive forms of nationalism and disciplinary measures of extreme violence were direct legacies of Japanese colonial rule. Under the Japanese occupation, Koreans had been subject to coercive power and surveillance, at risk of being killed for any expression of advocacy for independence. Kim states that the techniques for mass killings were inherited from the Japanese occupiers and used first in the post-1945 period by pro-Japanese right-wing Korean forces who felt cornered after Liberation,[19] which set off a reactive sequence of retaliatory violence. After Liberation, American authorities relied upon Japanese reports as they set up their occupation authority in the South and had little appreciation for the popular will strongly in favor of decolonization among Koreans, who had just survived the harshest years of wartime mobilization during the last decade of Japanese occupation. Rather than disbanding the widely despised colonial-era gendarmes, the USMGIK instead reinstated power to those who had worked in the police force under the Japanese. Regarding the Korean National Police, Su-kyoung Hwang writes, "even after liberation when the police were no longer entitled to summary jurisdiction, they continued to use colonial methods of third-degree interrogation, torture, and search without authorization."[20] The Korean National Police thereby wielded authority as a legacy of Japanese colonial power, reinforced by the occupation of the USMGIK, which had imposed martial law as early as February 1947 in anticipation of civil resistance.

Even after the creation of separate republics in 1948, it should be understood that the North and South were not stable states, as John Merrill explains, but rather each based their legitimacy on unifying the peninsula on their own terms, further pressured by the tensions that had been building since Korea's Liberation in 1945.[21] In other words, each side was driven by an exclusionary vision of ethnic nationalism—itself a phenomenon rooted in the polarizing circumstances of the Japanese colonial occupation—and such exclusionary nationalism was bent on negating its rival ideological counterpart. Kim Dong-Choon writes:

> [T]he massacres that occurred during the Korean War were so brutal and tragic because the war was not a conflict between states and nations, but between 'nationals' and 'non-nationals' . . . defenders of a blood-related community and those who betrayed that community. . . . The still largely agricultural society of Korea at the time consisted of clan and blood-related communities, and violence between individuals extended to confrontations between families and clans . . . when mixed with ideological confrontation, retaliations and assaults are extremely emotional and brutal.[22]

As discussed in chapter 1, both sides of the civil conflict invoked ethnic nationalism as an overriding rationale for unifying the peninsula, but such blood-based nationalisms were not of the nature that could furnish the symbolic ground for conciliatory compromise.[23] Rather than afford the possibility for reciprocal recognition, such oppositional forms of blood-based nationalism in Korea would undergird the mutually antagonistic logic for justifying the annihilation of the enemy.

HAZARDOUS CROSSINGS

Given such risks attached to ideologically based categories and exclusions in divided Korea, this chapter focuses on the perilous consequences of crossing the real and perceived boundaries that often determined criteria for belonging to one category or another. This analysis explores multiple forms of activity that have been interpreted as that of crossing a line or boundary—whether actual or metaphorical, temporary or permanent—but more specifically in order to explore the South Korean cultural idiom within which the meetings of wartime separated families have been constructed and understood. This analysis therefore includes: (1) the movement or displacement of individuals in what were thought to be temporary relocations prior to and during the 1950–1953 period, which was later denoted as a "crossing" after the stabilization of the inter-Korean dividing line; (2) the perceived transgressions of ideological lines imputed to those who took sides amid the multiple turn-overs of territorial control during the 1950–1951 period of the war; (3) the negotiation of the return of POWs and civilians to the other side of the border during the 1951–1953 Armistice talks, intended to conclude the war's major hostilities, but which became mired in a deadlock that prolonged the war; and (4) the development of temporary face-to-face reunions as a means to address the ongoing issue of war-separated families. Such crossings would prove to be fateful as consequential moments in the lives of the individuals who made such passages, which in turn would go on to define the identity of their extended families within categories that reflected the lived experiences of the global Cold War in divided Korea. How have such layered crossings of the inter-Korean divide figured into the historical construction of separated families?

In *DMZ Crossing: Performing Emotional Citizenship Along the Korean Border*, theatre-arts scholar Suk-Young Kim explores the cultural politics surrounding traversals of the restricted zone along the inter-Korean dividing line. She observes that "[f]or both South and North Koreans, one of the reasons the DMZ figures so prominently as national trauma is that so few are able to cross it."[24] In her analysis—which considers the wider category of border-crossers to include not only separated family members but also defectors, tourists, activists, war prisoners, participants in cultural exchanges, and others—Kim considers how such precarious acts of crossing the DMZ represent a form of both bodily and social performance, one which invokes the prerogatives of "emotional citizenship."[25] As Kim writes, "Crossing the DMZ becomes a crucial performance for these individuals who boldly claim the state's conventional right to define citizenship, often resisting the state's authority to define the border and the legitimacy of its crosser."[26] For Koreans on both sides, the stakes of such performances are inherent in the ways such crossings suggest alternative forms of citizenship based on creating affiliations that need not be primarily oriented toward justifying the legitimacy of one Korean state or the other.

In the post-Liberation period, particularly between 1945 and 1948 before the establishment of two separate Korean states, the border was still permeable. Indeed, there was considerable movement between North and South until 1948, when border clashes after the formation of separate regimes caused a tightening of security around the border. During this period, it was primarily intellectuals and artists who consciously chose to migrate from South to North. Charles K. Armstrong attributes this exodus of intellectuals to their disillusionment with the dominance of right-wing forces in South Korea, the relatively high degree of artistic freedom permitted by the government in the North until the spring of 1947, and also the significant resources that were committed to education, propaganda, and culture by the Soviets in the North as part of their strategy to foster a friendly regime.²⁷ Demographer Tai Hwan Kwon estimates that, during the period 1945–1953, approximately 286,000 Koreans went from the South to the North. This estimate includes (1) those who went voluntarily as self-identified leftists; (2) those who volunteered or were conscripted into the Korean People's Army; and (3) those who were kidnapped, including many prominent politicians and intellectuals who were abducted by the North Korean military as it was retreating from the southern part of the penninsula.²⁸

Although crossings occurred in both directions, the far larger number was that of Koreans moving south, with that group totaling approximately 1,390,000. In South Korea, the term "separated families" (*isan'gajok*) had been widely understood to refer exclusively to these *Wŏllammin*, those originally from northern Korean provinces (present-day North Korea) who migrated or fled south in the period between 1945 and 1953. In South Korea, the anticommunist *Wŏllammin* organizations have historically advocated hardline policies against North Korea. The first group of departures—about 740,000 people—occurred during the liberation period from August 15, 1945, to June 25, 1950. Among the reasons for their departure were the apprehensions raised by the Russian occupation but especially by the purging of wealthy landlords and Christians as part of the land reform and other political changes instituted by the communist party in the North. Another wave of departures, numbering roughly 650,000, occurred during the Korean War. Although Rhee's government in the South treated these figures as evidence that a majority of migrants were voting with their feet to choose the side of capitalism, sociologist Gwi-Ok Kim examines factors other than ideological identification that contributed to this southward migration, including widespread fears among Koreans during the war that the United States would deploy nuclear weapons in North Korea.²⁹

After 1953, different names would be ascribed to categories of separated families, which varied depending on the circumstances under which they became separated. This reflected how ideological identifications were associated with the direction of one's presumed "border-crossing." In South Korea, someone who "crossed over [the border] North"—or *wŏlbuk*—was generally presumed or suspected to be communist, and someone who "crossed over [the border] South"—or *wŏllam*—was presumed to be anticommunist. In the anthropological and sociological literature, analyses of issues surrounding separated families have engaged with the social and cultural changes that occurred at the turn of the millennium. Prior to the late 1990s, earlier studies concerning separated families focused on the symbolism or the ideology and structure of *Wŏllammin* communities, comprised of former war refugees who had fled from North Korea during the war.³⁰ In more recent work, anthropologist Soo-Jung Lee analyzes the mobilization of separated family members as "division subjects" in Cold War–era Korea. Analyzing how the sympathetic nationalist category of "separated families" (*isan'gajok*) had previously referred solely to the families of *Wŏllammin*, Lee traces the reconfiguration of this social field in the post–Cold War period to include *Wŏlbukcha* families, who had been marginalized and silenced.[31] Along with Lee's work, Gwi-Ok Kim and British sociologist James Foley each offer a comprehensive examination of the history and evolution of the category of separated families. James Foley's English-language study, *Korea's Divided Families*, includes a detailed demographic analysis and adopts a policy focus oriented toward finding a resolution to the problem of long-term Korean family separation.[32] In *Isan'gajok, "pan'gongjŏnsa" to "ppalgaengi" to anin* [Separated Families, Neither "Anticommunist Warriors" Nor "Reds"], Kim undertakes analyses of questions that had been generally overlooked in prior studies of separated families, including the North Korean side of the separated families issue, the voices of bereaved families, and the attenuation of *Wŏllammin* communities.[33]

Those who crossed the 38th parallel after Liberation in 1945 and during the war did so with no expectation that the national partition would endure for decades. It would be inaccurate, therefore, to describe as "defections" what were intended to be temporary internal migrations. Furthermore, such references to the wartime mobility of "crossing over" from one side to the other should not imply a stable border. Throughout the first year of the war when the internal migrations of refugees took place, lines dividing the territory under communist and U.S.–ROK control remained in flux. As discussed above, along with this volatility came intense forms of violence.

In *Southerners, Northerners* (*Namnyŏk Saram, Pungnyŏk Saram*), a fictionalized Korean War memoir, South Korean novelist Lee Ho-Chul depicts the war as not so much a military conflict as a tangle of individual fates. The narrative is loosely based on the life experiences of the author, who was recruited into the North Korean People's Army in July 1950 and later became a prisoner of war (POW) before settling in South Korea. Through the narrator's encounters with fellow soldiers and flashbacks to memories of village life, *Southerners, Northerners* explores the consequences of personal character when individuals are confronted with the upheavals of war and revolution as well as the vagaries of chance.[34]

The novel opens with scenes in the narrator's classroom, set during the period after Korea's liberation from colonial rule in 1945. By gauging the rise and fall of fortunes among schoolmates and teachers, the narrator comes to understand some of the transformations under the Soviet occupation in the North. After the war's outbreak, the narrator makes his way among a group of KPA army recruits, as some peers develop friendships and others clash. The narrator is charged with the responsibility of teaching "politics and ideology" to volunteers who traveled from various regions in the South, an assignment he finds absurd given his aversion for the new regime of rallies and study meetings. Nevertheless, he becomes intrigued by the demeanor and backgrounds of his counterparts from the South—each of whom suggests something about life under the U.S. occupation on the other side of the border, while also bearing his own secrets.

The early part of the book builds upon such interactions among a host of characters, and the narrative also includes passages that describe the experience of combat with jarring immediacy, such as this vivid recollection of a bombing raid from the ground:

> I will never forget the terror: the earsplitting roar of a mass of iron, weighing a thousand pounds or a ton, plummeting from the sky right above my head. We lay flat on our stomachs on the straw sacks we had spread inside the shelter, with both thumbs thrust in our ears, our other fingers pressing hard against our eyes, and our mouths open so wide our cheeks hurt. This was to prevent our eardrums from splitting at the noise of the bombs. But a ton of iron falling vertically above your head makes a sound as piercing as if the whole earth were about the crack apart, and seems to reach your eardrums not through your ears but through some other orifice. [35]

In the final two chapters, the novel's tone shifts. The narrator becomes more philosophical and introspective, a disposition in keeping with his relatively isolated circumstances as a POW. Recalling the memory of an atrocity, he initially defers its narration by referring to it obliquely and then discusses its consequences before he can bring himself to describing the "terrible incident" itself. He writes, "[W]hat's this? I'm still dragging my feet, and can hardly bring myself to relive that traumatic moment. Whether it's because such an act of excess could happen so suddenly, or because it left so little trace, I'm not sure." [36] The narrator does not dwell on the violence but weighs instead the myriad events, whether ominous or mundane, that led to the moment when a human life is cut short. In depictions of post-Liberation and wartime Korea in Lee's novel, it is evident that transitional periods and borderline states were not only associated with the passage from one set of circumstances to another. They also precipitated moments of uncertainty, confusion, and often perilous volatility.

ARMISTICE TALKS AND CONTESTED EXCHANGES

Like official boundaries, de facto borders are complex phenomena with spatial, territorial, and social dimensions, which are informed by the historical circumstances of their constitution and reconstitution over time. In the absence of an official Korean border, the power of the dividing line has been constructed through control over its passage, and that has been true since the inception of the Military Demarcation Line during the protracted 1951–1953 armistice talks. Given that a temporary ceasefire line would become the de facto inter-Korean border, it warrants consideration of how that divide was initially settled with the negotiated exchanges of, respectively, POWs and civilians in 1953. Although provisions pertaining to displaced citizens and separated families also factored into the truce negotiations, the Korean War armistice talks are primarily remembered for the deadlock over the policy regarding the release of POWs. That deadlock occurred ostensibly over conflicting interpretations of the Third Geneva Convention of 1949, particularly Article 118: "Prisoners of war shall be released and repatriated without delay after the cessation of active hostilities."[37] That article attempted to establish unequivocally that unjustified prolonging of POW captivity would violate the Convention, and its wording itself represented an evolution of responses to the changing nature of modern warfare. In a 1907 precedent, the Hague Conventions simply held that prisoners of wars should be repatriated as quickly as possible after peace was established, under the assumption that a peace treaty would be signed shortly after the close of hostilities. The 1919 Treaty of Versailles made this assumption explicit by calling for the repatriation of prisoners of war and civilian internees with the ratification of a treaty. However, that treaty illustrated the problem of the uncertain interval between war and peace, as the treaty was signed more than a year after an armistice had been reached. The Prisoners of War Convention of 1929 in turn stipulated that repatriation should occur upon the conclusion of an armistice. However, the dissolution of the German government at the end of World War II complicated the status of German POWs, many of whom were held in captivity by the Soviet Union long after the end of the war and were pressed into labor toward the postwar rebuilding of the Soviet Union. Article 118 in the Third Convention of 1949 therefore took into account the view that hostilities could end even without an armistice, though this change did not allow for flexibility in the event that prisoners might not want to return to the country that they had served as soldiers.

With respect to the Korean War armistice talks, the communist side initially proposed that all prisoners should be released on both sides, in keeping with a strict interpretation of Article 118. On humanitarian as well as on ideological grounds, the United States refused to repatriate prisoners by force against their will. The United States was also motivated by its recognition of the inherent instability on the peninsula that would remain in the wake of a negotiated settlement. An exchange of lists confirmed the presumption that the UNC held a far greater number of POWs than the Communists. An estimated 132,000 Communist soldiers and 37,000 civilian internees were prisoners of the UNC, compared to 7,142 South Korean POWs and 4,417 UNC troops detained by the Communists. To the UNC's military negotiators, the release and repatriation of all the POWs would contribute significantly toward restoring the KPA's former strength, a concern that would not have been as significant an issue had the war reached a more definitive resolution. While each side challenged the other's reported estimates of POWs as too low, the UNC continued to seek an alternative to the all-for-all exchange stipulated by the Geneva Convention.[38]

Also at issue was the uncertain ideological disposition of the captive prisoners. The ROK estimated forty thousand former South Korean residents who had been inducted into the KPA were among the POWs. To complicate the situation further, an estimated half of the Chinese Communist POWs had been former members of the Nationalist army. A compromise position was that the UNC would submit a new list after screening the POWs to determine which ones would not refuse repatriation, and that would be the basis for an all-for-all exchange. Despite indications that the Communist side may have been open to accepting this, the proposal unraveled when the screening results indicated only 70,000 out of more than 170,000 POWs expressed the wish to repatriate, which was a far lower number than previously estimated.[39] The Communists rejected the UNC proposal based on those new figures, and negotiations would remain bogged down over the POW issue for the following year.[40]

The armistice negotiations in 1951–1953 marked the first time that the two sides addressed the issue of separated families, albeit as a matter of returning displaced civilians, rather than as the task of reuniting families. The Armistice Agreement established the "Committee for Assisting the Return of Displaced Civilians," and Paragraph 59 of the Armistice Agreement places responsibility on the military commanders to "[call] upon the appropriate civil authorities to give necessary guidance and assistance to all such civilians who desire to return home."[41] The agreement distinguishes two groups of civilians: (1) those who wished to return home after ending up in territory under the military command of the side opposite of that which was their place of residence prior to June 25, 1950; and (2) civilians of foreign nationality who similarly wished to return to the other side of the Military Demarcation Line (MDL).

The Armistice Agreement set out the parameters for the Committee for Assisting the Return of Displaced Civilians, which was charged with publicizing the terms of the exchange and with coordinating and facilitating the return of the two groups of civilians, both Koreans and foreigners. However, these complex tasks fell to a small handful of four field officers. The committee was comprised of two military officers from each side and placed under the authority of the Military Armistice Commission. The committee held its first meeting on December 11, 1953, at the truce village P'anmunjom, where both sides agreed on details such as the location of exchange, the dates, and the criteria of kinship for accompanying family members. One point of contention was the numbers of people to be exchanged per day, where there was a significant discrepancy: the UNC proposed five hundred per day, while the

Communists proposed one hundred per day. Both sides met again for a second meeting on December 29, when the UNC side made a concession to the Communist side and agreed on exchanging one hundred persons a day with the UNC side. They also agreed that successful applicants for repatriation would return on the first day of March 1954, leaving the committee less than two months to publicize the exchange and review applications for repatriation.

The exchange involved far fewer numbers than had been originally anticipated. The UN command released thirty-seven people to North Korea, while the communist side sent nineteen to South Korea. The South Korean government had initially received a total of seventy-six applications in January and February, but two applicants were ruled out as North Korean espionage agents while thirty-seven reportedly changed their minds and decided against repatriation. Those returned by the North included no Koreans; instead they were foreigners, eight Russians and eleven Turks who had been captured by the North Koreans during its general offensive into the South in July 1950. Despite the clear inadequacy of this process for addressing the complex and politically sensitive problem of arranging for the return of displaced civilians, the March 1954 exchange would be the only one resulting directly from the Armistice Agreement. After that event, the committee was disbanded. As James Hoare and Susan Pares write, "With the repatriation of POWs and civilians, the line dividing the peninsula was effectively sealed."[42]

Since that exchange, the Korean Demilitarized Zone at the 38th parallel has been regarded as one of the most impenetrable and heavily armed "borders" in the world, although it would be more accurately termed a dividing line as it is not in fact an official border recognized by international treaty.[43] The sealing of the DMZ has meant not only a halt to the movement of people but also the inability for people to communicate or exchange information. As Roland Bleiker writes, both states have therefore been "able to promote and legitimize an unusually narrow approach to security issues, one that revolves almost exclusively around a military-based protection of the state apparatus."[44] For nearly fifty years after the armistice signing, relations across the divide were almost entirely controlled by the two states, as travel was halted and postal links and telecommunication connections were severed.

CATEGORICAL EXCLUSIONS

In South Korea, until the post-Summit period, the category of "separated family" was commonly understood to denote exclusively those war refugees who had left family behind in the North. "Separated family" therefore emerged as an anticommunist ideological construction denoting the quintessential "victims of division."[45] That category furthermore excluded other groups of people, such as the *Wŏlbukcha* families. After the Korean War, the families of those suspected to have gone to the North were subject to harassment by rightist youth groups and also underwent investigation by local authorities, who suspected them of maintaining ties with relatives on the other side of the border. The women left to head these households often lost their social standing within their extended kin networks, and were shunned within their own communities by neighbors and relatives who avoided association out of fear of being investigated also.[46] As the International Committee of the Red Cross has identified, among family members of those missing in war, women are disproportionately vulnerable because more men are killed, captured, or disappear in relation to armed conflict, and women are often the main initiators of requests for news of family members. Yet, when seeking information on missing relatives, women may confront barriers such as financial constraints and social taboos, and concerns for their own safety may inhibit their ability to access information from authorities such as the police or military.

These families were not only targeted by the state but also bore the intense psychological burden of social stigmatization and self-censorship amid accusations of being "Reds," or "*ppalgaengi*."[47] As South Korean literary critic Kim Jae-yong writes, "Because *wŏlbuk* families did not even recognize themselves as separated, they were silenced. With the influence of the Cold War, these families hid their family histories and would not say that their relatives went north but would insist that their family members were kidnapped to avoid discrimination. Such families could not call themselves separated nor dream of reunions."[48] The suppression of memory among these *Wŏlbukcha* families therefore occurred within the context of a "'cold' civil war"[49] in which social discrimination and practices by agents of the state left some groups silenced in the face of continuing national division.

In North Korea, those who moved to the South before or during the Korean War have been classified by the state as traitors. Their families are therefore regarded as part of the "hostile group" of society, or the "families who betrayed the fatherland." The DPRK Constitution indicates equality among all citizens, with Article 65 stating "Citizens enjoy equal rights in all spheres of State and public activities."[50] Yet several sources describe how, in practice, the North Korean government divides the population into three classes based on their family background and loyalty to the state. These class designations—"core," "wavering," and "hostile"—are passed down from one generation to the next, with those belonging to the "core" class receiving far greater access to education, employment, medical care, and other resources, while the members of the "hostile" class are subject to severe discrimination and persecution.[51] The Korean case is also exceptional because of the severe self-isolation policies adopted by North Korea beginning around 1960. Although access to knowledge about the outside world was also restricted in other Communist countries, North Korea was exceptional in the degree to which it imposed a reclusiveness on the majority of its own population, resulting from North Korea's unusual vulnerability as half of a divided state. The self-isolation policies were initially intended to guard against what was perceived as a dangerous "revisionism" characterizing the Soviet Union amid the process of de-Stalinization. However, North Korean leaders perceived as an even more serious threat the increasing material affluence and industrial development that comprised the so-called "economic miracle" in South Korea.[52] According to Andrei Lankov, the North Korean authorities went on to ban tunable radios and undertook a campaign to destroy most foreign books and other publications in the late 1960s, except for a cache of technical books to which access was restricted. Notably, the North Korean state made no exception for publications that came from fraternal countries, and contact between the population and foreigners was also severely curtailed. Lankov writes, "The North Korean authorities were aware that dangerous information could penetrate the country not only via media like radio or print but also through unsupervised personal interactions between the North Koreans and foreigners. They therefore took care to reduce such interaction to a bare minimum. North Koreans have always been aware that close contacts with foreigners outside one's clearly defined official duties would be seen as dangerous."[53] It is this self-imposition of not only an information blockade but also the isolation of the North Korean population that posed such a formidable obstacle for any unauthorized contact between those within the country and those on the outside.

BREAKTHROUGHS AND OPENINGS

In the late twentieth century, the development of two avenues—official and unofficial—for addressing the separated families problem reflected transformations in the inter-Korean relationship as well as the global Cold War. During the summer of 2000, the shock of discovering the survival of these relatives in North Korea was compounded by the fact that there had already been several alternative avenues available for at least a decade[54] for separated family members in the DPRK to exchange letters and to initiate contact for eventually arranging unofficial reunions. However, until the early 1970s, the two Koreas had virtually no contact. The continuation of mutual antagonism and rivalry defined the broader dynamic of inter-Korean relations, which in turn restricted the prospects for progress on the separated families issue. Each Korean state regarded the other as illegitimate and threatening, and each refused to maintain diplomatic ties with any foreign country that granted recognition to its rival state.

The external Cold War environment then underwent a dramatic transformation in the early 1970s. When the Nixon administration pursued normalized relations between the United States and the People's Republic of China, North Korea's closest ally, that development provided the chief catalyst for the two Koreas to begin direct negotiations with each other in 1971 as a hedge against reduced support from their respective patrons. [55] On the South Korean side, Park Chung Hee had already been anxious over the Nixon administration's retreat from Vietnam and its failure to preserve the United Nations seat held by the Republic of China. Previously, the Park administration had gained enormous political and economic advantage after it began dispatching South Korean troops in 1964 to fight in the Vietnam War, as Park's response to a White House request that would eventually direct billions of dollars to the ROK in the form of supplemental economic aid and military support from the U.S. government under Lyndon B. Johnson. [56] However, by 1970, as the Nixon administration sought to manage public perception surrounding a U.S. withdrawal from Vietnam, it settled upon Korea as another location in Asia where the United States would reduce its military commitments in order to create the appearance of a coherent broader policy. [57] In 1971, the Nixon administration withdrew twenty thousand troops from South Korea and cut back on U.S. economic aid, while also pressuring the ROK to maintain its own troop strength in Vietnam. Faced with this foreboding combination of U.S. actions, Park resorted to the 1971 decree of a State of National Emergency to preempt the possibility for his domestic opponents to gain political advantage through potential criticisms over the waning of U.S. support. [58]

The initial contact between both Koreas took place in 1971 through secret high-level negotiations. Because they occurred without public knowledge, it came as astonishing news when the first inter-Korean statement on reunification was released the following year. The July 4 Joint Communiqué would specify three main principles for reunification, stipulating that: (1) it would be attained through peaceful means, (2) which would transcend ideological differences, and (3) which would occur without foreign interference. Despite the dramatic impact of the Joint Communiqué as a bilateral declaration of imminent reunification, historian Tae Yang Kwak underscores how both Park Chung Hee and Kim Il-sung would shortly thereafter consolidate authoritarian political power for their respective regimes and unquestionably reinforce—not dismantle—the prevailing division system. [59]

Today, South Korea is by far the more powerful of the two Korean states in terms of economic strength and international diplomacy, but North Korea actually held a stronger position in terms of economic and military capacity through the early and mid-1960s. With the signing of the communiqué, the two sides established a South–North Coordinating Committee (SNCC) to address political, economic, and cultural affairs, and also opened Red Cross talks with the objective of reuniting members of separated families.[60] At the time of the Red Cross talks, the South Korean delegation pushed to restrict visits to those North Koreans who had blood relatives in the South, while the North Korean delegation called for the inclusion of a vague category of "friends," a proposal which the South rejected. As sociologist James Foley writes, the fear of the South Korean government was "that the North would use the pretext of divided family exchanges to infiltrate the South with its agents, build a 'fifth column' in the ROK and disrupt its society in preparation for a communist-inspired takeover and reunification."[61] Although the SNCC meetings would continue until 1975, as would the Red Cross talks until 1975, this initial period of substantive North–South contact eventually ended without progress on resolving the separated families issue.

After an attempt to revive official inter-Korean talks in 1979–1980 also proved fruitless, it was actually the spontaneous social phenomenon inspired by the 1983 KBS telethon that later created momentum to reopen the Red Cross talks in the mid-1980s, eventually leading to the first reunion of separated families across the Korean divide. With the tremendous response to the KBS marathon broadcast, as described earlier, that spike in public interest generated widespread momentum behind the movement to reunite families across the Korean divide. The KBS telethon both captured the national imagination and also drew sympathetic international interest, and such momentous inducements prompted the South Korean government to invest greater effort toward pursuing further inter-Korean Red Cross talks. In 1984, South Korea would go so far as to offer aid to North Korea, which the latter rejected and criticized as an attempt to undermine its society. However, when South Korea experienced extreme flooding a month later, North Korea responded with its own offer of assistance to South Korean flood victims. Although the ROK government similarly refused this overture, it reversed course within a few days, emphasizing that its acceptance of North Korean aid was not out of necessity but rather out of willingness on the part of the South "to open a road to a mutual cooperation between the brethrens [*sic*] . . . and improve inter-Korean relations."[62] That exchange of gestures in the 1980s led to a return to inter-Korean negotiations, and the May 1985 inter-Korean Red Cross talks resulted in the first-ever reunion among war-separated family members across the Korean divide in August 1985. Specifically, delegations of fifty separated family members from each side visited on September 20, 1985. Nevertheless, rather than augur an inter-state reconciliation, the 1985 reunions proved to reflect the prevailing Cold War atmosphere. As Soo-Jung Lee writes, "The 1985 reunion served mainly as a space of competition between the two Koreas,"[63] as the events were marred by ideological grandstanding on both sides.

Notably, out of the one hundred people involved in the exchange, only sixty-five family members were able to meet their relatives; that is, although fifty people were selected from each side to travel across the divide to Seoul and Pyongyang, reunions only occurred for thirty from the North and thirty-five from the South. During my own field research in 2000–2001, the most common interpretation I heard was that the low yield of the 1985 reunions, with so many unable to achieve a reunion, reflected how individuals were reluctant to come out in public to meet a relative from the other side, amid understandable fears of being subjected to new social risks within their everyday lives. Despite official plans to continue this reunion program, those efforts were halted after negotiations could not resolve differences between the two governments over South Korea's continued participation in annual joint "Team Spirit" military exercises with the United States. The 1985 reunion would therefore be the only official exchange of families between the two Koreas prior to 2000.

While official exchanges did not resume for another fifteen years, changes in both Koreas since 1990 allowed greater possibilities for private unofficial reunions of separated families to occur in third countries and also in North Korea. South Korea's economic takeoff during the 1980s translated to a shift in its foreign policy under President Roh Tae-woo, who pursued in the latter part of the decade what was called the "Northern Policy" or *Nordpolitik*. Taking as its model West Germany's *Ostpolitik* toward East Germany and the Soviet bloc, South Korea made diplomatic overtures toward North Korea's communist allies, successfully securing economic and diplomatic ties with Eastern European communist countries and, by 1990, with the Soviet Union. At a time when North Korea had fallen behind economically and was becoming increasingly isolated internationally after the disintegration of the communist bloc, this reconciliatory approach on the part of South Korea led to another opening for high-level inter-Korean talks.

During this period, the South Korean government also began permitting its citizens to pursue informal contact with their North Korean relatives. Given the impasse on a state level to arrange more exchange meetings, this amounted to a different strategy on the part of the South Korean government to address separated families by enabling more private reunions to take place among individual families. By 1990, the South Korean Ministry of Unification put in place the legal framework allowing South Koreans to meet with North Koreans without fear of punishment. Such meetings had previously been forbidden under the National Security Law, which prohibited any contact whether in person or via written correspondence. According to Article 3 of the "Laws on the Exchanges and Cooperation of North and South," an exception to the National Security Law could be granted if approval were secured from the Ministry of Unification for "communication, trade, interchange, and correspondence for South and North which contributes to the cooperation and exchange [between] the North and South."[64] Some separated families, mostly former war refugees, managed to exchange letters with and meet their North Korean families through private brokers or mediators who were mostly diasporic ethnic Koreans residing in China, Canada, or the United States. Following the normalization of diplomatic relations between the ROK and the PRC in 1992, China became the predominant point of contact for South Koreans seeking to arrange reunions with North Korean relatives in a third country. Indeed, within a decade, by 2002, ethnic Korean residents of China would broker an estimated 90 percent of such private meetings.[65]

In a further indication of the transformation of domestic and international conditions on the peninsula, the two Korean prime ministers held talks for the first time in 1990, negotiations which continued for several rounds before yielding two major accomplishments the following year: in September 1991, the ROK and the DPRK both became member states of the United Nations, and on December 13, 1991, they signed the "Basic Agreement on Reconciliation, Non-Aggression and Exchanges." As part of what is known simply as the "Basic Agreement," South Korea negotiated to include a specific article in which both sides committed to working toward the reunion of separated families. In the agreement, Article 18 reads: "South and North Korea shall permit free correspondence, movement between the two sides, meetings and visits between dispersed family members and other relatives, promote their voluntary reunion and take measures to resolve other humanitarian issues."[66] Inter-Korean Red Cross talks would resume in 1992, but they would be soon suspended after North Korea announced its withdrawal from the Nuclear Non-Proliferation Treaty (NPT) in March 1993, amid another rise in tensions on the Korean peninsula.

CONTEMPORARY TRANSFORMATIONS

The withdrawal from the NPT stemmed indirectly from the collapse of the Soviet Union in 1991, which meant that North Korea lost access to resources and supplies under the favorable terms that it had enjoyed with its key ally. During ensuing years, economic circumstances in the DPRK deteriorated rapidly. Under the increasing pressure of its worsening isolation and economic desperation, North Korea made an alarming announcement in March 1993 that it would withdraw from the Nuclear Proliferation Treaty, prompting a crisis that nearly precipitated war with the United States.[67] Ostensibly, North Korea was protesting what it perceived as a violation of sovereignty imposed by the International Atomic Energy Agency (IAEA) for nuclear inspections. Leon Sigal analyzes the withdrawal from the NPT as a gambit on the part of North Korea to provoke a crisis under the assumption that the United States would not ultimately resort to military means to resolve it, since such a course of action would risk the outbreak of another all-out war.[68] A last-minute mediation effort by former U.S. President Jimmy Carter helped to draw down further escalation of the crisis, and eventually the United States would meet with North Korea for unprecedented direct negotiations, which eventually led to the signing of the U.S.–DPRK Nuclear Framework Agreement on October 21, 1994. The Agreed Framework committed the United States and its allies to providing energy assistance to the DPRK—including two light-water reactors and supplies of heavy fuel oil—in exchange for international inspections of its nuclear facilities and a freeze on its nuclear program.

Although a primary motivation behind North Korea's signing of the Agreed Framework was its dire need for energy resources, another objective was to bring an end to U.S. economic sanctions against North Korea.[69] Lifting those sanctions was critical for North Korea to appeal for economic assistance from international financial institutions, such as the World Bank, International Monetary Fund (IMF), and Asian Development Bank. A key stipulation of the Agreed Framework was the improvement of relations between North and South Korea. Yet inter-Korean relations instead took a turn for the worse in the ensuing years, particularly after the death of the North Korean leader Kim Il-sung on July 8, 1994. The South Korean President Kim Young-sam chose not to send any message of condolence, instead placing the South Korean armed forces on high alert in anticipation of a possible collapse of the DPRK. At the time Kim Young-sam, along with many international observers, expected that North Korea would soon go the way of its Eastern bloc allies. Instead North Korea's durability defied those expectations, and no further progress on inter-Korean rapprochement was made for the remainder of the Kim Young-sam administration.

Formal talks between the two Koreas on the reunions of separated families issue did not resume until the beginning of the next South Korean administration under President Kim Dae-jung, who was elected to office by a narrow margin in 1997. A human rights activist and long-time opposition candidate, Kim Dae-jung assumed the presidency in South Korea's first peaceful democratic transfer of power to an opposition candidate, and the election had particular resonance with the generation of Koreans who had participated in the democratization movement in the 1980s. His administration brought a new approach toward peninsular issues by embarking upon the "Policy of Reconciliation and Cooperation with the North," widely known as the Sunshine Policy. Taking its nickname from one of Aesop's fables in which the elements compete to induce a man to take off his overcoat, the new policy's orientation toward engagement with the North invoked the metaphor of "sunshine" as the most effective way of bringing about a conciliatory atmosphere and defusing inter-Korean enmity. It drew upon the fable's moral that the warmth of sunshine, or a comprehensive approach to engagement, would win out over the bitterness of harsh winds in the form of threats and hostility. Under the Sunshine Policy, Kim Dae-jung's administration departed from the containment posture of prior regimes and pursued a new approach toward North Korea based on engagement, by emphasizing diplomatic dialogue, mutual recognition, peaceful reconciliation, and economic cooperation. After two years of overtures by the South toward the North, the breakthrough came with the historic June Summit between Kim Dae-jung and Kim Jong-il, the first meeting between the two Korean leaders since the republics were founded in 1948. In the June 15th Joint Declaration signed at the conclusion of the summit meeting, both sides called for greater economic cooperation, lessening of military tensions, the return of long-term North Korean political prisoners, and the reunions of North–South separated families.

International studies scholar Key-young Son argues that the Sunshine Policy, while drawing upon some aspects of prior unification policies pursued by predecessors Roh Tae-woo and Kim Young-sam, represented a significant departure from the past in at least three major respects: (1) it stated that South Korea would not seek to absorb North Korea; (2) it advocated the separation of economics and politics; and (3) it sought to transform South Korean identities as a means of supporting efforts toward inter-Korean reconciliation.[70] Kim Dae-jung's repeated declaration that the South has no "intention to undermine or absorb North Korea"[71] addressed one of the paramount fears in Pyongyang. The principle of non-absorption thereby removed this existential threat and also meant that the South was not counting on the imminent collapse of North Korean regime, as had been the expectation of the prior administration. The separation of economics and politics furthermore meant that economic and humanitarian aid was no longer dependent upon political progress between the two states.

In his inaugural address, Kim Dae-jung notably included a direct request to the North Korean government on behalf of separated families, emphasizing that the issue was one of his administration's highest priorities. He said, "I earnestly appeal to North Korean authorities. Numerous members of separated families have become old and are passing away. We must let relatives separated from their families in the South and North meet and communicate with each other as soon as possible. On this point, North Korea has shown some positive signs of late, and I am paying keen attention to developments."[72] His reference to "positive signs" acknowledged changes that had been occurring within North Korea at the time. Previously, since the 1980s, the North Korean state had begun encouraging visits from diasporic Koreans in Japan and other countries. However, in 1998, the North Korean government took a more proactive step by setting up an information center for gathering addresses and other contact information specifically to facilitate the process of locating separated family members within the DPRK.[73]

After Kim Dae-jung assumed the presidency in 1998, the South Korean government moved to include in the official designation of "separated families" the relatives of those who went north of the divide before or during the Korean War. This was not only a symbolic gesture but meant such families were then entitled to receive government assistance for private reunions in third countries such as China. Although the Kim Dae-jung administration at its outset had adopted this more inclusive definition, it did not publicize this change in policy, evidently to avoid the vigorous protests of political conservatives. Such families therefore remained in limbo; that is, although they were recognized by the government to receive assistance to locate their relatives, they were not informed of this new entitlement and therefore did not know to seek such aid. This unprecedented broadening of the category of "separated family," as officially recognized by the state in 1998, did not become widely known until the events surrounding the August 2000 reunions vividly dramatized this change.

NOTES

1. John Tirman, *The Deaths of Others: The Fate of Civilians in America's Wars* (Oxford: Oxford University Press, 2011), 318.
2. Tirman, *The Death of Others*, 320. In his review of the literature, Tirman laments the paucity of corroborated war-death numbers from the Korean War, and he observes the discrepancy among estimates of the war's death toll—including civilians and combatants from all sides—ranges from 770,000 to 5.5 million, though he discredits the low end of that range as implausible and disingenuous. That low figure appeared in a 1968 paper published by the Institute for Strategic Studies (ISS) in London, but the author, ISS researcher David Wood, makes no reference to any evidence or documentation. See also Leitenberg, "Deaths in Wars and Conflicts in the 20th Century," Cornell University Peace Studies Program, Occasional Paper #29 (3rd ed., 2006): 76. Leitenberg cites multiple sources in aggregate for his extensive compilation of mortality figures caused by post-1945 wars and conflicts; although the figure is not explicitly attributed, his apparent source for this Korean War-death estimate is Jon Halliday and Bruce Cumings, *Korea: The Unknown War* (New York: Pantheon, 1988).
3. Tirman, *The Deaths of Others*, 320.
4. Zhihua Shen, "China and the Dispatch of the Soviet Air Force: The Formation of the Chinese-Soviet-Korean Alliance in the Early Stage of the Korean War," *Journal of Strategic Studies* 33, no. 2 (2010): 211–30.
5. Cited in Rosemary Foot, *A Substitute for Victory: The Politics of Peacemaking at the Korean Armistice Talks* (Ithaca: Cornell University Press, 1990), 207–08; Cumings, *The Korean War*, 159.
6. Quoted in Marilyn Young, "Bombing Civilians from the Twentieth to the Twenty-First Century," in *Bombing Civilians: A Twentieth Century History* (New York: The New Press, 2010), 160.
7. Tirman, *The Deaths of Others*, 50; Cumings, *The Korean War* (New York: Random House, 2010), xv–xviii.
8. Quoted in Young, "Bombing Civilians," 160.
9. Cumings, *The Korean War*,149. Journalist Andrew Salmon's description of napalm's effects makes the statistic less abstract: "Whatever it touches, it adheres to, burning into vegetation, buildings, vehicles and people at a temperature of 800 degrees Celsius—eight times hotter than boiling water. Humans caught in such intense conflagrations become virtual fossils: In the Second World War, the heat generated by incendiaries baked and dehydrated the dead, turning humans into mummies. . . . So hotly does napalm ignite that it generates fifth-degree burns, scorching through skin, fat, muscle and bone; survivors suffer keloids, inerasable scars. Finally the intense heat of its ignition deoxygenates air, generating massive amounts of carbon

monoxide: Those victims at the centre of the blast who are not cooked end up killed by carbon monoxide poisoning." See *Scorched Earth, Black Snow: The First Year of the Korean War* (London: Aurum Press, 2011), 9.

10. "An Entirely New War," *Korea: The Unknown War*, Episode 4, first broadcast September 8, 1988, by Thames Television (London) in association with WBGH Boston, written by Jon Halliday and Bruce Cumings, and produced by Philip Whitehead. Cumings quotes this interview in *The Korean War*, 158–59.

11. Byung-Ook Ahn, *Truth and Reconciliation Activities of the Past Three Years*, trans. Sung-Soo Kim, Eun-Bok Kim, and Albert Park (Seoul: Truth and Reconciliation Commission, Republic of Korea, 2009), 86.

12. Dong-Choon Kim, *The Unending Korean War* (Larkspur, CA: Tamal Vista, 2009), 146–53; Suh Hee-kyung makes a similar argument in "Atrocities Before and During the Korean War: Mass Civilian Killings by South Korean and US Forces," *Critical Asian Studies* 42, no. 4 (2010): 553–88. For examples of recent South Korean scholarship based on oral histories regarding the Korean War, see Kim Kyŏng-hak, Pak Jŏng-sŏk, Yŏm Mi-kyŏng, Yun Jŏng-ran, and P'yo In-ju, *Chŏnjaeng kwa kiŏk: Maŭl kongdongch'e ŭi saengaesa* [Korean War, Community, and Residents' Memories] (Paju, Korea: Han'ul Ak'ademi, 2005); and Han'guk Kusulsa Hakhoe, *Kusulsa ro ingnŭn Han'guk Chŏnjaeng: Sŏul t'obagi wa mint'ongsŏn saramdŭl, chŏnjaeng mimangin kwa wŏlbuk kajok, kŭdŭl i mal hanŭn arae robut'o ŭi Han'guk Chŏnjaeng* (Seoul: Humanist, 2011).

13. John Merrill, "The Cheju-do Rebellion," *Journal of Korean Studies* 2 (1980): 151–52; Cumings, *The Korean War*, 121–22.

14. John Merrill, "The Cheju-do Rebellion," 155.

15. Ibid., 168.

16. Cumings, *The Korean War*, 121. See also Su-kyong Hwang, "South Korea, the United States and Emergency Powers During the Korean Conflict," *The Asia-Pacific Journal* 12:5 no. 1 (Feb. 2014); Yŏksa Munje Yŏn'guso, *Cheju 4.3 yŏn'gu* [Cheju, April 3rd: A Study] (Seoul: Yŏksa Pip'yŏngsa, 1999).

17. Hwang, "South Korea, the United States and Emergency Powers."

18. Heonik Kwon, "Korean War Traumas," *The Asia-Pacific Journal* 38:2, no. 10 (September 20, 2010). See also Suh Hee-kyung, "Atrocities Before and During the Korean War," 553–88.

19. Kim, *The Unending Korean War*, 207.

20. Hwang, "South Korea, the United States and Emergency Powers."

21. John Merrill, *Korea: The Peninsular Origins of the War* (Newark: University of Delaware Press, 1989).

22. Kim, *The Unending Korean War*, 207.

23. See Park Myung-Lim, *Han'guk chŏnjaengŭi palbal kwa kiwon* [The Outbreak and Origins of the Korean War] (Seoul: Nanam Press, 1996); Gi-Wook Shin, "Nationalism and the Korean War," in *Korea and the Korean War*, ed. Chae-Jin Lee and Young Ick Lew (Seoul: Yonsei University Press, 2002), 417–40.

24. Suk-Young Kim, *DMZ Crossing: Performing Emotional Citizenship Along the Korean Border* (New York: Columbia University Press, 2014), 7.

25. Elaine Lynn-Ee Ho, "Constituting Citizenship Through the Emotions: Singaporean Transmigrants in London," *Annals of the Association of American Geographers* 99, no. 4 (2009), 789, quoted in Kim, *DMZ Crossing*, 10–11. For a related analysis of the intersections between affective and political dimensions of the August 2000 reunions as border crossings, see chapter 4.

26. Kim, *DMZ Crossing*, 12–13.

27. Charles K. Armstrong, "The Cultural Cold War in Korea, 1945–1950," *Journal of Asian Studies* 62, no. 1 (2003): 67.

28. Tai Hwan Kwon, *Demography of Korea: Population Change and Its Components 1925–1966* (Seoul: Seoul National University Press, 1977).

29. Gwi-Ok Kim, *Wŏllammin ŭi saenghwal kyŏnghŏm kwa chŏnch'esŏng* (Seoul: Seoul National University Press, 2002); Kim, *Isan'gajok, "pan'gongjŏnsa" to "ppalgaengi" to anin* (Seoul: Yŏksabip'yŏngsa, 2004).

30. Cho Hyoung and Pak Myong-Son, *Pukhanchulsin wŏllammin ŭi chŏngchakkwajŏng ŭl t'onghaesŏ pon nambukhan sahoegujo ŭi pyŏnhwa* [The Change of Social Structure of South and North Korea through the Examination of the Process of Settlement of *Wŏllammin* from North Korea], in *Pundansidae wa han'guksahoe* [The Era of Division and South Korean Society] (Seoul: Kkach'i, 1985); Kang, Jeong-gu, *Haebang-hu Wŏllammin ŭi wŏllamtonggi wa kyegŭpsŏng e kwanhan yŏn'gu* [A Study of Class Backgrounds and the Motives for Coming to the South among *Wŏllammin* in the Post-Liberation Period], in *Han'gukchŏnjaeng kwa han'guksahoe pyŏndong* [The Korean War and Change in South Korean Society] (Seoul: P'ulbit, 1992).

31. Soo-Jung Lee, "Making and Unmaking the Korean National Division: Separated Families in the Cold War and Post–Cold War Eras," PhD dissertation (Urbana-Champaign: University of Illinois, 2006); Lee, "'T'alnaengjŏn minjok spekt'ŏk'ŭl': 2000-nyŏn yŏrŭm nambuk isan'gajok sangbong" ["Post–Cold War National Spectacle": Reunions of Separated Families in the Summer, 2000], *Minjok munhwa yŏngu* 59 (2013): 95–122.

32. James Foley, *Korea's Divided Families: Fifty Years of Separation* (London and New York: Routledge, 2004).

33. Kim, *Isan'gajok, "pan'gongjŏnsa" to "ppalgaengi" to anin*; Uhn Cho, "*Wŏllamgajok kwa Wŏlbukgajok ŭi chanyŏdŭl ŭi kusul ŭl chungsimŭro*" ["Remembering the Korean War and the Politics of Memory: Experiences of '*Wŏllam*' and '*Wŏlbuk*' Families' Descendants"] *Sahoewa yŏksa* [Society and History] 77 (2008): 191–229.

34. Lee Ho-chul, *Southerners, Northerners*, trans. Andrew Killick and Cho Sukyeon (Norwalk, CT: EastBridge, 2005). *Namnyŏk saram, pungnyŏk saram* was originally published in Korean in 1996, when it garnered both the Daesan Literature Prize and the National Academy of Arts Prize.

35. Ibid., 46.

36. Ibid., 186.

37. *International Conventions on Protection of Humanity and Environment*, eds. Günter Hoog and Angela Steinmetz (Berlin and New York: Walter de Gruyter, 1993), 183.

38. Rosemary Foot, *A Substitute for Victory: The Politics of Peacemaking at the Korean Armistice Talks* (Ithaca, NY: Cornell University Press, 1990), 88–89.

39. For an in-depth analysis and interpretation of the POW screening process, see Monica Kim, "Empire's Babel: US Military Interrogation Rooms of the Korean War," *History of the Present* 3, no. 1 (Spring 2013): 1–28.

40. Another recurring pressure for the United States during the armistice negotiations concerning the POW issue was the strain that the U.S. position caused with its allies. As Steven Hugh Lee writes, by May 1953, "[m]ore than any other issue during the Korean War, the debate over the best means of achieving an armistice, in the context of apparent Chinese concessions, threatened the allied effort in Korea." See Steven Hugh Lee, *Outposts of Empire: Korea, Vietnam, and the Origins of the Cold War in Asia, 1949–1954* (Montreal and Kingston: McGill-Queen's University Press, 1995), 181.

41. Korean War Armistice Agreement, Treaties and Other International Agreements, Series #2782, General Records of the United States Government, Record Group 11, National Archives Building, Washington, DC (1953).

42. James Hoare, and Susan Pares, *Conflict in Korea: An Encyclopedia* (Santa Barbara, CA: ABC-CLIO, 1999), 32.

43. Valérie Gelézeau, "The Inter-Korean Border Region—'Meta-Border' of the Cold War and Metamorphic Frontier of the Peninsula," in *The Ashgate Research Companion to Border Studies*, ed. Doris Wastl-Walter (Farnham, U.K.: Ashgate Publishing, 2011).

44. Roland Bleiker, *Divided Korea* (Minneapolis: University of Minnesota Press, 2005), 18.

45. Kim, *Isan'gajok, "pan'gongjŏnsa" to "ppalgaengi" to anin*; Lee, "Making and Unmaking the Korean National Division."

46. Ryong-kyong Lee, "War and Women's Lives: On the Experience of Bereaved Women of Left-related Victims of the Korean War," *The Review of Korean Studies* 6, no. 1 (2003): 85–108.

47. Jae-yong Kim, "*Isan'gajok munje ŭi chŏngch'isŏng kwa indojuŭi*," *Yŏksa pip'yŏng* 6 (1998): 137; Taek-Lim Yoon, "The Politics of Memory in the Ethnographic History of a 'Red' Village in South Korea," *Korea Journal* 32, no. 4 (1992): 65–79.

48. Jae-yong Kim, "*Isan'gajok munje ŭi chŏngch'isŏng kwa indojuŭi*," 137.

49. Timothy G. Ashplant et al., *The Politics of War Memory and Commemoration* (London and New York: Routledge, 2000), 27.

50. Yonhap News Agency, *North Korea Handbook* (Armonk, NY: M. E. Sharpe, 2002), 1018.

51. Elim Chan and Andreas Schloenhardt, "North Korean Refugees and International Refugee Law," *International Journal of Refugee Law* 19, no. 2 (2007): 215–45.

52. Andrei Lankov, *The Real North Korea: Life and Politics in the Failed Stalinist Utopia* (New York: Oxford University Press, 2013), 43.

53. Ibid., 44.

54. See discussion below regarding the changes since 1990 when the ROK government began to allow its citizens to pursue private unofficial reunions in third countries without fear of punishment under South Korean law.

55. Charles K. Armstrong, "Inter-Korean Relations in Historical Perspective," *International Journal of Korean Unification Studies* 14, no. 2 (2005): 3.

56. Tae Yang Kwak, "The Nixon Doctrine and the Yusin Reforms: American Foreign Policy, the Vietnam War, and the Rise of Authoritarianism in Korea, 1968–1973," *The Journal of American-East Asian Relations* 12, no. 1/2 (2003): 34.

57. Ibid., 46.

58. Ibid., 50.

59. Kwak, "*Han'guk ŭi Betŭnam chŏnjaeng chaep'ŏngga*" [Reevaluating Korean Participation in the Vietnam War] *Yŏksa pip'yŏng* [Critical Review of History] 107 (Summer 2014): 202–32.

60. Gabriel Jonsson, *Towards Korean Reconciliation: Socio-cultural Exchanges and Cooperation* (Aldershot, U.K.: Ashgate, 2006), 55–56.

61. Foley, *Korea's Divided Families*, 89.

62. *Taehanjŏksipchasa* 1986, 54–57, quoted in Lee, "Making and Unmaking," 48.

63. Lee, "Making and Unmaking," 49.

64. Jae-Jean Suh, "The Reunion of Separated Families Under the Kim Dae-jung Government," *The Journal of East Asian Affairs* 16, no. 2 (2002): 357.

65. Suh, "The Reunion of Separated Families," 357.

66. Ministry of Unification, Republic of Korea, *Peace and Cooperation: White Paper on Korean Unification* (Seoul: Ministry of Unification, 2001), 246.

67. In Don Oberdorfer's 2001 popular history of divided Korea, a striking revelation was that, at the height of this crisis, the risk of escalation toward war was in fact more severe than had been generally perceived at the time. See *The Two Koreas: A Contemporary History* (New York: Basic Books, 2001), chapter 13.

68. Leon V. Sigal, *Disarming Strangers: Nuclear Diplomacy with North Korea* (Princeton, NJ: Princeton University Press, 2009), 64.

69. Selig S. Harrison, *Korean Endgame: A Strategy for Reunification* (Princeton, NJ: Princeton University Press, 2009), xvii.

70. See Key-young Son, *South Korean Engagement Policies and North Korea* (London and New York: Routledge, 2006), 4–5; Dong-won Lim, *Peacemaker* (Stanford, CA: Stanford University Asia-Pacific Research Center, 2012), 164–68.

71. Young Whan Kihl, *Transforming Korean Politics: Democracy, Reform, and Culture* (Armonk, NY: M. E. Sharpe, 2004), 249.

72. John Kie-chiang Oh, *Korean Politics: The Quest for Democratization and Economic Development* (Ithaca, NY: Cornell University Press, 1999), 236.

73. Kim, *Isan'gajok*, 137.

Part II

Centering the Margin

Chapter Three

Anti-Commemorations

In South Korea, the Korean War is known as *yugio* ("6-2-5"), and the period of the Korean War is called "the time of June 25," or literally "6-2-5 time" (*yugio ttae*). Such naming reflects the orthodox historical interpretation in South Korea that blames the Korean War entirely on Communist aggression when North Korea launched a general invasion along the 38th parallel on the day of June 25, 1950. The common vernacular reference obscures a more complex understanding of the war's origins. As John Merrill argues, the North Korean invasion in June 1950 did not represent a sudden break in a stable relationship between two established Korean states but was rather the violent eruption of political tensions that had been accumulating since the post-1945 division following Korea's liberation.[1] Bruce Cumings points to a 1947 report in which an ACLU representative, after visiting U.S.–occupied Korea and reading U.S. intelligence reports, concluded that a "state of unde-clared civil war" had already existed there.[2] Kim Dong-Choon substantiates this point by citing Merrill's assessment that, prior to the North Korean invasion, approximately one-hundred thousand people had been killed "in conflicts between tenant farmers and landlords, labor disputes, extreme con-frontations and retaliations between leftists and rightists, and civilian massa-cres committed by the military and the police to subdue communist guerril-las."[3] Even the Republic of Korea's official Korean War Memorial in Seoul implicitly challenges the war's conventional periodization by beginning its list of war-dead with names of those who died in 1945.[4] Nevertheless, a close identification has prevailed within the South Korean vernacular between the war's outbreak and the year 1950 on a single fateful date. In this formulation, June 25th serves as a synecdoche for the entire three-year period of the war's major military hostilities.

Given the ubiquity of references to "6-2-5" ("*yugio*") as part of everyday language in South Korea, I therefore assumed during the year 2000 when I was conducting fieldwork in Seoul that the 25th of June would be a day filled with fifty-year commemorations of the Korean War and other activities linked to official national memory in South Korea. Instead, it was striking to experience how quietly the historic milestone passed. The South Korean Defense Ministry cancelled its annual parade of hundreds of Korean War veterans for the first time since the war, angering the veterans who had congregated in Seoul for the commemoration that was to have featured a reenactment of the 1950 Inchŏn landing.[5] The Defense Ministry replaced the planned ceremonies and anticipated fanfare with a restrained official observance held outside the Korean War Memorial near the U.S. 8th Army Base in Seoul, a decision described by a ministry spokesperson as a goodwill gesture toward the North, an effort to support the public mood favoring inter-Korean peace.[6]

The timing of the historic inter-Korean Summit, which had ended just ten days earlier in the North Korean capital city, helped displace public attention in Korea away from the legacies of a divisive and destructive war. The two-day summit, held on June 13–15, 2000, was the first meeting between the two Korean heads of state since the respective republics were established in 1948. The resulting Joint Declaration, signed by South Korean President Kim Dae-jung and North Korean leader Kim Jong-il,[7] would be known by the date of its completion. It was immediately dubbed the "June 15th Declaration" (*yugilo sŏnŏn*). In the days following the summit, I noticed people often expressing confusion about whether the Joint Declaration referred to June 25th or June 15th, *yugio* or *yugilo*. In interviews and conversations, I would hear people pausing deliberately or even laughing over the alliterative confusion as they stressed "*not* June *25th*, I mean June *15th*" ("*yugio malgo, yugilo maliya*"), enunciating the words carefully to distinguish the two, which sound nearly identical in Korean.

That these dates are virtually homonyms is indeed ironic, given the fact that this would not have been the case had the summit occurred on the dates upon which the two sides had initially agreed. Whether or not this is a coincidence depends on how one interprets the timing of the summit's last day, when such official agreements are conventionally signed. That is, the summit was originally planned to take place from June 12–14, but at the last minute, the North Koreans requested a postponement to the start of the summit by one day. With no explanation forthcoming, this delay spurred widespread speculation in the South Korean media regarding its possible rationale, what kinds of preparations were still being made, or whether the summit would actually happen at all. However, the summit otherwise went as planned, only one day later, and the upshot of the delay was that the name of the summit's concluding inter-Korean Joint Declaration would be known by the date of June 15th, *yugilo*, and not June 14th, *yugilsa*. The resulting phonetic similarity between June 25th and June 15th created a linguistic slippage between these two landmark dates, despite their diametrically opposed historical meanings: one widely regarded as signifying the outbreak of the Korean War in 1950, and the other recognized as the most monumental breakthrough of the inter-Korean peace process to date in 2000. Indeed, the occlusion effected by these near homophones provides an apt metaphor for how the unprecedented events in inter-Korean reconciliation at the turn of the millennium would overshadow official Korean War commemorations that had been a fixture of South Korean war memory in the second half of the twentieth century.

LUDIC TRANSGRESSIONS

The June Summit could accordingly be regarded as what historian Alf Lüdtke calls an "anti-commemoration," in that it sought effectively to efface the enmity that the war had engendered.[8] The historic meeting in Pyongyang between the leaders of the two Koreas was celebrated as a success in both Koreas for yielding the June 15th Joint Declaration and, above all, for exhibiting a spirit of amity rather than hostility. While images of the convivial handshake between the two Korean leaders were circulated throughout the world, a South Korean journalist friend remarked that an even more remarkable sight was the footage showing the two Korean entourages together singing "Our Wish is Unification" (*Uri e sowŏn ŭn t'ongil*), which became an unofficial anthem for the period of inter-Korean reconciliation. She laughed and asked, "Where else can you find leaders from opposing hostile states meeting to drink together and sing songs?"

Yet such scenes were not universally greeted with approval. When I was walking home from the subway station during the week of the June Summit meeting, I ducked into my neighborhood's mom-and-pop corner store, where its elderly proprietor was watching the television news. After exchanging greetings, I asked him his thoughts about the upcoming summit. His face suddenly reddened with anger, and he shook his finger at the television screen, saying, "Did you see all those people coming out to see Kim Jong-il?" He was referring to the crowds of people who could be seen in the official news footage from Pyongyang as they lined the streets cheering zealously while Kim Jong-il's entourage passed. "You know those people were commanded to do that. In the North, if someone says, 'Do this!' you cannot question anything. No one is free there." When I asked him what he thought of the fact that people were treating the summit as a breakthrough in North–South relations, he dismissed the event as simply a vehicle for North Korean propaganda. His comment reflected a deep mistrust that was not uncommon in South Korea, particularly among his generation. The following week, I visited a close family friend, a woman in her seventies whose husband disappeared during the Korean War, at her apartment in a suburb outside of Seoul. She said she felt uneasy about the rapid political changes between the two states and added, "Dealing with the North is very dangerous. We must go slowly and be very careful."

Nevertheless, in the weeks leading up to and following the June Summit, examples in wider South Korean popular culture revealed a shift in attitudes toward reconciliation that went beyond political posturing or rhetoric. The public mood in South Korea toward the North was characterized not only by openness but a lighthearted irreverence that would have been unimaginable a few months earlier. On the evening variety programs, celebrities were quizzed on their knowledge of the North Korean equivalents for common words and phrases (e.g., *kirim bap*, or "oiled rice," instead of *bokkum bap*, for "fried rice"), and the jaunty North Korean song *"P'angapsŭmnida"* ("Pleased to Meet You") received wide airplay, with the South Korean girl-band Pinkel performing their own pop rendition.

A visually arresting television commercial, produced by a leading South Korean Internet search engine *Daum* (translated as "Next"), was frequently broadcast on the network channels that summer. Shot in somber sepia tones, the commercial opens by showing two soldiers facing off in a dreary downpour, standing yards from each other. One soldier wears a South Korean uniform, and his counterpart, a North Korean one. They are on duty at P'anmunjom, the site within the Korean Demilitarized Zone at the inter-Korean border where negotiations take place in stark institutional buildings. In the commercial, the layered staccato rhythms of the driving rain gradually intensify as the camera-view alternates between the two guards, each shown tensely and warily holding his ground. Next, across the screen appears a grey concrete strip, resembling an unpainted speedbump, where a tiny frog hops over and across. The camera angle then zooms out to an overhead shot, showing a replay of the frog as it leaps obliviously from one side to the other. The concrete strip is of course the marker that divides the two sides in the Joint Security Area. A close-up of the frog captures its landing on the boot of the South Korean guard, where it makes a little *ribbit*. Then a whistle blows, indicating a changing of the guard. The commercial ends with close-ups of each soldier, though they do not make eye contact. First the South Korean, peering out at a point off-screen, makes a small but affable smile. Then the camera shows the North Korean still at attention but relaxing visibly as he responds with his own smile, as if the two are appreciating a private friendly joke. The voiceover concludes, "We still have many boundaries to overcome. The Internet tears down the walls of the mind."

Another less subtle example of South Korean material culture that captured the shift in mood occasioned by the June Summit was an advertisement

Figure 3.1. "Mother, the Road to the North Is Finally Open." Full-color print advertisement published in *Screen* magazine, a monthly South Korean general-interest periodical, May 2000. © Wisebook.com

for a domestic online vendor of digital books, Wisebook.com. As part of a campaign that included full-color placements in South Korean magazines and posters displayed in subway cars throughout Seoul, the advertisement shows a young woman posing playfully next to a man dressed as a North Korean guard or soldier in uniform. She flashes a big dimpled smile, appearing cheeky and a little cheesy. In contrast, the man looks straight into the camera, his face carrying an impassive expression except for a slight purse to his lips. She is dressed in a crisp white seersucker summer dress with her hair styled into two tight buns, one on each side of her head, resembling a "Princess Leia" hairdo. She is standing just behind him and primly holding what at first looks like a school binder; on closer inspection, one can see it is a laptop computer. The tableau suggests that he is on duty standing guard and she is perhaps an exchange student or someone on a field trip getting her picture taken as a souvenir. The background is divided into two vertical fields of color: red on the left side, blue on the right. The North Korean guard stands squarely in the area with the red background. On the other side, the young woman is mostly in the blue area, but she has sidled over so that her figure extends across the divide between the two colors. Beyond the evident border-crossing metaphor, the visual scheme of the ad suggests the mixing of elements from both sides: its composition juxtaposes hues that predominate in both the North Korean and South Korean flags—primary red, primary blue, elemental white—while the font color adds punches of yellow, which picks up on the maize-colored accents of the military insignia on the soldier's uniform.

Running on the right-hand length of the ad, the headline reads, "Mother, the road to the North is *finally* open" [*"Ŏmoni, dŭdiŏ ibuk ŭro ganŭngil i yŏllimnida"*]. In Korean, this ad copy reads as an irreverent play on words; it is clearly intended to make whimsy out of the coincidence that the English loanword for electronic books, "e-book," is a homonym in colloquial Korean for the politically neutral term for North Korea, *"ibuk"* ["the North"]. The pun therefore suggests this young woman is publicly and rather gleefully expressing her intention to visit North Korea. By addressing this sentiment to her mother, it also implies that the daughter is fulfilling a wish that had been instilled in her since childhood by her family. That nuance is highlighted by the fact that the Korean word for "finally" (*dŭdiŏ*) is added in with an editor's caret; rather than signaling an afterthought, however, it seems to suggest both a belated emphasis and a sense of relief. Meanwhile, the audacity of this advertisement lies in how its cheekiness effectively pokes fun at the anachronism of South Korea's still-existing National Security Law, which have been used to interpret such a statement as an offense punishable by imprisonment.

The proliferation of such forms of popular culture and material culture—examples of what still technically amounted to contraband—raised hackles among political conservatives, who were dismayed by the rapid pace of political change and attendant trivialization of the North Korean threat. Yet, with its coy, ironic historical references, the digital bookseller's ad provides a revealing example of the millennial zeitgeist in South Korea that one could characterize as a juxtaposition between retro and futurist. It was as if to speculate that perhaps the twenty-first-century high-tech sensibility of a wired generation, which made anything seem possible, could finally break through the pathologies of national division that seemed to be forever throwing the nation back to what novelist Choi In-hun called the "Imprisoned Age" of the Korean War era.[9] Such a hopeful change in attitudes toward the promise and potential for inter-Korean contact in post-Summit South Korea would help to undo the demonized anticommunist caricatures that were still prevalent at the time. Providing the context in which the August 2000 reunions would unfold as critical events, this sense of new possibilities—not least as the easing of inherited Cold War burdens of distress, fear, and anxiety—would facilitate the transformation of North Koreans "from enemies to brethren" in the national imaginary.

FINANCIAL CRISIS AND THE OTHERWISE IMPOSSIBLE

While this shift in greater South Korean openness toward cooperation with North Korea can be traced to the impact of democratization and the end of the Cold War, the more immediate context for inter-Korean engagement was the aftermath of the 1997–1998 Asian Financial Crisis. Despite South Korea's formidable economic gains in the 1970s and 1980s, the tumultuous events of the 1997–1998 Asian Financial Crisis revealed a disturbing degree of underlying vulnerability, and it was a reminder of Korea's liminal status as a nation divided and technically still at war.[10] The "beginning" of that financial crisis is often traced to Southeast Asia on July 2, 1997, when the Thai central bank had depleted its hard-currency reserves in its attempts to offset months of massive attacks by global currency speculators.[11] The Thai government was left with little choice but to unpeg the *baht* from the dollar, which set off a rapid devaluation. Foreign investors, bankers, and market analysts lost confidence in Thailand's ability to manage its worsening balance of payments, as bubbles loomed ominously in asset prices and real estate markets. The collapse of the *baht* triggered a rapid spread of the crisis throughout Asia, sending stock markets crashing in Indonesia, Malaysia, the Philippines, South Korea, and elsewhere. Investors rushed to withdraw short-term investments, and foreign banks called in loans, refusing to roll them over, creating an environment in which these nations were unable to procure new funds at any price. Officials as high-ranking as the governor of the Bank of Korea grossly underestimated the figure of nonperforming loans at $20 billion, barely a quarter of the estimated $80 billion calculated by private analysts.[12] Despite attempts by the ROK treasury to prop up its currency, the *won* soon lost half its value, and South Korea's financial markets entered a state of meltdown.

Unlike other nations hit by the currency crisis, such alarm was intensified for South Koreans by fears that their sudden economic vulnerability could unleash a yet-greater nightmare if the moment were exploited by North Korea to launch a military attack. I was living in Seoul in late 1997, and recall how the country was gripped by an atmosphere that many people compared to the time of the Korean War. The corridors of Kimpo International Airport, normally thronged with travelers and their well-wishers, emptied out to the degree that it resembled the terminal to a ghost town. In shops and supermarkets, whole store shelves were cleared of their inventories as people began to hoard rice, bottled water, and basic necessities. I would often visit the home of two older family friends, a couple whom I would describe as comfortably middle-class, and their reaction to the crisis was one of forlorn resignation. They described how their retirement savings, which they had faithfully salted away over their adult lifetimes, virtually evaporated overnight. Eventually, a sense of unease gave way to fears of panic, and riot police were stationed outside of banks in case of possible unrest. As the financial crisis worsened, South Koreans were stunned to realize that their country, the eleventh-largest economy in the world, was suddenly in the grips of bankruptcy. The unfolding of the financial crisis furthermore coincided with the run-up to the 1997 presidential election, and the neck-and-neck race between the two leading candidates only added to the heady climate of suspense, uncertainty, and dread.

On December 18, 1997, barely two weeks after South Korea had signed a financial "rescue" agreement with the IMF, Kim Dae-jung was elected president, eking out a narrow victory over his conservative-party opponent. For Kim, an internationally known human rights activist, it was a poignant culmination of a political career during which he had been a leader in South Korea's anti-government opposition and had also survived several assassination attempts as well as periods of confinement as a political prisoner. For the country, it marked the first peaceful change of power to the opposition party in South Korea since the inception of the republic in 1948. Soon after his narrow win, Kim announced his government would pursue "the parallel development of democracy and a market economy,"[13] later outlining a plan of economic restructuring to meet the harsh terms of the IMF bailout. So it was all the more striking when he declared that another cornerstone of his administration would be to pursue peaceful coexistence and economic cooperation with North Korea, which at the time was a hostile enemy of its capitalist counterpart.

In other words, at the same time that South Korea's newly elected center-left president indicated that his administration would accommodate the regime of global capital, he also expressed a determination to establish direct and autonomous relations with a financially strapped state that was considered to be, politically and economically, among the most closed in the world. In certain respects, these two approaches are not as contradictory as they might seem. Standard and Poor's estimated that the threat North Korea posed toward South Korea in that period exceeded the severity of threat facing any other "investment grade sovereign," including Israel and Taiwan.[14] In the wake of the currency crisis and liquidity crunch, one security analyst described South Korea's first priority as that of reducing military tensions on the peninsula in order to lure back the capital that had fled the country.[15] Indeed, the reunions took place just as the South Korean economy was regaining its footing in the wake of the crisis, and the Kim Dae-jung adminis-tration acquired political leverage from that recovery. While the Kim and Roh governments are known for their progressive domestic social programs and their pro-engagement policies with North Korea, they also undertook an economic agenda that more aggressively integrated South Korea into the neoliberal world order.[16]

To grasp the context of post-crisis South Korea more fully, it is important to consider the implications of recent developments within neoliberalism itself. Neoliberalism is not a monolithic ideology, but rather a plurality of interests and ideologies, which broadly aims to transform relations of power such that the values and logic of the market would extend beyond the realm of economic transactions to become embedded in political life, social rela-tions, and individual subjectivity. Anthropologist Aihwa Ong has analyzed how neoliberalism translates into two kinds of technologies of governance oriented toward political and economic optimization: (1) technologies of subjectivity, which invokes a concept of the human subject as an autono-mous, self-directing agent, such that manifestations of neoliberal political rationality implicate a range of institutions and actors in the cultivation of an "entrepreneurship of the self" that enables citizens to navigate unpredictable market conditions; and (2) technologies of subjection, which shape political strategies aimed at regulating groups and populations in order to achieve optimal conditions for productivity.[17] Notably, ethnographic research in this area has brought theoretical tools of cultural analysis to an area of social and economic policy that had itself appropriated theoretical concepts of "cul-ture." Critical studies of development have analyzed the "cultural turn" in political economy that began in the late 1990s,[18] when the cultural subse-quently became an object of instrumentalization in neoliberal development theory and practice.[19]

Such a broader analysis helps to account for South Korean state interests in the separated-family reunions and the overall process of inter-Korean reconciliation as a response to global economic imperatives. In the aftermath of the crisis, the South Korean state—charged with the tasks of restructuring the financial sectors and reforming the big conglomerates (*chaebol*)—in many respects became more powerful than before, through its newly mandat-ed regulatory structures.[20] In other words, the resulting policies can be char-acterized as an aggressive expansion of long-term state intervention, rather than a weakening or curbing of state power.

What occurred in South Korea reflected the influence of the so-called "post-Washington Consensus," which figured highly in the neoliberal reform prescriptions in the wake of the Asian Financial Crisis. The post-Washington Consensus refutes the utopian premise of the "Washington Consensus" that markets are by nature universally efficient. As the orthodoxy of development policy during the Reagan-Thatcher era, the Washington Consensus favored classic economic liberal notions of free trade and financial deregulation. In contrast, the post-Washington Consensus instead advocates some degree of state intervention in order to avoid potential market failures. In a vindication of Polanyi, the post-Washington Consensus acknowledges the embeddedness of the market in social and institutional relations and recognizes that the viability of global and domestic markets relies on public consent.[21] These new assumptions therefore move beyond the state-market opposition that was a hallmark of earlier neoliberal policies. Although the post-Washington Consensus is sometimes described as a retreat of neoliberalism, Paul Cammack instead characterizes its emergence as representing a shift from "shallow neoliberalism," which stresses free markets and a diminishing role of the state, to "deep neoliberalism," whereby state actors attempt to shape social relations and institutions to support the efficiency and sustainability of markets.[22]

In this process, the concept of "social capital" has become integrated within the policy and prescriptions of the World Bank to signify the shift in development policy and practice from the sterile calculus of "getting the prices right" to a broader project of "getting the social relations right."[23] Deemed the missing link of development, "social capital" has been assimilated into the jargon of the development world and has become institutionalized since 1995 within the World Bank.[24] Michael Watts notes that the earlier intellectual genealogy of social capital as a concept—notably the work of Pierre Bourdieu and Peter Evans—was largely lost in the World Bank's appropriations of the term.[25] Instead, its economists strongly tended to deploy social capital "to complement, not fundamentally to reassess, existing economic prognoses."[26] Following the post-Washington Consensus, World Bank economists looked to social capital as the medium through which to strengthen bonds and form linkages in the early years of the millennium. This came with the understanding, according to Watts, that networks, associations, norms, values, and relations of trust are "the raw material of social capital" which proved to be key factors in, among other things, "making institutions work and securing access to markets."[27] Governments, institutions, and all manner of affiliations are therefore seen to encompass a wide-reaching network of social relations linked in their instrumental capacity to open new markets and to reduce economic transaction costs.

Furthermore, the various networks of support and meaning that market-systems require operate not only through leveraging "social capital" but also by underscoring sources of "cohesiveness" in a society.[28] An annual World Bank report entitled, "Knowledge for Development," recommended in 1998: "Institutions, broadly defined to include governments, private organizations, laws and *social norms*, can contribute to establishing recognized standards and enforcing contracts, *thus making possible transactions which might not otherwise occur*" (emphasis added).[29] In the World Bank report, the explicit inclusion of "social norms" on par with governments, organizations, and laws among potential institutional targets for neoliberal intervention sheds light on how the presumption of instrumentalizing sociality itself was very much in play for policymakers in post-crisis East Asia. This turn in neoliberalism prompts us to revisit and reconfigure older questions about how state actors attempt to engineer certain forms of social governance through interventions in public life. While strategies of mobilization such as political rituals and media events have long been subjects of academic study, it is important to examine how they continue to be deployed by states, set against ever denser implications of globalization.

POLITICAL WATERSHEDS AND THE CLAIMS THEY STAKE

As periods of liminality inevitably accompany transitions of power, dramatic public events are often crucial for establishing the legitimacy of the new order. In his study of post-apartheid South Africa, anthropologist Richard A. Wilson posits that the Truth and Reconciliation Commission (TRC) was itself a "liminal institution." Wilson argues that the TRC served to legitimize the newly democratizing South African government by occupying a liminal space, betwixt and between the old and new regimes. He observes that the TRC's transitory role blurred lines between legalism and religious moralism in ways that were at times contradictory. The liminal nature of the TRC afforded distance from the institutional legacies of apartheid and a degree of freedom from the legal strictures of formal court procedures. The amnesty hearings instead came to manifest "a theatricalization of the power of the new state," and Wilson argues that such theatricalization—with its emotive religious and moralizing overtones—held "more legitimizing potential" than would a dry official legalism bound by rules and the obscure language of the court.[30] Wilson comments, "Importantly, the ritualized and moral features of rituals of transition were the result of the failure of secular mechanisms (such as the law) to deal with conflict in society."[31] Salient here is Wilson's contention that the recourse to forms of emotive ritual in the public sphere—along with their moral overtones—may provide an alternative means of achieving legitimation for a new order where more conventional avenues for overcoming political conflict are unavailable.[32]

In the case of South Korea's Kim Dae-jung government, despite the post-crisis expansion of state regulatory power, the administration did not have a strong popular mandate to pursue reconciliation with the North. Indeed, when Kim first announced the Sunshine Policy, it was largely met with skepticism or cynicism as to whether his administration could induce North Korea to respond positively. At the time, the state's politically weak position with respect to its Northern policy also stemmed from ambivalent attitudes among South Koreans toward reunification and strong opposition from polit-ical conservatives. As I discuss below, the separated-family reunions in Au-gust 2000 were an integral part of the processes that would launch and rationalize the administration's program of economic cooperation with North Korea as well as sanction a new identity for the nation. This study therefore engages theoretical discussions about the appropriation of political ritual as a liminal event, particularly in those situations where other possibilities for legitimizing social and political change are presumed to be foreclosed.

As political rituals that elided national and familial idioms, these reunions focused on separated families as tragic victims of the war and division. By making visible such visceral emotional connections representing cross-bor-der ties of kinship and blood-based nationalism, the reunions were clearly organized with the aim of achieving the classic ends of political ritual: bring-ing about a greater sense of collective cohesion, reordering social relation-ships, and imparting moral legitimacy for a new order. It must be noted here that, following the June Summit and August family reunions, inter-Korean economic cooperation proceeded at a scale and with a rapidity that would have been unthinkable before 2000. In ways specific to the Korean context, it is therefore critical to bear in mind the orientation within neoliberal policy that attempts to shape networks of meaning and social norms in the service of enabling otherwise impossible transactions.

Building on the assumption that ritual is critical for establishing consen-sus with respect to legitimacy, analyses of national identity and mass media tend to focus on the ways in which ritual provides a context for reimagining social arrangements or collective identities through the opening afforded by liminal periods.[33] A widely known study of ritual phenomena in media stud-ies is that of Daniel Dayan and Elihu Katz, who developed the concept of "media events" following the work on ritual by Victor Turner. Invoking Turner's concept of liminality to explain the power of such "transformative ceremonies," Dayan and Katz describe a media event as "an expressive dra-matization, a modeling or an illustrating of the desirable state of affairs" in response to a crisis in society.[34] Compare this to the description of Turner's approach to ritual by anthropologist Catherine M. Bell, who characterizes it "as the means for acting out social conflicts in a series of activities through which people experience the authority and flexibility of the social order, the liminality and bonds of egalitarian communitas, and the passage from an old place in the social order to a new status in a reconstituted order."[35] In a subsequent article about televised political spectacle, Dayan and Katz's debt to Turner is even more explicit: "The ceremony itself represents a 'liminal' moment, a break in the routinized social time. . . . It offers society opportu-nity [*sic*] to discover that there are alternatives to its choices and, in doing so, it partially reveals the anxieties, the chaos, the effervescence of genesis."[36] In these studies, liminality affords an explanation to account for the transformative capacity to reorganize social relationships, which is ascribed to both political rituals and media events.

In classic theoretical analyses of political ritual, a dominant concern centers on the degree to which ritual offsets forces of destabilization by bringing about social cohesion and, by extension, achieving political stability. In *Negara*, Geertz describes how the Balinese state was in fact far less beholden to the mundane tasks of government than it was to the rituals that served to dramatize a cosmic order legitimizing the social hierarchy.[37] In an early review article on modern political ritual, Steven Lukes had similarly characterized Neo-Durkheimian analyses of political ritual along such functionalist lines but within the idiom of kinship and belonging, maintaining that political rituals such as coronations both express and constitute an integration of values by which "the whole society is felt to be one large family."[38] Ritual's role in legitimating and perpetuating political paradigms or *représentations collectives* may indeed contribute to the stability of the political system, by helping to define its nature and by obscuring its alternatives in what Lukes calls the "mobilization of bias." He warns, however, against the facile identification of political ritual as a means for achieving values-consensus in modern industrial societies. Instead, he calls for a reading of Durkheim that recognizes how ritual includes a cognitive dimension. Ritual renders "intelligible society and social relationships, serving to organize people's knowledge of the past and present and their capacity to imagine the future. In other words, it helps to *define as authoritative certain ways of seeing society*"[39] (emphasis added). Therefore, instead of taking for granted the creation or expression of social integration through political ritual, it would be more theoretically productive to analyze the grounds for making such claims and for authorizing the particular forms of vision that shape popular memory and imagination. What kinds of power—and limits on power—are suggested by such ritual practices and their prerogatives of visuality?

PRELIMINARY NECESSITY

In South Korea at the turn of the millennium, given that prior attempts to hold similar reunions had been thwarted several times in past decades, even after official agreements had been signed, the successful achievement of reunions among separated families carried unquestionably weighty political significance. It was chronologically the first concrete outcome of the June Summit agreement, and South Korean officials described the successful accomplishment of these family reunions as a prerequisite to fulfilling other aspects of an agenda of economic cooperation. The South Korean government nevertheless maintained that the reunions were strictly a "humanitarian" endeavor. Official sources declared that the government would approach the separated-families dilemma "as a task that has nothing to do with political or military issues."[40] Yet, in earlier unsuccessful negotiations regarding separated families in the late 1990s, South Korean government documents acknowledged the necessity to accommodate "North Korea's intention to link the separated-family issue with economic support,"[41] a position that was later downplayed or denied by South Korean officials regarding the August 2000 reunions.

Despite the public claims by the Kim Dae-jung administration about the depoliticized nature of the reunions, the August 2000 family meetings were indeed widely recognized in South Korea as a diplomatic contingency. The successful accomplishment of these family reunions was taken by the South Korean government as a sign that other aspects of the June 15th Joint Declaration could be taken in good faith. While speaking to South Korean government officials in the weeks following the June Summit, I was struck by how the reunions of separated families were repeatedly described as a linchpin for expanding inter-Korean projects. "Without them the South Korean government cannot implement economic cooperation," said one government official, who served as an advisor to President Kim Dae-jung on inter-Korean economic issues. I had met him a few years earlier at an academic workshop, as the friend of one of my relatives who is a fellow economist, and he agreed to be interviewed at his office in Seoul shortly prior to the August family meetings. Regarding the then-imminent reunions, his assessment was that unless the Kim Dae-jung administration showed publicly that it was working to resolve the humanitarian problem of separated families, it would be politically impossible for the South Korean government to follow through on economic cooperation. He said, "This is a democratic society. The separated families are a priority because the reunions are the prerequisite, the condition for any further progress."[42] Without the successful achievement of the separated-families exchanges, he explained, the administration could not initiate the economic parts of its inter-Korean agenda. Attempting to move ahead otherwise with those policies would seem too insensitive. Well aware of the potential for public outrage over such a delicate political issue, members of the Kim administration knew they could not risk appearing to ignore the suffering of separated families, which would jeopardize their other plans for inter-Korean relations. Acknowledging the small scale of the reunions—with only one hundred people chosen from each side for the August meetings—this government official emphasized that it nonetheless represented a symbolic first step.

Others in the Kim Dae-jung administration also characterized the reunions as integral to the pressing goal of national "survival." During my fieldwork that year, I sometimes met with a researcher working at the Ministry of Unification in central Seoul. Though friendly, he could be quite circumspect at times, given that much of the decision-making process behind the reunions program was undisclosed to the public. He surprised me one day by speaking more freely when I asked what he thought was the meaning of the reunions. He reflected a moment and said: "The separated-families issue is partly related to reconciliation, and it's also simply humanitarian because old people miss their families, and more are passing away. It's good to make progress, but there will be a big setback because separated families are dying now. The Ministry of Unification is trying to keep the process a humanitarian issue. If they all die, what next?" In his assessment, the South Korean government was not working toward reunification chiefly for the objective of reunifying families, but rather for more pragmatic ends. "It's the only way for both sides to survive. It's a matter of survival. After that, there can be prosperity. But for right now, that means we are holding these events partly to soften the minds of hardliners."

Such emphasis on "survival" reflected a widely held anxiety following the Asian Financial Crisis (known in South Korea as the "IMF crisis") about Korea's place in the global economy, hemmed in by competition with rich countries on one side and by developing countries on the other. In this researcher's view, for South Korea to escape this squeeze, which threatens its economic viability, eventual unification with North Korea was both obvious and necessary. That assumption was certainly in keeping with the assumptions that motivated the Kim administration, which regarded the program of economic cooperation between North and South Korea as instrumental for success in an increasingly competitive global market.[43] The logic of that strategy presumed lower labor costs in North Korea, and the relatively minimal expenses for transportation to and from the then-proposed industrial park in Kaesŏng offered the potential to restore some of the economic advantage that South Korea had lost to China over the prior decade. Yet for this government bureaucrat to acknowledge the reunions were being held "partly to soften the minds of hardliners" struck me as astonishingly frank. By "hardliners," the researcher was referring to conservatives who vehemently opposed reconciliation with the North. As analyzed in the following chapter, the objective of influencing public opinion meant that the South Korean state was invested in making the reunions as highly visible as possible, especially their most heart-rending scenes.

Studies of political rituals, particularly those addressing divided societies, reveal how counter-commemorations staged by various actors project competing interpretations of historical events or assert oppositional claims to political legitimacy.[44] In the symbolic framework undergirding inter-Korean reconciliation, the reuniting families from North and South would serve to signify embodiments of an imagined common "bloodline" that would encompass both Koreas, making explicit the assumptions behind a pan-Korean ethnic nationalism. Sheila Miyoshi Jager and Jiyul Kim have analyzed how, at the beginning of the twenty-first century, a contemporary form of ethnic nationalism emerged in the rise of pan-Korean nationalism and an opposition to the interference of Great Powers (*pan'yŏlgangjuŭi*).[45] The separated-family reunions were indeed framed by an expression of such blood-based nationalism, as they also implicitly resonated with the discourses of resistance against the influence of powerful countries insofar as overcoming national division itself signified resolving the consequences of past intervention by foreign governments. Like the June Summit two months prior, the August 2000 reunions would thereby serve as anti-commemorations of the Korean War, which promised to displace the prior enmity and alienation between the two Koreas by invoking a newly reascendant blood-based nationalism that reified the shared kinship lineages presumed to span both the North and the South.

NOTES

1. John Merrill, *Korea: The Peninsular Origins of the War* (Newark: University of Delaware Press, 1989), cited in Kim Dong-Choon, *The Unending Korean War* (Larkspur, CA: Tamal Vista, 2009), 146.
2. Bruce Cumings, *Korea's Place in the Sun: A Modern History* (New York: Norton, 2005), 208.
3. Kim, *The Unending Korean War*, 146.
4. Sheila Miyoshi Jager, *Narratives of Nation Building in Korea: A Genealogy of Patriotism* (Armonk, NY: M. E. Sharpe, 2003), 134.
5. Jager, *Narratives of Nation Building in Korea*, 117.
6. Telephone interview with the author, June 26, 2000.
7. Kim Jong-il's official title was Chairman of the National Defense Commission, the highest post in the DPRK after Kim Il-sung's death in 1994. The Supreme People's Assembly posthumously named Kim Il-sung the Eternal President of the Republic, so his son and successor never assumed the title of President.
8. Alf Lüdtke, "Histories of Mourning: Flowers and Stones for the War Dead, Confusion for the Living," in *Between History and Histories: The Making of Silences and Commemorations* (Toronto: University of Toronto Press, 1997), 174.
9. In-hun Choi, *A Grey Man* (Seoul: Si Sa Yong O Sa, 1988), 138.
10. Amid the ideological polarization of Korea's postwar period, the two halves of the peninsula followed opposing trajectories. Like Germany and other divided countries, the two halves competed for legitimacy vis-à-vis each other, engaging in not only diplomatic and military rivalry but also economic competition. While North Korea was initially more successful economically than its Southern counterpart through the 1960s, South Korea underwent aggressive economic development of heavy industries since the 1970s and received massive economic aid from the United States, which supported its ally as a bulwark against Communism. South Korea's rapid double-digit growth during the 1980s helped to make South Korea the eleventh-largest economy in the world by 1997. In contrast, North Korea has been economically strapped for resources especially following the collapse of the Soviet Union, whose favorable trade terms had partly subsidized the DPRK economy.
11. For discussions of the onset of the crisis in the region, see Steven Radelet and Jeffrey Sachs, "The East Asian Financial Crisis: Diagnosis, Remedies, Prospects," *Brookings Papers on Economic Activity* 1 (1998): 1–90.
12. Bruce Cumings, "The Asian Crisis, Democracy, and the End of 'Late' Development," in *The Politics of the Asian Economic Crisis* (Ithaca, NY: Cornell University Press, 1999), 25.

13. Kim Dae-jung, "Democracy and Market Economy: Two Wheels of a Cart," in *Democracy, Market Economy and Development: An Asian Perspective*, eds. Farrukh Iqbal and Jong-Il You (Washington, DC: World Bank, 2001), 7.

14. Seo Jee-yeon, "North Korea is 'World's Largest Contingent Liability,'" *Korea Times*, May 14, 2004.

15. L. Gordon Flake, "Moral Hazard Alert: US Perspectives on Inter-Korean Relations," in *The 2nd Korea-US Security Forum: The 2nd Bush Administration and the Korean Peninsula*, Jeju, Korea, March 30–April 2, 2005.

16. Kevin Gray, "Political Cultures of South Korea," *New Left Review* 79, January–February (2013): 85–101.

17. Aihwa Ong, *Neoliberalism as Exception: Mutations in Citizenship and Sovereignty* (Durham, NC: Duke University Press, 2006), 6.

18. Larry Ray and Andrew Sayer, eds., *Culture and Economy: After the Cultural Turn* (Thousand Oaks, CA: Sage, 1999); Scott Lash and John Urry, *Economies of Signs and Space* (Thousand Oaks, CA: Sage 1994).

19. Michael Watts, "Culture, Development, and Global Neo-Liberalism," in *Culture and Development in a Globalising World: Geographies, Actors and Paradigms*, ed. Sarah A. Radcliffe (London: Routledge, 2006), 30–57.

20. See Meredith Woo-Cumings, "The State, Democracy, and the Reform of the Corporate Sector in Korea," in *The Politics of the Asian Economic Crisis*, ed. T. J. Pempel (Ithaca: Cornell University Press, 1999), 116–142. See also Cho Hee-yeon, "The Structure of the South Korean Developmental Regime and its Transformation" *Inter-Asia Cultural Studies* 1, no. 3 (1999): 408–26.

21. Karl Polanyi, *The Great Transformation* (Boston, MA: Beacon Press, 1944); John Lie, "Embedding Polanyi's Market Society," *Sociological Perspectives* 34, no. 2 (1991): 219–35; Nicola Phillips and Richard A. Higgott, "Global Governance and the Public Domain: Collective Goods in a 'Post-Washington Consensus' Era," Centre for the Study of Globalisation and Regionalisation, Working Paper No.47/99 (Coventry, U.K.: University of Warwick, 1999).

22. Paul Cammack, "What the World Bank Means by Poverty Reduction, and Why it Matters," *New Political Economy* 9, no. 2 (2004): 189–211. See also Garry Rodan, "Neoliberalism and Transparency: Political Versus Economic Liberalism," Murdoch University Asia Research Centre Working Paper 112, Perth, Western Australia, 2004. These two stages also correspond with what Jamie Peck and Adam Tickell describe as "rollback" versus "rollout" neoliberalism in "Neoliberalizing Space," *Antipode* 34, no. 3 (2002): 380–98.

23. John Hariss, *De-Politicizing Development: The World Bank and Social Capital* (New York: Anthem Press, 2002), 81.

24. Ben Fine, "Social Capital: The World Bank's Fungible Friend," *Journal of Agrarian Change* 3, no. 4 (2003): 586–603.

25. Watts, "Culture, Development and Global Neo-Liberalism," 30–57.

26. Ben Fine, *Social Capital Versus Social Theory: Political Economy and Social Science at the Turn of the Millennium* (New York and London: Routledge, 2001), 156.

27. Watts, "Culture, Development and Global Neo-Liberalism," 36.

28. Fine, *Social Capital*.

29. Rodan, "Neoliberalism and Transparency," 13, emphasis added.

30. Richard Wilson, *The Politics of Truth and Reconciliation in South Africa* (Cambridge: Cambridge University Press, 2001), 20.

31. Wilson, *The Politics of Truth and Reconciliation,* 10.

32. Cf. the discussion of this concept of the theater state in relation to contemporary North Korea in Heonik Kwon and Byung-Ho Chung, *North Korea: Beyond Charismatic Politics* (Lanham, MD: Rowman & Littlefield, 2012), 45ff.

33. Bent Steeg Larsen and Thomas Tufte, "Rituals in the Modern World: Applying the Concept of Ritual in Media Ethnography," in *Global Media Studies—Ethnographic Perspectives*, eds. Patrick D. Murphy and Marwan M. Krady (New York: Routledge, 2003); Don Handelman, *Models and Mirrors: Towards an Anthropology of Public Events* (Oxford: Berghahn, 1998). Meanwhile, by 2005, a book-length survey of media anthropology singled out

"ritual" as the concept that received the widest application at the time in that subfield; see Eric W. Rothenbuhler and Mihai Coman, *Media Anthropology* (Thousand Oaks, CA: Sage, 2005).

34. Daniel Dayan and Elihu Katz, *Media Events: The Live Broadcasting of History* (Cambridge, MA: Harvard University Press, 1992).

35. Catherine M. Bell, *Ritual: Perspectives and Dimensions* (Oxford: Oxford University Press, 2009), 40.

36. Quoted in Rothenbuhler and Coman, *Media Anthropology*, 5.

37. Clifford Geertz, *Negara: The Theatre State in Nineteenth-Century Bali* (Princeton, NJ: Princeton University Press, 1980).

38. Edward Shils and Michael Young, "The Meaning of Coronation," *Sociological Review* 1 (1953): 78–79.

39. Steven Lukes, "Political Ritual and Social Integration," *Sociology* 9, no. 2 (1975): 301.

40. Ministry of Unification, Republic of Korea, *Peace and Cooperation: White Paper on Korean Unification* (Seoul: Ministry of Unification, 2001).

41. Korea Institute for National Unification, *The Unification Environment and Relations between South and North Korea, 1999–2000: 1999 Annual Report* (Seoul: Minjok T'ongil Yŏn'guwŏn, 2000), 151–52.

42. Interview with author on August 12, 2000, Seoul, Korea.

43. Soon-Young Hong, "Thawing Korea's Cold War: The Path to Peace on the Korean Peninsula," *Foreign Affairs* 78, no. 3 (1999): 8–12.

44. Sabelo J. Ndlovu-Gatsheni and Wendy Willems, "Making Sense of Cultural Nationalism and the Politics of Commemoration Under the Third Chimurenga in Zimbabwe," *Journal of Southern African Studies* 35, no. 4 (2009): 945–65; Yiannis Papadakis, "Nation, Narrative and Commemoration: Political Ritual in Divided Cyprus," *History and Anthropology* 14, no. 3 (2003): 253–70; Roger I. Simon, "Forms of Insurgency in the Production of Popular Memories: The Columbus Quincentenary and the Pedagogy of Counter-Commemoration," *Cultural Studies* 7, no. 1 (1993): 73–88.

45. Sheila Miyoshi Jager and Jiyul Kim, "The Korean War After the Cold War: Commemorating the Armistice Agreement in South Korea," in *Ruptured Histories: War, Memory, and the Post–Cold War in Asia*, eds. Sheila Miyoshi Jager and Rana Mitter (Cambridge, MA: Harvard University Press, 2007), 233–65.

Chapter Four

Threshold Rituals, Fragility, and National Intimacy

On August 15, 2000, in the affluent Kangnam (Gangnam) district of Seoul, a large banner festooned over the entrance to the Convention and Exhibition Center (COEX) proclaimed, "We Are One Bloodline, One Brethren, One Spirit" (*Uri nŭn Hanp'itchul, Han'gyŏre, Hanmaŭm*). Buses carrying a delegation of one hundred North Korean visitors from Kimpo (Gimpo) International Airport[1] were late for their scheduled arrival, apparently delayed in traffic. Preparations had been underway for two simultaneous gatherings of relatives in South Korea and North Korea, and both delegations were traveling by air to their respective destinations. Notably, their trip was *not* in fact a technical crossing of the DMZ, as their plane did not pass through the airspace over the demarcation line above the Korean peninsula itself. A direct flight between the two Korean capitals, which are only 195 kilometers apart, would have taken a mere fifteen minutes. Instead, the families were transported along an indirect route that would prolong the trip to last an hour. Rather than going directly from Pyongyang to Seoul, the plane followed a flight path resembling a sideways U-turn, initially heading westward into international airspace before turning south and then east to land on a runway at the international terminal at Kimpo. A single wide-body plane was used, flown by Air Koryo, the national flag carrier of North Korea. The flight that morning departed from Pyongyang with the North Korean delegation at ten o'clock. After the Northern delegation arrived and deplaned in Seoul, the Southern delegation boarded the same aircraft to fly back via an identical route in reverse to Pyongyang for the parallel set of reunions. In this way, the delegations were conveyed from one state to the other without making a literal border-crossing.

Such a deliberately arranged non-crossing seemed to suggest that, without any acknowledged limits, the partition that demarcated national division would presumably continue to extend indefinitely into space. That is, it was no longer simply a territorial line of division on the ground but one that became projected vertically into the sky. I later learned from a South Korean Ministry of Unification official that this deliberate detour around the inter-Korean demarcation, even in mid-air, came at the insistence of the North Korean side. Although the North Koreans' logic had not been explicitly discussed during preparatory negotiations for the reunions, the South Korean official understood this stipulation to mean that the other side was withholding permission for the families to make an overland crossing of the DMZ. Such a watershed was instead presumably deferred to retain as a bargaining chip that could figure into future negotiations over additional aid, as the two states also prepared to embark on expanded economic ties in response, as detailed in the previous chapter, to global neoliberal pressures. In so doing, the aerial circumvention of the barriers along the de facto border on the ground figuratively extended the inter-Korean divide indefinitely upward at the very moment that the boundary would prove newly porous. The moment thereby offered a vertiginous instance of what political theorist Wendy Brown has characterized as a "theatricalized" projection of the aura of sovereign power when state sovereignty itself is on the wane. [2]

Back in Seoul, members of the domestic and international press already staked out the location that was being prepared for the reunions. The event was to take place in an enormous conference-center hall, which normally would accommodate international trade shows and large-scale conventions. The event hall was instead arrayed with round tables covered in white tablecloths, each bearing a floral centerpiece of fresh flowers beside a wooden tray with snacks and bottled drinks. Off to one side of the room, a temporary press center had been set up to facilitate coverage of the event, comprised of a cluster of makeshift workstations where reporters could file their late-breaking dispatches. Given this combination of journalistic presence and an atmosphere of elegant hospitality, the location of the historic inter-Korean separated-family reunions resembled nothing so much as a high-profile celebrity wedding reception. Indeed, the one hundred tables were arranged at a generous distance from each other. Later it would become apparent that the extra space was needed for the media camera crews to move from one table to another. With each of the visitors from North Korea expected to meet with five of his or her relatives, all reunion participants wore lanyards with a laminated tag showing their family's assigned number. That corresponded with the number printed on a card displayed at each table, a coding system used throughout the reunion events to facilitate logistics on the part of the organizers. Initially, the numbering also served to avoid potential confusion by giving reunion participants a means to identify their long-separated relatives, even if they could no longer easily recognize one another. The initial reunions would occur inside the main hall of Seoul's COEX (*K'oekseu*), a then-state-of-the-art facility that had been completed three months prior to the family meetings in one of the most exclusive areas of the city. Operated by a subsidiary of the Korean International Trade Association, COEX was slated to host the trade talks of the Third Asia-Europe Meeting (ASEM) in October of that year, and in its more conventional capacity, COEX was marketed as a full-service venue for international trade shows. COEX's main hall is located near the Korean World Trade Tower, accessible on foot by passing through corridors lined with restaurants and retailers. In fact, these buildings were integrated with a larger shopping and entertainment complex that also included a multiplex cinema, an aquarium, and a discotheque. In Seoul, a city with a history that goes back over two thousand years, there were numerous other sites that would have gestured toward a shared cultural heritage for both Koreas. In contrast, COEX was the urban space that, more than any other building complex at the time in Seoul, represented the contemporary South Korean embrace of capitalist globalization.[3] With its main exhibition hall as the setting of the most anticipated event of the North–South separated-family meetings, the choice of COEX for this event would set up a juxtaposition between two apparently conterveiling impulses: on one hand, the priority accorded to conciliatory efforts toward resolving the painful legacies of Korea's past, and on the other, some degree of Cold War triumphalism conveyed by foregrounding the material culture of South Korea's prosperity.

The schedule for the evening was that the North Korean visitors would be transported from the airport directly to COEX for the initial reunions and a dinner reception, after which they would travel again by bus to stay at the five-star Sheraton Walker Hill Hotel while their South Korean relatives were put up at another location in more modest accommodations. I later spoke with a South Korean security official who was assigned to assist one of the families with whom I had become acquainted in prior weeks. He mentioned that the Walker Hill Hotel had been chosen because its relative seclusion made it more convenient for "security purposes." The implication was that it would lend itself more easily to surveillance, given the site's past associations with the U.S. military and KCIA.[4] That hotel's location on Seoul's eastern side also meant that the delegation from North Korea would be transported throughout the length of the city, first on its initial journey from Kimpo Airport, situated to the west, to Kangnam in the south, and later to the hotel in the east. In this way, North Koreans directly experienced the sprawl of Seoul's urban development and could grasp South Korea's standard of living through the massive number of automobiles that cause congestion on Seoul's urban expressways and thoroughfares. When the initial family meetings took place at COEX, the reunions were delayed because the tour buses ferrying the North Koreans got stuck in traffic several times en route. This security official said he had accompanied one of the buses on that drive through the heart of the city. He said throughout the trip, the visiting family members were careful to keep their heads facing forward so as not to gaze out the windows on either side.

At COEX, the waiting members of the South Korean families sat separately at individually assigned tables, and they seemed dwarfed by the enormity of the room with its vaulted ceilings and expansive dimensions. A large television monitor suspended above the entrances on one side of the room displayed news reports following the North Korean delegation's bus entourage. The originally scheduled time for the Northerners' arrival passed uneventfully due to the traffic delays, and later a participant commented that, knowing her family would be meeting with her brother for the first time in more than fifty years, it was not easy to have to wait yet another hour. When the group finally arrived and disembarked, they walked in a loose single file to an escalator that rose through an atrium lined with glass balconies, specialty shops, and couture boutiques. The North Korean visitors waved as camera flashes went off and bystanders applauded. Crowds of additional relatives, who were not included in the formal reunion group, waited outside the building and along the balconies. Many held handmade signs with their relatives' names written on them, and they called out as the delegation passed. Whenever one of the visitors recognized his or her name with waves and smiles, a cheer went up from a circle of relatives as cameras flashed.

Although direct access was closed to the public, the meetings occurred in full view of the media and other participating families, among those who were permitted into the vaulted hall that was the designated site of the reunions. Access was limited to a pre-selected group comprised of government officials, designated members of the press, and a sizeable Red Cross support team, including one Red Cross worker assigned to each of the participating families. I also received permission to observe the event as a researcher and gained entry to the convention hall, along with my colleague, anthropologist Soo-Jung Lee, though we were asked to abide by several restrictions. When we arrived at the COEX Center, we had to go through security screening, and we were met by a man in a business suit with an earpiece. He was one of the security officials, and he initially escorted us away from the event hall and up several flights of stairs to view the scene from an indoor balcony high above the room. After Soo-Jung and I realized that was supposed to be our perch for doing fieldwork, we pressed him to reconsider, as our vantage there would be worse than simply watching the coverage on television. Fortunately, Soo-Jung managed to persuade him that we needed to do our research observations at closer range, and he agreed to let us return to the ground level of the main room.

Once there, the security official made clear, however, that we were restricted to remaining literally at the margins. That is, the room's perimeter had been marked with tape on the floor, and we were to remain outside the large rectangle of space it enclosed, which included the area where the one hundred tables were arrayed. Lines of tape further divided that rectangular area into four quadrants, like blocking marks on the stage floor for the set of a play. I later found out that the zones divided up the event hall into designated sections for each of four major South Korean television networks to cover. Inside this demarcated area, the reunions would be covered by "pool reports," written by pre-selected journalists, who would share their dispatches with all the other news organizations.[5] Soo-Jung and I were only permitted in the "swing area" outside the taped lines. We were further restricted from taking written notes at the time, nor could we record any images with a camera or other device. We were asked also not to speak with the participating family members, although we each briefly greeted some of the family members that we had met previously. Otherwise, we observed literally from the sidelines. Like the Red Cross workers who had insignia badges pinned to their bright yellow vests, we were also given small Red Cross badges to wear, presumably to indicate our security clearance.

Around the perimeter of the room also stood about two dozen men, who appeared relatively young, in their late twenties and thirties. Wearing dark business suits and discreet earpieces, they looked as if they had been sent by central casting to play the part of fledgling spies. Judging from their steady attentive stances and stoical expressions, it was evident that these men were part of the event's security detail and likely represented a contingent of South Korean intelligent officials. Like us, they wore South Korean Red Cross badges on their lapels too, and I felt uneasy about the visual association, however sutble. While television crews weaved around the room—with some reporters carrying notebooks and others hoisting video cameras or boom mikes—it was the tense watchful presence of these men lent an atmosphere of surveillance more palpable than did the bustling activity of the journalists.

As word arrived that the delegation was finally approaching, some family members rose from their seats and started gathering near the entrances of the convention hall. Each visitor from North Korea was escorted by a "minder," presumably a DPRK intelligence officer, and they made their way toward the family's designated tables where the relatives would meet. Above an excited din, one could hear first the shouting of names and a small cluster of cries, soon followed by loud outbursts of sobbing. With so many families meeting simultaneously, it was impossible to grasp the unfolding scene within a single field of vision. Perhaps the closest one could gain to an overall impression of that moment was to try to capture its ambient sound. Despite having the acoustics of a huge room with a vaulted ceiling, a rolling crescendo of human voices quickly filled the space with a rising swell of aggrieved wails. All one hundred reunions took place within moments of each other, as family members sobbed intensely while clutching each other in tight embraces. Within a few moments, the mood had shifted in the room from restive anticipation to plaintive lamentation. One South Korean participant was overcome with emotion upon meeting her brother, shaking him so vigorously by the shoulders that they fell to the floor. She cried out:

> I thought you had been shot! So we didn't look for you. But your sister went to look for you. You don't know how long she's been looking for you. She climbed mountains and crossed rivers to look for you everywhere. But she couldn't find you. Mother was so happy to have you. You were the only son. She was always looking for you, even in her dreams. When she died, she didn't even close her eyes. How could you? How could you? You go tell her to close her eyes![6]

The Red Cross worker assisting the family eventually came over and eased the woman away from her brother, escorting her back to a chair. Similarly, after their initial encounters, families were gently coaxed to return to seats around their respective tables, and much of the next hour was more subdued. While anguished and tearful episodes still continued as the event went on, many of the gatherings soon resembled that of other families catching up with relatives after a very long absence: asking questions and telling stories, sharing family albums, pouring drinks for each other, laughing and taking pictures together, and simply holding onto each other.

For a South Korean audience, the reunions were experienced vicariously through coverage by their national media. Seoul-based press organizations had far greater access to the venue in their own city—compared to restrictions in Pyongyang on how they could cover the story—and this shaped the way the reunion events were witnessed and perceived by the South Korean public. Throughout the four-day event in Seoul, several hours of continuous programming were dedicated to the event on all the national broadcasting stations and cable news channels. While these meetings were still taking place, the network broadcasters quickly began airing edited compilations of the initial footage on national television, and not surprisingly, the selected video segments included only the most sensational clips. Several wrenching scenes depicting the outpouring of uncontrollable emotion were captured on tape and broadcast over and over again.

A clutch of siblings gripping their arms around each other, shuddering with sobs. An elderly man, his face streaked with tears, cradling the head of his mother. A man, kneeling on the floor, let out a tormented cry for his mother whom he just learned had already died. His hands trembled in the air before he lowered them unsteadily to the floor in a full ritual bow before his senile father in a wheelchair, who looked with a vacant expression. These

Figure 4.1. An image from the initial moments of the inter-Korean family meetings at the COEX Convention Center in Seoul, August 15, 2000. Reproduced with permission from the National Archives of Korea.

scenes were played repeatedly during newscasts, in between news segments, and on network talk shows for several days afterward.

With their ubiquity and repetition in the South Korean media at the time, these video montages seemed less like news coverage and instead furnished a loop of newly iconic images, a visual memorial in the making. They conveyed an emotional intensity to the family meetings that had exceeded their purpose as merely political rituals. Rather, as Kuan-Hsing Chen describes them, the reunions "cut into the affective space of the collective social."[7] Along with journalistic photographs, the media reiteration of such video footage highlighted a spectrum of grief that separated Korean families had endured for decades, for the most part in obscurity. In this chapter, I seek to reconcile these scenes of personal anguish among separated Korean family members with the fact of their public visibility and mass mediation. The public exposure of the reunions stemmed in part from their nature as political rituals, intended to confirm the June 15th Joint Communiqué and to launch a broader range of exchanges between the two Korean states. A ritual narrative was readily conveyed by media portrayals, with the reunions figured as transformative media events. In other words, these events could be read as collec-

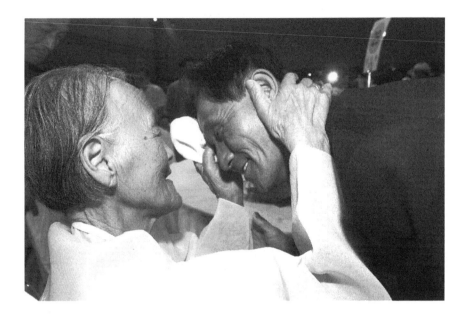

Figure 4.2.   This photograph of an elderly South Korean mother wiping away the tears of her North Korean son became widely circulated as one of the iconic images from the August 2000 reunions. Originally appeared on the front page of the Seoul-based daily newspaper *The Hankyoreh.* © Korea Press Photographers' Association.

tive rites of passage into a prospective post-division era, and the participating family members thereby became symbolically its first initiates.

Yet what are the implications of an official celebration of family bonds for the sake of reconfiguring Cold War suspicions across the 38th parallel, when these same ties of kinship had long rendered those families marginalized and "out of place" in South Korean society? How are we to understand the way in which these intensely emotional and intimate encounters among traumatized family members were made visible to national and international media audiences? In particular, how did these liminal figures of *Wŏlbukcha* (those who had crossed over to the North during the war) become transformed from their former status as vilified public enemies in South Korea, to become elevated as sympathetic figures emblematic of the nation? This transformation also extended to the South Korean families of wartime *Wŏlbukcha*, or those who remained behind in South Korea when a family member crossed to the North fifty years earlier. After they had been stigmatized in the past as social pariahs among South Koreans, members of such families suddenly found themselves in the media spotlight during the August 2000 reunions. Indeed, so prevalent were the iconic images and stories of the reunions at the time that several of the participants became the equivalent of instant media celebrities, at least insofar as they temporarily became highly visible in a positive light in the national news coverage.

In her ethnographic analysis of those reunions, anthropologist Soo-Jung Lee contends this period was the first time that these long-stigmatized families had been portrayed with a positive identification in South Korea.[8] She describes a shift in the expression of public nationalism around the time of the August 2000 reunions that resulted in a transposition of identities among different groups of separated family members. Lee argues that, under previous South Korean governments, the *Wŏllammin* were regarded as emblematic "victims of division" and represented the legitimacy of Cold War–era anticommunist nationalism—thus becoming what Ann Anagnost calls "enunciating subjects" or those who are positioned to "speak for" the nation.[9] However, during the summer of 2000, it was the *Wŏlbukcha* families who emerged instead as enunciated subjects, newly designated to represent the nation and to speak with the force of history.

With respect to this extraordinary reversal, it is salient to note that, in addition to the work of Van Gennep and Turner, the other major theoretical benchmark in the anthropology of liminality comes from Mary Douglas's classic work, *Purity and Danger*, published in 1966. Drawing upon Emile Durkheim's earlier work on classification, Douglas observed that "dirt"—or what any given society regards as pollution—is *not* something intrinsically unclean. Rather, it is deemed to be contamination for being "matter out of place." The notion of impurity therefore exists in inverse relation to socially constructed concepts of order, which presupposes both "a set of ordered relations and a contravention of that order."[10] Being "out of place" further implies not only marginality but also transgression, the crossing of a geographical border or cultural boundary. If pollution for Douglas is what arises from "category mixing" and other deviations from the normative rubric of inclusion and exclusion, liminality accounts for that which does not fit into socially recognized categories.

Similarly, in her work on the cultural subject-positions of those who suffer from chronic pain, medical anthropologist Jean E. Jackson builds upon Douglas's theorizations and analyzes how liminal beings are vulnerable to stigmatization *because* they are between categories. In the case of those who suffer from chronic pain, Jackson observes that Western society accords no designated identity for chronic–pain sufferers, who are viewed negatively, and the fact that they are neither properly well nor properly sick puts them "betwixt and between the statuses of sick and well." They are instead "marked" as outsiders or deviant when outside of a designated role or status.[11] As Douglas argued that rituals are necessary "to unify" those who disrupt the purity of the symbolic order, Jackson contends that "liminality is positively valued only when society provides a special status or role for the liminal object, state, or being."[12] At the same time, it is important to recognize that valorizing liminal beings through the designation of a "special status or role" effectively serves to recalibrate what has been hitherto marginal. Truly, such recalibration represents an inherently political act, particularly where marginal social categories are coded with charged ideological meanings—as has been and continues to be the case for separated Korean families.

With their kin ties caught between the two historically opposing states but also embodying a relationship that precedes the history of national division and inter-state hostility, these separated families divided between North and South Korea can be regarded as quintessential liminal subjects. If we consider displaced persons more generally, liminal beings are at least doubly marginalized in that they inhabit a space of danger peripheral to regimes of citizenship, and this vulnerability further calls them into question as figures that pose a political and symbolic threat to the prevailing social order.[13] This is particularly true of Korean separated families with non-normative kin relations, for whom it is not their own transgression but the known or alleged border-crossing of a member of their kin group that renders them marginal, as they were perceived as threatening sources of potential pollution in the context of anticommunist South Korea.[14]

As political rituals that elided national and familial idioms, the reunion events in 2000 focused on separated families as tragic victims of the war and division. Images issuing from these reunions were highly poignant and at times sensationalist, and the extensive media coverage collectively generated a national allegory of long-suffering South Korean mothers tearfully receiving the return of their anguished and repentant North Korean sons. Precisely because of the fact that this event involved an embodied, physical encounter between family members, it is critical to consider the gendered aspects of the North–South reunions. This was especially true of those involving elderly mothers, which contributed toward a disproportionate emphasis on the reunions in Seoul, as discussed below. Such representations portraying an idealized relationship between mothers and sons served to downplay the politically controversial aspects of the reunions, recasting the *Wŏlbukcha* families as sympathetic national figures, mediated through an appropriation of traditional gender roles in the Korean family. In light of the significance ascribed to the persistence of sentimental attachment among reuniting family members, the interplay between gender, nation, and affective intensity is fundamental to the construction of reunited separated families as representative national subjects in the milieu of inter-Korean reconciliation.

IRONIC VISIBILITY

At the moment when interest and visibility surrounding the issue of wartime family separation reached its peak in South Korea, those who became featured as *the* iconic "separated families" in media images and press accounts were those who, prior to that point, would not have even been recognized as belonging to the sympathetic nationalist category of "separated families" (*isan'gajok*). How did this ironic reversal occur? Such a turnabout is all the more striking when one considers that formerly non-normative and marginalized families became highly visible, while the former normative families became relatively obscured in the coverage of these events. That is, simultaneously with the Seoul reunions, a similar event of separated-family reunions was occurring in Pyongyang among one hundred visiting South Koreans, each of whom would also meet five of their relatives.

The reunions in Pyongyang were broadcast with far less fanfare, and that footage was delayed in part due to technical reasons. While there were also highly emotional scenes of tearful reunions in Pyongyang, the South Korean print and broadcast news outlets largely downplayed them, focusing instead on those held in Seoul.

This disparity in exposure stemmed in part from the discrepancy in logistical support for the journalists covering the events. Only twenty South Korean journalists were permitted to travel with the delegation that went to Pyongyang. In contrast to the many press restrictions in North Korea, the pool of reporters in Seoul had far greater access and freedom to shoot extensive on-site footage of the family meetings. The broadcasts of events taking place in Pyongyang would prove to be noticeably more subdued, compared to the relatively unrestrained and sensationalized reporting of events in Seoul, which also became the focus of the reunions' international media coverage.

Demographics also played a role in the disproportionate emphasis placed on the meetings in Seoul. The candidates for the reunions in South Korea were chosen by computer based on an algorithm that weighted criteria based on their age and the closeness of their relationship, with highest priority accorded to the elderly and those with parent-child ties. Therefore, those selected in the South—most of whom were in their late seventies and eighties—were too old to have surviving parents in the North. In what had initially appeared to be one exception, a seventy-six-year-old man residing in Busan was informed that he could expect to meet his mother, receiving the incredible news that she was still alive at the age of 110. Yet, within days, those reports of his mother's survival were found to be in error. Among the South Korean delegation who went to Pyongyang for reunions, all parent-child reunions therefore involved South Koreans meeting with their children in Pyongyang. Rather than joyous occasions, these meetings carried overtones of guilt for the parents who had left their offspring behind, even when the circumstances of separation were unavoidable due to the chaos of war. Such fraught emotional burdens posed considerable challenges for the media because the members of these families were far less inclined to be interviewed or to speak in front of the camera.

In the international media as well as in the South Korean news outlets, the events in Seoul would instead become representative of these historic family reunions. Indeed, meetings involving North Koreans returning to reunite with their elderly parents in Seoul lent themselves far more readily to the melodramatic media narratives favored in the South Korean coverage.[15] The majority of those who went north of the border during the Korean War—including students and military recruits, as well as leftist intellectuals—were significantly younger than the eldest survivors of the war refugee population, which had represented a far wider cross-section of those with origins in the northern provinces.[16] This demographic disparity partly explains why, at least during the "first-round" reunions in August 2000, no Southerners were able to meet their parents while the Northern delegation included twelve who had surviving parents in South Korea, ten mothers and two fathers. Furthermore, reunion participants from the North were chosen not by age but according to criteria of political status, party loyalty, and professional achievement. That is, selected on the basis of what were deemed their contributions to the state, members of the North Korean delegation included noted poet Oh Yŏng-Jae and prominent linguist Ryu Ryŏl, as well as high-ranking Party members and others with privileged positions in North Korean society.[17] The inclusion of prominent North Korean cultural figures also contributed to the disproportionate attention that the South Korean media placed on the Seoul reunions.

MOTHER POWER AND NATIONAL INTIMACY

Despite the diversity of family compositions and a disproportionately high number of siblings, the photographs and footage that became among the most representative of the inter-Korean family meetings in Seoul were those depicting a reunion between mother and son.[18] On the morning following the initial family meetings on August 15, the major national daily newspapers in South Korea ran their respective version of the seemingly timeless motif of *moja sangbong* (reunion between mother and son).

Under banner headlines that read "Pyongyang and Seoul Both Cried" and "A Sea of Tears," the images that captured the emotional nature of the scenes of these family meetings were dominated by variations on this theme, showing a mother and son in a tender embrace. The iconic value assigned to such images was evident in the initial coverage of the reunions, and it would become reinforced in later days and weeks. For example, in one major daily newspaper, all stories related to the reunions would be identified with a small inset graphic showing a widely circulated photographic image of an elderly mother wiping a tear from the cheek of her grown son. (See figure 4.2.) Meanwhile, on the Sunday immediately following the reunions, the state-run television station KBS devoted its most coveted prime-time slot to *Mother's Tears*, a documentary that featured vignettes about eight different South Korean mothers who had participated in the family meetings in Seoul.

The heavy exposure given to the stories of mothers in South Korea was hardly anecdotal, and instead reflected advance preparations on the part of the event's organizers as well as media crews. At the site of the reunions, journalists covering the Seoul event circulated photocopied diagrams depicting the room layout with a pattern of circles to represent the tables of the reuniting families. This makeshift blueprint was divided into quadrant, each labeled with the name of the broadcasting station responsible for its coverage—including the MBC and SBS networks, the twenty-four-hour news channel YTN, and the public broadcasting network KBS. Marked on the diagram were twenty circles highlighted for special attention; that is, families of prominent North Korean figures, as well as the ten families that included surviving mothers.

Recognizing the centrality of mothers to the meaning of the reunions was not, however, solely a media construction. In my own field interviews, it was not uncommon to hear a reunion participant emphasize what the meeting meant or would have meant to his or her mother when describing the impact of the event on their family. One reunion participant downplayed the significance of his own imminent reunion with his elder brother, acknowledging that the meeting would not mean as much as it would to a family with surviving parents. "A mother meeting her son and a younger brother meeting his elder brother is the difference between heaven and earth," he said, using a common Korean expression to characterize the disparity as worlds apart. Similarly, in the KBS documentary *Mother's Tears*, one man who was interviewed while preparing for the reunions expressed his gratitude toward his elder brother for living long enough to meet their mother during the reunions, thus relieving the *han*, or unresolved bitterness, she had carried from believing she had lost her first-born in the war. "This is really a matter between *ŏmŏni* and *hyŏng*," he said, referring to his mother and elder brother. "The rest of us are just supporters. We're all just supporting them."

Compared to the sentimental portrayal of mother-son stories in the coverage of the August reunions, the meetings between husbands and wives revealed notably more awkwardness and tension. Despite the idealization of reunited lovers in dissident historical narratives, actual attempts to bring together separated spouses from the North and South proved rather problematic. Because of the traditional stigma against the remarriage of widows, in most cases women never married again while their husbands began second families with new wives on the opposite side of the border after the Korean

War. In real life, bringing attention to a wife's chastity highlighted the double standard that allowed men in both Koreas to remarry without social recrimination, and suggested a betrayal toward the first wife and the children left behind. Nevertheless, in the discourses and imagery surrounding the separated-family reunions, faithful women emerge as central agents of reconciliation, although they did so more in the capacity as mothers than as wives.

In official and popular discourses, the invocation of motherhood as a symbol of social unity at moments of commemoration is not unique to Korea.[19] But the emotional intimacy of the relationship between mother and son bears a particular historical and cultural context there. Based on Confucian kinship norms surrounding the Korean patriarchal family, the father-son relationship was traditionally regarded as the core of the hegemonic patrilineal family system, as the *chip* (translated as "family" or "household") was to continue permanently through the connections formed over generations between father and son.[20] A strict demeanor characterized the normative disposition of fathers, withholding outward affection so as to instruct their sons with stern authority and, even in contemporary settings, grown Korean men often report feeling uncomfortable in their fathers' presence.

In contrast, the most intimate and enduring emotional ties could be found in the small, more cohesive unit that centered on the mother, or what anthropologist Margery Wolf has elsewhere described as the "uterine family." This alternative formation of kinship and belonging is understood to develop outside the norms of Confucian patriarchy. Wolf writes, "The uterine family has no ideology, no formal structure, and no public existence. It is built out of sentiments and loyalties that die with its members, but it is no less real for all that. The descent lines of men are born and nourished in the uterine families of women, and it is here that a male ideology that excludes women makes its accommodations with reality."[21] In a system of authority based on the father-son relationship, the mother forms the center of emotional security in the family through what Kwang-Kyu Lee calls an "affectional structure" provided by the mother-centered relationship.[22]

In considering the implications of the uterine family concept for Korean family separation, what is striking is the explicit assumption that the strongest sentimental ties will die out with the mother, leaving only ties of duty for the next generation. Insofar as the North–South separated families embody the affective bonds that would transcend national division, the most compelling motivations for family reunification are also subject to the relentless fact of human mortality.

Such was the implication behind a story that unfolded in the lead-up to the reunions, focusing attention on a one-hundred-year-old South Korean woman named Cho Wŏn Ho. There was speculation as to whether the great-grandmother, as the eldest person to participate in the reunions, would be able to recognize her son despite her impairment of sight, hearing, and memory. At the start of the reunions, relatives excitedly made way for this particularly momentous mother-son meeting. Yet rather than greet her son in sorrow or elation, Cho Wŏn Ho *Halmŏni* peered through her thick glasses and, in a slightly gravelly voice, asked him matter-of-factly, "Why are you coming so late like this?" Her response implied not only recognition of her son but also the chiding familiarity of maternal intimacy. By gently but firmly scolding him, she conveyed a tone that indicated how she had never questioned he was still alive. As Cho's son said after meeting his mother, "The reason for her long life was her will to see me." Indeed, a few families told of how their aged mothers had miraculously recovered from Alzheimer's disease upon hearing the news that they would meet their lost children again, and others described how their mothers adamantly had refused to change residences for the past fifty years out of fear that their missing child would not be able to find their way home.

Still, the reunions were not only a celebration of unlikely survival stories but also inevitably a time of mourning. This was particularly true for families who grieved the death of a long-suffering parent who had died in recent years or even recent weeks prior to the reunions. Among these families, the reunions were pervaded with a sense of melancholic belatedness because of the absence of those to whom the event would have carried the greatest meaning. For example, although two fathers participated in the Seoul reunions, the only meeting between father and son that received national television coverage occurred between Rim Jae-hyŏk and his ninety-year-old father, Rim Hui-kyŏng. The North Korean son was himself nearly seventy years old, but next to his father he looked younger than his age. "Father! It's me, Jae-hyŏk. I finally came!" shouted the son repeatedly, while the father looked blankly from his wheelchair and remained unresponsive to the events surrounding him. Due to his senility, the frail elder Rim was unable to recognize his son, and he sat impassively throughout the reunions. But rather than an encounter between father and son, this meeting became best remembered as a heartbreaking scene of mourning for the absent mother. The son knelt down to greet his father in a traditional deep bow, sobbing inconsolably while on his knees and wailing, "Where is Mother? Why is Mother not sitting beside you?" A vivid display of anguish and pathos, the scene was broadcast repeatedly on national television even several days after the reunions ended. Far less circulated was a question picked up on the audio feed of the initial coverage, when one of Rim's brothers asked him with an edge of bitterness, "What did you do in the North until our father became so old and unable to recognize you?"

Moreover, the physical presence and frailty of the most elderly mothers served to intensify the dramatic suspense of the reunions. An ongoing saga during the August reunions was whether the eighty-eight-year-old Kim Ae-ran, suffering from severe anemia, would be permitted to see her son, Yang

Han-sang. She had been scheduled to participate in one of the ambulance reunions, but her doctors subsequently ruled it out. It was reported that her condition made it dangerous for her to travel even the brief forty-minute ambulance ride to the reunion site. The North and South Korean Red Cross officials deliberated over the matter and agreed that Yang could not leave the hotel to visit his mother's home, since that was against the rules of the family exchange visits. Suspense built over whether an exception would be permitted, as video clips showed the elderly mother watching the reunion events on television from her bed at home. After three days of negotiation, the Red Cross officials agreed to permit Yang to meet his mother at a third location, provided it was not her home. At 4:00 a.m., six hours prior to his return to Pyongyang, the mother and son met for thirty minutes in a private hospital room at Shinchon Severance Hospital. When they met, Kim cried out, "Ah, who is this? Why are you so late [in returning]?" Yang knelt on the floor to bow, and then came over to embrace his mother where she was lying in the hospital bed, saying, "Forgive me, Mother. It's me, Han-sang. I am so sorry." At the end of their meeting, the son told his mother he had to depart, and she cried, "You can't go! You can't! Don't go! Where are you going without me?" He tried to comfort his mother, saying "You have to live for a very long time, Mother. I will come back." The son remained by his mother's bedside with his head bowed for several minutes, but then was told he had to leave.

While Kim Ae-ran *Halmŏni*'s story unfolded in an arc that played on melodramatic tropes, more visceral and fleeting scenes were among the most moving images captured during the reunions. These included the "ambulance reunions," which had been arranged for two mothers who were too frail to take part in the regular program. In the taped footage of one such reunion, a klieg light flashes into the ambulance's dim interior through a rear door, revealing the grown son sobbing and heaving with tears as he bent over the gurney bearing his debilitated mother, whose gaunt, brittle appearance gave the impression that she was barely alive. These family meetings took place at the outer physical limit of human survival. Their raw anguish provided particularly arresting and heartbreaking media images, evoking the countless separated family members who had not lived to see the reunions come to pass.

FAMILY MEETINGS IN PYONGYANG

On the planning side, considerable effort had gone into trying achieve a balance between the reunions in Seoul and those in Pyongyang, but the latter lacked such moments of emotional intensity. The start of those family meetings in Pyongyang was also delayed, though not by traffic. Instead, the family meetings were put on hold for an hour to ensure that they would occur at the same time as the Seoul events. Both sets of reunions occurred in ostensibly parallel circumstances, with a group of one hundred families meeting at separate tables in a hotel ballroom, though the Koryo Hotel could not compare with the outsized scale of the COEX setting. The footage from the North was broadcast on South Korean television, but the difference was immediately apparent, as the atmosphere during the Pyongyang reunions was markedly somber.

In Seoul, I was speaking with a South Korean Red Cross volunteer shortly after the initial reunions took place; she was relieved to see that the coverage of the events in Seoul were very positive. She said, smiling broadly, "Things were better on this side. It was better than the meetings in the North, which were more quiet. It was not as emotional as it was here." Her comment reflected how comparisons would inevitably be drawn between the simultaneous events, and the Seoul events were more successful in her eyes because they were more "emotional," as one would expect given the fraught circumstances.

Indeed, the starkest differences between the two events in Seoul and Pyongyang were affective. In his study of Korean separated families, the sociologist James Foley describes the extreme disappointment of one of the Pyongyang reunion participants who went to meet his wife and daughter in North Korea, only to encounter a chilly reception. His wife had no memory of him, and his daughter did not hide her misgivings about the reunion. The South Korean father said,

> To tell the truth, I didn't cry . . . couldn't cry. My feelings didn't come out. Why? Because "I have lived so well because of Kim Il-sung" that kind of thing. . . . We couldn't really communicate because of that. My wife, my siblings, our daughter, none of them could speak properly. . . . It wasn't the place for it. There wasn't the atmosphere for loving small talk. It wasn't because we were being watched, it was just that ideologically we were so different, how could we talk with feeling? I didn't talk much. On that side, what could I say to someone who was a Workers Party member and who had "lived his life for Kim Jong-il"?[23]

This father spoke about the feeling of "difference" (*ijilgam*) that results from the vast dissimilarities in education, politics, and culture in the two Korean societies.[24] He goes on to describe not only the lack of "loving words" among his family and jarring ideological rhetoric, but also an immediate overtone of resentment and recrimination from his North Korean daughter. He describes how they did not recognize each other at first. "Then I called my daughter's name, but she didn't run up to see me. She prostrated herself in a deep bow and said: 'Father, why have you come?'"[25]

His daughter's reproachful reception is understandable for several reasons. The father would have been resented for presumably having deserted his family. The families of those who departed from North Korea have historically been disfavored in North Korea's hierarchical society where class status is based on origin. In some cases their hardships could be surmised through physical appearance, such as a lean build, though all of the North Korean family members were dressed neatly—the women in traditional dresses and the men in Western-style suits. North Korea is a totalitarian state with a highly structured society where the social hierarchy is based on a system of social ranking, or *songbun*, which is assigned based on family origin and the perceived degree of loyalty to the state. North Koreans are divided into three main groups: "core" (*haekshim kyech'ung*), "vacillating" (*tongyo kyech'ung*), and "enemy" (*choktae kyech'ung*). Except for the core group, others are not regarded as completely trustworthy by the state. *Songbun* affected one's life chances by influencing access to education, housing, types of employment, and prospects for marriage.[26] This was particularly true prior to the death in 1994 of the first North Korean leader Kim Il-sung, and after his death the state exerted steadily less control over the daily activities of private life.[27] Those North Koreans who are part of separated families are generally regarded as belonging to the vacillating group; having relatives who fled South during the Korean War could be one reason for political and social discrimination, though this was not universally the case.[28]

The affective dimension of the reunions, which differed strikingly between the Seoul and Pyongyang locations, also suggested two different levels of ritual at work. On the South Korean side, the conventions of political ritual were in a sense exceeded by the emotional responses of the family members. On the North Korean side, in the formal context of the family meetings, there were also performances of state loyalty,[29] which the South Koreans reported as upsetting. The father who met his wife and daughter in Pyongyang conveys his alienation in the face of this profound incongruity: "My first words were: 'It must have been hard for you, how have you managed?' They answered coolly: 'Thanks to our Great General, we have lived well and without any worries.' At these words I went cold inside. . . . In such a situation, what was I going to say?"[30] In a widely cited definition of ritual in the anthropological literature, its chief characteristics are summarized as follows: a "patterned and ordered sequences of words and acts, often expressed in multiple media, whose content and arrangement are characterized in varying degree by formality (conventionality), stereotypy (rigidity), condensation (fusion), and redundancy (repetition)."[31] If one also adds the element of "compulsion" discussed by anthropologists Pascal Boyer and Pierre Lienard,[32] the properties of ritual closely align with South Korean expectations of the North Korean delegates prior to the reunions. In fact, the reunions in Seoul—compared to those in Pyongyang—made a such a powerful impact among South Koreans precisely because the spontaneous expressions of emotion and familial devotion went against assumptions that the Northerners would show little deviation from scripted social performances of state loyalty.

For the general public in South Korea, these scenes of remorse or anguish arguably did more to humanize North Koreans than perhaps any other single event up to that time. As critical events facilitating the transformation of North Koreans "from enemies to brethren" in the national imaginary, the reunions marked the highest point of approval among South Koreans for the Sunshine Policy, peaking at nearly 88 percent in favor of engagement with North Korea in August 2000, compared to 49 percent earlier that year in February and approximately 75 percent at the time of the June Summit.[33] On the day following the reunions, I spoke with a cab driver in his forties from Seoul who expressed it this way: "Do you know the word 'brainwashing'?" I had asked him his impression of the reunions, and from this question I was expecting him to criticize the North Koreans. Instead, he said something quite different. "We were taught that the North Koreans are brainwashed. But, you know, I think we were brainwashed, too." After a pause, he continued, saying that it was difficult to explain the depth of hatred that he, like other South Koreans, had been taught to have toward North Koreans. "When I was younger I really thought it's better for them to die. We wanted them to die as our enemies," he said. "But watching the reunions, I felt that kind of education was wrong." He spoke of South Korean anticommunist propaganda, in which North Koreans were demonized and portrayed literally with horns growing from their heads. Such propaganda is generally associated with the period under military authoritarian governments. However, even at the turn of the millennium in South Korea, progressive South Korean filmmaker Kim Dong-won describes in his documentary *Repatriation* how he was still felt residual effects of the trepidation and prejudice he had acquired from growing up with fearsome portrayals of North Koreans with horns and fangs.

Despite the generally positive reception of the August 2000 reunions in South Korea, the dramatic displays of emotion by members of the North Korean delegation was apparently not regarded favorably by DPRK authorities. At least, this is what can be surmised, judging from the change of behavior among the North Korean participants of the second round of reunions, which were held in mid-winter of that year (November 30–December 2, 2000). In contrast to the penitent supplications some North Koreans had made to their parents during the first round of reunions, no one asked for forgiveness or made comments about being unfilial during the second round. Also, the second group was also on average younger, and therefore fewer North Koreans had parents who were of advanced old age, compared to the first group. According to a Ministry of Unification official with whom I spoke afterwards, it was clear at the second round of reunions that the North Koreans made a deliberate attempt to appear happy. This official said it was as if they were told that this should be a joyful occasion and they have nothing to be sad about.

Another difference between the August and November reunions was that the second group seemed to be of a somewhat lower status in North Korean society than the first group. They therefore were apparently even less free to speak about their own personal lives or to show their emotions in public. Indeed, some of the South Korean family members expressed disappoint-ment afterwards over the fact that their relatives from North Korea shed no tears at the initial group reunion and instead talked continuously about reun-ification and the Great General. The adjective commonly used to describe such encounters was "stiff" (*ttakttakhae*), which implies they were unemo-tional and in this case ideological in tone. In another field interview, I spoke with a middle-aged Seoul resident who said such rigidity made it more pain-ful to meet. His elder brother's composed demeanor did falter, however, when their South Korean family members spoke about memories of their deceased mother, who wrote in her diary about him every day until she passed away. When they brought out the mother's diary to show him, the elder brother started to choke up and shut the book right away, making great efforts to restrain himself. It was only later, during the private reunions, that he read through their mother's diary more closely and cried among his family members, the younger brother said.

REUNIONS AND EMOTIONAL TRANSPARENCY

This contrast between the first and second round of reunions brings attention to the fact that, as affecting as the visible expressions of emotions were during the broadcast of the earlier August reunions, it was also unsettling to have such an intimate event fully televised in a public setting. At moments of extreme anguish or emotional distress, the reuniting family members were mobbed by camera crews and photographers. Many families complained about the press and said that they had tried to refuse giving interviews, but the reporters were unstoppable and they eventually gave in. "Time was so short, and the interviews took up our precious time," said one of the family members when recalling the reunions in the days afterward. When I asked a Ministry of Unification official about this sentiment, he replied that they had initially attempted to guard the families from the press but eventually gave up as well, saying that it was easier to protect the families by cooperating with the reporters than by trying to restrict them.[34]

Indeed, the access given via the national and international press to witness these heart-wrenching scenes exceeded the privacy that would have been accorded to normal citizens handling such emotionally complicated and often overwhelming personal matters. Yet because of the continuation of separate regimes that divides these families, these brief reunions were far from private matters. In South Korea, the extensive media exposure of participants in the separated-family reunions occurred at a time when government-level negotiations between the two Koreas were highly secretive. In a sense, the ostensibly "public" space of inter-state negotiations became private and concealed, while the "private" space of families was made public through extensive coverage of the family meetings in Seoul by a freewheeling South Korean press corps. Morris argues that such "alternative performances of transparency" can foster the understanding that secrets inevitably remain undisclosed elsewhere. [35]

In October 2000 came the announcement that President Kim Dae-jung won the Nobel Peace Prize, bringing global recognition to the inter-Korean breakthroughs and signifying the fulfillment of a long-held popular aspiration to have a South Korean join the ranks of Nobel laureates. Yet a damper on the public reaction was the criticism leveled against the engagement policy regarding the lack of openness about North–South Korean dialogue, which was not subject to public debate or scrutiny. On the one hand, given the sensitivities of dealing with North Korea in a politically divided climate, it would not have been realistic to expect the Kim Dae-jung administration to subject those ongoing negotiations to public scrutiny. On the other hand, that secrecy fueled rumors about what was being negotiated behind closed doors and gave rise to the expression, "*tonŭro satta*," or "it was bought with money." The insinuation was that the summit—and by extension the peace prize—came at the expense of the money given to the North Koreans in order to make them more amenable to South Korean engagement overtures. Even one of my informants who was openly supportive of the Sunshine Policy surprised me at lunch one afternoon by trying to calculate how much each family reunion cost, explaining that the reunions were obviously "paid for" through South Korean aid to the DPRK.

Such suspicions culminated in what became known as the "cash-for-summit" scandal when, in March 2003, a South Korean independent counsel began a formal investigation into $450 million in cash remittances made by the Hyundai conglomerate to North Korea shortly prior to the summit. Amid perceptions that this amounted to a quid pro quo arrangement, the reality was in fact more complicated. Related legal proceedings eventually led to eight indictments—of four government officials, two Hyundai executives, and two bank executives—for violating laws related to the process and disclosure of these transactions, and in concluding its investigation, the independent counsel found the remittances closely linked with the summit but stopped short of calling them bribes.

In *South Korean Engagement Policies and North Korea: Identities, Norms and the Sunshine Policy*, Son Key-young sorts out the complex issues surrounding these cash remittances in a detailed analysis.[36] Son explains the background to Hyundai's involvement and discusses how, from the outset of the Sunshine Policy, the Kim Dae-jung administration's agenda of comprehensive engagement had complementary interests with Hyundai's own projects in North Korea. Hyundai had undertaken a strategy of making massive investments in North Korea, whose infrastructure was badly in need of modernization, in order to secure rights to a wide range of large-scale development projects, including railways, power generation, and a joint venture to turn Mount Kumgang into a tourist destination. The conglomerate sought to monopolize those development projects and edge out competitors at a time when North Korea was beginning to form diplomatic ties with countries in Western Europe and elsewhere. That diplomatic opening itself reflected the growing influence at the time of a moderate group within the North Korean elite, represented by the KAPPC (Korea Asia-Pacific Peace Committee), which favored a pragmatic multilateral approach and supported engagement with South Korea. Officials within the KAPPC differed from the military hardliners who were focused almost exclusively on North Korea's relationship with the United States. By the time South Korean officials were searching to develop contacts for negotiation with their counterparts on the other side, Hyundai had already developed close relationships with North Korean officials who favored engagement.[37]

Inter-Korean negotiations to arrange the June Summit were therefore three-way negotiations that integrally involved Hyundai from the start. Meanwhile, Hyundai and North Korea reached a tentative deal on seven infrastructure projects on May 3, 2000, just six weeks before the summit. In connection with that deal, despite concerns among South Korean officials over the transfer of cash to North Korea, they helped Hyundai secure enormous preferential loans in order to make the remittances possible so as to provide a guarantee demonstrating the seriousness of the South's economic cooperation plans. Son quotes from his interview with Deputy Unification Minister Hwang Ha-soo: "The North Korean government started to believe the South Korean government, since it allowed Hyundai to pay the cash in spite of US objections. It reached the conclusion that the Kim administration was somewhat different from the previous governments."[38] When leaks about these transfers later emerged, South Korean conservatives cried foul and vigorously clamored for the launch of an independent probe. On February 22, 2003, President Kim Dae-jung would appear on national television to issue a formal apology, saying, "I am very sorry for causing such deep concern to our people because of a controversy over Hyundai's remittances." Emphasizing the need to prevent war on the Korean peninsula and to bring about peace and prosperity, he appealed for understanding from the public by saying, "The government allowed the payment despite a legal problem because it judged that doing so would benefit our national interest and work toward peace."[39] Again, this controversy reveals the repeated clashes within South Korea between those who accepted and rejected the policy of "comprehensive engagement"—or engagement through all possible means—as a strategy to overcome the state of unresolved war in Korea.[40]

For all its optimistic ambitions, the Kim Dae-jung administration could not simply undo the effects of five decades of anti–North Korean enmity and mistrust among the South Korean public to win enough support for the economic integration plan. Thus, when other forms of transparency were impossible, what separated family members possessed and were called upon to contribute to Korean reconciliation amounted to an emotional transparency. The reunions grounded the inter-Korean reconciliation process in the realm of direct experiences between relatives whose ties preceded national division. In this way, the reunions could be understood to reflect a larger process of working out a new model of "national intimacy,"[41] one that tied the intimacy of these family encounters to an emergent intimacy of the nation that could conceivably encompass both Koreas. With its repeated mass-mediated images affirming the ties of blood and affect that remained between the two Koreas, this model of national intimacy served to allegorize South Korea's economic embrace of North Korea.

Reunion images were highly poignant and at times sensationalistic, and the encounters among these family members revealed anguished cathectic bonds, which made possible a kind of agency for the state that no sterile cost-benefit analysis could offer. In light of the significance ascribed to the persistence of sentimental attachment among family members at the reunions, the interplay between gender, nation, and affective intensity is fundamental to the construction of reunited separated families as representative national subjects in the milieu of inter-Korean reconciliation. To demonstrate how a striking and palpable change had taken place in the state of North–South Korean relations, the reunions as a vehicle of affective transmission therefore appropriated the promise of ritual transformation, in which the separated families played a central role as liminal entities.

CODA: A MEMORIAL OF NAMES

At the site of the August 2000 family meetings in Seoul, an enormous mural ran along the entire length of one wall. The central figures appeared somewhat blurred and out of focus, as if to resemble a palimpsest. However, older South Koreans would readily recognize that it evoked a familiar image. It depicted a middle-aged man looking anguished while reaching for the hand of a placid-faced elderly woman, a son reuniting with his mother. This ex-

pressive photograph was taken during the first inter-Korean reunions of separated families in 1985, the only prior instance when such meetings had
taken place. In 2000, that portrait was enlarged and printed on a screen
measuring sixty meters wide. In the background of this famous mother-son
image, a faint pattern suggests the presence of an extraordinarily large audience, but one barely visible beyond the footlights of a stage. During the
August 2000 reunions in Seoul, this horizontal mural provided the backdrop
to the scene where members of one hundred separated families gathered after
a half-century of absence, uncertainty, and mourning. Seen from across the
room, the oversized print appeared hazy, as if stippled. Viewed up close, the
contours of the photographic image would give way to an expanse of tiny
Korean characters. The picture was in fact a mosaic of syllables, computer-
generated tiles of *hangŭl*, nearly all appearing in clusters of three. Given the
repetition of common Korean surnames, anyone familiar with the language
could recognize that this digitized rendering, which depicted a haunting image of reunion, was in fact comprised of an immense roster of personal
names. Each of the tens of thousands of names represented a South Korean
who had applied through the Red Cross or the Ministry of Unification in
hopes to arrange a meeting with a relative who they believed or surmised
may still be alive in North Korea.

   Totaling more than 116,000 names at the time, the South Korean appli-
cant pool of those who had originally applied for reunions was itself only a
fraction of the estimated overall number of separated families. In the days
after the August 2000 reunions, several people called into the current events
talk radio shows to comment on how the reunions program was woefully
inadequate for addressing the mammoth scale of the dilemma. It was common to hear the calculation that if there were reunions held every month
among one hundred families, it would take nearly a century for all the applicants to meet their relatives. With so many separated family members in their
advanced old age, it was clear that the great majority would not survive to
experience their own family reunions, whether temporary or permanent.

   Writing on the use of names in memorials, historian Daniel Sherman
observes that names signify the memory of individuals within collective
commemoration. The presence of names, he argues, represents the "fruits of
mass democracy," marking a fundamental shift from earlier modes of tribute
that glorified the memory of leaders while the rank-and-file soldiers were
relegated to oblivion in mass graves. Sherman writes, "In this dichotomy
names constitute signs of mourning, expressing an individual and communal
grief indifferent, if not actively hostile, to the ideology of patriotism and
military glory."[42] Implicit in the mosaic of personal names was this tension
between commemorating collective and individual losses. It offered a tribute
to surviving separated family members, while also anticipating a commemoration of the losses in the future, as it would be logistically impossible

to fulfill all of the submitted requests for reunion. Like a silent witness, the mosaic scaled high above the scene that centered on the reuniting family members as protagonists, surrounded by an entourage of Red Cross volunteers, state officials, intelligence agents, journalists, and other observers. Fashioned out of the names of those who could not themselves participate in this scene, the mosaic attested to the scale and urgency of an enduring crisis in kinship, which itself represented the legacies of war and division in Korea. The lengthy register of names, which made up the entirety of the mural's image, therefore carried an overtone of melancholic prolepsis, as if it were a memorial before its time.

NOTES

1. The airport is today named the Gimpo International Airport, with spelling that conforms to the Revised Romanization system released to the public by the South Korean government on July 7, 2000. At the time of the August 2000 reunions, the airport was still known by its old spelling, and it was by far South Korea's largest and most prominent international airport. That distinction would soon be taken over by the new Incheon International Airport when it opened on March 29, 2001. After that point, the older airport would retain its designation as an "international airport," but Gimpo would be mainly used for domestic flights within South Korea, as well some short-haul regional shuttles generally from lower-tier airports in China, Japan, and Taiwan. It should be noted that, in contrast to how it would likely be perceived today, the fact that the North Korean delegations during the 2000–2001 reunions all landed at Gimpo International Airport did not at the time either carry the connotation that it was necessarily a "domestic" Korean flight, or relegate the status of the Air Koryo flight to one originating from an "alternate" or minor airport.

2. Wendy Brown, *Walled States, Waning Sovereignty* (New York: Zone Books, 2010), 26.

3. As an indication of the plasticity of the urban landscape in Seoul, only a little more than a decade later, the COEX mall fell behind the trendy South Korean standards for premium retail space to the extent that it was overhauled for a full-scale renovation, requiring the entire mall to be closed for several months in 2013–2014.

4. The hotel is known today as the Sheraton Grande Walkerhill, a five-star hotel complex that also houses a casino and convention center. However, in the 1950s it catered initially to the U.S. military, as indicated by its namesake, Walton Walker, the first field commander of U.S. forces in Korea who died in a jeep accident in December, 1950. Historian Michael Seth describes the Walker Hill Hotel's subsequent status as a KCIA operation, "a gambling resort for foreigners used to gain access to foreign exchange." See Seth, *A Concise History of Modern Korea: From the Late Nineteenth Century to the Present* (Lanham, MD: Rowman & Littlefield, 2010), 156.

5. This was also the controversial approach to the press that the first Bush administration assumed during the first Gulf War, and the comparison is a reminder that the two Koreas are still technically at war.

6. Pool press report, Korean Overseas Information Service, Seoul, Korea (August 15, 2000).

7. Kuan Hsing Chen, *Asia as Method: Toward Deimperialization* (Durham, NC: Duke University Press, 2010), 116.

8. Soo-Jung Lee, "Making and Unmaking the Korean National Division," PhD dissertation, University of Illinois, 2006; see also "*T'alnaengjŏn minjok spekt'ŏk'ŭl,*" *Minjok munhwa yŏngu* 59 (2013): 95–122.

9. See Ann Anagnost, *National Past-Times: Narrative, Representation, and Power in Modern China* (Durham, NC: Duke University Press), 4.

10. Mary Douglas, *Purity and Danger: An Analysis of Concepts of Pollution and Taboo* (New York: Praeger, 1966), 48.

11. Jean E. Jackson, "Stigma, Liminality, and Chronic Pain: Mind-body Borderlands," *American Ethnologist* 32, no. 3 (2005): 332–53. As is true of much of the literature on social stigma, Jackson's work draws upon the seminal study by Erving Goffman, *Stigma: Notes on the Management of Spoiled Identity* (Englewood Cliffs, NJ: Prentice-Hall, 1963). Goffman defined stigma as "an attribute that is deeply discrediting" which reduces the bearer "from a whole and usual person to a tainted, discounted one" (3). Notably, Jackson's related analysis that liminal identity is itself a "mark," which can be negative or positive in meaning, contrasts with how the quality of being "betwixt and between" was celebrated in Turner's interpretations of liminality for its transformative capacity and *resistance* to categorization, as Turner put it, "without markings of differentiation or distinction."

12. Jackson, "Stigma, Liminality, and Chronic Pain," 333.

13. For an interpretation of Douglas's theoretical discussion with respect to the contemporary social and territorial displacement of refugees, see Liisa H. Malkki, *Purity and Exile: Violence, Memory, and National Cosmology Among Hutu Refugees in Tanzania* (Chicago: University of Chicago Press, 1995).

14. Kwon, Heonik, "Korean War Traumas," *The Asia Pacific Journal: Japan Focus* 38.2, no. 10 (2010), http://japanfocus.org/-heonik-kwon/3413.

15. The irony is that those who participated in the Seoul reunions would become the iconic representation of North–South Korean separated families, even though, as discussed in chapter 2, they had not previously been regarded as "*isan gajok*" [separated families], which excluded families of those who were suspected of going voluntarily to the North during the war.

16. Gwi-Ok Kim, *Wŏllammin ŭi saenghwal kyŏnghŏm kwa chŏnch'esŏng* (Seoul: Seoul National University Press).

17. Byeong-uk and Young-hui Kim, "Comparative Study of the Contacts of Divided Families in Korea and Germany," *North Korean Studies Review* 12, no. 1 (2009).

18. Lee, "Making and Unmaking the Korean National Division."

19. Susan R. Grayzel discusses, for example, the use of maternal imagery in war memorials after World War I. See *Women's Identities at War: Gender, Motherhood, and Politics in Britain and France During the First World War* (Chapel Hill: University of North Carolina Press, 1999), 226.

20. Laurel Kendall, "Korean Ancestors: From the Woman's Side," in *Korean Women: View from the Inner Room*, ed. Laurel Kendall and Mark Peterson (New Haven, CT: East Rock Press, 1983).

21. Margery Wolf, *Women and the Family in Rural Taiwan* (Stanford, CA: Stanford University Press, 1972), 37.

22. Kwang-Kyu Lee, *Korean Family and Kinship* (Seoul: Jipmoondang, 1997).

23. James Foley, *Korea's Divided Families* (London and New York: Routledge, 2004), 171.

24. See also Roy Grinker, *Korea and Its Futures* (New York: St. Martin's Press, 1998), 22.

25. Foley, *Korea's Divided Families*, 171.

26. Helen-Louise Hunter, *Kim Il-sŏng's North Korea* (Westport, CT: Praeger, 1999).

27. Andrei Lankov, *The Real North Korea* (New York: Oxford University Press, 2013).

28. Foley, *Korea's Divided Families*, 87.

29. Suk-Young Kim, *Illusive Utopia* (Ann Arbor, MI: University of Michigan Press, 2010).

30. Foley, *Korea's Divided Families*, 171.

31. Stanley J. Tambiah, "A Performative Approach to Ritual" (Paper presented at the Proceedings of the British Academy London, 1979), 119.

32. Pierre Liénard and Pascal Boyer, "Whence Collective Rituals? A Cultural Selection Model of Ritualized Behavior," *American Anthropologist* 108, no. 4 (2006): 814–27.

33. Jong Kun Choi, "Sunshine Over a Barren Soil: The Domestic Politics of Engagement Identity Formation in South Korea," *Asian Perspective* 34, no. 4 (2010): 134.

34. This problematic aspect of the reunions later resolved itself because of the waning of interest in this subject after the first reunion.

35. Rosalind Morris, "Intimacy and Corruption in Thailand's Age of Conspiracy," in *Off Stage, On Display: Intimacy and Ethnography in the Age of Public Culture*, ed. Andrew Shryock (Stanford, CA: Stanford University Press, 2004), 229.

36. The following discussion is based on chapter 4 of Son's *South Korean Engagement Policies* (New York: Routledge, 2006).

37. See also Sung Chull Kim and David C. Kang, *Engagement With North Korea: A Viable Alternative* (Albany, NY: State University of New York Press, 2009), 154–57.

38. Ibid, 121.

39. Shin Yong-bae, "President takes blame of 'payoff'; Kim says illicit payment to N.K. was necessary for peace," *Korea Herald*, February 15, 2003.

40. In contrast, Lee Jang-Hee cites a comparison with the process that eventually led up to the unification of divided Germany. He notes that no investigation was demanded by opposition parties after West Germany, in the period after a 1981 summit between the two German leaders, made loans to East Germany amounting to DM 1.95 billion or U.S. $750 million. Quoted in Son, 121.

41. Esra Özyrüek, *Nostalgia for the Modern: State Secularism and Everyday Politics in Turkey* (Durham, NC: Duke University Press, 2006), 67.

42. Daniel J. Sherman, "Bodies and Names: The Emergence of Commemoration in Interwar France," *American Historical Review* 103, no. 2 (1998): 443.

Part III

Crossing Over

Chapter Five

Impossible Returns

In the course of doing field research, the practice of asking "awkward questions"[1] is often unavoidable, though not always deliberate. At times one simply makes an outright faux pas, which by definition means the moment of realization is too late. While seeking out research participants, I once asked a question that I later recognized was not just awkward, but patently tactless: "Would it be possible for me to interview your mother-in-law?" It was during the early spring of 2000, after I had begun to focus more specifically on trying to learn more about the South Korean families of those who went to the North during the war. Gingerly, through word-of-mouth among personal friends, family friends, and other contacts, I tried to bring up the subject of my research. In the process, I soon heard more than a dozen anecdotal accounts of people with relatives believed to have gone to the North, ranging from hearsay to extended stories. But when I requested help in trying to secure an interview, it almost invariably went nowhere. Friends would quickly change the subject or simply shake their heads discouragingly. When I asked one woman, who had previously mentioned that her mother-in-law was from one of such families, she simply blanched. I met the woman at a meeting among a small group of former democracy activists, who occasionally gathered to discuss readings related to reunification issues, so my request was not entirely a non sequitur. But at the thought of my trying to arrange an interview with her mother-in-law, this woman with whom I was only a casual acquaintance gave me the kind of stunned look that made me question how I could have asked such a ridiculous question. When I quickly apologized with embarrassment, she said that it was all right, but she could not even imagine broaching the subject with her mother-in-law, let alone requesting an interview on my behalf. As another family friend put it, when I later relayed the incident, "Oh, yes, that's something which is *very* hush-hush."

During those early months in my field research, I searched for weeks in vain for an introduction to anyone from one of such families who might be willing to meet, if not grant an outright interview. One day while I was recounting my frustrations to a friend, whom I will call Hye-sung, she thought of someone who might be willing to chat with me. Hye-sung offered that an older colleague she knew quite well actually had an uncle who went to the North during the war. Sounding optimistic, Hye-sung volunteered to approach her during the coming week, and I waited with some hope that her colleague might be amenable to sharing at least a few comments from her perspective. Then I didn't hear back from my friend for several days until she called one afternoon to set up a time to meet over coffee. Hye-sung said she had something to tell me, but it would be better to speak in person. When we met the next day at a café, she explained that, though she had hoped to arrange a time for all three of us to get together, it would simply not be possible for her colleague to discuss this subject. Hye-sung explained that, when she had brought up the idea of meeting with me, she learned that her colleague had actually never meant to disclose the fact of having an uncle in North Korea. Hye-sung shared her best guess, that it must have slipped out accidentally while they were out socializing one night among their group of work buddies. Hye-sung seemed anxious that she had inadvertently disclosed what turned out to be, for her colleague, a closely held secret. Hye-sung had evidently gotten the picture that it would be best to forget that her colleague had said anything at all. While relaying that conversation, Hye-sung spoke slowly and deliberately to convey how surprised she too had been, but also to emphasize why there was no question as to whether her colleague would ever agree to speaking further. What Hye-sung learned was that having a lost uncle in North Korea was a secret that her colleague had never even told her own husband.

SEEKING FAMILY IN THE SOUTH

"Can you get to a television right away?"

It was early in the evening of July 16th, a month before the August reunions of 2000. I had just gotten off the subway in Seoul when I received a cell phone call from a friend and fellow researcher. "Did you hear? Names of the candidates for the North–South family reunions are going to be released to the public," she said brightly, adding that the list would include people I had been trying to find. "They'll be broadcast on television tonight." I raced home.

By the time I reached my apartment, the news reports had already started. "SEEKING FAMILY IN THE SOUTH . . . "

Under this heading appeared a name on the bottom of the television screen, followed by identifying details: hometown and a list of names— enumerated by relationship, such as father, mother, sister, brother—along with their ages. After a minute or so, another set of names appeared providing similar information, one after the other in succession. It was part of a special broadcast to locate the family members who had been selected as candidates to take part in the upcoming inter-Korean reunions. While the names at the bottom of the screen rotated, the headline persisted: "Seeking Family in the South" (*Namch'ŭkgajok ŭl ch'atsŭmnida*). For virtually all the families involved, this simple phrase represented the first communication, not to mention the first sign of life, through which they received word of survival regarding a relative who had been missing for fifty years. More precisely, it was the first indication that a family member presumed to be dead had somehow survived and was not in fact lost among the millions killed in a catastrophic war half a century earlier.

The television coverage also showed the initial reactions of notified families, expressing their incredulity that a long-lost family member had apparently just been discovered. Studio interviews of elated family members were interspersed with video reportage taped at people's homes. In one segment, an elderly woman showed a small array of yellowing black-and-white photographs, pictures of her elder brother in his adolescence. She explained that one morning during the war he had departed their childhood home to attend school and never returned. At the time, the initial news reports about the list of names sent from North Korea did not include any current images depicting those who had been listed. Without a recent photograph for the time being, all that visually represented the brother from North Korea in the news report was the image of him as a teenage student. The juxtaposition of a gray-haired grandmother holding the photograph of her youthful brother itself presented a poignant portrait revealing the embodied lapse of time since his disappearance from the South.

Truly, the unaged face on the photograph as a sole remaining trace of the brother would have ordinarily given the illusion of someone frozen in time, as if he had died young. However, the recent news of his unexpected survival instead suggested another temporal metaphor: the "twin paradox," which is often used to explain Einstein's theory concerning the relativity of time. In that thought experiment, one sibling stays earthbound while the other takes off in a spaceship, traveling to outer space at nearly the speed of light. The traveling sibling returns without having changed discernibly while the sibling who stayed at home has aged by several decades into an elderly person. According to the special theory of relativity, this dilation of time occurs because those who inhabit separate frames of reference, which move differently from one other, would also have disparate experiences of time. Similarly, without recent images of the brother revealed to be still alive in North

Korea, the woman in the KBS special broadcast who had preserved his photograph taken in the 1940s seemed to possess the youthful portrait of a time traveler soon to arrive from the distant past.

In all, two hundred families in South Korea were identified on the list sent by the DPRK Red Cross, based on information from those North Koreans selected to meet with their families in the upcoming reunions. The transmission of the list resonated with a message both intimate and impersonal. While intended to notify and locate these families for the purposes of preparing for the reunions, the televising of the list occurred during prime-time hours on the flagship channel of KBS, the national broadcaster. I later learned that the notification would effectively expose without prior warning, before a nationwide audience, family secrets that had been closely guarded for decades. The voiceover on the broadcasts repeated: "Those who thought their kin were dead have just learned their loved ones are alive. . . . " The television anchor instructed anyone who found their own name on the lists to call or visit the Red Cross headquarters in Seoul to confirm their current contact information and complete a formal application for family reunion.

I ran out to catch a cab to reach the KBS television station on Yŏŭido (Yeouido), the urban island in central Seoul that is home to a district of government buildings, including the location of the Republic of Korea National Assembly, as well as residential and shopping neighborhoods. I had wondered whether I could encounter any family members at the KBS Building in connection with the special broadcast, but I arrived only to find the main hall mostly darkened. The guard told me one person had arrived earlier that night, was briefly interviewed, and then went home. The interviews on the air at the time were coming from the regional stations out in provincial cities. After I returned to my apartment nearby, I saw that the broadcast of names were still cycling in a continuous loop on TV.

"Seeking Family in the South." The phrase resonated as a haunting enigmatic appeal. The two Korean Red Cross Societies had agreed to exchange lists of two hundred names, and each side was charged with verifying who was still alive among that group. One hundred families would eventually be selected from each side for the separated-family meetings from August 15 to August 18, 2000.[2] Following the broadcast of names, full-page charts appeared in the morning editions of the major South Korean newspapers, listing the information that had been sent from North Korea about the candidates for the reunions. Word quickly spread about members of this newly apparent group of North–South separated families, and news of the survival of those formerly presumed dead would reverberate in neighborhoods and communities throughout the country.

THE MOUNTAIN AND THE MISSING

In the heart of Seoul, the South Korean Red Cross headquarters occupies a modest office building near the foot of Namsan, the mountain that rises above the city's center. Following the provisions of the Geneva Conventions and its additional protocols, the International Committee on the Red Cross assists after conflicts with the reunification of separated family members and the tracing of missing persons.[3] Each of the two Korean states has its own Society of the Red Cross, and prior to the period of rapprochement that began in 2000, the Red Cross was the primary channel of inter-Korean contact and negotiation regarding humanitarian issues. At several junctures while conducting fieldwork from 1999 to 2001, I returned to the building that housed the South Korean Red Cross headquarters, meeting Koreans who had come to apply for assistance to locate family members. These individuals had disappeared during the war, and their families had reason to believe that they somehow ended up in North Korea, whether voluntarily or involuntarily, and all under the force of the extraordinary circumstances of war.

The neighborhood around that part of Namsan is not a residential area, and nearly all its visitors to the Red Cross headquarters had to travel there from somewhere else by car, taxi, or public transportation. Those coming by bus or subway must make the final ascent on foot up a steep hill, only to climb another flight of stairs once they arrived at their destination. The Red Cross location therefore offered little in the way of convenience, especially for the many elderly applicants who traveled there to apply for the reunions. The choice of this particular site nevertheless seemed entirely appropriate. Hour after hour, applicants would arrive at the Red Cross headquarters like sojourners on a pilgrimage. Many of them appeared visibly winded as they reached the top of the stairs, catching their breath and patting the perspiration off their brows with square-folded cotton handkerchiefs. Local residents from all directions—and many Seoulites who had been asked by relatives in the provinces to go on their behalf—converged upon the mountain at the geographical center of South Korea's capital city in order to claim their stake in a protracted crisis at the crux of the nation's division: the unresolved cases of families separated and persons still missing a half-century after the war's hostilities had ended.

When I arrived on the morning after the North Korean list was publicized, a handwritten sign directed prospective reunion applicants upstairs to the second floor. There, a meeting room had been temporarily converted into an makeshift administrative center, and the room was bustling with activity. Reporters, photographers, and a television camera crew mingled among a crowd of about forty people, mostly elderly, who were speaking to Red Cross staffers or filling out applications while seated around a cluster of conference tables at the center of the room. Along one wall of the room, another bank of three oblong tables were set up as an improvised reception counter, where staffers manned telephones and set about the work of processing applications and verifying vital information. During the three other times that I had visited this building in preceding months, the area devoted to receiving such applications was limited to a small cubicle in the corner of an office, and I had never seen any visitors there before. That made it all the more striking to encounter the buzz of excitement and anticipation as family members and journalists alike descended upon the Red Cross headquarters on that day and for several days thereafter.

As individuals called in on behalf of their families to confirm that they saw their family names on the publicized list, Red Cross workers each consulted a binder holding a set of forms with information about each individual. The Red Cross workers recorded the contact information of the callers and corrected any errors in the details regarding the surviving family members. Because so much time had passed, some of the information was understandably inaccurate, such as the ages of siblings or the names of relatives, particularly mothers and other female kin.[4] The Red Cross staff also verified who among the relatives listed was alive or the dates of death for those who passed away. The latter was traditionally regarded as vital information for a Korean kin-group in order to hold ancestor-worship memorials (*chesa*) at the proper time.

Although family members could confirm their details by phone, the advantage for those who came in person was to be able to see for themselves the photograph on the form sent from North Korea. That is, each person who made the strenuous trek to the Red Cross offices had the chance to see the actual form sent from the North, which included a small wallet-size photograph in the top right-hand corner. The picture had evidently been photocopied several times to the point that the image looked slightly blurred. But the photograph was still distinct enough to show the features of a face and to offer the first clues about the mystery behind a lost relative's reappearance.

I had been talking with one of the new applicants when we suddenly heard a desperate shout from across the room: "He's alive!" I looked up to see a tall elderly man reeling back, his face stricken. He ran to the back of the room, shrugging off reporters surrounding him, until he collapsed against a room divider. As a circle of photographers closed in on him with camera shutters clicking, their flurry of flashes momentarily cast a strobe effect over the man, now crumpled halfway to the floor. One of the Red Cross workers came to check on him and helped him sit down in chair, as he held his head in his hands, weeping. Reporters hovered, waiting for him to calm down enough to speak. Finally, the man said, "Until I actually saw the photograph, I didn't believe there was any way he could still be alive." After the man later regained his composure, he said that he had to come to the Red Cross head-

Figure 5.1. Family members and journalists converged on the Seoul headquarters of the Korean Red Cross after news broke that a detailed list of candidates for the first post-Summit reunions had been transmitted from North Korea. July 2000 © Yonhap News Agency.

quarters in person because he had assumed there must have been some mistake.

During the summer of 2000, those who had seen their names on television or in the newspaper lists were asked to visit the Red Cross headquarters in Seoul, where they could register directly to confirm that they had surviving relatives who could participate in the upcoming reunions. However, during this time, a sudden upsurge of applications occurred, as people whose family was not included on the list also came forward nevertheless, traveling to the Red Cross Headquarters to apply for reunions for the first time. While helping out some of these applicants, I asked why they had not applied previously. The common response was: "Not to cause them any harm." They did not want to make potential problems for their family members in the North. That is, simply by inquiring after family members through the process of application, they would bring attention to the fact that they had relatives on the other side of the de facto border. When I spoke with one elderly woman in late July at the Red Cross headquarters, she put it patly: "These people have been missing from here, and we've been missing from the other side."

This moment of resurfacing represented the first time that North Korea provided its southern counterpart with an official accounting of a substantially large number of those who were presumed to have died in the war, represented by those two hundred names included in the initial list. Through media reports following the publication of the list sent by the North Korean Red Cross, it quickly became apparent that all the reunion candidates from the other side were those who had gone to or ended up in the North at some point in wartime fifty years earlier. This unprecedented transmission of information came as an extraordinary development, and among South Koreans the collective shock caused by this news served as an indication that something had begun to unfold beyond what could have been imagined in the past.

EXILIC DIASPORA

At the turn of the millennium, it was under the extraordinary circumstances of the preparations for the separated-family reunions that the renewed relevance of a historically ambiguous identity emerged: namely, those who disappeared during wartime and lived on after the Korean War, but out of contact with their kin and former community on the other side of the divide. While resonating with other discourses of diaspora that have emerged from divided Korea, the extraordinary collective reappearance of those who had been formerly presumed among the war dead also proved to complicate the very concept of diaspora. In contrast to contemporary references to diaspora that commonly emphasize the maintenance of linkages across national boundaries and geographic spaces, the persistence of an older experience of diaspora is suggested by this reappearance en masse of those who had long been given up for deceased. That is, this phenomenon recalled the kind of *exilic diaspora* that is based not on connection, but rather on rupture and disconnection so profound that it had amounted to both a social death and a presumed death. Signifying the unexpected and unlikely return of these presumed war dead to South Korea, the list sent from North Korea was therefore an extraordinary revelation indicating the scope of an exilic diaspora, which had been all but impossible previously to trace or to apprehend collectively, precisely because its members had remained unaccounted for.[5]

The stories of Korean separated families that emerged during this period reveal lives jarred by displacement and the imposition of a diaspora caused by the destructive upheavals of the 1950–1953 period of the Korean War. Most incidents of family separation occurred during late 1950 and early 1951, when significant internal migration and movement was still possible and indeed necessary as the frontlines shifted rapidly. Wide-scale separation of Korean family members ensued when such instances of evacuation, necessary to escape the war's fighting, later became permanent inter-state relocations after 1953 when the border became impassable to citizens on either side. Accounts of family departure and separation from this period often describe hasty departures in which there was every expectation of return. "Everyone thought it would be temporary and they would be back," wrote Choi In-hun in the novel *The Grey Man*. "When the UN forces pulled out, the whole city was turned inside out. People who until the day before never dreamt of leaving found themselves rushing to the wharves."[6] Koreans who fled for refuge in wartime had little reason at the time to doubt that division would be temporary. For those who unavoidably took separate paths from their family members at the time, none could have imagined that, for more than fifty years, they could be left without the means to determine the fates of their kin never to be recovered from that war.

Sociologist Gwi-Ok Kim has observed that, in the twenty-first century, separated families in North and South Korea represent abiding examples of classic diaspora in the older sense of involuntary migration.[7] In its early usage, the term "diaspora" referred exclusively to experiences of collective exile among Jews displaced from the Holy Land and dispersed in various regions around the world. In contrast to this evocation of deracination and vulnerability, more recent interpretations of diaspora emphasize instead the creation of networks, identities, and consciousness that cross nation-state borders.[8] Since the 1990s diaspora has been largely discussed in globalized contexts as a hybridizing term, the use of which did not necessarily presume as normative its historical roots in the Jewish diaspora's exilic experience.[9] In light of modern means of transportation and electronic communication, a community's physical dispersion over geographical space has been more likely to suggest not atomization, but rather the agency of contemporary diasporic subjects to forge transnational identities and identifications.

Moreover, given the contemporary semantic evolution of the term of "diaspora," some Jewish studies scholars have suggested that the term for *galut*, or the perennial condition of forced homelessness and displacement, would now be more accurately translated as "exile."[10] In other words, the classic term of "diaspora" has come to take on such positive connotations that it arguably has lost the traumatic implications that are still conveyed by the modern concept of "exile."[11] Anthropologist Aihwa Ong writes, "More and more, diaspora becomes an emotional and ideologically loaded term that is invoked by disparate transnational groups as a way to construct broad ethnic coalitions that cut across national spaces." She argues that diaspora should not be regarded in the objective as a definable population, but instead as "an ethnographic term of self-description by different immigrant groups or publics."[12]

In contrast to "diaspora" in its current usage, revisiting its historical origins suggests other conceptual trajectories for theorizing diasporic experience beyond the construction of solidarity across spaces among those who identify with a physically dispersed collectivity. In *The Graves of Tarim*, anthropologist Enseng Ho conceptualizes diaspora as the "society of the absent," calling attention to how absence fundamentally shapes diasporic experience, evident in the abiding traces of migration left behind in places of origin and adopted temporary homelands. He writes, "Moving between places, mobility leaves in its wake a trail of absences. Important persons in one's life may be far away and hard to reach. When a mobile person leaves behind dependents, his or her absence may loom large in their daily existence."[13] According to Ho, diaspora's temporality actually far exceeds the length of a single lifetime, not to mention the heady instantaneity of globalization. Rather, diaspora unfolds over a long duration, spanning several generations. The absence of emigrants provokes debate over whether they will return, or whether the community will join them; and this is true even with respect to the absence of those emigrants who have died abroad. Ho argues that graves therefore remain vital sites for a diaspora, for the ways they mark "the truth of their presence in a land,"[14] a point of overlapping geographical and genealogical orientations to which descendants may someday return.

Whether one perceives diaspora chiefly through phenomena surrounding mobility, migration, or absence—both voluntary and involuntary—it is salient also to consider contemporary forms of diaspora defined not primarily by connectedness over distance and time, but instead by disruption. How does dispersion differ when experienced as an enduring break, comparable to the profound disconnection central to the experience of exile and older diasporas? Denoting the vulnerable isolation and deracinated alienation inherent to the banishment of exile, what one could call exilic diaspora would also preserve the nuance of diaspora as a term of collective social ascription. It would be misleading, however, to identify exilic diaspora too strongly with its roots as a Biblical term and a premodern concept. Indeed, despite the increasingly dense interconnectedness of the contemporary era, one cannot overlook how various disparate factors have led to the wholesale severing of ties and communication, whether among individuals, groups, or even populations cut off from one another. While the present study focuses on the circumstances of war, ideological polarity, and national division, other causes of such ruptures would include human trafficking, sudden evacuation from disasters, untimely deaths, closed adoption, a breakdown of relationships followed by estrangement, and other complicated circumstances of radical alienation.

The extent and nature of an exilic diaspora are difficult to perceive precisely because of the baffling circumstances surrounding the open-ended absences of those who departed or may have died, or both. Such elusiveness helps to establish how particularly extraordinary was the highly visible moment of unexpected return as part of preparations for the Korean separated-family reunions in the summer of 2000. Attesting to the existence of an exilic diaspora that had been previously obscured, the resurfacing of the presumed Korean War dead inspired recollections of others who disappeared during the course of that devastating catastrophe on the peninsula at the midpoint of the prior century. Such stories and intimations of stories would newly foreground how, alongside the relentless stalemate of ongoing military confrontation in divided Korea, there have always existed the evanescent realms of memory, ghostly hauntings, and ephemeral but unforgettable dreams. These comprise what anthropologist Stefania Pandolfo has elsewhere described as *barzakh*, "an intermediate imaginal realm, an *entre-deux* between absence and presence, spiritual and bodily existence, between self and other, the living and the dead."[15]

At the Red Cross headquarters in mid-July 2000, I spoke with Kwon *Ajumoni*, a woman in her early sixties who was poring over her application when I sat with her to offer help. I tried to pass along the small tips that I had picked up earlier that afternoon while speaking with the Red Cross staffers and helping out other applicants. As we talked, Kwon *Ajumoni* shared her story of how she was determined to find her brother, and she relayed a vivid memory from the day they were separated. It was when partisans fighting for the North Korean side came to her school and had all the students assemble in the schoolyard and sit on the ground. The partisans made speeches and called for volunteers to join them. Kwon *Ajumoni* said that a few of her classmates went forward and she nearly followed. She said, "I was about to raise my hand." At this point, she started acting out the memory by demonstrating how she lifted up her hand and bending her head forward while looking up watchfully. "But *Op'pa* (older brother) saw me and gave me a very sharp look," she said, suddenly hardening her eyes and furrowing her brow while bringing her hand down quickly. "He went forward instead. So *Op'pa* went instead of me." In Kwon *Ajumoni*'s story of how she was initially swayed by the rallying atmosphere and the actions of her peers, her brother appears to have stopped her from stepping forward by volunteering in her stead. She left it ambiguous whether her brother would have gone anyway or whether he went to distract the partisans from her attempt to volunteer. She looked stricken and went back to checking over her Red Cross family-tracing application while repeating under her breath, "I have to find him . . . I have to find him if he's still alive."

THE DANGER OF ABSENCE

After that midsummer special broadcast, reunion candidates quickly drew media attention, and these family members began to take for granted that they would be approached for interviews. However, prior to the release of the North Korean list, it had been extremely difficult to secure even a single introduction to a member of a so-called *Wŏlbukcha* family. I was only able to set up one extended interview. Through an introduction from a Korean litera-ture professor, I met the relative of a prominent North Korean novelist. In my fieldnotes, I refer to him as the "Author's Grandson," even though he was in his late seventies. His grandfather was one of the *Wŏlbukch'ak'ka*, or writers who were widely known to have crossed over to the North during the post-Liberation period.[16] Works by such intellectuals had been banned in South Korea, and except for copies that existed underground, the books they had authored were confiscated and destroyed. These blacklisted authors were dropped from histories of Korean literature until 1988, when censorship laws were eased. I first arranged a meeting with the Author's Grandson over the telephone, and I noticed that his address was an apartment building in an affluent part of Seoul. Had his family suffered discrimination in the past, they apparently managed somehow to become established enough to live in a desirable neighborhood. When I met him there along with my research assist-ant, we discovered that he actually lived with his son's family in a modest apartment. That suggested the family had devoted its resources toward pay-ing the high cost of living in an affluent neighborhood to ensure a good school district for the sake of the children.

The Author's Grandson was a trim elderly man who wore reading glasses and had a measured way of speaking. After exchanging introductions and discussing the background of my research, we spoke for a while about his own ongoing interest in trying to learn more about his grandfather. He spoke of a longstanding curiosity that went back to his youth. As a child, he had been given the impression that his grandfather was just a "third-rate writer," until an unexpected encounter one day when he learned for the first time about his grandfather's literary stature and how even mention of his name was taboo. He said:

> When I was in eighth grade, I was walking alongside my Korean literature teacher one day, and he told me, very quietly and quickly, that my grandfather was a famous writer. At that time, if anyone talked about my grandfather, they would be accused of being Communist. If I told anyone that my teacher men-tioned my grandfather, that teacher would have been dragged off. That was the

way it was. It was in the early '60s, right after. At that time, if you didn't like someone, you could report him as suspicious or strange. That was enough. Even now if there is any suspicion of Communists, I'd be in trouble, just because of my family background. At that time, it was much, much worse. Any word against you, it didn't need to be proved to put you under suspicion. If you tell the police that person is a little suspicious, that was enough for them to drag that person in for brutal interrogation and beat him half to death. Incredibly brutal. If you were a Communist or had any connection to Communism, it was unspeakably bad. But at the time even very insignificant cases were being pursued. Say your uncle somehow disappeared in the war or there was a rumor that he was mixed up in questionable things.

The Author's Grandson was referring to the early years under the regime of Park Chung-hee, who came to power in a coup on May 17, 1961, when a military junta seized power and closed the National Assembly. While Syngman Rhee had utilized national security to suppress his political opponents, a far more systematic consolidation of anticommunism as the ideology of the state occurred in South Korea under Park. He strengthened his regime's power through anticommunist and national security laws, including a "Political Activities Purification Law" in March 1962, which banned over four thousand politicians from seeking or holding political offices.[17] Families of those who were missing since the war as well as bereaved families of leftists killed in civilian massacres were placed under a regime of surveillance and discrimination known as *yŏnjwaje*, which operated according to the principle of guilt by association. In addition to regular surveillance, members of these families were blocked through background checks from gaining employment in public service, the military, and large companies. They were also prevented from traveling abroad because their passport applications would be denied. Thus they were excluded from both the avenues of power and social mobility in South Korean society, as well as the means to pursue alternatives outside the country.

Family members of leftists and those missing in the war therefore found themselves living in fear amid the consolidation of the anticommunist state during the 1970s. According to the Author's Grandson:

I didn't know when I was young, but as I grew older, I realized that I faced restrictions. If you have any family member who went to the North, there are many restrictions. If you're part of a *Wŏlbukcha* family, forget about getting a job in the government or military. That's how I got my job at G_____. In a way, I hid my family history to get hired. Background checks back then were really extreme. To apply for any job, they checked you. Even if you wanted to move, everything! During college, I really agonized over what kind of job I would get, what I would do. And my family was having financial difficulties, which added more pressure. I considered taking the exam for law, but then I realized it would be impossible. Even if I passed, they would catch me in the background check.

He left it unclear how he managed to circumvent the system of background checks to secure a stable job. Based on subsequent interviews, I learned that it was possible to evade detection if a friend or relative of a friend had the right connections and could vouch for you. Those with compromised family backgrounds who lacked such connections were effectively excluded from mainstream South Korean society. Because of the suspicion that *Wŏlbukcha* would return furtively to South Korea as spies, their families consequently became regarded as families of North Korean spies.[18] In the context of anti-communist discipline, *Wŏlbukcha* families would experience surveillance by police or government agents and could, without reason, be detained for several days. This system prohibited overseas travel and obstructed advancement in higher education and other fields to anyone with a "color problem," that is, anyone with a history of being tainted as a so-called "Red," not only through an ideological transgression but also on account of any accusations against them in the past or against one of their family members.

A couple of weeks after the June Summit, I met with Jae-won's Mother, a family friend who hosted me for lunch at her apartment in southern Seoul. Afterward, we talked while she was paring fruit and I was going over my field notes in order to ask her a few questions. She knew vaguely about my interests in separated families, but when I mentioned about how I wanted to learn more about the "other" group of families, she was intrigued. When I explained that I meant those who had been separated because someone went to the North, she raised her eyebrows and nodded. If *that* was what I was researching, she had a story to tell.

When Jae-won's Mother was in high school in Seoul during the late 1960s, she had been the "head student" of her class, a position that carried the responsibility of being acquainted with all of her classmates. Yet she recalled that there were always a few girls who kept to themselves. Though she had assumed they were shy, she said she had often wondered why they avoided contact with the other students. She said, "Whenever I tried to talk with them, they just shied away. I could understand that some people are not that social, but something about the way they avoided me and the other students seemed strange." In recalling this account from her schooldays, her voice had been steadily rising in energy and volume until she reached the main point of her story: "Many years later at our class reunion, I heard indirectly that *every one of those girls had a father who went to the North.*" With eyes widened now, she continued, "I remember one family in particular. The mother and children always looked so pale and sick. We were told to avoid that family because *there was TB* in that home." Jae-won's Mother ordinarily has a relaxed self-assured way of talking, but at this point, her voice rose in volume and started to break. Shaking her head, Jae-won's Mother said she had never questioned the rumors that the home was infected with tuberculosis. "I remember *we were told they had TB!*" she repeated emphatically, as if still in disbelief, and wiped away tears. "And grownups told us we should stay away from them, so we did." It was only many years later that she realized that the haggard appearance of these classmates' families must have resulted from their hardships of losing a father during the war, compounded by the toll of isolation their family endured from being subject to a social quarantine, set apart for having a relative suspected to have crossed over to the North.[19]

Oh Tae-suk's 1974 play, *Lifecord* (T'ae), is considered one of the most influential works in Korean modern theater. It is based on the true historical story of Tanjong, the fourth king of the Chosŏn dynasty, who at age fifteen in 1456 was usurped by his uncle, Sejo. Six royal academy scholars and loyal subjects made a failed attempt to return Tanjong to power, and for their actions all six men were condemned to death and their family lines were obliterated through execution of relations and affines according to the principle that "three families" must be destroyed to punish the crime.[20] In other words, accepted social conventions of the time meant that, in addition to executing each scholar's immediate family, the royal guard also executed the extended families on the father's side, mother's side, and wife's side. Although the play is set entirely in the fifteenth century, it makes oblique references to modern contexts. During a playwright's forum, Oh was questioned about his personal motivations for writing the play, and he referred to the kidnapping of his father and the disappearance of his uncle toward the outbreak of the war: "During the Korean War, my father and his two younger brothers all died, either kidnapped or unaccounted for, which is the same as being killed."[21] Deeming the condition of being among the war-missing as "the same as being killed," Oh's remarks recall how those who left for the North during the war were essentially dead to South Korean society, even if still alive across the border. The modern equivalent of kin-based punishment meant that Oh's missing kin from the war may not have been proven to be physically dead but, effectively, as social beings they were no longer alive.

Namsan, the mountain at the center of Seoul, is today known to foreign visitors largely as a tourist destination. There one can hike or ride a cable car to reach the foot of Namsan Tower, a defining landmark in the urban landscape of the capital city's metropolitan area. Visitors ascend the tower via a high-speed elevator to enjoy a stunning view that looks out over the expanse of Seoul's dense urban landscape in all directions. Yet Namsan also casts a densely layered shadow from Korea's historical past. The mountain was where the Japanese Government-General built its central Shintō shrine in 1925 as part of its strategy for spiritual assimilation of Koreans as colonial subjects. Today that site is the location for a statue and museum dedicated to

Korean independence movement leader Ahn Jung-geun, who assassinated Itō Hirobumi, the former Resident General of Korea, at the Harbin Railway Station in 1909.[22] Namsan also bears a more recent historical legacy as the site where the former Korea Central Intelligence Agency (KCIA) carried out brutal interrogations under past regimes of military dictators. Older Koreans still remember Namsan as a location associated with intimidation and torture, from the time when the mountain's name was synonymous with the KCIA.[23] After returning to the United States several months later, I talked about my fieldwork with a colleague who had emigrated more than twenty years earlier from Korea to Hawaii, and she mentioned that, even today, she still feels uneasy about visiting that part of Seoul because of its dark past and what "a trip to Namsan" used to connote.

For the Koreans who were seeking their relatives missing since the war, Namsan's association with the organization facilitating inter-Korean family reunions in the present existed alongside its implicit historical identification with an agency that had been infamous in the past for harshly interrogating individuals who belonged to families such as their own. The KCIA annex where democracy activists and other leftists were tortured was once located right next to the site of the present-day Red Cross Headquarters. The irony of these overlapping and opposing evocations shared by this precise vicinity reflects how, despite post-1993 advances in South Korea's democratization, socially progressive efforts endorsed by the liberal Kim Dae-jung administration were inescapably haunted by memories of state violence from an earlier era. Such memories would shadow the meanings called forth by the reunions. This ironic juxtaposition would be the context in which a small group of previously unaffiliated Korean families—those who had once been marginalized in their respective communities and subject to surveillance in their own homes—would become elevated collectively to represent, for a time, both the past and the future of the nation.

NOTES

1. Nayanika Mookherjee, "Friendships and Encounters with Left-Liberal Politics in Bangladesh," in *Taking Sides: Ethics, Politics, and Fieldwork in Anthropology*, ed. Heidi Armbruster and Anna Lærke (New York and Oxford: Bergahn, 2008), 66.

2. I later learned from staffers at the Red Cross headquarters that this preliminary screening step was intended to help avoid the situation that arose in 1985. That year, the only precedent to the inter-Korean reunions occurred, also with two delegations traveling to the opposite side to meet with relatives in meetings held simultaneously in Seoul and Pyongyang. At that time, no information about participants was circulated publicly in advance, and, out of a delegation of fifty visitors from each side, twenty from North Korea to Seoul and fifteen from South Korea to Pyongyang were unable to meet with any of their kin.

3. Simon Robins, *Families of the Missing: A Test for Contemporary Approaches to Transitional Justice* (New York and London: Routledge, 2013), 225.

4. Because mothers are rarely addressed in Korean by their given names but rather by teknonyms (e.g., *Yŏng-ju Ŏmma*, or Yŏng-ju's Mother) based on respective relationships, the names of women were more frequently inaccurate than those of male relatives.

5. This discussion both resonates with and departs from the body of scholarship exploring discourses and practices that endeavor to construct a transnational collective identity among diasporic Korean adoptees, whose transnational dispersion also keenly evokes a concept of diaspora based on rupture and disconnection. See Eleana Kim, *Adopted Territory: Transnational Korean Adoptees and the Politics of Belonging* (Durham, NC: Duke University Press, 2010); Tobias Hübinette, *Comforting an Orphaned Nation: Representations of International Adoption and Adopted Koreans in Korean Popular Culture* (Stockholm: Department of Oriental Languages, Stockholm University, 2005); Kim Park Nelson, "Mapping Multiple Histories of Korean American Transnational Adoption," Working Paper WP09-01, U.S.–Korea Institute at SAIS, January 2009; and Elise Prebin, *Meeting Once More: The Korean Side of Transnational Adoption* (New York: NYU Press, 2013).

6. Choi, *A Grey Man* (Seoul, Korea: Si Sa Yong O Sa, 1988), 57.

7. Gwi-Ok Kim, *Isan'gajok, "pan'gongjŏnsa" to "ppalgaengi" to anin* [Separated Families, Neither "Anticommunist Warriors" or "Reds"] (Seoul: *Yŏksabip'yŏngsa*, 2004), 3–5.

8. See Nina Glick Schiller et al., "From Immigrant to Transmigrant: Theorizing Transnational Migration," *Anthropological Quarterly* (1995): 48–63; Saskia Sassen, "Global Cities and Diasporic Networks: Microsites in Global Civil Society," *Global Civil Society* (Oxford: Oxford University Press, 2002); Steven Vertovec, "Transnationalism and Identity," *Journal of Ethnic and Migration Studies* 27, no. 4 (2001): 573–82; and Alison Blunt, "Cultural Geographies of Migration: Mobility, Transnationality and Diaspora," *Progress in Human Geography* 31 (2007): 684–94.

9. James Clifford, "Diasporas," *Cultural Anthropology* 9, no. 3 (1994): 302–38.

10. Roger Brubaker, "The 'Diaspora' Diaspora," *Ethnic and Racial Studies* 28, no. 1 (2005): 1–19.

11. Howard Wettstein, *Diasporas and Exiles: Varieties of Jewish Identity* (Berkeley: University of California Press, 2002), 2.

12. Aihwa Ong, "Cyberpublics and Diaspora Politics Among Transnational Chinese," *Interventions* 5, no. 1 (2003): 90.

13. Enseng Ho, *Graves of Tarim: Genealogy and Mobility Across the Indian Ocean* (Berkeley and Los Angeles: University of California Press, 2006), 18.

14. Ho, *Graves of Tarim*, 3.

15. She draws the term from the sacred writing of Islamic mystic, philosopher, and poet Ibn 'Arabi. See Stefania Pandolfo, *Impasse of the Angels: Scenes from a Moroccan Space of Memory* (Chicago: University of Chicago Press, 1997). Also regarding ephemeral but enduring legacies of the Korean War, another book that explores similar themes is Grace M. Cho's *Haunting the Korean Diaspora: Shame, Secrecy, and the Forgotten War* (Minneapolis: University of Minnesota Press, 2008).

16. In the post-Liberation period, particularly between 1945 and 1948 before the establishment of two separate Korean states, the border was still permeable and there was considerable movement between North and South. During this period, it was primarily intellectuals and artists who chose to migrate from South to North. Charles Armstrong attributes this exodus of intellectuals to their disillusionment with the dominance of right-wing forces in South Korea, a relatively high degree of artistic freedom until the spring of 1947, and also the significant resources that were committed to education, propaganda, and culture by the Soviets in the North as part of their strategy to foster a friendly regime. See Armstrong, "The Cultural Cold War in Korea, 1945–1950," *Journal of Asian Studies* 62, no. 1 (2003): 167. See also Hun Ch'ae, *Wŏlbuk chakka e taehan chaeinsik* [Reconsiderations of *Wŏlbuk* writers] (Seoul: Kip'ŭn Saem, 1995).

17. David Kang, "Bureaucracies and Rulers in South Korea," in *Transformations in Twentieth Century Korea*, ed. Yun-shik Chang and Steven Hugh Lee (New York and London: Routledge, 2006), 196.

18. Sungmi Cho, "*Wŏlbukchagajok ŭi saenghwalgyŏnghŏm*," MA thesis, Department of Sociology (2002), Ewha's Women's University, Seoul, Korea.

19. For a related discussion, see Ryong-kyong Lee, "War and Women's Lives: On the Experience of Bereaved Women of Left-Related Victims of the Korean War," *The Review of Korean Studies* 6, no. 1 (2003): 85–108; Uhn Cho, *"Wollam gajok kwa wŏlbuk gajokŭi chanyŏdŭlŭi kusulŭl chungsimŭro"* [Re-membering the Korean War and the Politics of Memory: Experiences of *"Wollam"* and *"Wolbuk"* Families' Descendants], *Sahoe wa yŏksa* [*Society and History*] 77 (2008): 191–229.

20. Ah-jeong Kim and R. B. Graves, *The Metacultural Theater of Oh T'ae-sŏk: Five Plays From the Korean Avant-Garde* (Honolulu: University of Hawaii Press, 1999), 6.

21. Kim and Graves, *The Metacultural Theater of Oh T'ae-sŏk*, 7.

22. As historian Todd Henry writes, "the continued prominence of anticolonial and anticommunist monuments on Namsan [points] to an ongoing engagement with the ghostly presence of Seoul's colonial spaces nearly seventy years after liberation from Japanese rule." Henry, *Assimilating Seoul: Japanese Rule and the Politics of Public Space in Colonial Korea, 1910–1945* (Berkeley and Los Angeles: University of California Press, 2014), 216.

23. Bruce Cumings, *Korea's Place in the Sun* (New York: Norton, 2005), 371. Note that the name of the KCIA was changed in 1981 to the Agency for National Security Planning (ANSP).

Chapter Six

Ethical Traversals

Chang *Halmŏni* described the initial shock of first discovering her brother was still alive, comparing it to a lightning strike. "Ttok!" She lifted her hand and let her knuckles fall square against her chest, repeating the onomatopoeia, "Ttok!" Without hope of their brother's survival during the war, Chang *Halmŏni* said she and her siblings had never looked into the possibility of whether he could be traced somewhere in the North, let alone applied for a reunion. So she had not given a second thought when the list of prospective reunion candidates was sent from North Korea in mid-July of 2000. Instead it was her husband who would be the first to spot the names of his in-laws when he happened to be watching the special broadcast. He broke the news to his wife by beckoning her to the television, saying, "Your brother is looking for you." Chang *Halmŏni* again replayed the gesture—"Ttok!"—as if reliving that bolt from the blue. She said she had never even imagined the separated-family meetings would have anything to do with her. Recounting her incredulity in the same terms I had heard over and over among others I met at the Red Cross headquarters, she said, "I kept asking myself, 'Is this a dream? Or is this reality?' (*hyŏnsil in'ga? kkum in'ga?*)."

I traveled to the outskirts of Seoul to meet Chang *Halmŏni* at her home during the month following the August 2000 reunions. We had met momentarily at the Red Cross headquarters, where initially she had brushed me off, but she did take my card. A few days later she called after seeing a small news article about my research, which had run in one of the daily newspapers. She apologized for being so brusque when we had met initially, explaining that she had felt too flustered to talk with anyone at the time. She also left quickly to avoid being approached by journalists, but she said she would be willing to speak to a student from abroad. Over the phone, she asked a few questions about me and then agreed to speak further, so we

161

arranged to meet at her home. After inviting me in and exchanging initial greetings, we walked past a corner of her apartment where she pointed out a low wooden table laden with a few books. Had I come a year prior, it would have been the spot where she could have shown me her mother's quilted prayer cushion. Chang *Halmŏni* explained that, virtually every day over many years and eventually decades, her mother had said prayers for her son's safety in the hope that he was somehow alive, a hope that the rest of the family had long abandoned. Chang *Halmŏni* said she had held onto the prayer cushion as a memento of her mother, who had passed away four years earlier, and she very much wished she could have given it to her brother when he visited Seoul for the reunions. But the cushion had been worn and threadbare, and she finally threw it away in a house-cleaning last year, a decision she now regretted.

Chang *Halmŏni* went on to explain that, after the news sunk in, her disbelief gave way to a mixture of emotions. "We are so glad. We are so glad that he did not die young as a student in the war and that he did not die in vain." Though she was clearly relieved that her brother had not died alone in his youth, Chang *Halmŏni* would repeatedly steer the conversation back to her utter confusion upon learning that he was alive. As we talked, Chang *Halmŏni* later said what she had most wanted to know from her brother was why he had not tried to contact his family in all those years. Sounding at first exasperated and then disappointed, she said, "Why couldn't he have sent even one letter? My parents would have died with their hearts more at peace, knowing that their son did not die young in the war."

QUIET WAITING

The way that Chang *Halmŏni* described her mother's rituals of remembrance echoed other stories of maternal devotion which circulated around the time of the August reunions. The South Korean media featured mothers who had adamantly refused to move for fifty years, for fear that their son or daughter might somehow find their way back home only to discover a household of strangers. One elderly woman went so far as to set out a place at the dinner table every night for her missing son.[1] Among these women, the refusal to give up on those who went missing decades ago in wartime in part reflects a profound investment in the stakes of embodiment and the presumption that one cannot mourn without receiving the body of the deceased. That is, they inhabited an abiding faith in their loved one's survival, a belief not to be relinquished without seeing evidence to the contrary.

This quiet and resolute practice of waiting occurred alongside the resignation of other family members and relatives who had long given up the war-missing for dead. In field interviews, I came across such discrepancies in attitudes within members of a kin group who differed in their opinions of whether their family was in fact among the war-bereaved. I would sometimes hear conflicting accounts and found that it was not uncommon for those among the same family to hold opposite views about the chances of a missing relative's survival. This came across in my encounters with one group of relatives whom I will call Yi *Halmŏni*'s family. Using information from the list of reunion candidates, I managed to get in touch by telephone with Yi *Halmŏni*'s daughter, who agreed to meet and invited me to visit them. The daughter lived with her husband in a small rural town about three hours south of Seoul by train and bus, and her mother lived nearby on their family's farm.

After I arrived in the morning, we gathered in the front room of Yi *Halmŏni*'s home along with her sister-in-law and brother-in-law, who also lived nearby. Yi *Halmŏni* was quiet but cheerful, saying, "It's so good, isn't it? We'll finally meet again. Can you believe it?" Her sister-in-law spoke admiringly of Yi *Halmŏni*, remarking on what a hard life she had led, running the farm as a widow and raising two children by herself. While we were talking, a neighbor dropped by to pay a visit. She came accompanied by another middle-aged woman whom she introduced as an acquaintance through a mutual friend. The visitors expressed their congratulations and chatted politely, but it was soon clear that the purpose of their social call was to ask Yi *Halmŏni* the favor of conveying a letter. The acquaintance explained that her father and two uncles also disappeared during the war, and she hoped that perhaps the letter might reach someone who knew them if Yi *Halmŏni* would be willing to pass it along during their family's upcoming reunion. The news about Yi *Halmŏni*'s husband had evidently caused a ripple effect in the surrounding area. It created a sense of possibility among others such as this visitor who came bearing her own rekindled hopes. Though this was a more personal and private form of appeal, the transmission of the letter among neighbors seemed comparable to the placards that were held up by bystanders who came to the sites of reunion events in Seoul. Those handmade signs showed the names and ages of still-missing family members, displayed in the hopes that a North Korean visitor might recognize one of the names.

Afterward, I spent time with Yi *Halmŏni*'s daughter separately while she was speaking with the friend who had paid a visit. Yi *Halmŏni*'s daughter commented how strange it would feel to call out "Appa!" ("Daddy!"). Growing up without a father, she never had occasion to say it before. She said she was trying to get used to it, and she pronounced the word aloud, as if calling out softly: "Appa." She said it again, listening to herself. She then repeated it a few times but did so facetiously, as if rehearsing a scene for a television drama, using different intonations and facial expressions. I was surprised by her lightheartedness, but she explained that even the thought of meeting her father seemed unreal. The next day, in a more serious moment, I was speaking with her alone at her home. She recalled how she had worried in the past about her mother, who would express the same sense of anticipation every winter during their New Year celebrations, saying, "I wonder whether this is the year your father will return?" Upon recounting this, Yi *Halmŏni*'s daughter looked at me and said, "Of course whenever I heard that, I thought it would be better for her to give up."

Before my visit with their family ended, I shared a car ride with Yi *Halmŏni*'s sister-in-law and, unsure of where she stood on the matter, I asked whether she had ever made any efforts to find out if her missing brother was still alive. She dismissed it out of hand, but since she spoke very quickly and jumped from one subject to another, I wanted to make sure that I had understood her correctly. I tried again during our conversation to bring up the question at a few points, phrasing it in different ways as best I could manage. By the third time I asked, she turned to me, looking a little exasperated, and said, "Why would we look? Didn't I tell you we thought he had died?"

Based on even just this small handful of interactions, it seemed reasonable to gather that Yi *Halmŏni* felt as much conviction in her belief in her husband's survival, as other family members were assured of the likelihood of his death. I thought again of the media stories about the mothers who lived in waiting, who had defied what everyone around them had presumed to be good sense. What is striking about these stories is how they narrated the unlikely vindication of women who were ultimately proven to have been right all along in holding out hope against tremendous odds.[2] Notably, by focusing on the women who had impractically held onto hope for the survival of a lost loved one, these stories overlook the reasons why other, mostly younger family members would have felt compelled to resign themselves to the loss of those who were missing. When Yi *Halmŏni*'s daughter told me that she had often thought in the past that it would have been better for her mother to come to terms with her father's death, she clearly struck me as expressing concern for her mother's peace of mind, along with her own frustration over what she took to be her mother's obstinacy and melancholia. The daughter had no reason to doubt her own past perception of reality regarding the composition of her extant family. However, in this instance and other similar cases of those given up for dead, left unspoken—or perhaps not overtly taken into consideration—was the danger that would have been attached to any hope for the survival of a family member or relative who went missing during the chaos of war fifty years earlier. That is, it went without saying that to wish for their survival was tantamount to acknowledging that they could still be alive in the North, which would have risked rendering their kin group stigmatized as a "Red family" in the present.

GOOD DEATH, BAD DEATH

To avoid the risk of stigmatization, it was not uncommon for family members of those missing during the war to presume their kin as dead. Several families I interviewed referred to having submitted a death report, after which they proceeded to "straighten out" their official household registers (*hojŏk chŏngni rŭl haessŏyo*), which became a pragmatic means of coping with the already difficult circumstances they faced. Some families went even further, as one reunion participant described removing all official traces of his missing brother: "At first, we regarded him as missing. And after that we took him out of our family records. Later in the war, the *hojŏk* was destroyed in a fire. So when we reconstructed it, we didn't even consider including his name." During the period of recovery from the devastation of the war, to conceal the fact of being related to anyone who left for the North, these families formalized the death of the missing family member not only by submitting a death report but also by performing ceremonial ancestral rites (*chesa*) to memorialize him or her. Because the date of death was unknown, the families I interviewed explained that they held the memorials on the relative's birthday or date of disappearance. In such cases, even if there was a chance that the person in question might still be alive, his or her family brought about a social death in order to eliminate the possible cause of anticipated harm. In *Precarious Life: The Powers of Mourning and Violence*, Judith Butler poses a question that is highly salient here: "What counts as a livable life and a grievable death?"[3] Among these separated families, the tenuous possibility for improving one's life-chances was enabled by the social death of the one who had gone missing, whose actual death could not be verified and therefore could not be truly grieved. In other words, for the family to submit a death report for one who had not died meant that the person herself or himself had to be forgotten. It forced what O Song-chan called "forgetting as cure for trauma of the event."[4]

In a tragic twist to their moral dilemma, however, the gesture of renunciation that offered these families a measure of safety in a Cold War ideological climate put them at great risk in a metaphysical sense. That is, to submit a death report for a missing person was to declare that the relative had a "bad death" (*hoengsa*). In contrast to a "good death" (*hosang*), which is to die at one's home surrounded by one's family and friends after having led a full life, the worst kinds of death in the traditional Korean worldview include: death on the road (*kaeksa*), alone or among strangers; and death while still young, unmarried, and childless.[5] A great many of the cases of the war-missing would in fact represent a combination of all of these circumstances that characterize a bad death. Also included in this category are those killed by violence, accidents, or drowning, and those who died during childbirth or who committed suicide. Their spirits are known as *wŏnhon*, or spiteful souls, which are unable to receive proper funeral ceremonies. These dead therefore remain "ritually unclean" and threaten to become dangerous ghosts or spirits, as their spirits are liable to become lost and disoriented.[6] Unable to enter the next world, they are trapped in a "middle void" where they are condemned to wander the world, bringing illness and misfortune. According to anthropologist Seong-nae Kim, "The spiritual status of those dead souls are considered as abnormal and thus tragic according to the standard of Confucian morality, the status that could unexpectedly bring about a danger to the descendants. The malice of these unquiet souls is imagined to be much more fearful than any regrettable memory of those ancestors who had normal deaths."[7] For countless separated families, their relative's crossing over the border during the war in life made it uncertain whether he or she would be able to cross over to the next world in death, itself a cause for emotional anguish but also regarded as a source of ongoing spiritual peril.

This cultural context explains why many people who had come to the South Korean Red Cross headquarters in July 2000 described themselves as "*choein*," meaning "sinner" or "guilty person," after realizing they had prematurely mourned the loss of their missing family member decades ago. That is, from a Korean perspective, to perform ancestral rites for someone not confirmed as dead is itself a grievous transgression; it is the moral violation of abandoning one's own living kin. These separated families therefore faced a catch-22. If they chose to submit a death report without verifying that their relative had died, they risked betraying their missing family member by colluding in the state's obliteration of his or her memory. Yet, if they refused to submit a death report on grounds of principle or out of devotion to their missing kin, they faced another form of risk by jeopardizing the prospects of stability in their own lives, threatening their own livelihoods as well as the futures of their children and even their descendants. As discussed earlier, the families of those who disappeared or were believed to have gone to the North during the war have only recently been regarded as part of the sympathetic category of "separated family."[8] For decades following the 1950–1953 Korean War, they occupied an ambiguous subject position, which became a place of danger in the period of anticommunist state formation.

Their vulnerability recalls Seong-nae Kim's extensive research investigating cultural legacies and commemorative practices regarding the 1948 Cheju April Third Massacre. Kim evokes the traumatic memories recalling the indiscriminate killings and sexual violence that haunt survivors of the "Red hunt" and their descendants.[9] Civilians with family connections to the guerrillas were regarded as guilty by association, vilified as the "bodies of the Reds" which threatened to reproduce ever more "Reds." As Kim writes: "It was not only the individual communists who were targeted in the extermination campaign, but anyone who fell under the category of 'Reds,' be they the entire extended family of someone who fled to the hills."[10] Even those simply trying to escape the scorched-earth campaign were therefore rendered suspect, or simply anyone who had the misfortune of inhabiting the interior part of the island, which was declared enemy territory. "Even after April Third, once it had been given, the mark 'Red' or 'insurgent' persisted as a burden on the surviving family members or relatives who were thereafter known as the 'Red family' or the 'rebel family,' and were persecuted under the Law of Complicity."[11] Kim asserts that the same hatred that rationalized "the massacre by the public authority of the state" during the Cheju April Third Incident continued long afterward "in the form of continuing tortures, terrorizing, and murders of leftists and other dissidents." Kim regards this collective hatred to be structurally tantamount to racial or genocidal hatred and argues "the anticommunist state of South Korea established its identity with the tactic of *racial* annihilation of the 'Reds.'"[12]

Beyond mere ideological enmity, the logic underpinning South Korean anticommunism comprised a systematic rationalization of state repression through the vilification of leftists and alleged leftists—and by extension their families—as potential threats to the political order, irrespective of their actual actions or beliefs. It should be noted that, during the period after the South Korean state was established in 1948, arrests of those labeled as "leftist" were so indiscriminate as to give rise to a new term: "a government-created communist."[13] Despite such dubious means of ideological categorization, the harrowing fate suffered by National Guidance League [*Kungmin podo yŏnmaeng*] members illustrates how fateful and lethal an identification as "leftist" could be. A state-established organization, the National Guidance League (NGL) ostensibly offered former or "converted" communists in the South another chance for returning to the fold of mainstream society, but in fact the NGL primarily served to keep its members under surveillance and control. As NGL recruitment expanded, many were strongly persuaded to join either through social pressure or by the lure of practical incentives. In her memoir, *Who Ate Up All the Shinga?*, acclaimed South Korean novelist Park Wan-Suh speculates what circumstances motivated her brother's decision to join the NGL: "It's never been clear to me whether he joined the National Guidance Alliance to land a job or he became a member once he started working, but I believe there was a psychological and material relation between the two."[14]

Eventually the NGL would not only be comprised of former leftists but also those from rural areas who had had little meaningful contact with political activities, with more than 70 percent of the NGL rank and file are estimated to have been peasants with "no consistent political identity or ideology."[15] Then, in the days and weeks after the North Koreans invaded in June 1950, NGL members were rounded up as "suspected communists" or "traitors" to be jailed and summarily executed by the ROK police and military police.

Historical sociologist Kim Dong-Choon, former Standing Commissioner of the Truth and Reconciliation Commission–ROK, argues that the scale and brutality of these mass killings of NGL members dwarfed that of other massacres committed during the Korean War. He estimates that a total of one hundred thousand to two hundred thousand deaths resulted from a pattern of killing that began in Suwon and Inchŏn and was soon thereafter repeated in cities and villages throughout South Korea.[16] Regarding the aftermath of such atrocities, political scientist Lee Ryong-kyong writes:

> Afterwards, no one was allowed to speak of the civilian massacres, and via the guilt-by-association system (*yŏnjajwe*), victims' families were identified as "targets for surveillance" and watched closely by the KCIA. The guilt-by-association system meant that members of the NGL and left-related victims' families were characterized as national enemies, potential political dissidents or traitors to state power, and thus the system served as the institutional foundation for various types of repression and expulsion.[17]

Although the "guilt-by-association" system may have officially ended in 1980, it should not be surprising that—given its role as a fundamental element of repressive state anticommunism that had been translated into and reproduced within the social realm—its effects continue to reverberate into the present.

FORGETTING, REMEMBERING, AND THEIR POSSIBILITIES

After receiving the news in mid-July 2000 that his paternal uncle was alive, Mr. Na debated whether or not he would come forward to participate in the reunions. I met the Na family in their Seoul hotel room on the evening of the second day during the August 2000 family meetings. Mr. Na lived in another part of the city, where he ran a small company, and his elderly aunts and uncle had traveled together from their rural hometown several hours away. They were all staying at the Olympic Parktel, a modestly appointed though comfortable hotel in the southeastern part of Seoul where they had received gratis accommodations during the reunions, along with the other South Korean participants.[18] I spoke first with Mr. Na's relatives in their hotel room in Seoul shortly after the first family meeting with their brother from North Korea. I had been initially introduced to the elderly siblings by the Red Cross volunteer designated to help them, and she later mentioned to me in an aside that I should try to speak with their nephew separately if I had the chance. The Red Cross volunteer mentioned that he was thoughtful and well spoken, and although Mr. Na was too young to have ever met his uncle who went to North Korea, she thought that he would likely have things to say. She added that he had apparently attended a university in Seoul and was a pro-democracy activist during the 1980s, something that he later confirmed. I eventually had the chance to speak with Mr. Na on a few occasions, and during one interview, he spoke about his initial reservations about meeting his uncle from the North, which were influenced by the difficulties that had shaped his own life.

It was several weeks after the reunions, and we were at a café as he was recounting his family's story. Mr. Na described the ironic position regarding his own identity as *"changnam,"* the eldest son of an eldest son and traditional position of family heir in a patriarchal kinship order. His father tried to instill in him a keen sense of Confucian values, to which his father was deeply committed. Mr. Na explained that his father also felt very strongly that they must maintain the hope of finding his uncle and thus not submit a death report. He said that, as a young man, he despaired over his father's refusal to alter that position, which effectively meant inviting discrimination against their wider family while effectively foreclosing his own life chances.

Filing a death report would also mean crossing out the lost brother's name in the clan genealogy, a step which Mr. Na's father was unwilling to take. In light of the highly competitive nature of South Korean society, it is notable that Mr. Na's father's decision not to forsake his brother amounted to rejecting the chance to help his son. Mr. Na described agonizing about the consequent dimming of prospects for his future, which sent him into a deep depression, as he felt forced to give up his ambitions to pursue a job where he could apply his abilities. "I hated my life. But I couldn't get a passport, which meant I was trapped in this system," he said. "My uncle had to die so that I could live, but my father refused." At issue between father and son was the struggle over what Clifford Geertz called "genealogical amnesia,"[19] whereby the son tried to persuade the father to partake in an act of forgetting that would afford the younger generation possibilities that would otherwise be ruined by remembering the uncle. This is a conflict in the "politics of forgetting" that balances the obligations of filial duty toward past generations or absent family members with those of protecting the well-being of one's offspring and descendants.[20]

I was struck by how much Mr. Na's story contrasted with what I had heard from his relatives when we had spoken during our earlier group interview at the Olympic Parktel. Evidently, other members of the family had given their lost relative up for dead based on the logic that he would have otherwise managed to send word of his survival somehow. Despite the fact that their late brother, Mr. Na's father, had caused so much strife for his son by refusing to report his missing brother as dead, the other siblings never imagined that he had survived the war. One sister said they had felt guilty because they had essentially forgotten about their brother. Another sibling relayed how surprised they all were to learn that their brother had several children and nearly a dozen grandchildren, meaning that their family was far larger than they had imagined. During the two-hour meeting with their brother, they largely exchanged inquiries about health and caught up on the news regarding their extended family. Mr. Na's uncle said, "The thing he was most happy about was that his siblings were so healthy. I probably don't need to tell you this, but a lot of North Koreans say that people in South Korea are not doing very well. Our brother thought that before, but then he saw that we were all happy and secure and that we were not poor." When these siblings talked among themselves, they joked about their good fortune for being part of a bigger clan than they had been aware of, suggesting traditional notions of Korean prosperity based on the number of children and descendants. One after the other, they continued to marvel at the suddenly expanded number of their close relatives, as they were evidently still taking in their astonishment toward this news and happily recalibrating their sense of family identity.

In contrast, what preoccupied Chang *Halmŏni* after the reunions was not an enlarged sense of family but rather a keen awareness of her brother's own isolation in North Korea over so many years since he had disappeared in 1950. During their meeting, when Chang *Halmŏni* asked her brother why he could not send one letter, he replied that it would be difficult for her to understand. She said, "He tried to explain that North Korea was a 'structured society,' and you have to move within the structure." She remembered being struck by the fact that her brother seemed burdened about not fulfilling his duty as eldest son to care for his parents in their old age. She recounted how he felt he had compensated for his absence in the only way he saw available to him, by attempting to bring honor to his family in a Confucian sense by becoming a scholar. "He said to us, 'Because I was unable to take care of my parents, I am indeed an unfilial son. But for that reason, I studied very hard and received my doctorate to become a professor. You could say that was a kind of filial duty.'" Despite what he said, Chang *Halmŏni* instead took his academic accomplishments as cause to wonder whether he took that path because, being alone without family or relatives, "he could only study." She continued, "When we were talking, he asked about our entire family, even distant relatives that even we had not contacted for a while. He knew their names and remembered small details, such as the birthdays of relatives like our *Chagŭn ŏmma* [the wife of their father's younger brother]." Chang *Halmŏni* said their immediate family in South Korea had actually fallen out of touch with the relatives he asked after. It was something that made her feel embarrassed during their meeting, given that nothing had truly prevented the relatives in the South from being in contact with each other. She added, "He must have really missed having a family, and being so lonely he had vivid memories of all these relatives." Even later, as I prepared to depart, Chang *Halmŏni* remarked again at how astounded she was that her brother had remembered the particulars of so many members of their extended family. It was a feat of memory that had clearly left a moving impression upon her, a performative trace of her brother's wistful solitariness during their fifty years apart.

A CONFLICT OF LOYALTIES TO KIN AND STATE

Past experiences of social isolation was also a recurring motif in the narratives of South Koreans who came forward to participate in the Seoul reunions during August 2000. I met on two occasions with Mr. Koh, whose father's name appeared on the first list of reunion candidates sent from North Korea. I met him along with his brother at Mr. Koh's apartment, and they readily acknowledged their family's past financial struggles while they were growing up without a father. But Mr. Koh felt that what was even worse was the social isolation. "Our mother always kept to herself. Her hobby was needlework, and she did things alone," he said. "We were different from other families. Think about it. How do you make friends? You talk about your children, your family. But for my mother, I suppose it was easier not to get into that kind of awkward situation."[21] What is revealing is how he referred obliquely to the taboo surrounding kin ties with North Korea. This differed from a common perception I had heard from friends and colleagues, that in Cold War South Korea any connection with North Korea was rendered taboo because the North was associated with evil. While families like Mr. Koh's were indeed often subject to stigmatization as "Red families," Mr. Koh described the everyday predicament of having a relative suspected to be in the North through memories of experiencing social sanctions not through Manichean anticommunist discourses of good-versus-evil, but rather in more sublimated forms. He remembered them not as direct condemnations, which could conceivably have been deflected or dismissed, but rather as the lived experiences of marginalizing phenomena whose unseen nature rendered them yet more insidious: self-exclusion, insularity, and loneliness.

In the remainder of this chapter, I consider how the social liminality in South Korea imposed upon families related to known or suspected leftists— including those believed to have gone north of the border before or during the war—comprised a significant means through which anticommunist state policy was translated into everyday life in South Korea.[22] Living under a taboo against speaking about one's kin was particularly isolating given the norms of Korean sociality, whereby asking after and speaking about one's family is often among the first topics of conversation among those getting to know one another or simply being friendly. This most basic means of social interaction was effectively denied or forbidden among these families. While speaking with those affected by politically sensitive kin ties, I encountered recurring references to such social exclusion, not only in terms of an infringement of rights, but also in terms of various mundane but nonetheless substantially consquential forms of social interaction.

Indeed, among the most insidious aspects of division's effects in Korea are those that prove also to be the most elusive, such as fear and suspicion in everyday life. South Koreans commonly refer to a so-called "Red complex" which has been defined as "the exaggerated distorted terror toward the threat of Communism"[23] that stems from decades of anticommunist state discipline. This term also encapulates the social psychology induced by such terror, which justified the violence and intimidation against leftists and their families within South Korean society under state anticommunism.[24] Such attitudes exacerbated the disadvantages that non-normative separated families already faced to gaining access to the social networks upon which Koreans rely extensively in everyday life, networks essential for building an intersubjective life-world through everything from exchanging small favors, to securing employment, to finding eligible marriage partners for one's children.[25]

The pressure created by such discrimination once came up in passing during another interview that autumn with a woman who recalled the tense political atmosphere around the time she and her husband had gotten married, saying, "When we were younger, families of missing persons received severe treatment. Park Chung Hee was in power at the time and had I known about my husband's father being in the North, I might have reconsidered marrying him. Not that it matters now." Among those with whom I spoke, none described being subject to abuse as severe as the atrocities that occurred during the Cheju April Third Massacre or the killings of the NGL members, but many described a sense of psychological anguish and personal turmoil that resulted from experiencing harsh forms of harassment, surveillance, and social discrimination, particularly during the 1970s, when consolidation of the anticommunist state intensified.

Among separated families bearing what anthropologist Heonik Kwan has called "non-normative kin relations," relatives therefore had to wrestle with the decision of whether to report their kin as dead in order to escape discrimination and stigmatization in the historical contexts of South Korean anticommunist nationalism. In the years following the Korean War and during the Park Chung Hee era, leftists and their families were socially marginalized as potential sources of contamination that threatened ideological purity.[26] What were the ethical implications of the kin relationships that were brought to light by the encounter of the North–South family reunions? How did such separated families in South Korea negotiate the tension between both their status as citizens of a national security state within a divided nation, and their quandary as actual and potential victims of ideologically based social risks for having kin on the other side?

Sophocles's tragedy *Antigone* asks a parallel question in terms familiar to classical Greek antiquity: Which takes precedence, *physis* (natural or divine law) or *nomos* (human custom or man-made law)? The play is set in the wake of civil war, after the two sons of Oedipus clashed over the crown of Thebes in a battle that left them both dead. Their uncle, Creon, as the new Theban king, has sided with one brother, Eteocles, whom he honors with a hero's funeral, while condemning the other brother, Polyneices, to remain unburied on the battlefield. Their older sister, Antigone, feels bound by sacred duty to bury her brother Polyneices, which would allow his soul to be released to the underworld. Antigone therefore defies Creon's decree, but she is eventually caught and sentenced to death. Regarding Antigone's predicament to be an allegory for the crisis of kinship, Judith Butler interprets this crisis in terms of which losses receive recognition and sanction as socially legitimate. If kinship is established through being-in-relation, a crisis of kinship follows from severing the recognition of this relationship through "publicly ungrievable loss."[27] Arguing that Antigone's act exposes the contingent nature of kinship and challenges the separability of the state from the politics of kinship, Butler writes, "Can there be kinship . . . without the support and mediation of the state? Can there be the state without the family as its support and mediation?" Antigone here stands as an archetypal figure occupying the liminal spaces between life and death and between the family and the state, embracing kinship outside what man-made law has established as the normative family.[28]

Caught within the conditions of family separation and exilic diaspora, Korean separated family members are similarly figures of liminality insofar as their subject-position makes their families liminal to both states of the divided nation. How is kinship practiced without the support and mediation of the state, or indeed *against* the foundational *nomos* of the state? The reality of Korean family separation at the turn of the millennium moreover raises the question of what happens when it serves the interests of the state to support and mediate precisely the kind of kinship ties that had previously been rendered taboo and outlaw under a prior government. In Seoul during August of 2000, the reunions afforded such an occasion to observe a remarkable reversal, whereby the state under a new leadership actively promoted kinship ties that had been previously stigmatized and persecuted as integral to the consolidation of the anticommunist South Korean state.[29]

In *The Other Cold War*, Heonik Kwon discusses the reconciliatory role that social memory and kinship identity can play in societies that were violently divided by the Cold War and underwent the destructive experience of civil war. At issue for both the political community at large and also for individuals was "the reconciliation of ideologically bifurcated genealogical backgrounds or ancestral heritages" whether the dichotomy was framed as either "'Red' Communists versus anticommunist patriots" or "revolutionary patriots versus anticommunist 'counterrevolutionaries.'" Kwon writes, "In these societies, kinship identity is a significant site of memory for past political conflicts and can also be a locus of creative moral practices."[30] For Kwon, despite the divisive legacy of warfare and internecine violence, both intimate and public dimensions of kinship identity can provide a cultural resource for retrieving social memory across a deeply charged and polarizing ideological divide.

However, the significance of the family as a site of post-conflict reconciliation in South Korea is complicated by a lengthy history of moralizing state appropriations of filial piety discourses. For example, under the regime of Park Chung Hee, the South Korean state of the 1960s and 1970s sought to promote filial piety, much as did the Chosŏn dynasty, as a manifestation of loyalty to the state.[31] In his ethnography *Kyŏngju Things*, anthropologist Robert Oppenheim considers the state promulgation of the Silla Cultural Festival shortly after the 1961 coup that brought Park to power. Analyzing the political pretensions to grandeur appropriated through cultural references to the ancient Silla kingdom, Oppenheim describes how Park participated in opening ceremonies modeled on Confucian ritual observance, playing a role consistent with that of an eldest son in an attempt to garner legitimacy through a stylization as heir to the Silla crown.[32] Moreover, anthropologist Cho Han Hae-Joang also cites Park's earlier mobilization of Confucian values in order to explain the uneasiness among intellectuals and other South Koreans toward the phenomenon of Confucian revivalism dating to the mid-1990s, given that Park's injunctions to preserve loyalty and filial piety too easily blurred with a mandate for state compliance and conformity.[33]

In South Korea's ideologically charged modern context, the notion of filial piety is therefore not a neutral cultural concept, and an exploration of the ethics of kinship here gains clarity from elucidating the distinctions between morality and ethics. *Morality* generally denotes the codes that determine what is permitted or forbidden, or the prescriptions that gauge the positive or negative value of one's behavior; in contrast, *ethics* relates to the individual working out the relevance of moral codes to one's own circumstances and responses. As discussed by Michel Foucault, ethics concerns how the individual constitutes her- or himself as a moral subject of her or his own actions. In *The Use of Pleasure*, Foucault identifies four aspects to this concept of ethics as the relationship of the self to itself. The first concerns what part of the self or one's behavior is concerned with moral conduct. The second addresses what Foucault terms the "mode of subjectivation" (*mode d'assujettissement*), which is "the way in which people are invited or incited to recognize their moral obligations," such as through divine law, natural law, or rational rule. The third aspect pertains to the question of the means one can employ to change oneself to become an ethical subject; in other words, what comprises the "self-forming activity" that one must undergo in order to behave ethically. This entails what Foucault elsewhere calls "techniques," the practices deployed on the self to remake itself. Finally, the fourth aspect asks what is the *telos* of ethical action—what kind of being does one aspire to become when acting in a moral way?[34]

While Foucault sets out to trace a genealogy of ethics in classical Greek philosophy and Western Christianity, his discussion of ethics and its four aspects offers a useful rubric of inquiry for considering the circumstances facing separated families with non-normative kin relations in contemporary Korea. Under the extraordinary conditions of long-term wartime family separation that culminated in improbable reunion, how did the participating families sort out and determine their notions of what comprises ethical action regarding kin, family, and self, while also taking into consideration the values and beliefs they held about the meaning of being citizens, community members, and human beings? In the following sections, I draw upon field interviews with separated families who participated in the Seoul reunions in the early 2000s, to trace how these individuals responded to their circumstances by critiquing, reinventing, or redefining ethical norms, including practices conventionally identified with filial piety. In the process, they would redefine the meaning of kin-based obligation and, by extension, what it means to have acted ethically in a social milieu shaped by the local and intimate consequences of the global Cold War.

PARSING THE FIGURE OF *WANGDDA*

There is a kind of pariah that Koreans call *"Wangdda."* A widely used slang word in vernacular Korean, the term means someone shunned as a social outcast but also targeted for bullying. The term derives from the transitive verb, *wang ddadollinda*, which means "to greatly ostracize" or "to collectively harass and ostracize a person." Since the 1990s, in South Korea *"Wangdda"* has resonated as a one-word signifier for the serious social problem of bullying, affecting students from grade school to high school and beyond.[35] But like references to any social ill, *Wangdda* could also be appropriated for the sake of humor. For example, I recall such an instance while out one night in Seoul among friends and colleagues, when I heard a few of them use the term *"Wangdda"* spontaneously in what amounted to a collective performative joke. The group included several who were long-time friends with each other, and they were sending off a mutual colleague before her departure for a year's research leave abroad. At one point later in the evening, it was apparent that a few of the friends wanted to go home, instead of continuing on for another round of drinking and merrymaking. When it was clear that those opting out would not be persuaded otherwise, the companions turned on them as would-be pariahs, humorously taunting them in mock scorn with jeers of "*Wangdda!*" or "*Paeshinja!*" (traitor). The temporary outcasts received this abuse in sheepish good humor and had little choice but to accept their verdict—for the crime of being antisocial—by slinking off toward sobriety, duly chastened.

This scene called to mind an explanation I had once heard from Kim Dong-Choon, who traced the origins of the contemporary usage for "*Wangdda*" to a context far from humorously playful, that was instead politically and ideologically charged. According to Kim, such usage arose out of the pressures to choose sides before and during the Korean War at the risk of being ostracized by one's peer group.[36] Such pressures were clearly evident in several oral-history accounts I heard from family members who had participated in the inter-Korean family meetings, including one man who had discovered his brother was alive in the North through the reunions program. Describing the time when his brother had disappeared, he recalled an atmosphere of confusion during the period immediately after the outbreak of the war in 1950, when South Korean communist partisans suddenly took over their local district office:

> We didn't know what was going to happen. I didn't know which side to take. It was the experience of living in a kind of stateless twilight zone. . . . If we sided with the People's Republic, would the South Korean army retreat, meaning that the communists would truly take over the country? Or might there be another attack by the South? And what else could we do but go to work if we had jobs?

Amid this profound insecurity about the future, Koreans were forced to take sides, and in this climate, those who actively chose or were involuntarily conscripted to go to the North would become branded as traitors. That left their families to be identified as the relatives of traitors, rendering them as *Wangdda*—or those made available to be beaten, ridiculed, and otherwise punished as those marked for exclusion from the inchoate social order of the new South Korean state.

Because of the term's harsh implications, I therefore found it ironic and surprising when I came across a *positive* interpretation of *Wangdda* in my field interviews with one of the *Wŏlbukcha* family members. It was Mr. Na who mentioned *Wangdda*, linking the notion to a logic characterized not simply by exclusion but also by ethical action. It came up while he was retelling the circumstances under which his uncle disappeared during the war. Mr. Na said:

> In the old days, there was a saying that "You would follow your friend across the Han river" (*ch'inggu ddara Kangnam kanda*). On the one hand, you could say, in Korean there's an expression that you're turning your back on me, which is very commonly used among friends, or in Chinese [characters]

"*Wangdda*,"[37] which means you can't be relied on and you're selfish. So there were of course situations where they sacrifice for others. On the other hand, you could say, "I come first. I come before others."

Mr. Na's uncle was separated from his family when he was apparently recruited or conscripted into the North Korean People's Army along with his friends at school. When the war broke out, mass recruitments occurred at schools and workplaces, resulting in the disappearance of many students or young people who had migrated from the countryside to Seoul for education or work. Regarding these collective recruitment or conscription drives, most families referred to them with expressions of ambiguity about the circumstances under which their relative joined the North Korean army.

About such cases, I often heard the same proverb, "*ch'inggu ddara Kangnam kanda*," which can also be translated as "out of loyalty to a friend, one would go to the ends of the earth." Another common expression was "*cha ŭi pan, ta ŭi pan*," meaning "half one's own intention, half that of another." The implication was that their relative did not take up arms entirely of his or her own volition but was influenced by friends, teachers, or the general atmosphere of the time. For those who disappeared when they were younger, their family members would often ask a rhetorical question along the lines of "He was only fifteen at the time. What did he know?" They therefore distanced their relative from any political or ideological motivation for crossing the divide, a gesture which bears similarities to the sentiment that anthropologist Nancy Abelmann found among the rural villagers of Koch'ang regarding their political allegiances during the war. She writes, "As one man said, during the Korean War 'ignorant people couldn't be reds—you had to know something. We [i.e., ignorant people] just went there if they said 'go there' and the other way if they said 'go the other way.'"[38]

In contrast, Mr. Na's interpretation of the validity of acting out of loyalty to one's friend presumed that such actions were not naïve, ignorant, or even coerced. Rather, he framed it as instead an admirable choice in contrast to the refusal to stick with one's friends. According to Mr. Na, the latter represented selfishness and betrayal, which he deemed understandable grounds for ostracism, and *Wangdda* was therefore a means to enforce the ethic of loyalty among friends. When I asked him the meaning of "*Wangdda*," he thought for a moment before replying:

It's a bad word. It's when you make one of your friends the fool. You make such a fool out of him that he can't even show his face at school. . . . It's collective, mob thinking, group pressure. For instance, if you have five people who come together, you have more pressure. And of course one is really nothing compared to the five, so you pretty much destroy him. The kids also beat them up and pull their hair. You make the kid not want to come to school anymore.

His vivid description of the concept of *Wangdda* struck me as ironic because the scenes of taunting and beatings he described were characteristic of those I had learned of elsewhere, in which the objects of abuse were people like himself, the family members of known leftists.

However, in Mr. Na's account, he eschews taking the perspective of the victim, implying that he identifies with those who felt justified in marginalizing an outcast for the sake of upholding a larger principle of loyalty. In a sense, Mr. Na turns the significance of *Wangdda* on its head. That is, to consign someone to the fate of *Wangdda* is not only a means of bullying the weak and imposing social controls on those deemed misfits, but it can in fact be a mode of subjectification in a Foucauldian sense, in inciting a moral subject to ethical action.

The striking political implication of Mr. Na's perspective is that it recognizes how intense peer pressures existed at the time that the *Wŏlbukcha* made his or her fateful decision to choose one side over another during the war. It also implies a degree of absolution toward that relative for the terrible consequences that the choice eventually yielded for his family in later years and decades. The general perception of *Wŏlbukcha* in South Korean society is that they were overly zealous in their ideological views to have chosen their ideology over the welfare of their families. I heard this sentiment when speaking among journalists who were covering the story when the lists of family members were first sent via the Red Cross. While I was doing field interviews at the Red Cross headquarters, one of the journalists asked me, "Don't you think they were too extreme? To have abandoned their family for their ideology?" Yet, this judgment reflects the influence of later South Korean depictions of *Wŏlbukcha* as enemies of the state and presupposes a teleological understanding of national history as one inevitably directed toward anticommunism. In contrast, Mr. Na moderates their position, recognizing how those who chose to side with the communists in the late 1940s or early 1950s did so during a period characterized by deep uncertainty over the political future.

SELF-MAKING AND ITS LIMITS

Despite Mr. Na's explanation of the compensatory and ethically complex aspects of *Wangdda*, it was far more common for families of those who crossed to the North during the war to narrate experiences of social exclusion and stigmatization from the viewpoint of the victim. For example, another method of social exclusion was a system of background checks that prevented the relatives of *Wŏlbukcha* and other leftists from gaining positions in the government, military, and established companies. The impact of the background check could be devastating to their careers and their chances to pursue a secure livelihood, preventing them from regular employment in main-stream society. I noticed that many of those whom I interviewed were running their own small businesses. Indeed, entrepreneurship was one coping mechanism for economic survival, although surely a difficult path given the limited social networks which such families generally had available.

I met Mr. Han and his wife at the Red Cross office, where they had come to confirm the family identity and contact information after seeing the name of Mr. Han's brother on the list sent from North Korea. I spoke with them briefly and then met for a longer interview at their home several days later. After we briefly chatted about my own family, Mr. Han began to talk about his brother, who had disappeared in 1950 at the age of sixteen:

> I don't know whether *Hyŏng* (Older Brother) went North or just ended up in the North. What I know is that at the time he was attending H___ Middle School in his third or fourth year, I can't exactly remember. . . . What I found out later was that the North Korean army gathered at that school, and they say it was used as a staging area for assembling troops (*chip'kyŏlchi*). At that time he said he was going to school and did not return. And we were also out of our right senses, caught up with trying to stay alive during the war. After that, we guess that *Hyŏng* went to the North. I was ten years old. When he disappeared, especially my mother was deeply aggrieved. Now it's been a year since she died, the 14th [of August] is her one-year memorial, and *Hyŏng* arrives on the 15th. It's too ironic.

Unlike most of the reunion participants, Mr. Han was aware that his brother was alive in North Korea, something his family learned through a chain of events in the mid-1960s. One day a mysterious letter arrived from Japan in his ancestral hometown, a small village where several of his relatives were still living. The letter was sent to the home where Mr. Han had grown up, but it never reached his family. Rather than attempting to forward it to Mr. Han's father, who was the addressee, a local postal clerk evidently surmised the letter might have come from the missing brother and reported it to the police. Mr. Han said that, after that point, his family suffered "all kinds of hardships," including being placed under surveillance and regularly visited by the police. He recounted trying to obtain an entry-level position at several companies, but wherever he applied, the existence of his brother would come up in a background check. Then, in a fluke, Mr. Han managed to secure a job in a forestry agency. He said, "I worked for only three days. But then they went back and repeated my background check, and I couldn't go back to the office after the third day. So for one year I stayed at home and laid low, doing nothing. My father decided to support me to start whatever I might not otherwise be able to do. . . . I agonized about what to do." Eventually, he started his own business in car repair, and added, "Even now I have been afflicted by all kinds of things, but I have no regrets."

In addition to repeating "I have nothing to hide," Mr. Han also returned to this phrase, "I have no regrets" (*huhoe ka opsŏyo*), several times during our conversation. I found those two statements striking because he was responding not to any question or comment that I posed, but rather he seemed to be denying the assumptions that other Koreans would likely have made about him and his family. I noticed how he would state these pronouncements with a tone of conviction, saying each word firmly and sometimes making a sweeping gesture with his hand. These simple statements therefore came across as a kind of reflexive performance of defiance. He was at once making a verbal negation of the suspicion that had been directed toward his family during decades of surveillance, and also a denial of the resentment that others might easily ascribe to *Wŏlbukcha* families. It was as if he had inhabited these two negations, simultaneously rejecting the presumed resentment that might be expected of him and instead appropriating its contradiction as a gesture of willed self-making.

Mr. Han's remarks suggest how kinship represents something beyond a system of moral obligation toward those with whom one is related, and instead constitutes what anthropologist Lamia Karim calls "a generative structure of possibilities and impossibilities of self-making."[39] While individuals do not possess limitless agency in self-making, they are also not wholly determined by subjection to moral precepts, social structures, or state policy. Among such marginalized Korean separated families, the endeavors to make and unmake the possibilities of "specific kinds of selves" went beyond the dynamic between normative community values—such as *hyo*, or filial piety—on the one hand, and the families' "performative responses"[40] on the other. Instead, participants in the reunions negotiated competing and conflicting normative prescriptions for behavior.

Similarly, Mr. Na spoke of how his father was preoccupied with protecting the traditional principles of the family and lineage; however, the traditional obligations against forgetting one's blood relations could not be reconciled with the Cold War political and ideological environment without subjecting one's family to terrible risks. Another reunion participant, Mr. Chun, explained that his family had no choice but to abandon hope about his older brother, as they were too preoccupied with their own survival: "When I say 'give up,' it was not really a matter of giving up. It was simply impossible to meet. We had to leave it far behind us and forget. If we needlessly kept thinking about our inability to meet each other, it would totally debilitate us physically and for no reason. So psychologically we had to live as if it never happened. We had no choice." Again an ethos of survival under hostile circumstances offered up forgetting as the cure, and to Mr. Chun it seemed self-evident that a problematic absence in one's family would be most sensibly transformed into kinship with oblivion.

   Such willed forgetting resonates with anthropologist Sonia Ryang's exploration of the concept of consanguinity (blood relation) in a contemporary
transnational milieu. She observes that the "dissolution of 'traditional family'
is happening beyond the west or the US (as in Korea or Japan), if not necessarily because of divorce and separation, but because of historically generated conditions of international relations of power such as colonialism, civil
war, immigration, and the Cold War. Furthermore, these two factors—domestic dissolutions of the family and the world-historical factors—coincide
and converge to configure and rationalize the new partitions and unities of
the family."[41] Notably, such convergences of factors could also conspire to
make the very conditions of family separation effectively unseen or presumed to be beyond the threshold of death, so that immediate kin could well
be unwitting of their own identity as individuals with living family members
on the other side of the Korean divide.

   In domestic and international press coverage of the August 2000 reunions, media images replayed and sensationalized their most heartrending
moments, while on a national scale the reunion participants were fêted as
their family meetings were hailed as an unequivocal milestone in the inter-
Korean peace process. However, the celebratory atmosphere of these breakthrough family meetings was shadowed by accounts of reunion participants
who spoke of discrimination, persecution, and atomization experienced during the decades after the war. As family members came forward to reclaim
those presumed to have been dead for fifty years, the reappearance of lost
family members during these exchange meetings brought buried social identities and relationships back to life. Such resurfacings were conditioned by
the existential and political liminality that shaped lives among the fraught
circumstances of belonging for circles of kin. They had been unable to confirm the fates of their missing family members while they had also been
stigmatized for their blood relationship with those same relatives.

   In Korea, the losses stemming from catastrophic war are sweeping in
scale, and the legacies of the Korean War's staggering death toll still remain
unresolved amid the ongoing territorial division and hostile confrontation
between the two states on the peninsula. However, the reunions participants'
stories also gave witness to far more mundane losses of a personal and
quotidian nature, which were nonetheless central to their situated experiences
of liminality in a divided nation—including discrimination, derailed careers,
economic hardship, diminished life-chances, and a sense of thwarted personal fate due to social isolation. Their narratives reveal how individuals facing
such circumstances repeatedly endeavored to grasp, if not fulfill, the ethical
obligations they had to kindred both living and dead on both sides of the
border, in part to compensate for how their lives and relationships had been
distorted by war and division.

As their stories first came to wider public attention in South Korea during the August 2000 reunions, such non-normative separated families took on a double-signification through their collective identity as liminal entities who had long been marginalized as social pariahs until their temporary elevation to a designated high-profile role sanctioned by the state through the inter-Korean family meetings.[42] The families who participated in the Seoul reunions thereby came to signify an inversion of their negative subject position, no longer "matter out of place" as during the military authoritarian period, but instead valorized in the hopeful moment of millennial post-Summit optimism. Through this unexpected reversal of fortunes, these families emerged in August 2000 as the visible and embodied link between two inverse agendas by different governments in South Korea's modern past—the consolidation of the anticommunist state under Park Chung Hee, and the pursuit of reconciliation with the North during the Sunshine Era under Kim Dae-jung.

In other words, what they evoked was the oppositional relationship between these two historical moments, while also highlighting the parallels and contradictions between them. The eras symbolized respectively by Park and Kim may have been characterized by political objectives that were diametrically opposed. However, both Park and Kim in their own time similarly deployed state-directed cultural policies that promoted developmentalist agendas, which sought to mobilize national subjects through the invocation of traditional values. No other reunion event, before or since, more clearly or dramatically represented this reciprocal dynamic in South Korea between, on the one hand, inter-Korean rapprochement and, on the other, a domestic process of reconciliation regarding the social, cultural, and personal legacies of anticommunist state formation. That is because the participants in the August 2000 reunions in Seoul were readily recognized among Koreans as those who could bear direct witness to both historical periods through indelible personal experiences. Indeed, members of these separated families were those individuals previously marginalized under state anticommunism who, at a moment of unprecedented promise for reconciliation, briefly rose to prominence in a new and privileged role, thereby revealing in a double sense their legibility and vulnerability as liminal subjects.

NOTES

1. These extended practices of waiting—such as the ritual of repeatedly preparing a favorite meal in anticipation of a loved one's return—are dramatized in Kang Je-Gyu's poignant short film, "Awaiting" (*Minu-ssi Onŭnnal*, 2014).

2. For married women like Yi *Halmŏni*, the phenomenon of waiting is particularly gendered. Conservative Confucian attitudes would have influenced Yi *Halmŏni*'s generation, including the restrictive cultural expectation that idealized widows who remained chaste wives for the rest of their lives, although the same obligation was in no way expected of widower husbands. However, it should be noted that such unequal standards for chastity were challenged

as early the late 1930s by pioneering Korean feminist intellectuals. See, for example, "Paek Ch'ŏl: A New View on Chastity," in *New Women in Colonial Korea: A Sourcebook*, ed. Hyaeweol Choi (London and New York: Routledge, 2012), 148–52. Notably, the position of these "New Women" in colonial Korea critiqued the norms of chastity not only for widows but also for women whose husbands or lovers had fled the country. See Theodore Jun Yoo, *The Politics of Gender in Colonial Korea: Education, Labor, and Health, 1910–1945* (Berkeley and Los Angeles: University of California Press, 2008), 81–82.

3. Judith Butler, *Precarious Life: The Powers of Mourning and Violence* (London: Versa, 2006), 146.

4. Quoted in Seong-nae Kim, "Lamentations of the Dead: The Historical Imagery of Violence on Cheju Island, South Korea," *Journal of Ritual Studies* 3, no. 2 (1989): 251–85.

5. David Prendergast, *From Elder to Ancestor: Old Age, Death and Inheritance in Modern Korea* (Leiden, NL: BRILL/Global Oriental, 2005), 180.

6. See also Heonik Kwon's parallel discussions of the condition of displaced afterlife and the concept of "death in the street" in *The Ghosts of War in Vietnam* (New York: Cambridge University Press, 2008), chapter 1 and 85–90.

7. Kim, "Lamentations of the Dead," 238.

8. See chapter 2.

9. Seong-nae Kim, "Sexual Politics of State Violence: On the Cheju April Third Massacre of 1948," in *"Race" Panic and the Memory of Migration*, ed. Meaghan Morris and Brett De Bary (Hong Kong: Hong Kong University Press, 2001), 259–83; Seong-nae Kim, "Women, Mourning, and the Ritual of Death in the Family," in *Gender and Family in East Asia*, ed. Siumi Maria Tam, Wai Ching Angela Wong, and Danning Wang (New York and London: Routledge, 2014).

10. Kim, "Sexual Politics of State Violence," 266. The term "Red" here is a literal translation of *bbalgaenggi*, but its usage in the South Korean vernacular connotes a more malevolent pejorative, closer to the combination of "Commie" in American slang modified by a hateful adjective.

11. Ibid., 267.

12. Ibid., 268.

13. Namhee Lee, "Anticommunism, North Korea, and Human Rights in South Korea: 'Orientalist' Discourse and Construction of South Korean Identity," in *Truth Claims: Representation and Human Rights*, ed. Mark Philip Bradley and Patrice Petro (New Brunswick, NJ: Rutgers University Press, 2002), 45.

14. Park Wan-Suh, *Who Ate Up All the Shinga?* (New York: Columbia University Press, 2009).

15. Dong-Choon Kim, "Forgotten War, Forgotten Massacres—The Korean War (1950–1953) as Licensed Mass Killings," *Journal of Genocide Research* 6, no. 4 (2004): 534.

16. Ibid., 535. Kim acknowledges that other scholars estimate the death toll reached as high as three hundred thousand people, based on an estimated NGL membership of 350,000 immediately prior to the war's outbreak.

17. Lee Ryong-kyong, "War and Women's Lives: On the Experience of Bereaved Women of Left-Related Victims of the Korean War," *The Review of Korean Studies* 6, no. 1 (2003): 91.

18. Meanwhile the visiting North Korean family members were put up in a different part of Seoul at a separate hotel, the Walker Hill Sheraton, which was more luxurious and far better equipped for security purposes; for more details, see chapter 4, note 3.

19. Clifford Geertz, "Ideology as a Cultural System," in *Ideology and Discontent*, ed. David Apter (New York: Free Press, 1964), 55.

20. Janet Carsten, "The Politics of Forgetting: Migration, Kinship and Memory on the Periphery of the Southeast Asian State," *Journal of the Royal Anthropological Institute* 1, no. 2 (1995): 317–35.

21. Similarly, regarding the bereaved families of left-identified victims of political violence, Lee discusses the agonizing phenomena of social banishment and the dissolution of communities. See "War and Women's Lives," 96–100.

22. In a "mirror" effect typical of divided Korea, *Wŏllammin* (those who crossed over to the South during the Korean War) separated families were categorized by the North Korean state as

reactionaries and counterrevolutionaries. For a discussion of how the separated families issue has been regarded in North Korea, see Gwi-Ok Kim, *Isan'gajok, "pan'gongjŏnsa" to "ppalgaengi" to anin* (Seoul: Yŏksabip'yŏngsa, 2004), 116–29.

23. Jun-man Kang, ed., *Redŭ k'omp'ŭlleksŭ: Kwangki ka namgin ahopkae ŭi ch'osang* [Red Complex: Nine Portraits That the Madness Left Behind] (Seoul, Korea: Samin, 1997), 7.

24. Ibid., 7. For a comparative discussion of the parallel phenomenon that exists in North and South Korea in this regard, see Hae-joang Cho-Han and Suhaeng Kim, *"Pan'gong/Panje kyuyul sahoe ŭi munhwa/kwŏllyŏk"* [Culture and Power in Anti-Communist/Anti-Imperialist Disciplined Society], in *T'albundan sidae rŭl yŏlmyŏ* [Opening an Era of Post-Division], ed. Cho-Han Hae-joang and Lee Woo-young (Seoul: Samin, 2000), 116–63.

25. See Uhn Cho, *Ch'immukŭro chiŭn chip* [The House Built by Silence] (Paju, Korea: Munhak Dongnae, 2003); Uhn Cho,*"Wŏllamgajok kwa wŏlbukgajok ŭi chanyŏdŭl ŭi kusul ŭl chungsimŭro,"* [Remembering the Korean War and the Politics of Memory: Experiences of *"Wollam"* and *"Wolbuk"* Families' Descendants], *Sahoe wa yŏksa* [Society and History] 77 (2008): 191–229.

26. Heonik Kwon, "The Korean War and the Political Life of Kinship," paper presented at the British Association of Korean Studies conference, Asia House, London, United Kingdom, November 2010.

27. Judith Butler, *Antigone's Claim: Kinship between Life and Death* (New York: Columbia University Press, 2013 [2000]), 24.

28. Ibid., 5. See also Kwon's related discussion of Antigone, Hegel, and Butler, in *Ghosts of War in Vietnam*, 158 ff.

29. Soo-Jung Lee, *"T'alnaengjŏn minjok spekt'ŏk'ŭl minjok munhwa yŏngu"* 59 (2013): 95–122, and "Making and Unmaking the Korean National Division," PhD dissertation, Urbana–Champaign: University of Illinois, 2006. For an historical comparison, consider the South Korean government's efforts to promote marriages in the early 1990s between Korean farmers and ethnic Korean or *Chosŏnjok* women in northeastern China, using government-funded matchmakers and sponsored "marriage tours" in an attempt "to redress the shortage of rural brides." See Caren Freeman, *Making and Faking Kinship: Marriage and Labor Migration between China and South Korea* (Ithaca, NY: Cornell University Press, 2011).

30. Kwon, *The Other Cold War* (New York: Columbia Universityt, 2010), 113.

31. Roger L. Janelli, and Dawnhee Yim, "The Transformation of Filial Piety in Contemporary South Korea," in *Filial Piety: Practice and Discourse in Contemporary East Asia* (Stanford, CA: Stanford University Press, 2004).

32. See Robert Oppenheim, *Kyŏngju Things: Assembling Place* (Ann Arbor, MI: University of Michigan Press, 2008), 57.

33. Cho Hae-Joang, "Constructing and Deconstructing 'Koreanness,'" in *Making Majorities: Constituting the Nation in Japan, Korea, China, Malaysia, Fiji, Turkey, and the United States*, ed. Dru C. Gladney (Stanford, CA: Stanford University Press, 1998), 73–91. Recent literature on the Park Chung Hee period has explored the interplay of the era's prevailing ideologies: anticommunist statism, national developmentalism, and patriarchal familism. See Hyung-A Kim and Clark W. Sorensen, eds., *Reassessing the Park Chung Hee Era, 1961–1979: Development, Political Thought, Democracy, and Cultural Influence* (Seattle: University of Washington Press, 2011); Chihyung Jeon, "A Road to Modernization and Unification: The Construction of the Gyeongbu Highway in South Korea," *Technology and Culture* 51, no. 1 (2009): 55–79; and Seung-Mi Han, "The New Community Movement: Park Chung Hee and the Making of State Populism in Korea," *Pacific Affairs* 77, no. 1 (2004): 69–93.

34. Michel Foucault, *The History of Sexuality, Volume 2: The Use of Pleasure* (New York: Knopf Doubleday, 2012 [1990]), 25–28.

35. There is an extensive literature on this topic in counseling, psychology, public health, and medicine; for example, Young Shin Kim et al., "School Bullying and Suicidal Risk in Korean Middle School Students," *Pediatrics* 115, no. 2 (2005): 357–63.

36. Kim Dong-Choon, interview with author, October 20, 2000.

37. By "Chinese characters," Na *Sŏnsaengnim* is noting the etymology of *wangdda* as a Sino-Korean word.

38. Nancy Abelmann, *Echoes of the Past, Epics of Dissent: A South Korean Social Movement* (Berkeley: University of California Press, 1996), 100.

39. Lamia Karim, "A Kinship of One's Own," in *The Ethics of Kinship: Ethnographic Inquiries*, ed. James D. Faubion (Lanham, MD: Rowman & Littlefield, 2001), 101.

40. Ibid., 100.

41. Sonia Ryang, "A Note on Transnational Consanguinity, Or Kinship in the Age of Terrorism," *Anthropological Quarterly* 77, no. 1 (2004): 750.

42. See related discussion in chapter 5 of research on the liminality of chronic pain sufferers by medical anthropologist Jean E. Jackson, who contends "liminality is positively valued only when society provides a special status or role for the liminal object, state, or being." In Jackson, "Stigma, Liminality, and Chronic Pain," *American Ethnologist* 32, no. 3 (2005): 333.

Conclusion

Meeting with the Past

In the opening scenes of the 2004 South Korean blockbuster film *Tae Guk Gi: The Brotherhood of War* (*T'aegŭkki hwinallimyŏ*), directed by Kang Je-gyu, an elderly man receives a phone call from someone who soon apologizes for what he takes to be a case of mistaken identity. The caller is a member of a South Korean army excavation team seeking next of kin after unearthing a set of battlefield remains, which they had identified as someone bearing the same name, Lee Jin-seok. The conversation sends the elderly man to the excavation site because he suspects what they found is actually the skeleton of his elder brother, Jin-tae, who has been missing for over fifty years since the war. This is the frame-story of the film, whose main narrative is told as an extended flashback when the two brothers are in their youth. That extended central part of the film begins at the time of the war's major outbreak in June 1950, when the idyllic world of their family is shattered as both brothers are swept into conscription.

Assigned to the same unit, the elder brother Jin-tae, an unschooled shoe-maker, takes it upon himself to protect the younger Jin-seok, a promising student on whom their family has pinned their future hopes. Jin-seok is bewildered and disturbed to see his brother often putting his own life in danger, unaware that Jin-tae has secured a promise from his commanding officer: in exchange for Jin-tae winning the Medal of Honor, Jin-seok would then be sent home. Jin-tae goes on to pull off several feats of daring that border on suicidal, eventually securing him the medal, but it proves useless for achieving his ultimate aim of relieving his brother of duty. Due to the unexpected turn of the tide following China's entry into the war, the deal is off. Moreover, by that point, the younger brother had become disgusted by

187

Figure 6.1. In the film *Tae Guk Gi: The Brotherhood of War* (*T'aegŭkki hwinallimyŏ*), protagonists Jin-seok (Won Bin) and Jin-tae (Jang Dong-gun) are brothers conscripted into the army and forcefully separated from their family. *Tae Guk Gi: The Brotherhood of War*, directed by Kang Je-gyu, 2004 © Samuel Goldwyn Films.

the elder brother's recklessness, which had put other soldiers in danger and had cost the life of at least one mutual friend, whose battle death would leave behind a young child to grow up fatherless.

The film challenges orthodox nationalist narratives by suggesting that those fighting the war were largely motivated by loyalty to their families and closest friends, rather than out of commitment to the state or ideology.[1] But it also shows how complicated were many of the circumstances that led to the separation of families during the war, representing a manifold array of causes resulting from coercion, volition, and happenstance, amid brutal violence that occurred on and off the battlefield. In one scene after the South Korean army retakes Seoul, the brothers return separately to the vicinity of their family home, but the visit soon turns into a crisis when Jin-tae's fiancée Young-shin is abducted by pro-government thugs and accused of being a communist. When Young-shin learns she has been targeted because her name appeared on a list of people who had attended pro-North rallies, she explains in exasperation that she did so to obtain food, rather than allow her family to starve. Ultimately, Jin-tae is unable to save her from being summarily executed, and he later is led to believe that Jin-seok dies while incarcerated in a military prison that is deliberately set on fire by retreating South Korean troops. Unbeknownst to the elder brother, Jin-seok does survive, though he is injured and is sent to a veterans' hospital for his convalescence. While recovering, the younger brother learns from military officials that Jin-tae has crossed over to fight for the other side, an act of treason by a decorated Southern soldier that represents a huge propaganda coup for the North.

Realizing that Jin-tae would have switched sides out of the rage he must have felt over the perceived murders of both his fiancée and his brother, Jin-seok volunteers to find his older brother and bring him back to the South. After surviving hand-to-hand combat while searching on the battlefield, Jin-seok improbably finds Jin-tae, who does not initially recognize the younger brother whom he believes to be dead. Only after an extended struggle and Jin-seok's desperate pleas invoking their naïve former aspirations for their family, does Jin-tae come to his senses. But the two brothers become separated again on the battlefield, where Jin-tae resumes his earlier role as a protective martyr to allow the younger brother to escape back to southern lines. The film ends in the present with the elderly protagonist Jin-seok speaking at the excavation site in present-day South Korea and lamenting the fate of his absent brother who could not keep his promise to return. The camera then shifts perspective to show a full-dress military ceremony honoring the burial of Jin-tae's remains at the film's close.

Breaking box-office records in 2004 as the highest-grossing film then to date in South Korea, *The Brotherhood of War* became the first major hit among a new generation of South Korean war films whose themes about the war's human costs marked a departure from Cold War interpretations of the war and reflected the warming of relations between the Koreas.[2] It is notable that the film, which would garner global attention, is readily recognized as a story of a war-separated family, even though it confounds what had long been the traditional notion of separated families in anticommunist South Korea. That the protagonist who crossed over to the North was not portrayed as a villain or an ideologue further reflected a reconsideration of the complexity of wartime identifications.[3] Given the importance accorded to these aspects of the narrative, the film's runaway success demonstrated how, despite the recurring challenges facing the political aspects of inter-Korean rapprochement, the reconciliatory events that had taken place at the turn of the millennium clearly left a profound and enduring cultural impact in South Korea.

REFRAMING SOUTH KOREAN COSMOPOLITANISM

Truly, the family meetings that took place in August 2000 served as a watershed political ritual imbued with the hopes of prospective national reunification, as well as the possibilities of radical inclusion implicit in the process of reconciliation. In this way, I argue that the reunions signaled the *cosmopolitan* orientation of South Korea's most proactive decade of engagement with North Korea, though highlighting its relation to cosmopolitanism might initially seem counter-intuitive. In the context of contemporary South Korea, cosmopolitan subjectivity is a complex phenomenon. On the one hand, cosmopolitanism is one of the most coveted markers of personal identity, the brass ring in an intensely competitive society, where strategies for class reproduction and aspirations for social mobility are attuned to a globalized milieu. Cosmopolitanism in this sense primarily denotes the fluid crossing of national boundaries and an urbane transcendence of parochial affiliations and ethnic nationalism, a perspective that simultaneously takes for granted elitist neoliberal sensibilities of competitiveness, risk-taking, and self-management. It is epitomized by the cultural capital ascribed to education abroad and the widespread strenuous efforts to have one's children master multiple global languages, particularly English.[4] North Korea, if it figures at all into this competition-focused perspective, is met with a sense of indifference[5] or regarded with condescending disdain and annoyance.

On the other hand, other concepts at the heart of cosmopolitanism have received far less attention with respect to South Korea, particularly the ideals of "openness," tolerance, the moral incorporation of the other, the ethical abjuring of partiality, and the desire to remove longstanding boundaries and borders. This broader philosophical understanding of cosmopolitanism is particularly salient for South Korea where a hostile opposition to North Korea was formative to its national identity, an enmity that continued in official state policy until the Kim Dae-jung administration.[6] If one were to interpret cosmopolitanism as an overcoming of boundaries, the concept also holds special resonance for those South Koreans whose life-chances had been limited by obstacles to gaining employment or access to overseas travel due to their problematic family connections. The ability to travel abroad during the Cold War period was not only an economic class distinction; such freedom of transnational mobility also signified the confirmation of an ideologically "pure" bloodline, one that was untainted by allegiances to or sympathy with leftist groups among one's family members and extended kin. Notably, during the period immediately after Korea's liberation from colonial rule in 1945, it was arguably the most cosmopolitan group of intellectuals and educated youth whose universalist political convictions had compelled them to cross North in the period prior to and during the Korean War, and later anticommunist state policies of "guilt-by-association" sought to parochialize the family members and extended kin they left behind in South Korea by limiting their social mobility and restricting their movement beyond state borders.

In his article, "Ghosts of War and the Spirit of Cosmopolitanism," Heonik Kwon traces a concise conceptual trajectory of cosmopolitanism in European intellectual history to describe how the rise of nation-states supplanted a prior cosmopolitan worldview rooted in local collective memory. Following historian John Gillis, Kwon explains this by way of the concomitant existence of two worlds—one agrarian and feudal, and the other urban and multicultural—during the late medieval and early modern period in Western Europe. That is, collective memory could be at once cosmopolitan *and* local because it reflected extant parallels across space, a sense of continuity which later became disrupted and subsumed by burgeoning nationalisms. As Kwon writes, "[I]t is, historically, through the invention of modern national consciousness that the local and the cosmopolitan are perceived to be on separate spatial scales."[7] Kwon develops a related discussion in his book *Ghosts of War in Vietnam*, citing anthropologist Richard Werbner's characterization that, with the incorporation of collective memory into national memory, what follows is "the state's encompassment of the personal identities of citizens."[8] Notable here is Kwon's *reversal* of the temporal relationship conventionally ascribed to cosmopolitanism and nationalism. That is, in the recent anthropological and sociological literature, cosmopolitanism is usually regarded as moving *beyond* national allegiances; in contrast, Kwon portrays the spirit of cosmopolitanism as an ethos that *precedes* the nation and can be recovered or revived as a rightful inheritance.

This temporal move underpins his reading of Antigone as well as writings by Kant, Hegel, and others, to illuminate rituals in postwar Vietnam that commemorated the marginalized spirits of dead family members who had fought on the opposite side. He writes, the "act of claiming the rights of kinship to remember the dead, against the background of a civil war, is simultaneously that of empowering the universal ethics of commemoration."[9] Here, Kwon's line of argument opens the possibility to consider kinship *not* as inevitably partial, another counterintuitive intervention in the discourse on cosmopolitanism. In other words, invocations of kinship can in fact motivate ethical action in the service of broadly shared common ends, rather than narrow interests. To appreciate more fully the implications of this interpretation, consider two key questions that arise from the logic of a more inclusive cosmopolitanism, which are clearly relevant to the ethical challenges raised by post-conflict reconciliation in divided Korea and beyond: Why care for the stranger and the enemy? Why care for distant others, when I have obligations to my own kith and kin?

To legitimize mass killing, modern warfare depends upon a sustained process that renders one's enemy less than human through mechanisms of dehumanization that are not only militarized in the obvious senses but also in ways that are psychological, linguistic, and socio-cultural. Reconciliation in war's aftermath therefore requires a means by which to reinstate the humanity of the enemy. In *Political Crime and the Memory of Loss*, anthropologist John Borneman writes of how reconciliation is contingent upon creating the conditions that go beyond simply developing a sense of trust but also make possible a sense of *caring* for the enemy. He writes that trust "must be reestablished under new conditions of the production of truth, conditions that embed the individual, the ethnic group, and the truth-effects in larger and more global concentric circles—networks—of others. Caring for the enemy, then, becomes an essential aspect of any ongoing reconciliation."[10] Suggestive here is how the building of trust is not represented as merely an escalating series of quid pro quo transactions, but rather a widening of the social imagination. If caring for the enemy is also a central concern of a more inclusive cosmopolitanism, one way to analyze the significance of the meetings in August 2000 among Korean separated family members is to consider how they characterized a concerted attempt to mobilize this kind of broader cosmopolitan memory in post-Summit South Korea.

TENSIONS SURROUNDING LATER REUNIONS

As the reunion events among separated families were intended to mediate the inter-Korean transition between enmity and reconciliation, soon after they were successfully concluded, economic cooperation projects proceeded apace. In the months following the August reunions, representatives from the two Koreas proceeded with working-level meetings to hammer out details, a process that would culminate in the signing of four major agreements on inter-Korean economic cooperation at the Fourth Inter-Korean Ministerial Talks in December 2000.[11] Among the cooperative projects that resulted from increased bilateral economic ties between the two Koreas was the establishment of two Special Economic Zones (SEZs), Mt. Kŭmgang Resort and the Kaesong Industrial Complex (KIC).[12] With these two projects comprising the core of inter-Korean economic cooperation, the Kaesong Industrial Complex represented a cooperative venture focused on manufacturing—combining North Korean land and labor with South Korean capital and expertise—while the Mt. Kŭmgang Resort was chiefly regarded as a source of tourism revenue for North Korea. Mt. Kŭmgang, or "Diamond Mountains," known for dramatic vistas with jagged peaks, is regarded in both legend and cultural vernacular as the most scenic mountain setting on the Korean peninsula.[13] Inaccessible to South Koreans for a half-century after the peninsula was divided into two states, the storied destination became the focus of investment and a key site for the development of the tourism industry in North Korea as part of the economic opening that began in 2000. Beginning with the fourth round of the reunions, Mt. Kŭmgang would also be established as the new venue for several subsequent separated-family meetings, with a permanent reunions center constructed in 2008. Meanwhile, logistics for continuing the reunions program would become intertwined with efforts to promote tourism to North Korea.[14]

However, following the first round of reunions in August 2000, meetings among North–South separated families would never again capture the national imagination to the degree that they had in those months immediately following the June Summit. In the years since 2000, the cultural meaning of inter-Korean family meetings changed dramatically as the reunions became more marginal, less visible, and repeatedly complicated by cross-border relations. Despite the advances of the early Sunshine Period, the reversal of U.S. support for inter-Korean reconciliation that occurred with the election of George W. Bush was a major setback. In contrast to the mood of hopeful aspiration that greeted the June Summit and particularly the August 2000 reunions, a heightened preoccupation with national security would alter the international climate after September 11, 2001, and this would inevitably impinge upon the inter-Korean family meetings. As described below, the controversy and uncertainty that marred the planning of the fourth round of reunions provide a clear illustration of how the adverse international geopolitical environment significantly soured the relationship between the two Koreas and by extension constrained the possibilities for the inter-Korean reunions program.

The first three reunions in 2000–2001 had been negotiated to take place in Seoul and Pyongyang as part of the agreement signed between the two Korean leaders at the June Summit. However, there was no stipulation for such an exchange of delegations across the de facto border for further rounds and, beginning with the fourth round, the reunions would only take place in North Korea. This restriction in part reflected the fact that only a very limited number of separated family members in the North would come from a position high enough in that society be granted permission to travel outside of the country without posing a defection risk. The fourth reunion had been scheduled to take place in October 2001, and the two sides had exchanged lists of candidates for confirming the survival of prospective reunion participants, as they had done for the prior three rounds. However, less than a week prior to its scheduled start on October 16, the North abruptly canceled the events, protesting the heightened security in the South. The increased security measures in the South, put in place after the September 11 terror attacks in the United States, were viewed by North Korean sources as targeted against the DPRK. A Pyongyang statement criticized Seoul's moves to strengthen security as "dangerous acts that severely incite us" and described the cancellation of the reunions as a temporary postponement that would only be removed once South Korea were to lift its special alert status. North Korea demanded a peaceful atmosphere for exchanges, rather than a "situation on the verge of war."[15] The two sides eventually renegotiated the fourth reunion to take place the following spring, from April 28 to May 3, 2002, but the subsequent reunions would be shadowed by the tensions of nuclear and military crises. Then, in 2008, a South Korean tourist, a fifty-three-year-old woman named Pak Wang Ja, was shot and killed by a North Korean soldier while she was taking an early morning walk and had wandered into a restricted zone. Anthropologist Christian Park notes that, while no one regarded this as an act of war, unanswered questions led to an increase in suspicions between the two states. Following this incident, tours to Mt. Kŭmgang would be suspended altogether.[16]

Clearly, after the first three rounds of reunions, circumstances for inter-Korean family meetings became more uncertain and contentious amid the deterioration of the inter-Korean relationship in the post–9/11 milieu. The continuation of the reunions program itself nevertheless marked an unprecedented breakthrough in that a recurring family-reunion program had never been sustained between the two Koreas prior to 2000.[17] In all, nineteen face-to-face meetings have been held among reuniting families, with the most recent as of this writing held in February 2014, after a hiatus of three years. Even during periods of increased tensions, the proposal from one side or the other to restart negotiations in order to hold another round of family meetings came to signify the intention to dial down inter-state hostility. Holding such family meetings, which had long posed a major stumbling-block in inter-Korean negotiations prior to 2000, has subsequently come to be regarded as a relatively "easy" goal, compared to other objectives such as military trust-building. This itself could be taken as an indication of the program's success, or so one might think. However, ironically, the significance of the August 2000 reunions as a cultural resource in this respect has been obscured by the very continuation of subsequent family meetings.

That is, while later rounds of inter-Korean family meetings were characterized by circumstances markedly less celebratory, the relative frequency of the reunions also meant that they became normalized; they would no longer draw the same kind of widespread public interest and public sympathy as did the initial rounds that took place in the months following the June Summit. However, the fact that the later reunions occurred under less advantageous and more limited conditions should not detract from an appreciation of the impact of the initial family meetings. In other words, it would be misleading to assume that later rounds of inter-Korean family meetings in 2001–2014 were essentially repetitions of earlier reunions; and this is actually an understandable mistake given the way that subsequent media images looked very similar to the photographs and video footage from earlier rounds of reunions. While there may be parallels in format and representation, I argue that the subsequent inter-Korean family meetings are of an entirely different nature than the reunions that occurred in August 2000. To explain, again John Borneman's analysis proves illuminating. He describes the multiple ways that individuals and groups seek to give new meaning to their losses, primarily through four modes of accountability: (1) retribution; (2) restitution/compensation; (3) performative redress; and (4) rites of commemoration.[18] Particularly salient is how Borneman distinguishes "rites of performative redress," which are singular events of cultural accountability, from "rites of commemoration," which are expected to continue indefinitely. In the case of the Korean family meetings, the reunions in August 2000 served the purpose of shifting perspectives on the war away from a search for retribution, as had historically dominated war memory on both sides for decades. Unlike the more obscure repetitions of later rounds, the most prominent of such family meetings that took place in the months immediately following the June Summit effectively served as *a rite of performative redress* that was intended to acknowledge the devastating human losses of the Korean War on both sides of the divide.

Moreover, an unexpected dimension of these reunions in South Korea was how they also served to provide a public acknowledgment of the suffering of those separated families who had been never been recognized as part of the sympathetic category of "separated families" per se, and who were instead marginalized and persecuted during the Cold War period. Anthropologist Soo-Jung Lee has analyzed how the participants in the Seoul reunions, as former targets of state anticommunism in South Korea, underwent a reversal of signification.[19] Emerging from obscurity as those formerly silenced and socially stigmatized, these individuals were suddenly elevated to high-profile visibility so as to become *the* iconic figures of national reconciliation at a historic juncture in North–South engagement. In this way, the reunions illustrated how measures undertaken by the two states to realize inter-Korean rapprochement served to highlight a reckoning with the suppressed legacies of Cold War–era repression against leftists and their families within South Korea.

In ensuing years, increased interaction between the two sides yielded both opportunities and challenges that underscored the liminal condition at the heart of Korea's division. The family reunions program was no longer at the symbolic forefront of the efforts toward reconciliation and cooperation, and instead it would become embroiled in a combination of inauspicious factors: the erratic nature of the inter-Korean relationship, which itself reflected regional and international tensions in conjunction with complications stemming from expanded economic transactions across the 38th parallel. As discussed earlier, Korea's geopolitical liminality as a divided nation has cast the peninsula into chronic uncertainty, subject to the historically contingent nature of its relationships with the powerful nations that bear a strategic interest in the peninsula. If the inter-Korean Summit indicated direct and mutual recognition that is crucial to conciliatory work, those unprecedented bilateral negotiations were nonetheless facilitated by an international climate at the time that was more conducive to inter-Korean rapprochement than that of any other period before or since.

This book has revisited the events during the immediate post-Summit period in order to grasp the affective dimensions of what makes reconciliation possible in a society still divided by the legacies of a brutal civil war. The August 2000 reunions proved to be the only reunions to take place amid an unprecedented combination of conditions: the most favorable international climate to date for the Korean peace process; an unusually high level of domestic optimism toward North–South reconciliation; and the impact of the unexpected simultaneous resurfacing of hundreds of those presumed to have died during the Korean War. The reappearance of those presumed dead signified a dramatic break from past assumptions and practice, one demonstrated not only through political rhetoric and gestures but also at the level of vernacular experience and physical embodiment. These events therefore exceeded the scope of mere political rituals; they touched the lives of ordinary civilians and transformed the possibility for war memory to aid rather than thwart the process of reconciliation.

FAMILY STATE AND THE TRANSMISSION OF AFFECT

The reunions thus added further complexity to the ideological polarization concerning North–South relations by allowing the Kim Dae-jung administration to advance its engagement policy through invocations of the moral politics of the family, which had often been previously appropriated by conservatives in South Korean political debates. Sociologist Kyung-Sup Chang has described how the political use of the moral discourse on the family in South Korea relies upon a socially conservative outlook in which the nuclear family is stereotyped as a self-serving form of affiliation, representing the ills of individualism.[20] As a scapegoat for the insecurities attending modern society, the nuclear family compares unfavorably to the extended family, which is by contrast idealized as comprising a mutual support network built on the Confucian virtues of familial solidarity, filial piety, and self-sacrifice. A narrow self-interested focus on the nuclear family is blamed for the decline of filial piety and by extension held responsible for an array of major contemporary social problems, including widespread poverty and psychological difficulties among children and the elderly. Although rapid industrialization and urbanization did indeed break down prior cooperative relationships,[21] Chang contends that exaggerated distortions of the nuclear family's impact serve a larger purpose as an ideological construct, by attempting to deflect political pressure away from calls for a progressive expansion of social welfare.[22]

While the larger process of inter-Korean reconciliation and cooperation arose as a consequence of contemporary phenomena—namely, the passing of the global Cold War and the concomitant economic pressures of globalization—the reunions also played out the metaphor of the nation as family in a manner that symbolically responded to the assumptions of Korean modernity. On one register, it invoked the "family state." A metaphor with enduring relevance to contemporary society, the family state characterized traditional Korea with its basis in family-centered production and values of filial piety rooted in Confucian ideology.[23] Regarding the symbolic significance of separated families in divided Korea, anthropologist Roy Richard Grinker observes that the rhetoric of the nation is never far from the language and imagery of the family. He writes: "Given the importance of filial piety, it is perhaps not surprising that many south Korean discourses on division and unification are framed within the idiom of the family. Koreans often construe division not only as the separation of the nation but also as the separation of families, and as a result unification is construed as the reunion of separated family members. The nation is the family writ large."[24] In keeping with the logic of this metaphor, the relatives participating in the North–South family meetings were arguably figured and projected as the first subjects of a prospective reunified national community.

The meetings between family members therefore produced a space that exposed national division as an artificial demarcation violating the most fundamental familial relationships. The reunions would instead serve to posit—and, in turn, allow a national audience to witness—the irreducibility of the embodied relationships that antedated the artificiality of the national division which had disrupted and estranged these prior attachments. In other words, the reunions could be understood as a nationally broadcast litmus test to gauge the potential for increased contact and sociability between the people of the two Koreas, or to address the question, *how different are they from us?* That was something potentially far more meaningful, in terms of anticipating a common future beyond Korean reunification, than even an official signed agreement reached between state leaders. Grinker writes: "South Koreans question whether North Koreans have remained similar to them or have changed forever. If it is only the state that has changed, then unification will bring families back together as they should be; if the state has been able to dramatically transform people and values . . . then unification may not truly unite divided families."[25] Because separated families are among those with presumably the greatest personal stake in reunification, whether or not they are capable to "truly unite" would augur well or ill for the future prospects of a reunified nation as a whole.

However, even before the August reunions were realized, conservatives in South Korea were already challenging the June 15th Agreement by insisting upon "reciprocity" from the North Koreans. That is, they were demanding concessions from the North that would be commensurate to the millions of dollars in aid committed by the Kim administration. Indeed, one of the reasons often cited by South Koreans for a gradual approach to rapprochement was the financial burden that the North would inevitably impose. Given the staggering disparity in the size of the two states' respective economies, projections at the time of the combined cost to South Korea of unification and related crisis management exceeded $561 billion.[26] Resulting apprehensions over the potential economic burden facing the South warrant consideration of what Foucault calls "the perspective of population."²⁷ This is the logic underpinning modern governmentality, which reoriented the notion of economy away from prior prevailing social models based on the family and toward one that concerns aggregate phenomena such as epidemics, levels of mortality, and rates of productivity and wealth. In contrast, the Korean separated-family reunions instead privileged the family as the central metaphor of the nation, embracing the integrity of the traditional family over the authority of modern economic rationality. Such symbolic invocation of the nation-as-family therefore served to answer the rationalist objections in South Korea to projected plans for inter-Korean economic cooperation and the wider engagement policy toward North Korea.

Further insight into the symbolic capital of the family in the relationship between the state and the populace may be found in a historical debate surrounding the etymology of *kukka*, the term commonly translated as "state." If one considers the word *kukka*, which denotes "state, nation, body politic," the first character *kuk* means "state or country," and the second character *ka* means "family." Historian Kyung Moon Hwang has explored the reformulation of *kukka* during the Korean enlightenment period, 1896–1910. At a time when intellectuals in Korea were trying to define the nature of the Korean political system, a controversy arose over the meaning and implications surrounding the usage of *kukka*. The debate polarized those who favored a more statist interpretation centered on the dynastic family or ruling authority, and those who argued that the concept referred to a collective entity belonging to all the people. The latter contingent promoted the idea of the "nation as family," a concept that still informs present-day usage of *kukka*, which "refers just as much to the collectivity of government, land, and people."²⁸ The approach of the Kim Dae-jung administration in executing its engagement policy with North Korea therefore illustrates tensions that still underlie these two conceptualizations of *kukka*: one statist, and the other familial. With respect to separated families, the high profile accorded to the collective national character of the family meetings compensated in a sense for the otherwise opaque, inaccessible process of North–South dialogue where decision-making power was centered on the designated elites within the two states.

The reunions could furthermore be understood to have projected what Lauren Berlant has elsewhere called an "intimate public sphere,"²⁹ tied to an emergent intimacy of the nation, which in this case could conceivably encompass both Koreas. The emergence of this public sphere reflected a larger process of working out a new model of "national intimacy,"³⁰ based on an enduring kinship that transcended the enmity of national division while defying immediate economic imperatives and the challenge posed by pecuniary calculations. As discussed in chapter 4, a key limitation of the Kim Dae-jung administration's Sunshine Policy was its own political weakness as a minority government, which posed obstacles for realizing its far-reaching ambitions for promoting not only reconciliation but also dramatically increased cooperation and contact between the two Koreas. This dilemma of pursuing a bold inter-Korean agenda with a weak political base also affected the policy concerning separated families. In 1998, the Kim administration did move to make the category of "separated families" more inclusive, allowing the *Wŏlbukcha* families (related to those who went to North Korea during the war) access to some of the government benefits previously afforded only to the *Wŏllammin* families (wartime refugees from the North), such as financial support to arrange for a meeting in a third country.[31] However, out of apprehension that it would spark a backlash among conservative right-wing groups, administration officials chose not to publicize this change in policy at the time.

Given the Kim administration's limited ability to maneuver politically in a hostile, ideologically polarized climate, I have analyzed how the apparent transparency of affect during the reunions—and the visibility of these fraught, highly emotional encounters—served to offset the lack of political and financial transparency in inter-Korean negotiations. In South Korea, the extensive media exposure of the individual participants occurred at a time when government-level negotiations between the two Koreas were highly secretive. In a sense, the ostensibly "public" space of inter-state negotiations became private and concealed, while the "private" space of families was made public through virtually unrestricted coverage of the family meetings in Seoul. The use of ritual as liminal events in social and political processes where other avenues were foreclosed[32] is therefore a salient rubric for assessing the reunions' role in the Kim Dae-jung administration's efforts to construct and legitimize a new South Korean identity consistent with inter-Korean reconciliation. However, such an approach was not without its risks and critics.

INTERSTITIAL VIGNETTE: FREEZING RAIN

A woman was the first to answer the phone. It was the winter of 2000, and a new list of reunion families had appeared in the newspapers for candidates in another round of reunions to be held in Seoul. The woman was not a direct relative of the person who would be visiting from the North, but rather the daughter-in-law. She said it would be better not to speak with her husband, but she agreed to meet with me. The woman gently insisted that she would be able to answer everything I needed to know.

My research assistant, Sungmi Cho, had arranged for us all to meet in front of the entrance to a royal tomb in the northern part of the city, and I presumed the woman had other business to do nearby there since it was far from her own neighborhood. When I got out of the cab, I couldn't see Sungmi anywhere, so I called her cellphone and was surprised to find out that they were actually inside the grounds of the tomb. It was overcast and the third day of a cold snap which coincided with the official beginning of winter. I saw them ahead, Sungmi walking briskly a few steps behind the woman, and at first I wasn't sure if they were together. It seemed strange that they were not waiting up for me. The woman was dressed fashionably but conservatively, wearing a trench coat over a blouse and slacks. She seemed a little nervous and did not greet me with the customary polite bow or friendly salutations. Instead, she took off ahead of us and hurriedly directed us toward a picnic area near the concession stand. I had been wondering which café we might hurry into so that we could get out of the cold, but when I saw them ahead of me tilting back the plastic chairs which had been leaning forward in storage around one of the patio tables, I realized that this interview would take place outside.

When Mrs. Hwang[33] settled down at the table with us, she apologized for not being able to host us more comfortably in her home. She confided that her family was unaware of our meeting, saying they would not have been happy about the idea. "This is still a difficult subject for my husband and his family to discuss," she said. By then a light drizzle of freezing rain had started, and Mrs. Hwang suggested that we head to a café after all. We got up and headed for the gate again but she stopped herself, saying "This is not the kind of thing we should discuss where there are a lot of people, so let's just talk here." We went back inside the grounds to the picnic area. Out of her purse, Mrs. Hwang took out a small stack of paper cups, and she pulled down the sleeve of plastic off the cups before opening an aluminum thermos to make us instant coffee with filter bags.

I don't drink coffee, but I accepted her offer gladly so that I could warm my hands around the steaming cup. It was a kind gesture to show us that she had put forethought into providing some hospitality, even if under these awkward circumstances. For the first few minutes it felt strange to hold a conversation while sitting outside in the cold. While others had simply re-fused an interview, Mrs. Hwang decided to speak in a place where our conversation could not be overheard. Since we had already spoken over the phone, she did not spend much time asking about our own situations and family backgrounds, as other research participants had done. Without our prompting, she began to talk about her husband and his family, saying, "I didn't even know that he was alive. My husband said that his father died in the Korean War. But because they never found a corpse, they just filed a death certificate." Mrs. Hwang had considered the separated-families issue as unrelated to her own family in the past but, since receiving the news, she had begun pulling together memories of observations and overheard comments she had gleaned over the years which had suggested that the fate of her husband's father was something of a mystery.

Mrs. Hwang described that she had heard her father-in-law was an intellectual who graduated from a top university. The family was well off before the war and came from an elite background, from a line of scholars. During the summer after the war broke out, her husband's father left one night and disappeared without a trace. In subsequent years, the family had always assumed that the father's family had reported him dead after the war. But they later discovered that no death report had been made, and Mrs. Hwang surmised that her husband's grandfather must never have gotten to it while looking after a large family that fell upon hard times during the war years. She continued, "Even now, my husband is still scarred. When my husband graduated . . . he passed the first round of the exam but failed after the interview. That's when he realized what had happened to his father."[34] Soon afterward the family submitted a death report, but the damage had already been done. Several times during our conversation, Mrs. Hwang mentioned her husband's abandonment of his graduate training, which seemed a pivotal event, not only because it changed the family's circumstances so dramatically but it also suggested a "mark" that had been hidden to themselves but had forced upon the family an ambiguous social status.

The rain started coming down a little harder, and my fingers were numb with cold as I tried to scratch down notes discreetly. During the few times we reached a pause in the conversation she would turn to me and ask if there is anything else I wanted to know. I asked Mrs. Hwang if she could tell us more about her late mother-in-law, and she described a very private person who attended church but did not have many friends and confidantes. In the years after the war, her mother-in-law led a difficult life, raising her son alone. Mrs. Hwang said that her husband rarely spoke about his father, but they began holding memorial rites when their daughters were of school age because they thought it was important for the younger generation to remember their grandfather. They started by saying prayers on major holidays and also prepared a gravestone in a cemetery. "We didn't start because of missing him. It started simply for educational purposes for the kids," she said. Mrs. Hwang explained that when their elder daughter was in grade school, she started receiving homework assignments where she had to find out about their family.

When I asked whether her mother-in-law helped to educate the children about their grandfather, Mrs. Hwang replied, "No. So I just tried to do as much as I could as a daughter-in-law and took care of my children's questions," she said. Her blunt assertion that memorials were initiated for practical reasons ("simply for educational purposes") rather than for sentimental ones ("because of missing him") indicated that she was distinguishing her family's kinship practice from the ones implied though the prevalent discourse about separated family members which depicted them as "filled with longing." She also commented that during the first reunions there were few families shown who brought young people with them. Instead, they were mostly older people.

Mrs. Hwang and her husband had received the news about the reunions from a family friend who had seen her husband's name in the newspaper listing. When friends and relatives began calling with congratulations, Mrs. Hwang said that it was unexpectedly a relief that everyone already knew about their situation rather than having to find a way to tell others. She said, "My husband says that he's not sure whether this will be an entirely good thing to have happened to us. But he said he was going to the meeting for his father's sake." The family had started gathering family pictures to collect into a photo album as a gift for her father-in-law. Since receiving news about his father, she said, on the outside her husband pretends to be composed and normal, but she can tell that he has been crying often lately when he is alone. She said that she sometimes hears it when he is lying down or she can tell in his face, though he doesn't say so openly.

> At first, I was excited. For my husband, he might have really been missing him. I don't know whether we'll be able to travel back and forth freely in the event of reunification, but for now I think it's just a tool for breaking down the 38th parallel. Politically we're being used to support the government's policy. This is also an extremely important event for my husband and those involved. But in truth I don't have a great deal of longing. His father is alive, but because of that person, we endured so much hardship. Will there be any great advantage to us? My husband is meeting out of respect toward his blood relative.

Her analysis of the reunions was unsentimental. She said matter-of-factly that families like hers had very little to gain personally, and if it were for their own sake, the organizers would construct a meeting place and allow families to reunite privately. She continued:

> We are participating in order to do the courteous thing. It's because the situation is part of process of reunification. Through the meetings, the number of cases of contact with the North will increase. Because the North dislikes press reports about material aid, reporting about these kinds of events is more acceptable to the North. They could have gone about this in a quiet manner, but they are making a big commotion because they taking advantage of this as a tool. To us there is really no great benefit. On the contrary, it could even be harmful to us.

Mrs. Hwang initially said she could only meet for an hour, but we talked well past noon, and she mentioned that she had been shunning reporters. She explained that one of the reasons she was willing to meet with us was because she felt that she would want others to help her daughters if they were ever to do research in the future. I had heard this before from other research participants, and it reflects not only a broad understanding of reciprocity but also reveals a kind of transferable sympathy based on a sense of responsibility to one's own family. I was struck by how this ethos of concern can be extended to total strangers, out of the hope that other people would one day help their own children. I gathered that perhaps she had hoped that we could help them in some way. As we parted, Mrs. Hwang asked that we contact her via mail in the future rather than over the telephone because she worried that a possible misunderstanding could upset her family. We sent a note of thanks, requesting another time when we might be able to speak with her again, but no reply ever came.

Though I would continue to meet with several other families that winter, Mrs. Hwang was the most bluntly candid in expressing her criticisms of the reunions program, as well as the most open in voicing her wariness toward the risks that the reunions represented for her family. This likely reflected her insider/outsider status as someone whose life was directly impacted by the reunions but who had a limited emotional investment in them personally. Still, whether she was self-conscious about discussing her affinal relatives' complicated personal histories, or whether she was exercising understandable caution about speaking in public about such sensitive matters, ours was an encounter that took place out in the cold. As I grasped the strangeness of those circumstances at the time, I realized how improbable it was to have been able to speak with her at all.

REUNIONS AND THE VISIBLE PAST

Here a theoretical detour is in order before weighing the costs of visibility, such as those related in Mrs. Hwang's account, as well as the imperatives of the unseen. In an essay on the politics of the rights of Korean-Chinese in the process of South Korean democratization, sociologist Hyun Ok Park has considered the contradictory disposition toward neoliberalism that emerged during the presidencies of Kim Dae-jung and Roh Moo-hyun, both former democracy activists. Among South Korean social movement activists, why did a consensus emerge about the state's embrace of market-driven neoliberalism, despite the fact that these same activists decried the economic inequality and social precarity that such an economic system creates?[35] To unravel this contradiction within neoliberal democracy, Park theorizes what she terms "a new state-centrism."[36] Following the Lacanian work of Slavoj Žižek, Park distinguishes between two forms of identification with the state: (1) "imaginary identification," denoting an "identification with the objects in an image," and (2) "symbolic identification," which is "identification with the gaze that produces the image, and thus is not only socially located elsewhere from the depicted objects but may be animated and organized by very different desires and social forces."[37]

In Park's adaptation of Žižek's analysis, the latter, symbolic identification with the democratic state under Kim and Roh and their two liberal center-left administrations in South Korea, relies upon a temporal standpoint "located elsewhere." If viewed with a gaze from the past, the democratic present may be regarded from the vantage of former decades under military dictatorship. Park writes, "This identification is wedded to their memories of the past primarily in terms of terror, loss, and repression. Seen from this view of the past, the present signifies indisputable political progress. The gaze from the past renders former and still committed activists impotent to observe the continued dominance in different forms of state power, market forces, and global relations."[38] Among progressive activists, the legitimacy of the state therefore does not derive from its "actuality," but rather stems from the *symbolic* meaning of the state as emblematic of the triumph of the democracy movement.

Within this formulation reside two notable assumptions. One is that traumatic losses incurred by past state terror and repression are *inherent* to the contemporary identification with the populist democratic state. The affective residue of the Cold War is thereby insinuated into an ostensibly triumphalist democratic project. A second assumption concerns the resulting effect of blindness or paralysis, such that the evocation of traumatic Cold War memory leaves contemporary political subjects helpless to recognize—let alone act upon—the collusion of South Korean state practice with global market forces under the liberal Kim and Roh administrations in the early twenty-first century.[39] Notably, the "consensus" that formed around neoliberal democracy coalesced around a utopian vision of market-driven unification. Two central tenets underpinning neoliberal democracy are (1) that unification is essential for Korea to achieve genuine democracy and (2) that a unified Korea could better compete in global markets by combining South Korea's international networks and its technical and managerial expertise with North Korea's disciplined and controlled labor force as well as its natural resources and undeveloped land.[40] So while many questionable aspects of the reunions did indeed render these events as political spectacle, the logic behind making the reunions does not necessarily reduce to sheer cynicism about media exploitation or political instrumentality. Anthropologists Jean and John Comaroff have commented that postcolonial states in particular have increasingly relied upon "mass-mediated ritual excess" in order to "produce state power, to conjure national unity, and to persuade citizens of the reality of both."[41] The separated-family reunions in Korea can therefore be understood within this larger pattern at the intersection of media specularity and postcolonial cultural politics.

In addition, other family members who participated in the reunions themselves saw the value in having the events publicized. As the date of the reunions drew nearer, I had increasing difficulty arranging meetings with the participating family members because they had become overwhelmed with inquiries from journalists. Prior to the August reunions, I tried several times to reach Hong Gil Soon, who was to meet with her daughter, prominent North Korean dance professor Hong Ok Bae. Although she declined to be interviewed, I spoke with her son, a South Korean psychologist, in his office in a trendy university neighborhood in western Seoul. He explained that his mother was most concerned with maintaining contact with the press, saying, "We are trying to be very positive. It's important to keep the media interested in the subject and to keep them motivated. Public opinion is extremely important. We can't refuse an interview. We need to keep this issue alive, and people must not forget our situation." His family's proactive recognition of their involvement in maintaining media interest contrasted with criticisms of an overly aggressive press and of the South Korean state's complicity in the media overexposure, such as those voiced by Mrs. Hwang. Yet, when the August 2000 reunions actually occurred, the families that became the focus of heightened media attention from journalists were limited in number, including the ten families with surviving elderly mothers and a handful of those related to prominent cultural figures in the North. Beyond that group, the members of other families received little-to-no broadcast exposure, despite the marathon coverage and ubiquitous press presence throughout the events. When I spoke with one of the participants in the Seoul family meetings at her apartment a few weeks later, she actually expressed her disappointment about her family being excluded from the broadcasts, saying in exasperation, "I asked our youngest son to stay home from work to record the TV for four days, and we didn't see our family even once! My friends are asking me, 'Were you really there?'"

In carrying out ethnographic research during that period, I found myself facing an ethical dilemma, torn between the belief that all of the reunion participants should have been afforded the option of having more privacy, and the fact that I benefited by gaining access to informants who would otherwise have been difficult, if not impossible, for me to reach. When the plans for the reunions were announced and separated families suddenly became a subject of news interest, I found that those formally marginalized and silenced as members of non-normative separated families were not only willing to speak, but now expected to be interviewed. Indeed, the main limitation was the fact that they were often pressed for time because they were also fielding a barrage of inquiries and requests for interviews from South Korean reporters covering the unfolding story. Meanwhile, that intense media attention also created an atmosphere of openness and raised hopes for political change, which allowed these historically invisible families to come forward to claim their lost kin.

Even if the operative vision was for these events to achieve a measure of ritual healing for a nation still deeply divided, we are still left to consider why the visibility of the reunions would be presumed as favorable, even essential. In that sense, the reunions of separated families may be understood in terms similar to that of the relationship of symbolic identification, which Park uses to describe social movement activists vis-à-vis the democratic South Korean state. However, I would argue the reunions represent a *reversal* of the gaze from the past. Particularly for Koreans too young to remember the Korean War in the 1950s, or for those too jaded to care about the democracy struggles of the 1980s, the reunions evoked a broad identification among those who watched the unfolding of these heartrending, tearful reunions with a gaze "located elsewhere" from what they perceived. In other words, that temporal standpoint is not a gaze from the past, but rather a *gaze from the present*. To witness the reunions of separated families with a gaze from the then-present was to have looked upon the traumatic past of Korea's modern history and to regard the suffering of those still bound to that past: to render visible those who had been socially effaced through their irrevocable losses during the Korean War and through the legacies left by repression and social exclusion under military authoritarian regimes. To offer public witness to how Korea's legacies of profound loss and terror persist, in the intimate spaces of individual and ordinary families, should be understood as an attempt to reverse the historical amnesia that itself represents a cultural inheritance of the Cold War. This therefore reveals an aspiration to imbue Korea's present with a sense of a shared, visible, and agonizing past, thus striving to initiate the necessary affective groundwork for both consensus and reconciliation.

DIVISION TEMPORALITIES

South Korea's engagement policy, which pertained directly to inter-Korean relations, in this way responded to and shaped the setting for a process of domestic reckoning regarding controversial aspects of historical memory.[42] In striking contrast to the ways that the North Korean threat had previously been used in order to justify the suppression of dissenters by South Korean military authoritarian governments, reconciliation with North Korea in the new millennium coincided with the breaking of social taboos surrounding previously silenced South Koreans who had faced discrimination and persecution by the anticommunist state. The August 2000 reunions—as the first inter-Korean reconciliation event to involve civilians during the Sunshine Era—publicly reinforced this connection between inter-Korean reconciliation and a key moment in the process of domestic reconciliation with South Korea's anticommunist past.

Though national attention would diminish for the later rounds of reunions, the preparations and realization of the initial post-Summit reunions informed the cultural context of reconciliation with the North. In wider South Korean popular culture, more humanized cinematic portrayals of North Koreans had already begun to appear at the turn of the millennium with the release of two blockbuster films, *Shiri* (1999) and *Joint Security Area* (2000).[43] During the 2000s, representations of Northerners would further depart from earlier portrayals of them as rigid one-dimensional automatons, vicious spies, and comparable figures of the enemy "Other," which had been the mainstay of anticommunist education and popular culture during prior decades in South Korea.[44] Instead, in depicting humane interactions among Koreans who hail from opposite sides of the North–South divide, there emerged a trend in film and television, as well as in literary fiction, music videos, and advertisements, whereby South Korean portrayals would relax to the point that they were frequently characterized by humor. For example, cultural critic Stephen Epstein notes how 2003 saw the release of three different comedic B-movies representing romantic couples comprised of a North Korean woman and a South Korean man; he also describes how the 2007 documentary *Planet B-Boy* puts a twist on the militarized mirroring that occurs at the Joint Security Area in P'anmunjom by staging the Northern and Southern soldiers as competing breakdancing crews.[45] Meanwhile, mainstream programs on network television informed South Korean viewers about actual everyday life in North Korea, including schools, food culture, differences in language, and cultural trends.[46] Epstein attributes the rise of this cultural phenomenon to the greater openness toward the North that characterized the Kim and Roh administrations, as well as the presence of a larger population of North Koreans refugees (*t'albukcha*) or "new settlers" (*saet'omin*).[47] Yet I have argued that, in this transformation, the summer of 2000 signified a pivotal period of dramatic cultural change. Although the domestic and international political environment would soon thereafter grow more challenging for the Sunshine Policy, the developments in popular culture and social discourse in the months following the Summit and culminating with the August 2000 reunions helped to mark a break from the dominant hold of anticommunism and anti-North enmity as culturally hegemonic in South Korea. This departure in turn helped to highlight counternarratives in popular memory that would endure even after the decade of engagement, as an alternative to the inter-Korean confrontation of a mutual war-footing amid the return to volatile hostilities that grew particularly intense in 2010.

As ritualized media events of national reconciliation, the state-sponsored family meetings in August 2000 projected reimaginings of the nation based on "blood and tears" metaphors of shared kinship and mutual longing. By foregrounding the suffering endured by ordinary people, these events deflected attention away from memories of the war's catastrophic destruction and horrifying atrocities, displacing the cycle of blame and recrimination, which had theretofore perpetuated the mutual animosity between the two Koreas. The reunions therefore signaled a form of belonging that was figured as extending beyond mere mutual political recognition, to affirm instead reimagined ties of biological relatedness, collective historical trauma, and shared destiny.

Yet, it is important here to distinguish the "post–Cold War" period from the "post-division" period on the Korean peninsula, even though these terms are sometimes used interchangeably. Significantly, the reunions marked the expansion of a reconciliation agenda spearheaded by greater inter-Korean economic cooperation.

Indeed, while goods and capital could subsequently move more freely across the Korean border, the territorial aspects of division were to be maintained, including restrictions on place of residence in North Korea and limitations on contact between the populations of the two Korean states. Reflecting this incongruity inherent to the reconciliation framework, the heart-wrenching reunions unfolded in full view of press cameras in 2000 only to be followed by another separation, when the family members had to part again after only four days together. These circumstances recall how Van Gennep's and Turner's classic analyses of "rites of passage" elicited a critique by French sociologist Pierre Bourdieu, who argued that, in elaborate rituals of crossing, what is affirmed is not so much the passage, but rather the existence of the *line*. According to Bourdieu, such events were revealed to be, not rites of passage, but rather *rites of institution*, which "tend to consecrate or legitimate an arbitrary boundary, by . . . encouraging a recognition of it as legitimate" and by obscuring the border's arbitrary nature.[48] While rites of passage may ostensibly focus on the sanctioned transgression of boundaries, they actually have the effect of reinforcing those very boundaries. Similarly, as much as the reunions of Korean separated families were celebrated as prefiguring imminent national reunification and a passage into a post-division era, what they instead established most immediately was the integrity of the boundary.

Even after the emotional meetings and rekindled connections, all of the reunion participants returned to the other side at the end of four days. Indeed, in an interview with a Ministry of Unification official during the week following the August reunions, I learned that one of the key factors by which she and her colleagues at the MOU regarded the reunions as a success was that there were no attempts to defect on either side.[49] While this lack of controversy was unquestionably beneficial for supporting the progress of inter-Korean cooperation, it also underscored that the border remained as an impassable divide that even ties of kinship and affection could only surmount for a very brief span of time. In this way, while the reunions renewed hopes for reconciliation and eventual reunification, they also served for the time being to consecrate the border's durability.

Apparent here is the paradox at the center of the North–South Korean family meetings. No one could witness these emotional meetings without recognizing how they were circumscribed by highly restrictive conditions, including limits on time and place; the assumption by participating families that they were under state surveillance, a sense exacerbated by the pervasive presence of media cameras; and, most significantly, the lack of any guarantee or indication that the family members would be able to maintain contact or to meet again. In other words, for all their fanfare as humanitarian events reuniting long-separated kin, for all their promise as a newly mediated model of intimacy evoking the possibilities of eventual reunification of the nation, the reunions lasted only a few days before the families were again forced to separate again and suspend contact on opposite sides of the border. The reunions, though widely recognized in South Korea as a breakthrough in inter-Korean reconciliation, also appeared to shore up some aspects of national division and arguably served to ritualize division's continuation.

To grasp these contradictions, it is helpful to turn to theorizations of Korea's division system by South Korean literary critic Paik Nak-chung. Paik argues that the particular nature of Korean division differentiates it from other precedents, with a division structure more stable than that of Vietnam but which, unlike Germany, had involved both civil war and a postcolonial struggle.[50] Overcoming division in Korea would therefore require not military means or rapid annexation, but rather a gradual process marked by many smaller steps, including an intermediate stage of a loose union or confederation of the two existing states.[51] Given that the process of rapprochement between the two Koreas during the engagement period was predicated upon the assumption of such a confederation model, the reunions of separated family members held a significant symbolic place. That is, the projected national future of "coexistence through economic cooperation" stipulated that it was necessary to maintain for the time being a high degree of separation between the two Korean populations in working toward a gradual vision of reunification in the long run. In that way, the parting scenes of each round of inter-Korean family meetings dramatically confirmed the presumption of this continued separation for the present time. The fact that even those who underwent these emotional reunions would shortly be separated again to opposite sides of the border meant that the process of inter-Korean reconciliation would, for the time being, *not* undermine the power of the dividing line but rather serve to reaffirm it.

In theorizing the division system in Korea, Paik has furthermore characterized the relationship between North and South as not only oppositional but also symbiotic, where each side is dependent upon the other for perpetuating the status quo. According to Paik, the symbiosis at the root of the division system stems from an antidemocratic logic that favors those with vested interests on each side while alienating a majority of the population across the Korean peninsula by maintaining circumstances of unending war. Paik argues that overcoming the division system can only be achieved through means that extend well beyond state politics to encompass everyday life in the form of multidimensional civic participation.[52] Indeed, the crossings of the separated-family reunions became the precursor to subsequent North–South Korean civilian contacts that followed during the Kim and Roh administrations among civic organizations, labor organizations, linguists, and other groups. In this way, the reunions marked the shift away from a state-centered approach to rapprochement and a departure from the decades-long precedent whereby inter-Korean relations were overwhelmingly controlled by the two states. Indeed, the diplomacy analyst Roland Bleiker has assessed that "the most radical but often underestimated element of the Sunshine Policy is its attempt to loosen state control over security by promoting more interaction, communication, and information exchanges between the two parts of the divided peninsula."[53] By offering a glimpse of post-division society, the reunions therefore served to shift the space of inter-Korean reconciliation beyond the state to the intimate relations among families and individuals, encompassing the sentiments and identities of ordinary people.[54]

Given that these events carried the intention to secure greater South Korean support behind a reconciliation agenda, the reunions among separated families served as political rituals that provided a symbolic rationale for South Korea's moral incorporation of the other—the transformation of enemies into brethren—reflecting a logic crucial to a newly cooperative inter-Korean economic strategy in response to global economic pressures. The series of breakthroughs in inter-Korean relations during 2000 were indeed the direct fruit of an ambitious vision of economic integration framed as both a survival strategy and postcolonial destiny for North and South Korea. South Korea, for its part, stipulated the resumption of separated-family reunions, without which the government would have lacked the mandate among its own society to proceed with North–South economic cooperation. However, the participating family members had few expectations of their families being permanently reunited in their lifetimes. These family meetings therefore served as threshold rituals to mark a new era of inter-Korean reconciliation while they simultaneously signified the ritualization of continued national division. In so doing, they revealed how the losses of the fratricidal Korean War and ensuing decades of national division had created a profound and ongoing crisis in kinship, compelling ordinary Koreans to reconfigure an ethics of kinship which could exceed the limitations of that divide.

NOTES

1. Don Baker, "Exacerbated Politics: The Legacy of Political Trauma in South Korea," in *Northeast Asia's Difficult Past: Essays in Collective Memory*, ed. B. Schwartz and M. Kim (New York: Palgrave-McMillan, 2010), 197.

2. Leonid Petrov, "Historiography, Media and Cross-border Dialogue in East Asia: Korea's Uncertain Path to Reconciliation," in *East Asia Beyond the History Wars: Confronting the Ghosts of Violence*, ed. Tessa Morris-Suzuki et al. (New York: Routledge, 2013), 53–56. See also Suk-Young Kim, "Crossing the Border to the 'Other' Side: Dynamics of Interaction between North and South Koreans in *Spy Li Cheol-jin* and *Joint Security Area*," in *Seoul Searching: Culture and Identity in Contemporary Korean Cinema* (Albany, NY: SUNY Press, 2007), 219–42; Theodore Hughes, "Planet Hallyuwood: Imaging the Korean War," *Acta Koreana* 14, no. 1 (2011): 197–212; and Benjamin Joinau, "Sleeping with the (Northern) Enemy: South Korean Cinema and the Autistic Interface," in *De-Bordering Korea: Tangible and Intangible Legacies of the Sunshine Policy*, ed. Valérie Gelézeau et al. (New York: Routledge, 2013), 172–88.

3. Compare this with, for example, an earlier one-dimensional portrayal in Park Sang-ho's 1965 film *DMZ*, where a ruthless soldier in the process of crossing from South to North attempts to abduct two children and ends up killing one of them. See Suk-Young Kim, *DMZ Crossings* (New York: Columbia University Press, 2014), 54.

4. Nancy Abelmann, Jung-Ah Choi, and So Jin Park, *No Alternative?: Experiments in South Korean Education* (Berkeley: University of California Press, 2012); So Jin Park and Nancy Abelmann, "Class and Cosmopolitan Striving: Mothers' Management of English Education in South Korea," *Anthropological Quarterly* 77, no. 4 (2004): 645–72.

5. Hyeon Ju Lee, "Remembering and Forgetting the Korean War in the Republic of Korea," *Suomen Antropologi: Journal of the Finnish Anthropological Society* 35, no. 2 (2010): 48–55.

6. Sang-jin Han, "From the Asian Value Debate to Cosmopolitanism: An Active Interpretation of the Political Thoughts of Kim Dae-jung," *Korea Journal* 51, no. 3 (2011): 196–222.

7. Kwon, "The Ghosts of War and the Spirit of Cosmopolitanism," *History of Religions* 48, no. 1 (2008): 24.

8. Richard Werbner, "Smoke from the Barrel of a Gun: Postwars of the Dead, Memory, and Reinscription in Zimbabwe," in *Memory and the Postcolony: African Anthropology and the Critique of Power*, ed. Richard Werbner (New York: Zed Books, 1998), 72. Quoted in Kwon, *Ghosts of War in Vietnam* (New York: Cambridge University Press, 2008), 62.

9. Kwon, *Ghosts of War in Vietnam*, 163.

10. John Borneman, *Political Crime and the Memory of Loss* (Bloomington, IN: Indiana University Press, 2011), 70.

11. Jhe Seong-Ho, "Four Major Agreements on Inter-Korean Economic Cooperation: Legal Measures for Implementation," *East Asian Review* 16, no. 4 (2004): 19–40.

12. Ralph Michael Wrobel, "Inter-Korean Cooperation in Special Economic Zones: Developments and Perspectives," in *Towards a Northeast Asian Security Community*, ed. Bernhard Seliger and Werner Pascha (New York: Springer, 2011); Semoon Chang and Hwa-Kyung Kim, "Inter-Korean Economic Cooperation," in *The Survival of North Korea: Essays on Strategy, Economics and International Relations*, ed. Suk Hi Kim, Terence Roehrig, and Bernhard Seliger (Jefferson, NC: McFarland, 2011).

13. Tessa Morris-Suzuki, *To the Diamond Mountains: A Hundred-Year Journey through China and Korea* (Lanham, MD: Rowman & Littlefield, 2010).

14. See Christian J. Park, "Crossing the Border: South Korean Tourism to Mount Kŭmgang," in *De-Bordering Korea: Tangible and Intangible Legacies of the Sunshine Policy*, ed. Valérie Gelézeau, Koen De Ceuster, and Alain Delissen (New York and London: Routledge, 2013). Mt. Kŭmgang has also served as the venue for inter-Korean dialogue on various occasions both non-governmental and governmental, and from late 1998 through 2008, nearly 1.95 million tourists visited the mountain.

15. Korean Central News Agency, "S. Authorities Urged to Create Conditions for Meeting of Separated Families," October 16, 2001.

16. Park, "Crossing the Border," 46–47.

17. As discussed in chapter 1, the sole precedent of smaller-scale inter-Korean family exchange visits occurred in 1985, but that program did not continue amid a re-escalation of Cold War hostilities.

18. John Borneman, *Political Crime and the Memory of Loss*, 3.

19. Soo-Jung Lee, *"T'alnaengjŏn minjok spekt'ŏk'ŭl"* [Making and Unmaking the Korean National Division], PhD dissertation, Urbana-Champaign: University of Illinois, 2006.

20. Kyung-Sup Chang, "The Neo-Confucian Right and Family Politics in South Korea: the Nuclear Family as an Ideological Construct," *Economy and Society* 26, no. 1 (1997): 22–40.

21. Dongno Kim, "The Transformation of Familism in Modern Korean Society: From Cooperation to Competition," *International Sociology* 5, no. 4 (1990): 409–25.

22. Chang, "The Neo-Confucian Right"; see also Kyung-Sup Chang, *South Korea Under Compressed Modernity: Familial Political Economy in Transition* (London and New York: Routledge, 2010).

23. Hae-Joang Cho ("Male Dominance and Mother Power—The Two Sides of Confucian Patriarchy in South Korea," *Asian Women* 2 [1996]: 77–104) contends that family-centeredness was exacerbated by socio-political instability, which dates back to the latter part of the Yi Dynasty. She faults the persistence of such exclusive familism today for the conservative social system in South Korea.

24. Roy Richard Grinker, *Korea and Its Futures* (New York: St. Martin's Press, 1998), 102.

25. Grinker, *Korea and Its Futures*, 100.

26. Young-Sun Lee, "The Cost and Financing of Korean Unification," in *Perspectives on Korean Unification and Economic Integration*, ed. Young Back Choi, Yesook Merrill, Yung Y. Yang, and Semoon Chang (Cheltenham, U.K.: Edward Elgar, 2001), 42.

27. Michel Foucault et al., *The Foucault Effect: Studies in Governmentality* (Chicago: University of Chicago Press, 1991), 99.

28. Kyung Moon Hwang, "Country Or State? Reconceptualizing *Kukka* in the Korean Enlightenment Period, 1896–1910," *Korean Studies* 24, no. 1 (2000): 13.

29. Lauren Berlant, *The Female Complaint: The Unfinished Business of Sentimentality in American Culture* (Durham, NC: Duke University Press, 2008).

30. Esra Özyürek, *Nostalgia for the Modern: State Secularism and Everyday Politics in Turkey* (Durham, NC: Duke University Press, 2006).

31. Gwi-Ok Kim, *Isan'gajok, "pan'gongjŏnsa" to "ppalgaengi" to anin* (Seoul: Yŏksabip'yŏngsa, 2004).

32. Richard A. Wilson, *The Politics of Truth and Reconciliation in South Africa: Legitimizing the Post-Apartheid State* (Cambridge: Cambridge University Press, 2001).

33. At her request, I addressed her as "Mrs. ___," and here I replace her real name with a pseudonym to call her "Mrs. Hwang." In other words, she had us address her by the commonly used English loan-word "Mrs." (*Misesŭ*) as a courtesy title that indicated the formality of our relationship.

34. Here there are parallels with others from non-normative separated families. For example, as Namhee Lee writes, "The well-known novelist Yi Mun-yŏl is rumored to have failed the Korean bar exam because his father went to North Korea when Yi was three years old." Lee, "Anticommunism, North Korea, and Human Rights," in *Truth Claims*, ed. M. P. Bradley and P. Petro (New Brunswick, NJ: Rutgers University Press, 2002), 64 fn.16.

35. Jesook Song in her work has also raised the issue of the difficulty that these activists faced in examining their own liberalism. See Song, *South Koreans in the Debt Crisis* (Durham, NC: Duke University Press, 2009).

36. Hyun Ok Park, "For the Rights of 'Colonial Returnees': Korean Chinese, Decolonization, and Neoliberal Democracy in South Korea," in *New Millennium South Korea: Neoliberal Capitalism and Transnational Movements*, ed. Jesook Song (London and New York: Routledge, 2011), 123.

37. Slavoj Žižek, *The Fragile Absolute: Or, Why Is the Christian Legacy Worth Fighting For?* (London: Verso, 2001), 50.

38. Park, "For the Rights of 'Colonial Returnees,'" 123. This overlays with Cho Han Hae-Joang's earlier analysis of South Korean subjectivity and the hegemonic construction of *kuk-*

min, or "a member of the nation," which conflated nationalism and modernity in such a way that even left-wing intellectuals were generally reluctant to oppose market-first policies in the 1970s and 1980s in the drive to build a powerful nation. See Cho Han, "You Are Entrapped in an Imaginary Well," *Inter-Asia Cultural Studies* 1, no. 1 (2000): 57–59.

39. Cf. Jong Bum Kwon, "Forging a Modern Democratic Imaginary: Police Sovereignty, Neoliberalism, and the Boundaries of Neo-Korea," *positions* 22, no. 4 (2014): 71–101.

40. Minkyu Sung challenges the identity politics of popular nationalist discourses by analyzing how they can serve to naturalize what he calls "the normality of nationalism" which uncritically serves to endorse an agenda of economic developmentalism. See "The 'Truth Politics' of Anti-North Koreanism: The Post-Ideological Cultural Representation of North Korea and the Cultural Criticisms of Korean Nationalism," *Inter-Asia Cultural Studies* 10, no. 3 (2009): 439–59.

41. Jean Comaroff and John Comaroff, "Nations With/Out Borders: Neoliberalism and the Problem of Belonging in Africa, and Beyond," in *Border Crossings—Grenzverschiebungen und Grenzüberschreitungen in einer Globalisierten Welt*, ed. Shalini Randeria (Zurich: VDF, 2008), 142.

42. Other related developments included the South Korean Truth and Reconciliation Commission and the "Settling the Past" historiographical movement. See Gi-Wook Shin et al., *Rethinking Historical Injustice and Reconciliation in Northeast Asia: The Korean Experience* (New York: Routledge, 2007); HunJoon Kim, "Seeking Truth After 50 Years: The National Committee for Investigation of the Truth About the Jeju 4.3 Events," *International Journal of Transitional Justice* 3, no. 3 (2009): 406–23; Dong-Choon Kim, "The Long Road Toward Truth and Reconciliation: Unwavering Attempts to Achieve Justice in South Korea," *Critical Asian Studies* 42, no. 4 (2010): 525–52; Jae-Jung Suh, "Truth and Reconciliation in South Korea: Confronting War, Colonialism, and Intervention in the Asia Pacific," *Critical Asian Studies* 42, no. 4 (2010): 503–24; and Jae-Jung Suh, ed., *Truth and Reconciliation in South Korea: Between the Present and Future of the Korean Wars* (London and New York: Routledge, 2012). See also Koen De Ceuster, "When History is Made: History, Memory and the Politics of Remembrance in Contemporary Korea," *Korean Histories* 2, no. 1 (2010): 13–33; and Dong-Choon Kim, "Korea's Movement to Settle the Issues of the Past and Peace in East Asia," *Korea Journal* 50, no. 4 (2010): 152–85.

43. Jake Bevan, "Welcome to Panmunjeom: Encounters with the North in Contemporary South Korean Cinema," *New Cinemas: Journal of Contemporary Film* 8, no. 1 (2010): 45–57.

44. Suk-Young Kim, "Crossing the Border," 222–24.

45. See "The Axis of Vaudeville: Images of North Korea in South Korean Pop Culture," *The Asia-Pacific Journal* 10, no. 2 (2009). *Planet B-Boy* was directed by Canadian filmmaker Benson Lee.

46. Samuel Gerald Collins, "Train to Pyongyang: Imagination, Utopia, and Korean Unification," *Utopian Studies* 24, no. 1 (2013): 120.

47. Byung-Ho Chung, "Between Defector and Migrant: Identities and Strategies of North Koreans in South Korea," *Korean Studies* 32, no. 1 (2009): 1–27; Hae Yeon Choo, "Gendered Modernity and Ethnicized Citizenship: North Korean Settlers in Contemporary South Korea," *Gender and Society* 20, no. 5 (2006): 576–604.

48. Pierre Bourdieu, "Rites of Institution," in *Language and Symbolic Power* (Cambridge, MA: Harvard University Press, 1991), 118.

49. The Ministry of Unification official said they were not only worried about this risk on the North Korean side. There was also considerable concern about one elderly South Korean man of very modest means who had no relatives on this side of the border, and the officials were reportedly relieved that man did not attempt to stay with his family in North Korea.

50. Nak-chung Paik, *The Division System in Crisis: Essays on Contemporary Korea* (Berkeley: University of California Press, 2011), 20–21.

51. Paik, *The Division System in Crisis*, 35–36.

52. Nak-chung Paik, "Toward Overcoming Korea's Division System through Civic Participation," *Critical Asian Studies* 45, no. 2 (2013): 279–90.

53. Roland Bleiker, *Divided Korea: Toward a Culture of Reconciliation* (Minneapolis: University of Minnesota Press, 2005), xli.

54. Cho Han Hae-Joang and Lee Woo-young, eds., *T'albundan sidae rŭl yŏlmyŏ* [Opening an Era of Post-Division] (Seoul: Samin, 2000).

Epilogue

The Afterlife of Division

Regarding historically controversial events, the passage of fifty years is a momentous occasion for commemoration, when witnesses have the chance to leave a collective imprint on the legacy of public remembrance before large numbers of their generation begin to pass away. Although the contemporary "memory boom"—or the rapid expansion of academic scholarship in memory studies—can be dated to the 1980s and earlier, it received considerable impetus in the 1990s when widespread commemorations were timed with the fifty-year anniversaries of various milestones associated with the Second World War. Truly, the half-century anniversary offers a compelling temporal marker, providing a balance between distance and proximity: contested incidents are far enough in the past to be revisited with more perspective, and yet those events still remain within living memory.[1]

However, in the traditional East Asian worldview, it is the anniversary of sixty years that betokens a more meaningful milestone. Reaching sixty years of age represents a full life-cycle,[2] reflecting the completion of five iterations of the classic twelve-year astrological cycle. For Koreans, *hwan'gap*, or the sixtieth anniversary of an elder's birth, was traditionally marked with a festive gathering as a counterpart to the *dol*, the celebration of an infant's first birthday. Both could be understood as key rites of passage in the collective recognition of personhood among one's family and one's community.

In recent decades in South Korea, because of longer life expectancies, the milestone of *hwan'gap* has become downplayed, and instead families would generally wait another decade or two to fête their elder with a grand birthday party. Notably, among those for whom the Korean War's major hostilities violently upended a formative period in their lives as teens and young adults

215

in 1950–1953, the sixtieth-year commemorations of the war in 2010 would occur when they were in their mid-seventies and eighties or older. For the Korean War generation, then, the contemporary equivalent of a full life-cycle would coincide with the passing of sixty years since the life-altering upheavals that occurred at the midpoint of the twentieth century.

If one compares these two significant milestones at the fifty-year and sixty-year marks, 2000 and 2010 could hardly be more different with respect to the official memory of the Korean War in South Korea. A comparison of the political contexts is striking: if 2000 promised the beginning of a new era of reconciliation and cooperation between the two Korean states, 2010 underscored the continuation of an old war. It was in May of that year that the sinking of the *Cheonan* touched off a vehement clash of interpretations regarding the meaning of the conflict in the two Koreas, generating a controversy that still resonates in 2015.[3] After a tense summer and early fall, the resumption of reunions among separated Korean families in late October and early November 2010 appeared to signal a modest improvement in inter-Korean cooperation at the time, raising hopes that a program of cross-border family meetings would not only continue, but also expand. Yet those hopes were dashed only weeks later when an alarming military crisis brought the two Koreas to what many believe was the brink of war, or at least perilously close to the point of reigniting large-scale conflict. At the time, brinkmanship did not ultimately trigger the inexorable escalation toward cataclysm that each side had threatened, but the crisis served to raise worldwide alarm over the risk of a second Korean War and focused global attention on a triangular maritime area of contested waters to which both Koreas lay claim.[4]

In late February 2014, after a hiatus of more than three years, the inter-Korean family meetings resumed at the reunions center located at Mt. Kŭmgang on North Korea's eastern coast. These family meetings were the nineteenth round of reunions to occur since the June Summit of 2000. They were realized only after the resumption of high-level talks between the two sides, which were the first such negotiations to be held since liberal rule had ended in South Korea in 2008. In fact, up until nearly the moment that the family meetings actually occurred in February 2014, it was uncertain whether they would happen at all.[5] The reunions therefore proved again to serve as a kind of threshold ritual, but one of far more modest significance than those that took place in 2000. Following each rupture in inter-Korean relations, the reunions have served as a conciliatory gesture toward the abatement of hostility and tension on the peninsula. Indirectly, they have served to indicate as well that a parallel diplomatic track has been restarted behind the scenes.

Despite disruptive changes over time, there have also been continuities in the tensions and negotiations related to these family meetings. For example, in the case of the 2014 reunions, North Korean negotiators had initially stipulated that the family meetings would not go forward unless the United

States and South Korea canceled their joint military exercises, a condition that North Korea would eventually take off the table in order to allow the reunions to proceed. That would seem to draw a stark contrast with 2010, when the reunions were suspended after the shelling of *Yŏnp'yŏng* Island. Yet while the shelling itself was widely condemned as a provocation by the South Korean and Western media, the North Koreans regarded their actions as a response to circumstances surrounding the joint military activities. In a similar vein, it should be noted that in 1985, when the first North–South family exchange meetings took place as the sole precedent to the contemporary reunions program, North Korea decided against continuing with further exchanges as a way of protesting the joint U.S.–South Korean "Team Spirit" military exercises. While these precedents indicate that U.S.–South Korean war games exercises have represented a long-running concern for the North Koreans, it also shows how the connection between the reunions and these military exercises goes back nearly thirty years. The "life-span" of Korea's long war can therefore be understood in vying opposition to that of the separated family members, while the phenomena surrounding both military confrontation and family separation are among the most immediate symptoms of unending war on the peninsula.

Uncertainty over the continuation of such reunions also arose during the engagement period. For example, the fourth round of reunions in 2001 was initially cancelled by the North side, which had objected to what it perceived as increasingly hostile measures undertaken by the South in the wake of 9/11. Yet, after a stabilization of the reunions program, there set in a more predictable rhythm to the North–South family meetings. With an average of two per year, the reunions became regularized in the later rounds during the engagement period, and they no longer attracted interest from the media or general public. However, that quiet regularity ended in 2008, following the election in South Korea of conservative Lee Myung-bak, when Lee's assumption of a hostile policy toward the North ensured North Korea's own return to belligerence against the South. The resulting tenuousness of relations between North and South Korea resulted in the ongoing uncertainty surrounding the family meetings program in subsequent years.

BELATED CONVEYANCES
AND AN EPISTEMIC BOUNDARY

With respect to the indefinite and irregular continuation of inter-Korean family meetings, it is important to distinguish between the reunions as a political technology and the reunions as a social and cultural phenomenon. Indeed, these family meetings figure significantly into the calculus of aid and diplomacy between the two states. For example, during the period when reunions

occurred in February 2014, the South Korean government approved a ship-
ment of humanitarian aid to North Korea by two Seoul-based civic groups,
which were permitted to send the equivalent of $988,000 in powdered milk
and medicine.[6] Also, for the sake of separated family members who are frail
from old age and passing away in ever-rising numbers, the urgency of continuing these reunions is an issue upon which both conservatives and progressives in South Korea agree.

These meetings, however, represent more than a political means to address a humanitarian problem. As the reunions continue intermittently and
without certainty, what they signify above all is a ritual acknowledgment of
the passing of the Korean War generation,[7] in the absence of any imminent
likelihood of their seeing a conclusion to the war itself. That is, these encounters capture the tragically poignant reality that, no matter how resilient these
elderly Korean War survivors may be, they will not live long enough to see
the resolution of a conflict that has shaped nearly their entire lives. The
pained acknowledgment of such is expressed in the parting consolations that
separated family members have offered to each other, such as "Please stay
alive until reunification!" and "May you live to be one hundred years old so
that we will see each other again!" With each new round of reunions, the
decline in the number of reunions applicants becomes a defining reference
point for the attenuation of a generation for whom the Korean War is a
formative living memory. With each new military crisis or flare-up of tensions on the peninsula, the oppositional dynamic of Korean division reveals
itself to be relentlessly recursive and indifferent to the limits of human fragility.

After the Korean War Armistice Agreement was signed in 1953 and final
exchanges were negotiated to formalize the sealing of the border, post-
conflict reconstruction in divided Korea was predicated upon the wholesale
erasure of those missing from each society. This led to a proliferation of
social deaths where physical deaths were impossible to prove or to disprove.
In the early twenty-first century, the reunions of North–South separated families thereby served to reveal how the lived experience of Korea's division
has concerned far more than the enforcement of territorial boundaries. The
reunions provided a space to reflect on how the meaning of national partition
has extended even beyond the post-1945 geographical mapping of an inter-
Korean ideological divide. While its historic roots in landlord-tenant relations predated the colonial period, that ideological opposition would be intensely exacerbated by colonization and division, before it was transformed
into another order of enmity altogether with the catastrophic violence of the
Korean War.

What these family meetings instead foregrounded was how national division for ordinary Koreans has existed as an *epistemic* boundary, a limit to
what was knowable or could be determined about the fates of those who had

disappeared in wartime. In the Cold War climate that prevailed in subsequent years and decades, lacking such knowledge about a relative was the source of risk and danger to oneself as well as to one's family and extended kin. The reunions opened a window onto multigenerational stories that described a range of local practices for coping with such risk, including ostensible mourning for those given up for dead, hidden mourning for deaths that could not be grieved in public, as well as implicit waiting for news about the war-missing among family members who privately still hoped or expected them to be alive. Division as an epistemic boundary therefore led to the cultural production of new ambiguous forms of life and death, while blurring the distinctions between them.

THE FRACTAL LIMINAL

Since August 2000, the North–South separated-family meetings have marked a historic moment when the process of inter-Korean reconciliation precipitated the encounter between those who had been lost to their families for decades on one side of the peninsular divide, and those who had lived long enough and had overcome enormous odds for reunion on the other. In this way, the reunions brought together survivors of both the destruction of war and the exigencies of division that has itself lasted nearly a human lifetime. As discussed earlier, despite their emotionally fraught nature, these family meetings should not be regarded as occasions of unremitting tragedy. Participants also describe these encounters in terms of joy and gratitude for their relative's survival, recognizing that for them to meet is to celebrate the improbable presence of the other. At the same time, these encounters are also the occasion to mourn those who had died while waiting for such a moment, and to lament the impossibility of lives that they were unable to have lived.

Given that an enormous number of deaths during the Korean War were unaccounted for and unable to be properly grieved, the staggering scale of such disquieting mystery suggests yet another dimension to the liminality of Korea's divided condition. To grasp the complexity of this condition, consider the analogy of divided Korea's liminality as having properties akin to those of a fractal. In the realm of mathematics, a fractal denotes a geometric pattern that is repeated at ever-smaller scales, exhibiting self-similarity across all scales. Beyond its relevance to the abstract reasoning of geometry and computer simulations, fractals also occur empirically in nature, as can be seen in multi-scalar repetitions patterned in ice crystals, tree branches, and coastlines. To think of Korea's liminality through the metaphor of a fractal, then, is to consider how the political, social, and ontological limbo imposed by the Korean War's irresolution inexorably structures interrelated aspects of Korean society and ordinary life—repeating itself, as it were, under several

Figure 6.2. At the meetings of war-separated families, it was common for participants to bring portraits of deceased parents who passed away prior to having the chance for reunion, despite having waited for several decades in anticipation of any news about a son or daughter missing since 1950–1953. Seoul, November 2000. Reproduced with permission from the National Archives of Korea.

levels of magnification. Among other dimensions, this would include: the macro level of regional geopolitical risk and tension; the peninsular condition of "peacelessness"[8] between war and not war; in both Korean states, the social level of stigmatization toward those deemed "out of place" as a means of enforcing ideological normativity; and the existential level of limbic ambiguity in which the boundary between life and death has been rendered uncertain. Encompassing both the patterned and the chaotic, such complexity serves as an important reminder that, for the elderly members of separated families and other survivors of the Korean War, their trauma of loss is not reducible to what can be appropriated in the service of a securitized or militaristic logic in the contemporary moment on either side of the Korean divide. Indeed, the irony of any such appropriation is evident, given that the provenance of the aggrieved collective suffering among these separated and bereaved families is the merciless destructiveness of war. To shed further light on the contradictory meanings surrounding the Korean separated-family reunions, it is worth considering another theoretical challenge to the assumption that rituals ultimately restore social and political solidarity. In a book-length essay entitled *Imaginative Horizons*, anthropologist Vincent Crapanzano observes how ritual can serve instead to reveal the disjunctions borne of the risks and rifts in the lives of communities and individuals. In ceremonies of transition, ritual entails not only the passage from one status to another, but also the gap between the two positions. The existence of this breach, as Crapanzano stresses, always leaves open the potential for an incomplete passage:

> They are the defining moments of rites of passage, healing ceremonies, sacred and secular investitures of power and authority. . . . They are risky and some-times dangerous. . . . They may mark a change of status in their participants; they often involve the exchange of objects, real or symbolic, which hover "possessionless" for an instant. Indeed, there is in any exchange a disjunctive moment in which the object is neither given nor received and the participants are not yet givers nor receivers. There is always the risk of default and an ensuing rupture of relationship. And there are moments, the most dramatic of all, when the participants are trapped in a between that they cannot even define—in which there is no crossing.[9]

In any rite of passage, the most critical moments occur when the risks of an unfulfilled crossing become apparent. This may be particularly true in cere-monies of epochal transition, in which there arises the promise of a new state of affairs, new relationships, and possibilities for new social configurations. That is, in such passages there also lies the sobering potential that liminal entities will remain caught in "the between," ensnared in a fate of ontological suspension that defies closure and strains comprehension.

In Korea, while the initial circumstances of family separation can be attributed to the chaos and upheaval of war, the decades-long continuation of this phenomenon is rooted in the political rationality of ongoing national division. The peninsula's territorial divide represents a case of extreme social division whereby the two populations were not only separated but also sealed off from each other. Unable to confirm the fates of their lost kin, these families were also burdened with a truncated personal history, in which close relatives could not be properly remembered or properly mourned. The separ-ated-family reunions thereby revealed a crisis of kinship brought about by division and deepened by the lived consequences of "publicly ungrievable losses."[10]

If the "inability to mourn" the catastrophic losses of the Korean War has arguably perpetuated the systems that have maintained Korea's division,[11] the August 2000 reunions of separated families figured into a new perspec-tive informed by a shared legacy of bereavement that transcended the penin-sular divide. Occurring at a particular and extraordinary historical moment, these emotionally charged political rituals opened liminal spaces for Koreans in which to reckon in unprecedented ways with the traumas of national division, family separation, and a devastating war's unresolved nature. Thus, these family meetings would reveal a committed refusal to accept prevailing versions of the national past as fixed and complete on either side.[12] Amid these new partitions and unities of the family, the traces of politically charged silences and forgetting have a particular poignancy in a Korean context, where remembering one's ancestors is so vital to concepts of the interconnection between the living and the dead. As a liminal space for collective mourning over everything that both sides lost, the separated-family reunions therefore yielded an opening for newly recognizing the humanity of those long vilified as enemies, and for fathoming how legacies of violent turmoil in Korea's modern history have permeated ties of kinship across the longstanding divide. With their overlapping dimensions as sites of memory and history—with implications at once national, personal, intersubjective, and transnational in significance—these engagements with the traumatic past would generate new possibilities for reimagining the future.

NOTES

1. Gustav Niebuhr, "Whose Memory Lives When the Last Survivor Dies?" *New York Times*, January 29, 1995; Tessa Morris-Suzuki, *The Past Within Us: Media, Memory, History* (New York: Verso, 2005), 44. For an analysis of the memory boom in historical studies and its precedents earlier in the twentieth century, see Jay Winter, *Remembering War: The Great War between Memory and History in the Twentieth Century* (New Haven: Yale University Press, 2006).

2. As Kang Jeong-Koo describes, "In Korea, the 60th birthday has traditionally been characterized as a milestone that signals the commencement of a new life—one that is qualitatively different from that of the previous 60 years." Kang was discussing the 60th anniversary of the Armistice Agreement as a landmark among peace activists in their efforts to realize a peace agreement. See Christine Hong, "The First Year of Peace on the Korean Peninsula," *Foreign Policy in Focus*, Institute for Policy Studies (October 11, 2012), http://fpif.org/the_first_year_of_peace_on_the_korean_peninsula/.

3. See Scott Snyder and See-Won Byun, "*Cheonan* and Yeonpyeong: The Northeast Asian response to North Korea's provocations," *The RUSI Journal* 156, no. 2 (2011): 74–81; Jae-Jung Suh, "Race to Judge, Rush to Act: The Sinking of the *Cheonan* and the Politics of National Insecurity," *Critical Asian Studies* 42, no. 3 (2010); Mark E. Caprio, "Plausible Denial? Reviewing the Evidence of DPRK Culpability for the *Cheonan* Warship Incident," *The Asia-Pacific Journal* 30.4, no. 10 (2010).

4. Nan Kim, "Korea on the Brink: Reading the *Yŏnp'yŏng* Shelling and Its Aftermath," *The Journal of Asian Studies* 70, no. 2 (2011): 344–45.

5. Plans for a prior set of reunions fell through the previous year, when the North suspended the program indefinitely in a move aimed at criticizing political conservatives in the South for approaching inter-Korean relations "with hostility and abuse."

6. Figure quoted in U.S. dollars. See Choe Sang-hun, "South Korea Aids North as Families Are Reunited," *New York Times*, February 22, 2014.

7. According to the Ministry of Unification, 46.5 percent of those who applied for family reunions had passed away by August 2014. This mortality rate—representing 60,312 out of 129,575 people—dwarfs the number of those who had been reunited since 2000 through the reunions program, which totals only 3,094 families. Furthermore, those in their eighties or older comprised 51.7 percent of the applicants still alive at the time. See "More than 60,000 S. Koreans likely died before meeting separated family in North," Yonhap News Agency.

8. The term "peacelessness" here is taken from the international conference, "Configuration of Peacelessness on the Korea Peninsula: Dialogue between Humanities and Social Sci-

ence," organized by the Institute for Peace and Unification Studies (IPUS) of Seoul National University, and held at the Plaza Hotel in Seoul on July 25, 2012.

9. Vincent Crapanzano, *Imaginative Horizons: An Essay in Literary-Philosophical Anthropology* (Chicago: University of Chicago Press, 2004), 61.

10. Butler, *Antigone's Claim* (New York: Columbia University Press, 2013), 24.

11. In this contention, anthropologist Roy Richard Grinker in *Korea and Its Futures: Unification and the Unfinished War* (New York: St. Martin's Press, 1998) draws upon the work of the literary critic Paik Nak-chung. See, for example, Paik's *The Division System in Crisis: Essays on Contemporary Korea* (Berkeley: University of California Press, 2011).

12. David L. Eng and David Kazanjian, *Loss: The Politics of Mourning* (Berkeley: University of California Press, 2003). See in particular Eng and Kazanjian's interpretation of Walter Benjamin's "Theses on the Philosophy of History," in which they refute the negative implications of melancholia; instead, they recognize it as a sustained form of mourning that can give rise to a hopeful and creative engagement with past losses by creating an active and open relationship with history (1–6).

Bibliography

Abelmann, Nancy. *Echoes of the Past, Epics of Dissent: A South Korean Social Movement.* Berkeley: University of California Press, 1996.
———. *The Melodrama of Modernity: Women, Talk and Class in Contemporary South Korea.* Honolulu: University of Hawaii Press, 2003.
Abelmann, Nancy, Jung-Ah Choi, and So Jin Park. *No Alternative?: Experiments in South Korean Education.* Berkeley: University of California Press, 2012.
Agamben, Giorgio. *Homo Sacer: Bare Life and Sovereign Power.* Translated by Daniel Heller-Roazen. Stanford: Stanford University Press, 1998.
Ahn, Byung-Ook. *Truth and Reconciliation Activities of the Past Three Years.* Translated by Sung-Soo Kim, Eun-Bok Kim, and Albert Park. Seoul: Truth and Reconciliation Commission, Republic of Korea, 2009.
Anagnost, Ann. *National Past-Times: Narrative, Representation, and Power in Modern China.* Durham, NC: Duke University Press.
Armstrong, Charles K. "The Cultural Cold War in Korea, 1945–1950." *Journal of Asian Studies* 62, no. 1 (2003): 71–100.
———. *The North Korean Revolution: 1945–1950.* Ithaca, NY: Cornell University Press, 2004.
———. "Inter-Korean Relations in Historical Perspective." *International Journal of Korean Unification Studies* 14, no. 2 (2005): 1–20.
———. *The Koreas.* London and New York: Routledge, 2007.
———. "Contesting the Peninsula." *New Left Review* 51 (2008): 115–36.
Ashplant, Timothy G., Graham Dawson, and Michael Roper. *The Politics of War Memory and Commemoration.* London and New York: Routledge, 2000.
Baker, Don. "Exacerbated Politics: The Legacy of Political Trauma in South Korea." In *Northeast Asia's Difficult Past: Essays in Collective Memory,* edited by Barry Schwartz and Mikyoung Kim, 193–212. New York: Palgrave-McMillan, 2012.
Bell, Catherine M. *Ritual: Perspectives and Dimensions.* Oxford: Oxford University Press, 2009.
Berdahl, Daphne. *Where the World Ended: Re-Unification and Identity in the German Borderland.* Berkeley: University of California Press, 1999.
Berkofsky, Axel. *A Pacifist Constitution for an Armed Empire: Past and Present of the Japanese Security and Defense Policies.* Milan: FrancoAngeli, 2012.
Berlant, Lauren. *The Female Complaint: The Unfinished Business of Sentimentality in American Culture.* Durham, NC: Duke University Press, 2008.
Bevan, Jake. "Welcome to Panmunjeom: Encounters with the North in Contemporary South Korean Cinema." *New Cinemas: Journal of Contemporary Film* 8, no. 1 (2010): 45–57.

Bhabha, Homi. *The Location of Culture.* New York: Routledge, 1994.

Bleiker, Roland. *Divided Korea: Toward a Culture of Reconciliation.* Minneapolis: University of Minnesota Press, 2005.

Blunt, Alison. "Cultural Geographies of Migration: Mobility, Transnationality and Diaspora." *Progress in Human Geography* 31 (2007): 684–94.

Bodnar, John. *Remaking America: Public Memory, Commemoration, and Patriotism in the Twentieth Century.* Princeton, NJ: Princeton University Press, 1994.

Borneman, John. *Belonging in the Two Berlins: Kin, State, Nation.* Cambridge: Cambridge University Press, 1992.

———. "Reconciliation After Ethnic Cleansing: Listening, Retribution, Affiliation." *Public Culture* 14, no. 2 (2002): 281–304.

———. *Political Crime and the Memory of Loss.* Bloomington, IN: Indiana University Press, 2011.

Bourdieu, Pierre. "Rites of Institution." In *Language and Symbolic Power*, 117–26. Cambridge, MA: Harvard University Press, 1991.

Bowie, Katherine A. *Rituals of National Loyalty: An Anthropology of the State and the Village Scout Movement in Thailand.* New York: Columbia University Press, 1997.

Brown, Wendy. *Walled States, Waning Sovereignty.* New York: Zone Books, 2010.

Brubaker, Rogers. "The 'Diaspora' Diaspora." *Ethnic and Racial Studies* 28, no. 1 (2005): 1–19.

Butler, Judith. *The Psychic Life of Power: Theories in Subjection.* Stanford: Stanford University Press, 1997.

———. *Antigone's Claim: Kinship between Life and Death.* New York: Columbia University Press, 2013 [2000].

———. *Precarious Life: The Powers of Mourning and Violence.* London: Verso, 2006.

Calman, Donald. *Nature and Origins of Japanese Imperialism: A Re-Interpretation of the 1873 Crisis.* London and New York: Routledge, 1992.

Cammack, Paul. "What the World Bank Means by Poverty Reduction, and Why It Matters." *New Political Economy* 9, no. 2 (2004): 189–211.

Caprio, Mark E. "Plausible Denial? Reviewing the Evidence of DPRK Culpability for the *Cheonan* Warship Incident." *The Asia-Pacific Journal* 30.4, no. 10 (2010).

———. "Silent Voices: The Wartime Views of George McCune and Andrew Grajdanzev for Post-Liberation Korea." Paper presented at the Center for Korean Studies Colloquium. University of Hawaii, Honolulu, HI. March 4, 2014.

———, and Yoneyuki Sugita. *Democracy in Occupied Japan: The U.S. Occupation and Japanese Politics and Society.* New York and London: Routledge, 2007.

Carsten, Janet. "The Politics of Forgetting: Migration, Kinship and Memory on the Periphery of the Southeast Asian State." *Journal of the Royal Anthropological Institute* 1, no. 2 (1995): 317–35.

Ch'ae, Hun. *Wŏlbuk chakka e taehan chaeinsik* [Reconsiderations of *Wŏlbuk* writers]. Seoul: Kip'ŭn Saem, 1995.

Chan, Elim, and Andreas Schloenhardt. "North Korean Refugees and International Refugee Law." *International Journal of Refugee Law* 19, no. 2 (2007): 215–45.

Chang, Kyung-Sup. "The Neo-Confucian Right and Family Politics in South Korea: The Nuclear Family as an Ideological Construct." *Economy and Society* 26, no. 1 (1997): 22–40.

———. *South Korea Under Compressed Modernity: Familial Political Economy in Transition.* London and New York: Routledge, 2010.

Chang, Semoon, and Hwa-Kyung Kim. "Inter-Korean Economic Cooperation." In *The Survival of North Korea: Essays on Strategy, Economics and International Relations*, edited by Suk Hi Kim, Terence Roehrig, and Bernhard Seliger. Jefferson, NC: McFarland, 2011.

Chen, Jian. *China's Road to the Korean War.* New York: Columbia University Press, 1996.

Chen, Kuan Hsing. *Asia as Method: Toward Deimperialization.* Durham, NC: Duke University Press, 2010.

Cho, Grace M. *Haunting the Korean Diaspora: Shame, Secrecy, and the Forgotten War.* Minneapolis: University of Minnesota Press, 2008.

Cho, Hae-Joang. "Male Dominance and Mother Power—The Two Sides of Confucian Patriarchy in South Korea." *Asian Women* 2 (1996): 77–104.

———. "Constructing and Deconstructing 'Koreanness.'" In *Making Majorities: Constituting the Nation in Japan, Korea, China, Malaysia, Fiji, Turkey, and the United States,* edited by Dru C. Gladney, 73–91. Stanford, CA: Stanford University Press, 1998.

Cho Han, Hae-Joang. "'You Are Entrapped in an Imaginary Well': The Formation of Subjectivity Within Compressed Development—A Feminist Critique of Modernity and Korean Culture." *Inter-Asia Cultural Studies* 1, no. 1 (2000): 49–69.

———, and Kim Suhaeng. "*Pan'gong/Panje kyuyul sahoe ŭi munhwa/kwŏllyŏk*" [Culture and Power in Anti-Communist/Anti-Imperialist Disciplined Society]. In *T'albundan sidae rŭl yŏlmyŏ* [Opening an Era of Post-Division], edited by Cho Han Hae-Joang and Lee Woo-young, 116–163. Seoul: Samin, 2000.

———, and Woo-young Lee, eds. *T'albundan sidae rŭl yŏlmyŏ* [Opening an Era of Post-Division]. Seoul: Samin, 2000.

Cho, Hee-yeon. "The Structure of the South Korean Developmental Regime and Its Transformation: Statist Mobilization and Authoritarian Integration in the Anticommunist Regimentation." *Inter-Asia Cultural Studies* 1, no. 3: 408–26.

Cho, Hyoung, and Pak Myong-Son. *Pukhanchulsin wŏllammin ŭi chŏngchakkwajŏng ŭl t'onghaesŏ pon nambukhan sahoegujo ŭi pyŏnhwa* [The Change of Social Structure of South and North Korea through the Examination of the Process of Settlement of *Wŏllammin* from North Korea]. In *Pundansidae wa han'guksahoe* [The Era of Division and South Korean Society]. Seoul: Kkach'i, 1985.

Cho, Sungmi. *Wŏlbukchagajok ŭi saenghwalgyŏnghŏm kwa wolbuk ŭi ŭimich'egye* [Life Experiences of *Wŏlbukcha* Families and the Meaning System of "*Wŏlbuk*"]. MA thesis, Department of Sociology (2002). Ewha's Women's University. Seoul, Korea.

Cho, Uhn. "*Ch'immuk kwa kiŏk ŭi yŏksahwa: yŏsŏng, munhwa, ideollogi*" [Historicizing Silence and Memory: Women, Culture, Ideology]. *Ch'angjak kwa bip'yŏng* [Creation and Criticism] 112 (Summer 2001): 76–90.

———. *Ch'immukŭro chiŭn chip* [The House Built by Silence]. Paju, Korea: Munhak Dongnae, 2003.

———. "*Wŏllamgajok kwa wŏlbukgajok ŭi chanyŏdŭl ŭi kusul ŭl chungsimŭro*" [Remembering the Korean War and the Politics of Memory: Experiences of "*Wollam*" and "*Wolbuk*" Families' Descendants]. *Sahoe wa yŏksa* [Society and History] 77 (2008): 191–229.

Choe, Sang-hun. "South Korea Aids North as Families Are Reunited." *New York Times*, February 22, 2014.

Choi, In-hun. *A Grey Man.* Seoul, Korea: Si Sa Yong O Sa, 1988.

Choi, Jong Kun. "Sunshine Over a Barren Soil: The Domestic Politics of Engagement Identity Formation in South Korea." *Asian Perspective* 34, no. 4 (2010): 115–38.

Choo, Hae Yeon. "Gendered Modernity and Ethnicized Citizenship: North Korean Settlers in Contemporary South Korea." *Gender and Society* 20, no. 5 (2006): 576–604.

Chung, Byung-Ho. "Between Defector and Migrant: Identities and Strategies of North Koreans in South Korea." *Korean Studies* 32, no. 1 (2009): 1–27.

Chung, Yong-Wook. "War and Memory in Korean History." *The Review of Korean Studies* 7, no. 3 (2004): 3–14.

———. "The Emergence of 'North Korea' in Cold War United States." Working Paper No. 03/05, The Mario Einaudi Center for International Studies, Cornell University, 2005, http://einaudi.cornell.edu/system/files/03-2005.pdf (accessed April 24, 2011).

Clark, Donald N. *Living Dangerously in Korea: The Western Experience, 1900–1950.* Norwalk, CT: EastBridge, 2003.

Clifford, James. "Diasporas." *Cultural Anthropology* 9, no. 3 (1994): 302–38.

Collins, Samuel Gerald. "Train to Pyongyang: Imagination, Utopia, and Korean Unification." *Utopian Studies* 24, no. 1 (2013): 119–43.

Comaroff, Jean, and John Comaroff. "Nations With/Out Borders: Neoliberalism and the Problem of Belonging in Africa, and Beyond." In *Border Crossings: Grenzverschiebungen und Grenzüberschreitungen in Einer Globalisierten Welt,* edited by Shalini Randeria. Zurich: VDF, 2008.

Connerton, Paul. *How Societies Remember.* Cambridge, MA: Cambridge University Press, 1989.

Coronil, Fernando. "Beyond Occidentalism: Towards Non-Imperial Geohistorical Categories." *Cultural Anthropology* 11, no. 1 (1996): 51–87.

Couldry, Nick. *Media Rituals: A Critical Approach.* London and New York: Routledge, 2002.

Crapanzano, Vincent. *Imaginative Horizons: An Essay in Literary-Philosophical Anthropology.* Chicago: University of Chicago Press, 2004.

Cumings, Bruce. *The Origins of the Korean War, Volume 1: Liberation and the Emergence of Separate Regimes, 1945–1947.* Princeton, NJ: Princeton University Press, 1981.

———. *The Origins of the Korean War, Volume II: The Roaring of the Cataract, 1947–1950.* Princeton, NJ: Princeton University Press, 1990.

———. "The Asian Crisis, Democracy, and the End of 'Late' Development." In *The Politics of the Asian Economic Crisis,* edited by T. J. Pempel, 17–44. Ithaca: Cornell University Press, 1999.

———. *Korea's Place in the Sun: A Modern History.* New York: Norton, 2005.

———. *The Korean War: A History.* New York: Random House, 2010.

———. *North Korea: Another Country.* New York: The New Press, 2011.

Das, Veena. *Critical Events: An Anthropological Perspective on Contemporary India.* Oxford: Oxford University Press, 1995.

Dayan, Daniel, and Elihu Katz. *Media Events: The Live Broadcasting of History.* Cambridge, MA: Harvard University Press, 1992.

de Bary, Wm. Theodore and JaHyun Kim Haboush, eds. *The Rise of Neo-Confucianism in Korea.* New York: Columbia University Press, 1985.

De Ceuster, Koen. "When History is Made: History, Memory and the Politics of Remembrance in Contemporary Korea." *Korean Histories* 2, no. 1 (2010): 13–33.

Deuchler, Martina. *The Confucian Transformation of Korea: A Study of Society and Ideology.* Cambridge, MA: Harvard University Press, 1992.

Dikötter, Frank. *The Discourse of Race in Modern China.* Stanford, CA: Stanford University Press, 1992.

Douglas, Mary. *Purity and Danger: An Analysis of Concepts of Pollution and Taboo.* New York: Praeger, 1966.

Dudden, Alexis. *Japan's Colonization of Korea: Discourse and Power.* Honolulu: University of Hawaii Press, 2005.

———. *Troubled Apologies Among Japan, Korea, and the United States.* New York: Columbia University Press, 2008.

Duncan, John B. *The Origins of the Chosŏn Dynasty.* Seattle: University of Washington Press, 2000.

———. "Uses of Confucianism in Modern Korea." In *Rethinking Confucianism: Past and Present in China, Japan, Korea, and Vietnam,* edited by Benjamin A. Elman, John B. Duncan, and Herman Ooms, 431–62. Los Angeles: University of California, 2002.

Duus, Peter. *The Abacus and the Sword: The Japanese Penetration of Korea, 1895–1910.* Berkeley: University of California Press, 1998.

Em, Henry H. "Nationalism, Post-Nationalism, and Shin Ch'ae-ho." *Korea Journal* 39, no. 2 (1999): 283–317.

———. *The Great Enterprise: Sovereignty and Historiography in Modern Korea.* Durham, NC: Duke University Press, 2013.

Eng, David L., and David Kazanjian. *Loss: The Politics of Mourning.* Berkeley: University of California Press, 2003.

Epstein, Stephen. "The Axis of Vaudeville: Images of North Korea in South Korean Pop Culture." *The Asia-Pacific Journal* 10, no. 2 (2009).

Faubion, James D. "Introduction: Toward an Anthropology of the Ethics of Kinship." In *The Ethics of Kinship: Ethnographic Inquiries,* edited by John Borneman and James D. Faubion, 1–28. Lanham, MD: Rowman & Littlefield, 2001.

Feldman, Allen. "Securocratic Wars of Public Safety: Globalized Policing as Scopic Regime." *Interventions* 6, no. 3 (2004): 330–50.

Fine, Ben. *Social Capital Versus Social Theory: Political Economy and Social Science at the Turn of the Millennium.* New York and London: Routledge, 2001.

———. "Social Capital: The World Bank's Fungible Friend." *Journal of Agrarian Change* 3, no. 4 (2003): 586–603.

"First Deliberative Polling in Korea: Issue of Korean Unification, Seoul, South Korea." Center for Deliberative Democracy of Stanford University (January 25, 2012) http://cdd.stanford.edu/polls/korea/2012/kr-results-summary.pdf.

Flake, L. Gordon. "Moral Hazard Alert: U.S. Perspectives on Inter-Korean Relations." In *The 2nd Korea-U.S. Security Forum: The 2nd Bush Administration and the Korean Peninsula,* Jeju, Korea, March 30–April 2, 2005.

Foley, James. "'Ten Million Families': Statistic or Metaphor?" *Korean Studies* 25, no. 1 (2001): 96–110.

———. "'Sunshine' Or Showers for Korea's Divided Families?" *World Affairs* 165, no. 4 (2003): 179–84.

———. *Korea's Divided Families: Fifty Years of Separation.* London and New York: Routledge, 2004.

Foot, Rosemary. *A Substitute for Victory: The Politics of Peacemaking at the Korean Armistice Talks.* Ithaca, NY: Cornell University Press, 1990.

Foucault, Michel. *The History of Sexuality, Volume 2: The Use of Pleasure.* New York: Knopf Doubleday, 2012.

Foucault, Michel, et al. *The Foucault Effect: Studies in Governmentality.* Chicago: University of Chicago Press, 1991.

Freeman, Caren. *Making and Faking Kinship: Marriage and Labor Migration between China and South Korea.* Ithaca, NY: Cornell University Press, 2011.

Freud, Sigmund. "Mourning and Melancholia." In *Standard Edition of the Complete Psychological Works of Sigmund Freud,* edited by James Strachey. Vol. 14 (1914–1916): 154–167. London: Hogarth Press, 1917.

Frühstück, Sabine. *Uneasy Warriors: Gender, Memory, and Popular Culture in the Japanese Army.* Berkeley and Los Angeles: University of California Press, 2007.

Fujitani, T., Geoffrey White, and Lisa Yoneyama, eds. *Perilous Memories: The Asia Pacific War(s).* Durham, NC: Duke University Press, 2001.

Geertz, Clifford. "Ideology as a Cultural System." In *Ideology and Discontent,* edited by David Apter, 47–76. New York: Free Press, 1964.

———. *Negara: The Theatre State in Nineteenth-Century Bali.* Princeton, NJ: Princeton University Press, 1980.

Gelézeau, Valérie. "The Inter-Korean Border Region—'Meta-Border' of the Cold War and Metamorphic Frontier of the Peninsula." In *The Ashgate Research Companion to Border Studies,* edited by Doris Wastl-Walter, 325–48. Farnham, U.K.: Ashgate Publishing, 2011.

———, Koen De Ceuster, and Alain Delissen, eds. *De-Bordering Korea: Tangible and Intangible Legacies of the Sunshine Policy.* New York and London: Routledge, 2013.

Gillis, John R. *Commemorations: The Politics of National Identity.* Princeton, NJ: Princeton University Press, 1994.

Ginsburg, Faye D., Lila Abu-Lughod, and Brian Larkin. *Media Worlds: Anthropology on New Terrain.* Berkeley: University of California Press, 2002.

Gluckman, Max. *Politics, Law and Ritual in Tribal Society.* Oxford, U.K.: Basil Blackwell, 1971.

Goffman, Erving. *Stigma: Notes on the Management of Spoiled Identity.* Englewood Cliffs, NJ: Prentice-Hall, 1963.

Goncharov, Sergei, John Lewis, and Xue Litai. *Uncertain Partners: Stalin, Mao, and the Korean War.* Stanford, CA: Stanford University Press, 1994.

"Gov't to Raise Financial Support for Separated Families." *Korea Times,* March 2, 2000.

Gray, Kevin. "Political Cultures of South Korea." *New Left Review* 79 (January–February, 2013): 85–101.

Grinker, Roy Richard. *Korea and Its Futures: Unification and the Unfinished War.* New York: St. Martin's Press, 1998.

Haboush, JaHyun Kim. *A Heritage of Kings: One Man's Monarchy in the Confucian World.* New York: Columbia University Press, 1988.
————. "The Confucianization of Korean Society." In *The East Asian Region Confucian Heritage and Its Modern Adaptation*, 84–110. Princeton, NJ: Princeton University Press, 1991.
Halliday, Jon, and Bruce Cumings. *Korea: The Unknown War.* New York: Pantheon, 1988.
Han, Jong-woo, and Tae-hern Jung, eds. *Understanding North Korea: Indigenous Perspectives.* Lanham, MD: Lexington Books, 2013.
Han, Sang-jin. "From the Asian Value Debate to Cosmopolitanism: An Active Interpretation of the Political Thoughts of Kim Dae-jung." *Korea Journal* 51, no. 3 (2011): 196–222.
Han, Seung-Mi. "The New Community Movement: Park Chung Hee and the Making of State Populism in Korea." *Pacific Affairs* 77, no. 1 (2004): 69–93.
Handelman, Don. *Models and Mirrors: Towards an Anthropology of Public Events.* Oxford: Berghahn, 1998.
Han'guk Kusulsa Hakhoe. *Kusulsa ro ingnun Han'guk Chŏnjaeng: Sŏul t'obagi wa mint'ongsŏn saramdŭl, chŏnjaeng mimangin kwa wŏlbuk kajok, kŭdŭl i mal hanŭn arae robut'oŭi Han'guk Chŏnjaeng.* Seoul: Humanist, 2011.
Hanley, Charles J., Sang-Hun Choe, and Martha Mendoza. *The Bridge at No Gun Ri: A Hidden Nightmare From the Korean War.* New York: Henry Holt, 2001.
Hariss, John. *De-Politicizing Development: The World Bank and Social Capital.* New York: Anthem Press, 2002.
Harrison, Selig S. *Korean Endgame: A Strategy for Reunification.* Princeton, NJ: Princeton University Press, 2009.
Hein, Laura. "Savage Irony: The Imaginative Power of the 'Military Comfort Women' in the 1990s." *Gender & History* 11, no. 2 (July 1999): 336–72.
Henderson, Gregory. *Korea: The Politics of the Vortex.* Cambridge, MA: Harvard University Press, 1968.
Henry, Todd. *Assimilating Seoul: Japanese Rule and the Politics of Public Space in Colonial Korea, 1910–1945.* Berkeley and Los Angeles: University of California Press, 2014.
Herr, Ranjoo Seodu. "Is Confucianism Compatible With Care Ethics? A Critique." *Philosophy East and West* 53, no. 4 (2003): 471–89.
Ho, Elaine Lynn-Ee. "Constituting Citizenship Through the Emotions: Singaporean Transmigrants in London." *Annals of the Association of American Geographers* 99, no. 4 (2009): 788–804.
Ho, Enseng. *Graves of Tarim: Genealogy and Mobility Across the Indian Ocean.* Berkeley and Los Angeles: University of California Press, 2006.
Hoare, James, and Susan Pares. *Conflict in Korea: An Encyclopedia.* Santa Barbara, CA: ABC-CLIO, 1999.
Hobsbawm, Eric. *Nations and Nationalism Since 1780.* New York: Cambridge University Press, 1990.
Hong, Christine. "The First Year of Peace on the Korean Peninsula." *Foreign Policy in Focus.* Institute for Policy Studies. October 11, 2012. http://fpif.org/the_first_year_of_peace_on_the_korean_peninsula/ (accessed October 17, 2012).
Hong, Soon-Young. "Thawing Korea's Cold War: The Path to Peace on the Korean Peninsula." *Foreign Affairs* 78, no. 3 (1999): 8–12.
Hoog, Günter, and Angela Steinmetz, eds. *International Conventions on Protection of Humanity and Environment.* Berlin and New York: Walter de Gruyter, 1993.
Hübinette, Tobias. *Comforting an Orphaned Nation: Representations of International Adoption and Adopted Koreans in Korean Popular Culture.* Stockholm: Department of Oriental Languages, Stockholm University, 2005.
Hughes, Theodore. "Planet Hallyuwood: Imaging the Korean War." *Acta Koreana* 14, no. 1 (2011): 197–212.
————. *Literature and Film in Cold War South Korea: Freedom's Frontier.* New York: Columbia University Press, 2012.
Hunter, Helen-Louise. *Kim Il-sŏng's North Korea.* Westport, CT: Praeger, 1999.

Hwang, Kyung Moon. "Country Or State? Reconceptualizing *Kukka* in the Korean Enlightenment Period, 1896–1910." *Korean Studies* 24, no. 1 (2000): 1–24.

Hwang, Sok-yong. *The Guest*. Translated by Kyung-Ja Chun and Maya West. New York: Seven Stories Press, 2005 [2002].

Hwang, Su-kyoung. "South Korea, the United States and Emergency Powers During the Korean Conflict." *The Asia-Pacific Journal* 12.5, no. 1 (February 3, 2014).

Ikels, Charlotte, ed. *Filial Piety: Practice and Discourse in Contemporary East Asia*. Stanford, CA: Stanford University Press, 2004.

Im, Hyug Baeg. "Faltering Democratic Consolidation in South Korea." *Democratization* 11, no. 5 (2004): 179–98.

Institute for Foreign Policy Analysis. *Northeast Asian Security after Korean Reconciliation or Reunification: Preparing the U.S.–Japan Alliance*. Cambridge, MA and Washington, D.C.: February 2002.

Jackson, Jean E. "Stigma, Liminality, and Chronic Pain: Mind-Body Borderlands." *American Ethnologist* 32, no. 3 (2005): 332–53.

Jager, Sheila Miyoshi. "Time to End the Korean War: The Korean Nuclear Crisis in the Era of Unification." 2006. www.nautilus.org/fora/security/0693MiyoshiJager.html.

———. *Narratives of Nation Building in Korea: A Genealogy of Patriotism*. Armonk, NY: M. E. Sharpe, 2003.

———. *Brothers At War: The Unending Conflict in Korea*. New York: W. W. Norton & Company, 2013.

Jager, Sheila Miyoshi, and Rana Mitter. *Ruptured Histories: War, Memory, and the Post–Cold War in Asia*. Cambridge, MA: Harvard University Press, 2007.

———, and Jiyul Kim. "The Korean War After the Cold War: Commemorating the Armistace Agreement in South Korea." In *Ruptured Histories: War, Memory, and the Post–Cold War in Asia*, edited by Sheila Miyoshi Jager and Rana Mitter, 233–65. Cambridge, MA: Harvard University Press, 2007.

Janelli, Roger L., and Dawnhee Yim. "The Transformation of Filial Piety in Contemporary South Korea." In *Filial Piety: Practice and Discourse in Contemporary East Asia*, 128–52. Stanford, CA: Stanford University Press, 2004.

———, and Dawnhee Yim Janelli. *Ancestor Worship and Korean Society*. Stanford, CA: Stanford University Press, 1982.

Jeon, Chihyung. "A Road to Modernization and Unification: The Construction of the Gyeongbu Highway in South Korea." *Technology and Culture* 51, no. 1 (2009): 55–79.

Jeon, Seung-Hee. "War Trauma, Memories, and Truth: Representations of the Korean War in Pak Wan-So's Writings and in 'Still Present Pasts.'" *Critical Asian Studies* 42, no. 4 (2010): 623–651.

Jervis, Robert. "The Impact of the Korean War on the Cold War." *Journal of Conflict Resolution* 24, no. 4 (1980): 563–92.

Jhe, Seong-Ho. "Four Major Agreements on Inter-Korean Economic Cooperation: Legal Measures for Implementation." *East Asian Review* 16, no. 4 (2004): 19–40.

Joinau, Benjamin. "Sleeping with the (Northern) Enemy: South Korean Cinema and the Autistic Interface." In *De-Bordering Korea: Tangible and Intangible Legacies of the Sunshine Policy*, edited by Valérie Gelézeau et al., 172–188. New York: Routledge, 2013.

Jong-Ho, Ho, Kang Sok-Hui, and Pak Thae-Ho. *The U.S. Imperialists Started the Korean War*. Pyongyang: Foreign Languages Publishing House, 1993.

Jonsson, Gabriel. *Towards Korean Reconciliation: Socio-Cultural Exchanges and Cooperation*. Aldershot, U.K.: Ashgate, 2006.

Jun, Suk-ho, and Daniel Dayan. "An Interactive Media Event: South Korea's Televised 'Family Reunion.'" *Journal of Communication* 36, no. 2 (1986): 73–82.

Jung, Jin-heon. "State and Church in the Making of Post-Division Subjectivity: North Korean Migrants in South Korea." MMG Working Paper 11–12, Göttingen, Germany: Max Planck Institute for the Study of Religious and Ethnic Diversity, 2011.

Kallendar, George. *Salvation through Dissent: Tonghak Heterodoxy and Early Modern Korea*. Honolulu: University of Hawaii Press, 2013.

Kang, Jeong-gu. *Haebang-hu Wŏllammin ŭi wŏllamtonggi wa kyegŭpsŏng e kwanhan yŏn'gu* [A Study of Class Backgrounds and the Motives for Coming to the South among *Wŏllammin* in the Post-Liberation Period]. In *Han'gukchŏnjaeng kwa han'guksahoe pyŏndong* [The Korean War and Change in South Korean Society]. Seoul: P'ulbit, 1992.

Kang, Jun-man, ed. *Redŭ k'omp'ŭlleksŭ: Kwangki ka namgin ahopkae ŭi ch'osang* [Red Complex: Nine Portraits That the Madness Left Behind]. Seoul: Samin, 1997.

Karim, Lamia. "A Kinship of One's Own." In *The Ethics of Kinship: Ethnographic Inquiries*, edited by James D. Faubion. Lanham, MD: Rowman & Littlefield, 2001.

Kaufman, Sharon R., and Lynn M. Morgan. "The Anthropology of the Beginnings and Ends of Life." *The Annual Review of Anthropology* 34 (2005): 317–41.

Katsiafacas, George. *Asia's Unknown Uprisings, Vol. 1: South Korean Social Movements in the 20th Century*. Oakland, CA: PM Press, 2012.

Kendall, Laurel. "Wood Imps, Ghosts, and Other Noxious Influences: The Ideology of Affliction in a Korean Village." *The Journal of Korean Studies* 3 (1981): 113–45.

———. "Korean Ancestors: From the Woman's Side." In *Korean Women: View From the Inner Room*, edited by Laurel Kendall and Mark Peterson, 97–112. New Haven, CT: East Rock Press, 1983.

———. *Shamans, Nostalgias and the IMF: South Korean Popular Religion in Motion*. Honolulu, HI: University of Hawaii Press, 2009.

Kihl, Young Whan. *Transforming Korean Politics: Democracy, Reform, and Culture*. Armonk, NY: M. E. Sharpe, 2004.

Kim, Ah-jeong, and R. B. Graves. *The Metacultural Theater of Oh T'ae-sŏk: Five Plays From the Korean Avant-Garde*. Honolulu: University of Hawaii Press, 1996.

Kim, Byeong-uk, and Young-hui Kim. "Comparative Study of the Contacts of Divided Families in Korea and Germany." *North Korean Studies Review* 12, no. 1 (2009).

Kim, Choong Soon. *Faithful Endurance: An Ethnography of Korean Family Dispersal*. Tucson: University of Arizona Press, 1988.

Kim, Dae-Jung. "Democracy and Market Economy: Two Wheels of a Cart." In *Democracy, Market Economy and Development: An Asian Perspective*, edited by Farrukh Iqbal and Jong-Il You. Washington, DC: World Bank, 2001.

Kim, Dong-Choon. "Forgotten War, Forgotten Massacres—The Korean War (1950–1953) as Licensed Mass Killings." *Journal of Genocide Research* 6, no. 4 (2004): 523–44.

———. *The Unending Korean War: A Social History*. Translated by Sung-ok Kim. Larkspur, CA: Tamal Vista, 2009.

———. "Korea's Movement to Settle the Issues of the Past and Peace in East Asia." *Korea Journal* 50, no. 4 (2010): 152–85.

———. "The Long Road Toward Truth and Reconciliation: Unwavering Attempts to Achieve Justice in South Korea." *Critical Asian Studies* 42, no. 4 (2010): 525–52.

Kim, Dongno. "The Transformation of Familism in Modern Korean Society: From Cooperation to Competition." *International Sociology* 5, no. 4 (1990): 409–25.

Kim, Eleana. *Adopted Territory: Transnational Korean Adoptees and the Politics of Belonging*. (Durham, NC: Duke University Press, 2010).

Kim, Eunshil. "The Cultural Logic of the Korean Modernization Project and its Gender Politics." *Asian Journal of Women's Studies* 6, no. 2 (2000): 50–77.

Kim, Gwi-Ok. *Wŏllammin ŭi saenghwal kyŏnghŏm kwa chŏngch'esŏng* [The True Character of the Life Experience of Refugees From the North]. Seoul: Seoul National University Press, 2002 [1999].

———. *Isan'gajok, "pan'gongjŏnsa" to "ppalgaengi" to anin* [Separated Families, Neither "Anti-Communist Warriors" Nor "Reds"]. Seoul: Yŏksabip'yŏngsa, 2004.

Kim, Ha-gie. "A Perfect Meeting" (*Wanjŏnhan mannam*). *Korea Journal* 32, no. 4 (1992): 119–34.

Kim, Hosu. "Korean Birthmothers Lost and Found in the Search-and-Reunion Narratives." *Cultural Studies—Critical Methodologies* 12, no. 5 (2012): 438–49.

Kim, Hun-Joon. "Seeking Truth After 50 Years: The National Committee for Investigation of the Truth About the Jeju 4.3 Events." *International Journal of Transitional Justice* 3, no. 3 (2009): 406–23.

Kim, Hyun Mee. "Work, Nation and Hypermasculinity: The 'Woman' Question in the Economic Miracle and Crisis in South Korea." *Inter-Asia Cultural Studies* 2, no. 1 (2001): 53–68.

Kim, Hyun Sook. "History and Memory: The 'Comfort Women' Controversy." *positions* 5, no. 1 (1997): 73–108.

Kim, Hyung-A, and Clark W. Sorensen, eds. *Reassessing the Park Chung Hee Era, 1961–1979: Development, Political Thought, Democracy, and Cultural Influence.* Seattle: University of Washington Press, 2011.

Kim, Jae-yong. *"Isan 'gajok munje ŭi chŏngch 'isŏng kwa indojuŭi."* *Yŏksa pip 'yŏng* 6 (1998): 136–59.

Kim, Janice C. H. *To Live to Work: Factory Women in Colonial Korea, 1910–1945.* Stanford, CA: Stanford University Press, 2009.

Kim, Jiyul. "Pan-Korea Nationalism, Anti-Great Power-ism and US–South Korean Relations." *Japan Focus*, December 13, 2005. http://www.japanfocus.org/-Jiyul-Kim/1679.

Kim, Key-Hiuk. *The Last Phase of the East Asian World Order: Korea, Japan, and the Chinese Empire, 1860–1882.* Berkeley: University of California Press, 1980.

Kim, Kwang-ok. "The Making and Indigenization of Anthropology in Korea." In *The Making of Anthropology in East and Southeast Asia*, 253–85. New York and Oxford: Berghahn Books, 2004.

Kim, Kyŏng-hak, Jŏng-sŏk Pak, Yŏm Mi-kyŏng, Yun Jŏng-ran, and P'yo In-ju. *Chŏnjaeng kwa kiŏk: Maŭl kongdongch 'e ŭi saengaesa* [Korean War, Community, and Residents' Memories]. P'aju-si, Korea: Han'ul Ak'ademi, 2005.

Kim, Mikyoung, and Barry Schwartz, eds. *Northeast Asia's Difficult Past: Essays in Collective Memory.* New York: Palgrave-Macmillan, 2010.

Kim, Monica. "Empire's Babel: U.S. Military Interrogation Rooms of the Korean War." *History of the Present* 3, no. 1 (Spring 2013): 1–28.

Kim, Nan. "Korea on the Brink: Reading the *Yŏnp 'yŏng* Shelling and Its Aftermath." *The Journal of Asian Studies* 70, no. 2 (2011): 337–56.

Kim, Seong-nae. "Lamentations of the Dead: The Historical Imagery of Violence on Cheju Island, South Korea." *Journal of Ritual Studies* 3, no. 2 (1989): 251–85.

———. "Sexual Politics of State Violence: On the Cheju April Third Massacre of 1948." In *"Race" Panic and the Memory of Migration*, edited by Meaghan Morris and Brett De Bary, 259–83. Hong Kong: Hong Kong University Press, 2001.

———. "The Work of Memory: Ritual Laments of the Dead and Korea's Cheju Massacre." In *A Companion to the Anthropology of Religion*, edited by Janice Boddy and Michael Lambek. London: Wiley Blackwell, 2013.

———. "Women, Mourning, and the Ritual of Death in the Family." In *Gender and Family in East Asia*, edited by Siumi Maria Tam, Wai Ching Angela Wong, and Danning Wang. New York and London: Routledge, 2014.

Kim, Seseoria. "The Meaning of 'Filial Piety' and Ethics of Care in the Korean Family." *The Review of Korean Studies* 10, no. 3 (2007): 9–34.

Kim, Seung-kyung, *Class Struggle or Family Struggle?: The Lives of Women Factory Workers in South Korea.* Cambridge: Cambridge University Press, 1997.

Kim, Suk-Young. "Can We Live as One Family? Rethinking the Two Koreas' Kinship in John Hoon's Kang Tek-koo." *Theatre Research International* 3 (2004): 267–83.

———. "Crossing the Border to the 'Other' Side: Dynamics of Interaction between North and South Koreans in *Spy Li Cheol-jin* and *Joint Security Area*." In *Seoul Searching: Culture and Identity in Contemporary Korean Cinema*, 219–242. Albany: SUNY Press, 2007.

———. *Illusive Utopia: Theater, Film, and Everyday Performance in North Korea.* Ann Arbor, MI: University of Michigan Press, 2010.

———. *DMZ Crossing: Performing Emotional Citizenship Along the Korean Border.* New York: Columbia University Press, 2014.

Kim, Sung Chull, and David C. Kang. *Engagement With North Korea: A Viable Alternative.* Albany, NY: State University of New York Press, 2009.

Kim, Suzy. *Everyday Life in the North Korean Revolution, 1945–1950.* Ithaca, NY: Cornell University Press, 2013.

Kim, Yong-sŏp. "The Landlord System and the Agricultural Economy during the Japanese Occupation Period." In *Landlords, Peasants, and Intellectuals in Modern Korea*, edited by Ki-jung Pang, Michael D. Shin, and Yong-sŏp Kim. Ithaca, NY: Cornell University Press, 2005.

Kim, Young Shin, Yun-Joo Koh, and Bennett Leventhal. "School Bullying and Suicidal Risk in Korean Middle School Students." *Pediatrics* 115, no. 2 (2005): 357–63.

Kirk, Don. "Seoul Leader Pressed on Funds Sent to North." *New York Times*, February 1, 2003. http://www.nytimes.com/2003/02/01/world/seoul-leader-pressed-on-funds-sent-to-north.html.

Koh, Byong-ik. "Confucianism in Contemporary Korea." In *Confucian Traditions in East Asian Modernity: Moral Education and Economic Culture in Japan and the Four Mini-Dragons*, edited by Tu Wei-ming. Cambridge, U.K.: Harvard University Press, 1996.

Korea Institute for National Unification. *The Unification Environment and Relations between South and North Korea, 1999–2000: 1999 Annual Report*. Seoul: Minjok T'ongil Yŏn'guwŏn, 2000.

Korea: The Unknown War. Episode 4. "An Entirely New War." First broadcast September 8, 1988, by Thames Television (London) in association with WBGH Boston, produced by Philip Whitehead and written by Jon Halliday.

Korean Central News Agency. "S. Authorities Urged to Create Conditions for Meeting of Separated Families." October 16, 2001. www.kcna.co.jp/item/2001/200110/news10/16.htm (accessed November 30, 2001).

Korean Overseas Information Service (KOIS). "Exchange Visits by Separated Families in South and North Korea." Press pool report, unpublished typescript, Seoul, Korea, August 15, 2000.

Korean Red Cross (Republic of Korea). "Inter-Korean." http://www.redcross.or.kr/eng/eng_activity/activity_interkorean.do (accessed May 20, 2014).

Korean War Armistice Agreement. Treaties and Other International Agreements, Series #2782. General Records of the United States Government, Record Group 11, National Archives Building, Washington, DC (1953).

Kwak, Tae Yang. "*Han'guk ŭi Betŭnam chŏnjaeng chaep'ŏngga*" [Reevaluating Korean Participation in the Vietnam War]. *Yŏksa pip'yŏng* [Critical Review of History] 107 (Summer 2014): 202–32.

———. "The Nixon Doctrine and the Yusin Reforms: American Foreign Policy, the Vietnam War, and the Rise of Authoritarianism in Korea, 1968–1973." *The Journal of American-East Asian Relations* 12, no. 1/2 (2003).

Kwon, Heonik. "The Ghosts of War and the Spirit of Cosmopolitanism." *History of Religions* 48, no. 1 (2008): 22–42.

———. *Ghosts of War in Vietnam*. New York: Cambridge University Press, 2008.

———. "Korean War Traumas." *The Asia Pacific Journal: Japan Focus* 38 no. 2 (2010).

———. *The Other Cold War*. New York: Columbia University Press, 2010.

———. "The Korean War and the Political Life of Kinship." Paper presented at the British Association of Korean Studies conference, Asia House, London, United Kingdom, November 2010.

———. "Legacies of the Korean War: Transforming Ancestral Rituals in South Korea." *Memory Studies* 6, no. 2 (2013): 161–73.

———, and Byung-Ho Chung. *North Korea: Beyond Charismatic Politics*. Lanham, MD: Rowman & Littlefield, 2012.

Kwon, Insook. "A Feminist Exploration of Military Conscription: The Gendering of the Connections Between Nationalism, Militarism and Citizenship in South Korea." *International Feminist Journal of Politics* 3, no. 1 (2000): 26–54.

Kwon, Jong Bum. "Forging a Modern Democratic Imaginary: Police Sovereignty, Neoliberalism, and the Boundaries of Neo-Korea." *positions* 22, no. 4 (2014): 71–101.

Kwon, Tai Hwan. *Demography of Korea: Population Change and Its Components 1925–66*. Seoul: Seoul National University Press, 1977.

Lankov, Andrei. *The Real North Korea: Life and Politics in the Failed Stalinist Utopia*. New York: Oxford University Press, 2013.

Larsen, Bent Steeg, and Thomas Tufte. "Rituals in the Modern World: Applying the Concept of Ritual in Media Ethnography." In *Global Media Studies—Ethnographic Perspectives*, edited by Patrick D. Murphy and Marwan M. Krady. New York and London: Routledge, 2003.

Lash, Scott, and John Urry. *Economies of Signs and Space*. Thousand Oaks, CA: Sage, 1994.

Lee, Ho-chul. *Southerners, Northerners: A Novel (Namnyŏk Saram, Pungnyŏk Saram)*. Translated by Andrew P. Killick and Sukyeon Cho. Norwalk, CT: EastBridge, 2005.

Lee, Hyeon Ju. "Remembering and Forgetting the Korean War in the Republic of Korea." *Suomen Antropologi: Journal of the Finnish Anthropological Society* 35, no. 2 (2010): 48–55.

Lee, Hyo-Jae. "National Division and Family Problems." *Korea Journal* 25, no. 8 (1985): 4–18.

Lee, Jee Sun E. "Post-Unification Korean National Identity." Working Paper 09/03. Asiatic Research Center, Korea University. Washington, DC: U.S. Korea Institute at SAIS, 2009.

Lee, Jongsoo James. *The Partition of Korea After World War II: A Global History*. New York: Palgrave Macmillan, 2007.

Lee, Kwang Kyu. *Korean Family and Kinship*. Seoul: Jipmoondang, 1997.

———. "Confucian Tradition in the Contemporary Korean Family." In *Confucianism and the Family*, 249–66. Albany, NY: State University of New York Press, 1998.

Lee, Namhee. "Anticommunism, North Korea, and Human Rights in South Korea: 'Orientalist' Discourse and Construction of South Korean Identity." In *Truth Claims: Representation and Human Rights*, edited by Mark Philip Bradley and Patrice Petro, 43–72. New Brunswick, NJ: Rutgers University Press, 2002.

———. *The Making of Minjung: Democracy and the Politics of Representation in South Korea*. Ithaca, NY: Cornell University Press, 2007.

Lee, Ryong-kyong. "War and Women's Lives: On the Experience of Bereaved Women of Left-Related Victims of the Korean War." *The Review of Korean Studies* 6, no. 1 (2003): 85–108.

Lee, Soo-Jung. "Making and Unmaking the Korean National Division: Separated Families in the Cold War and Post–Cold War Eras." PhD dissertation, Urbana-Champaign: University of Illinois, 2006.

———. "*Kukka p'ant'aji wa kajok ŭi kulle: wŏlbukcha kajok ŭi namhan kungmin toegi*" [Fantasies of State, Bonds of Family: *Wolbukcha* Family Stories]. *Pigyomunhwa yŏngu* [*Comparative Cultural Studies*] 16, no. 1 (2010): 163–93.

———. "The Korean War and the Politics of Memory." *Korean Social Sciences Review* 3, no. 2 (2013): 101–27. (Translated from *Korean Cultural Anthropology* 44, no. 1 [2011], with permission from the Korean Society for Cultural Anthropology).

———. "'*T'alnaengjŏn minjok spekt'ŏk'ŭl': 2000-nyŏn yŏrŭm nambuk isan'gajok sangbong*" ["Post–Cold War National Spectacle": Reunions of Separated Families in the Summer, 2000]. *Minjok munhwa yŏngu* 59 (2013): 95–122.

Lee, Steven Hugh. *Outposts of Empire: Korea, Vietnam, and the Origins of the Cold War in Asia, 1949–1954*. Montreal and Kingston: McGill-Queen's University Press, 1995.

———. *The Korean War*. New York: Longman, 2001.

Lee, Young-Sun. "The Cost and Financing of Korean Unification." In *Perspectives on Korean Unification and Economic Integration*, edited by Young Back Choi, Yesook Merrill, Yung Y. Yang, and Semoon Chang. Cheltenham, U.K.: Edward Elgar, 2001.

Leitenberg, Milton. "Deaths in Wars and Conflicts in the 20th Century." Cornell University Peace Studies Program, Occasional Paper #29 (3rd ed., 2006).

Lew, Young Ick. "The Conservative Character of the 1894 Tonghak Peasant Uprising." *Journal of Korean Studies* 7, no. 1 (1990): 149–80.

Li, Chenyang. "The Confucian Concept of *Jen* and the Feminist Ethics of Care: A Comparative Study." *Hypatia* 9, no. 1 (1994): 70–89.

Lie, John. "Embedding Polanyi's Market Society." *Sociological Perspectives* 34, no. 2 (1991): 219–35.

———. *Han Unbound: The Political Economy of South Korea*. Stanford, CA: Stanford University Press, 2000.

Liénard, Pierre, and Boyer, Pascal. "Whence Collective Rituals? A Cultural Selection Model of Ritualized Behavior." *American Anthropologist* 108, no. 4 (2006): 814–27.

Liem, Ramsay. "History, Trauma, and Identity: The Legacy of the Korean War for Korean Americans." *Amerasia Journal* 29, no. 3 (2003–2004): 111–29.
———. "Silencing Historical Trauma: The Politics and Psychology of Memory and Voice." *Peace and Conflict: Journal of Peace Psychology* 13, no. 2 (2007): 153–74.
Lim, Dong-won. *Peacemaker: Twenty Years of Inter-Korean Relations and the North Korean Nuclear Issue.* Stanford, CA: Stanford University Asia-Pacific Research Center, 2012.
Lone, Stewart, and Gavan McCormack. *Korea Since 1850.* New York: St. Martin's Press, 1993.
Lüdtke, Alf. "Histories of Mourning: Flowers and Stones for the War Dead, Confusion for the Living." In *Between History and Histories: The Making of Silences and Commemorations*, 149–79. Toronto: University of Toronto Press, 1997.
Lukes, Steven. "Political Ritual and Social Integration." *Sociology* 9, no. 2 (1975): 289–308.
Malkki, Liisa H. *Purity and Exile: Violence, Memory, and National Cosmology Among Hutu Refugees in Tanzania.* Chicago: University of Chicago Press, 1995.
Mansourov, Alexandre Y. "Stalin, Mao, Kim, and China's Decision to Enter the Korean War, September 16–October 15, 1950: New Evidence from the Russian Archives." *Cold War International History Project Bulletin* (Winter 1995): 94–107.
Masco, Joseph. *The Nuclear Borderlands: The Manhattan Project in Post–Cold War New Mexico.* Princeton, NJ: Princeton University Press, 2006.
———. "'Survival is Your Business': Engineering Ruins and Affect in Nuclear America." *Cultural Anthropology* 23, no. 2 (2008): 361–98.
———. "Engineering the Future as Nuclear Ruin." In *Imperial Debris: On Ruins and Ruination*, edited by Ann Laura Stoler. Durham, NC: Duke University Press, 2013.
McNamara, Laura A., and Robert Rubinstein, eds. *Dangerous Liaisons: Anthropologists and the National Security State.* Santa Fe, NM: School for Advanced Research Press, 2011.
Memory of Forgotten War. Directed by Deann Borshay Liem and Ramsay Liem. DVD. Berkeley, CA: Mu Films, 2012.
Merrill, John. "The Cheju-do Rebellion." *Journal of Korean Studies* 2 (1980): 151–52.
———. *Korea: The Peninsular Origins of the War.* Newark: University of Delaware Press, 1989.
Ministry of Unification, Republic of Korea. *Peace and Cooperation: White Paper on Korean Unification.* Seoul: Ministry of Unification, 2001.
Mookherjee, Nayanika. "Friendships and Encounters with Left-Liberal Politics in Bangladesh." In *Taking Sides: Ethics, Politics, and Fieldwork in Anthropology*, edited by Heidi Armbruster and Anna Lærke. New York and Oxford: Bergahn, 2008.
Moon, Chung-in. "From Symbols to Substance: Comparing the 2000 and 2007 Inter-Korean Summits." *Global Asia* 2, no. 3 (2007).
———. *The Sunshine Policy: In Defense of Engagement as a Path to Peace in Korea.* Seoul: Yonsei University Press, 2012.
Moon, Katharine H. S. "South Korean Movements Against Militarized Sexual Labor." *Asian Survey* (1999): 310–27.
Moon, Seungsook. *Militarized Modernity and Gendered Citizenship in South Korea.* Durham, NC: Duke University Press, 2005.
Morris, Rosalind. "Intimacy and Corruption in Thailand's Age of Conspiracy." In *Off Stage, On Display: Intimacy and Ethnography in the Age of Public Culture*, edited by Andrew Shryock, 225–243. Stanford, CA: Stanford University Press, 2004.
Morris-Suzuki, Tessa. *The Past Within Us: Media, Memory, History.* New York: Verso, 2005.
———. "Remembering the Unfinished Conflict: Museums and the Contested Memory of the Korean War." *The Asia-Pacific Journal* 29, no. 4 (2009).
———, Morris Low, Leonid Petrov, and Timothy Tsu. *East Asia Beyond the History Wars: Confronting the Ghosts of Violence.* New York and London: Routledge, 2013.
Myers, Ramon Hawley, and Mark Robert Peattie. *The Japanese Colonial Empire: 1895–1945.* Princeton, NJ: Princeton University Press, 1984.
Nelson, Christopher. *Dancing With the Dead: Memory, Performance, and Everyday Life in Postwar Okinawa.* Durham and London: Duke University Press, 2008.

Nelson, Laura. *Measured Excess: Status, Gender, and Consumer Nationalism in South Korea.* New York: Columbia University Press, 2000.

Newendorp, Nicole. *Uneasy Reunions: Immigration, Citizenship and Family Life in Post-1997 Hong Kong.* Stanford, CA: Stanford University Press, 2008.

Niebuhr, Gustav. "Whose Memory Lives When the Last Survivor Dies?" *New York Times,* January 29, 1995.

Ndlovu-Gatsheni, Sabelo J., and Wendy Willems. "Making Sense of Cultural Nationalism and the Politics of Commemoration Under the Third Chimurenga in Zimbabwe." *Journal of Southern African Studies* 35, no. 4 (2009): 945–65.

Oberdorfer, Don. *The Two Koreas: A Contemporary History.* New York: Basic Books, 2001.

Oh, John Kie-chiang. *Korean Politics: The Quest for Democratization and Economic Development.* Ithaca, NY: Cornell University Press, 1999.

Oh, Kongdan. "The Problem and Promise of Inter-Korean Economic Cooperation." In *Korea Briefing: Toward Reunification,* edited by David R. McCann. Armonk, NY: M. E. Sharpe, 1996.

Oh, Yeon-Ho. *"Ch'oech'ochŭngŏn Ch'amchŏn Mikun ŭi Ch'ungbuk Yŏngdong Yangmin 3-paek Yŏmyŏng Haksal Sakŏn"* [First Testimony: Massacre of 300 Villagers by American Soldiers During the Korean War in Yŏng-dong Ch'ungbuk]. *Monthly Mal* (July 1994): 36–45.

O'Neill, Mark. "Soviet Involvement in the Korean War: A New View from the Soviet-Era Archives." *OAH Magazine of History* 14, no. 3 (2000): 20–24.

Ong, Aihwa. *Flexible Citizenship: The Cultural Logics of Transnationality.* Durham, NC: Duke University Press, 1999.

———. "Cyberpublics and Diaspora Politics Among Transnational Chinese." *Interventions* 5, no. 1 (2003): 82–100.

———. *Neoliberalism as Exception: Mutations in Citizenship and Sovereignty.* Durham, NC: Duke University Press, 2006.

Oppenheim, Robert. *Kyŏngju Things: Assembling Place.* Ann Arbor, MI: University of Michigan Press, 2008.

———. "On the Locations of Korean War and Cold War Anthropology." *Histories of Anthropology Annual* 4 (2008): 220–59.

Özyürek, Esra. *Nostalgia for the Modern: State Secularism and Everyday Politics in Turkey.* Durham, NC: Duke University Press, 2006.

Paik, Nak-chung. *The Division System in Crisis: Essays on Contemporary Korea.* Berkeley: University of California Press, 2011.

———. "Toward Overcoming Korea's Division System through Civic Participation." *Critical Asian Studies* 45, no. 2 (2013): 279–90.

Pandolfo, Stefania. *Impasse of the Angels: Scenes from a Moroccan Space of Memory.* Chicago: University of Chicago Press, 1997.

Pang, Ki-jung, Michael D. Shin, and Yong-sŏp Kim. *Landlords, Peasants, and Intellectuals in Modern Korea.* Ithaca, NY: Cornell University Press, 2005.

Papadakis, Yiannis. "Nation, Narrative and Commemoration: Political Ritual in Divided Cyprus." *History and Anthropology* 14, no. 3 (2003): 253–70.

Park, Christian J. "Crossing the Border: South Korean Tourism to Mount Kŭmgang." In *De-Bordering Korea: Tangible and Intangible Legacies of the Sunshine Policy,* edited by Valérie Gelézeau, Koen De Ceuster, and Alain Delissen. New York and London: Routledge, 2013.

Park, Eugene Y. "Imagined Connections in Early Modern Korea, 1500–1894: Representations of Northern Elite Miryang Pak Lineages in Genealogies." *Seoul Journal of Korean Studies* 21, no. 1 (2008): 1–27.

Park, Hyun Ok. "For the Rights of 'Colonial Returnees': Korean Chinese, Decolonization, and Neoliberal Democracy in South Korea." In *New Millennium South Korea: Neoliberal Capitalism and Transnational Movements,* edited by Jesook Song, 115–29. London and New York: Routledge, 2011.

Park, Insook Han, and Cho, Lee-Jay. "Confucianism and the Korean Family." *Journal of Comparative Family Studies* 26, no. 1 (1995): 117–34.

Park, Myung-Lim. *Han'guk chŏnjaengŭi palbal kwa kiwon* [*The Outbreak and Origins of the Korean War*]. Seoul: Nanam Press, 1996.

Park, So Jin, and Nancy Abelmann. "Class and Cosmopolitan Striving: Mothers' Management of English Education in South Korea." *Anthropological Quarterly* 77, no. 4 (2004): 645–72.

Park, Soon Won. *Colonial Industrialization and Labor in Korea: The Onoda Cement Factory.* Cambridge, MA: Harvard University Press, 1999.

Park, Wan-Suh. *Who Ate Up All the Shinga?: An Autobiographical Novel.* New York: Columbia University Press, 2009.

Park Nelson, Kim. "Mapping Multiple Histories of Korean American Transnational Adoption." Working Paper WP09-01. U.S.–Korea Institute at SAIS. January 2009.

Peck, Jamie, and Adam Tickell. "Neoliberalizing Space." *Antipode* 34, no. 3 (2002): 380–398.

Petrov, Leonid. "Historiography, Media and Cross-Border Dialogue in East Asia: Korea's Uncertain Path to Reconciliation." In *East Asia Beyond the History Wars: Confronting the Ghosts of Violence*, edited by Tessa Morris-Suzuki, Morris Low, Leonid Petrov, and Timothy Y. Tsu, 40–59. London and New York: Routledge, 2013.

Phillips, Nicola, Richard A. Higgott. "Global Governance and the Public Domain: Collective Goods in a 'Post-Washington Consensus' Era." Centre for the Study of Globalisation and Regionalisation, Working Paper No.47/99. Coventry, U.K.: University of Warwick, 1999.

Polanyi, Karl. *The Great Transformation.* Boston, MA: Beacon Press, 1944.

"Politburo Decision to Confirm the Following Directive to the Soviet Ambassador in Korea." September 24, 1949, History and Public Policy Program Digital Archive, AVP RF, Fond 059a, Opis 5a, Delo 3, Papka 11, listy 75–77. http://digitalarchive.wilsoncenter.org/document/112133.

Prebin, Elise. *Meeting Once More: The Korean Side of Transnational Adoption.* New York: NYU Press, 2013.

Prendergast, David. *From Elder to Ancestor: Old Age, Death and Inheritance in Modern Korea.* Leiden, NL: BRILL/Global Oriental, 2005.

Price, David. *Anthropological Intelligence: The Deployment and Neglect of American Anthropology in the Second World War.* Durham, NC: Duke University Press, 2008.

Radelet, Steven, and Jeffrey Sachs. "The East Asian Financial Crisis: Diagnosis, Remedies, Prospects." *Brookings Papers on Economic Activity* 1 (1998): 1–90.

Ray, Larry, and Andrew Sayer, eds. *Culture and Economy: After the Cultural Turn.* Thousand Oaks, CA: Sage, 1999.

Renfro-Sargent, Matthew. "The Borderlands of Community: Refugee Camps, Intentional Communities, and Liminality." In *Intentional Community: An Anthropological Perspective*, edited by Susan Love Brown, 83–105. Albany, NY: State University of New York Press, 2002.

Robins, Simon. *Families of the Missing: A Test for Contemporary Approaches to Transitional Justice.* New York and London: Routledge, 2013.

Robinson, Kenneth R. "Centering the King of Chosŏn: Aspects of Korean Maritime Diplomacy, 1392–1592." *The Journal of Asian Studies* 59, no. 1 (2000): 109–25.

Robinson, Michael E. "Colonial Publication Policy and the Korean Nationalist Movement." In *The Japanese Colonial Empire: 1895–1945*, edited by Ramon H. Myers and Mark R. Peattie. Princeton, NJ: Princeton University Press, 1984.

———. *Cultural Nationalism in Colonial Korea, 1920–1925.* Seattle: University of Washington Press, 1988.

———. *Korea's Twentieth Century Odyssey.* Honolulu: University of Hawaii Press, 2007.

———, and Gi-Wook Shin. *Colonial Modernity in Korea.* Cambridge, MA: Harvard University Press, 1999.

Rodan, Garry. "Neoliberalism and Transparency: Political Versus Economic Liberalism." Working Paper 112. Murdoch University, Perth, Australia: Asia Research Centre, 2009.

Rothenbuhler, Eric W., and Mihai Coman. *Media Anthropology.* Thousand Oaks, CA: Sage, 2005.

Ryang, Sonia. "A Note on Transnational Consanguinity, Or, Kinship in the Age of Terrorism." *Anthropological Quarterly* 77, no. 1 (2004): 747–70.

Ryang, Sonia, ed. *North Korea: Toward a Better Understanding.* Lanham, MD: Lexington Books, 2009.

Salmon, Andrew. *Scorched Earth, Black Snow: The First Year of the Korean War.* London: Aurum Press, 2011.

"Samsung Corporate Profile." September 2007, http://www.samsung.com/cn/aboutsamsung/corporateprofile/download/2007_9_corporate%20citizenship-coprosperity-greenmanagement.pdf.

Sassen, Saskia. "Global Cities and Diasporic Networks: Microsites in Global Civil Society." In *Global Civil Society*, 217–40. Oxford: Oxford University Press, 2002.

Scalapino, Robert A., and Chong-Sik Lee. *Communism in Korea, 2 Vols.* Berkeley and Los Angeles, CA: University of California Press, 1972.

Schattschneider, Ellen. "Family Resemblances: Memorial Images and the Face of Kinship." *Japanese Journal of Religious Studies* 30, nos. 1–2 (2004).

Schiller, Nina Glick, Linda Basch, and Cristina Szanton Blanc. "From Immigrant to Transmigrant: Theorizing Transnational Migration." *Anthropological Quarterly* (1995): 48–63.

Schmid, Andre. *Korea Between Empires: 1895–1919.* New York: Columbia University Press, 2002.

Seth, Michael. *A Concise History of Modern Korea: From the Late Nineteenth Century to the Present.* Lanham, MD: Rowman & Littlefield, 2010.

Shen, Zhihua. "China and the Dispatch of the Soviet Air Force: The Formation of the Chinese-Soviet-Korean Alliance in the Early Stage of the Korean War." *Journal of Strategic Studies* 33, no. 2 (2010): 211–30.

Sherman, Daniel J. "Bodies and Names: The Emergence of Commemoration in Interwar France." *American Historical Review* 103, no. 2 (1998): 443–466.

Shils, Edward, and Michael Young. "The Meaning of Coronation." *Sociological Review* 1 (1953): 63–81.

Shima, Mutsuhiko. "In Quest of Social Recognition: A Retrospective View on the Development of Korean Lineage Organization." *Harvard Journal of Asiatic Studies* 50, no. 1 (1990): 87–129.

Shin, Gi-Wook. *Peasant Protest & Social Change in Colonial Korea.* Seattle, WA: University of Washington Press, 1996.

———. "Nationalism and the Korean War." In *Korea and the Korean War*, edited by Chae-Jin Lee and Young Ick Lew, 417–440. Seoul: Yonsei University Press, 2002.

———. *Ethnic Nationalism in Korea: Genealogy, Politics, and Legacy.* Stanford, CA: Stanford University Press, 2006.

———, Soon-Won Park, and Daqing Yang. *Rethinking Historical Injustice and Reconciliation in Northeast Asia: The Korean Experience.* London and New York: Routledge, 2007.

Shu, Catherine. "Samsung Reportedly Tried to Suppress a Film Critical of its Safety Record." *Tech Crunch*, February 25, 2014. http://techcrunch.com/2014/02/25/samsung-another-family/.

Sigal, Leon V. *Disarming Strangers: Nuclear Diplomacy With North Korea.* Princeton, NJ: Princeton University Press, 2009.

Simon, Roger I. "Forms of Insurgency in the Production of Popular Memories: The Columbus Quincentenary and the Pedagogy of Counter-Commemoration." *Cultural Studies* 7, no. 1 (1993): 73–88.

Smith, Anthony D. *The Ethnic Origins of Nations.* New York: Basil Blackwell, 1986.

Snyder, Scott, and See-Won Byun. "*Cheonan* and Yeonpyeong: The Northeast Asian response to North Korea's provocations." *The RUSI Journal* 156, no. 2 (2011): 74–81.

Soh, C. Sarah. *The Comfort Women: Sexual Violence and Postcolonial Memory in Korea and Japan.* Chicago: University of Chicago Press, 2008.

Sohn, Ho-min. *Korean Language in Culture and Society.* Honolulu: University of Hawaii Press, 2006.

Sohn, Yul, and Kang Won-taek. "South Korea in 2012: An Election Year under Rebalancing Challenges." *Asian Survey* 53, no. 1 (2013): 198–205.

Son, Key-young. *South Korean Engagement Policies and North Korea: Identities, Norms and the Sunshine Policy.* London and New York: Routledge, 2006.

Song, Jesook. *South Koreans in the Debt Crisis: The Creation of a Neoliberal Welfare Society.* Durham, NC: Duke University Press, 2009.

Sorensen, Clark W. *Over the Mountains Are Mountains: Korean Peasant Households and Their Adaptations to Rapid Industialization.* Seattle: University of Washington Press, 1988.

Stafford, Charles. *Separation and Reunion in Modern China.* Cambridge: Cambridge University Press, 2002.

Suh, Dae-Sook. *The Korean Communist Movement, 1918–1948.* Princeton, NJ: Princeton University Press, 1967.

Suh, Hee-kyung. "Atrocities Before and During the Korean War: Mass Civilian Killings By South Korean and U.S. Forces." *Critical Asian Studies* 42, no. 4 (2010): 553–88.

Suh, Jae-Jean. "The Reunion of Separated Families Under the Kim Dae-jung Government." *The Journal of East Asian Affairs* 16, no. 2 (2002): 352–84.

Suh, Jae-Jung. "Truth and Reconciliation in South Korea: Confronting War, Colonialism, and Intervention in the Asia Pacific." *Critical Asian Studies* 42, no. 4 (2010): 503–24.

———. "Race to Judge, Rush to Act: The Sinking of the *Cheonan* and the Politics of National Insecurity." *Critical Asian Studies* 42, no. 3 (2010).

———, ed. *Truth and Reconciliation in South Korea: Between the Present and Future of the Korean Wars.* London and New York: Routledge, 2012.

———, Sunwon Park, and Hahn Y. Kim. "Democratic Consolidation and Its Limits in Korea: Dilemmas of Cooptation." *Asian Survey* 52, no. 5 (2012): 822–44.

———. ed. *Origins of North Korea's Juche: Colonialism, War, and Development.* Lanham, MD: Lexington Books, 2013.

Sung, Kyu-tak. "Measures and dimensions of filial piety in Korea." *The Gerontologist* 35, no. 2 (1992): 240–47.

Sung, Minkyu. "The 'Truth Politics' of Anti-North Koreanism: The Post-Ideological Cultural Representation of North Korea and the Cultural Criticisms of Korean Nationalism." *Inter-Asia Cultural Studies* 10, no. 3 (2009): 439–59.

Tambiah, Stanley J. "A Performative Approach to Ritual." Paper presented at the Proceedings of the British Academy London, 1979.

Tarlo, Emma. *Unsettling Memories: Narratives of the Emergency in Delhi.* Berkeley: University of California Press, 2003.

Theidon, Kimberly. *Intimate Enemies: Violence and Reconciliation in Peru.* Philadelphia, PA: University of Pennsylvania Press, 2012.

Tikhonov, Vladimir. "The Race and Racism Discourses in Modern Korea, 1890s–1910s." *Korean Studies* 36 (2012): 31–57.

Tirman, John. *The Deaths of Others: The Fate of Civilians in America's Wars.* Oxford: Oxford University Press, 2011.

Turner, Victor. "Betwixt and Between: The Liminal Period in Rites of Passage." In *Betwixt and Between*, 3–19. La Salle, IL: Open Court Press, 1987.

Turner, Victor W. *The Forest of Symbols: Aspects of Ndembu Ritual.* Vol. 101, Ithaca, NY: Cornell University Press, 1967.

———. *Dramas, Fields and Metaphors: Symbolic Action in Human Society.* Ithaca, NY: Cornell University Press, 1975.

———. *The Ritual Process: Structure and Anti-Structure.* New Brunswick, NJ: Transaction, 1995.

Uchida, Jun. *Brokers of Empire: Japanese Settler Colonialism in Korea, 1876–1945.* Cambridge, MA: Harvard University Asian Center/Harvard University Press, 2011.

United States Department of State. *The Korea Problem at the Geneva Conference, April 26–June 16, 1954,* Publication 5609. Washington, DC: U.S. Government Printing Office, 1954.

———. "United States National Security Policy: Estimates of Threats to the National Security; The Extension of Military Assistance to Foreign Nations; The Preparation of NSC 68, 'United States Objectives and Programs for National Security.'" In *Foreign Relations of the United States, 1950, National Security Affairs; Foreign Economic Policy, Volume I,* 126–149. Washington, DC: U.S. Government Printing Office, 1950. http://digicoll.library.wisc.edu/cgi-bin/FRUS/FRUS-idx?id=FRUS.FRUS1950v01 (accessed August 28, 2008).

Van Gennep, Arnold. *The Rites of Passage.* Chicago: University of Chicago Press, 1909.

Vertovec, Steven. "Transnationalism and Identity." *Journal of Ethnic and Migration Studies* 27, no. 4 (2001): 573–82.

Wada, Haruki. "The Korean War, Stalin's Policy, and Japan." *Social Science Japan Journal* 1, no. 1 (1998): 5–29.

———. *The Korean War: An International History.* Lanham, MD: Rowman & Littlefield, 2013.

Waterston, Alisse, and Barbara Rylko-Bauer. "Out of the Shadows of History and Memory: Personal Family Narratives in Ethnographies of Rediscovery." *American Ethnologist* 33, no. 3 (2006): 397–412.

Watts, Michael. "Culture, Development and Global Neo-Liberalism." In *Culture and Development in a Globalising World: Geographies, Actors and Paradigms,* edited by Sarah A. Radcliffe, 30–57. London and New York: Routledge, 2006.

Weathersby, Kathryn. "Soviet Aims in Korea and the Origins of the Korean War, 1945–1950: New Evidence From Russian Archives." Working Paper 8. Woodrow Wilson International Center for Scholars (1993). http://www.wilsoncenter.org/sites/default/files/Working_Paper_8.pdf (accessed August 28, 2008).

———. "New Russian Documents on the Korean War." *Cold War International History Project Bulletin* (Winter 1995): 30–84. http://www.wilsoncenter.org/sites/default/files/ACF1A6.pdf (accessed August 28, 2008).

Werbner, Richard. "Beyond Oblivion: Confronting Memory Crisis." In *Memory and the Postcolony: African Anthropology and the Critique of Power,* edited by Richard Werbner, 1–17. New York: Zed Books, 1998.

———. "Smoke from the Barrel of a Gun: Postwars of the Dead, Memory, and Reinscription in Zimbabwe." In *Memory and the Postcolony: African Anthropology and the Critique of Power,* edited by Richard Werbner, 71–102. New York: Zed Books, 1998.

West, Philip, and Ji-moon Suh. *Remembering the Forgotten War: The Korean War Through Literature and Art.* Norwalk, CT: M. E. Sharpe, 2001.

Wettstein, Howard. *Diasporas and Exiles: Varieties of Jewish Identity.* Berkeley: University of California Press, 2002.

Wilson, Richard. *The Politics of Truth and Reconciliation in South Africa: Legitimizing the Post-Apartheid State.* Cambridge: Cambridge University Press, 2001.

Winstanley-Chesters, Robert, and Christopher Green. "A Bifurcated Review of De-Bordering Korea: Tangible and Intangible Legacies of the Sunshine Policy." *Sino-NK,* May 12, 2014. http://sinonk.com/2014/05/12/a-bifurcated-review-of-de-bordering-korea-tangible-and-intangible-legacies-of-the-sunshine-policy/.

Winter, Jay. *Remembering War: The Great War between Memory and History in the Twentieth Century.* New Haven, CT: Yale University Press, 2006.

Wolf, Margery. *Women and the Family in Rural Taiwan.* Stanford, CA: Stanford University Press, 1972.

Woo-Cumings, Meredith. "The State, Democracy, and the Reform of the Corporate Sector in Korea." In *The Politics of the Asian Economic Crisis,* edited by T. J. Pempel, 116–142. Ithaca, NY: Cornell University Press, 1999.

Wrobel, Ralph Michael. "Inter-Korean Cooperation in Special Economic Zones: Developments and Perspectives." In *Towards a Northeast Asian Security Community,* edited by Bernhard Seliger and Werner Pascha. New York: Springer, 2011.

Yang, Hyunah. "Re-membering the Korean Military Comfort Women: Nationalism, Sexuality, and Silencing." In *Dangerous Women: Gender and Korean Nationalism,* edited by Elaine Kim and Chungmoo Choi, 123–40. London and New York: Routledge, 1998.

Yonhap News Agency. *North Korea Handbook.* Armonk, NY: M. E. Sharpe, 2002.

Yoo, Theodore Jun. *The Politics of Gender in Colonial Korea: Education, Labor, and Health, 1910–1945.* Berkeley and Los Angeles: University of California Press, 2008.

Yoon, Taek-Lim. "The Politics of Memory in the Ethnographic History of a 'Red' Village in South Korea." *Korea Journal* 32, no. 4 (1992): 65–79.

Yoshimi, Yoshiaki. *Comfort Women: Sexual Slavery in the Japanese Military During World War II.* Translated by Suzanne O'Brien. New York: Columbia University Press, 2000.

Young, Marilyn. "An Incident at No Gun Ri." In *Crimes of War: Guilt and Denial in the Twentieth Century*, edited by Omar Bartov, Atina Grossman, and Mary Nolan, 242–58. New York: The New Press, 2002.

———. "Bombing Civilians from the Twentieth to the Twenty-First Century." In *Bombing Civilians: A Twentieth Century History*, edited by Yuri Tanaka and Marilyn Young, 154–174. New York: The New Press, 2010.

Yuh, Ji-Yeon. "The Korean War: A Still Present Past." In *Still Present Pasts: Korean Americans and the "Forgotten War,"* 23–31. Catalog accompanying eponymous exhibit, A Project of the Channing and Popai Liem Education Foundation and the Korean American Memories of the Korean War Oral History Project, Boston College, 2005.

Zamindar, Vazira Fazila-Yacoobali. *The Long Partition and the Making of Modern South Asia: Refugees, Boundaries, Histories.* New York: Columbia University Press, 2007.

Žižek, Slavoj. *The Fragile Absolute: Or, Why is the Christian Legacy Worth Fighting For?* London: Verso, 2001.

Index

Acheson, Dean, 57, 59
activism, 49, 51, 158, 169, 203–204, 206
agricultural modernization, 44, 63n15
Ahn Jung-geun, 158
Allied negotiations (1945), 50
Anagnost, Ann, 121
Another Family, xix
anti-commemorations, 97, 110
anticommunism: family separation and, 79–80, 121, 154–157, 164–168, 171–175, 182, 183n21–183n22; guilt-by-association system and, 168; *isan'gajok* as cipher of, xxiv; isolation and, 69–81; in KBS broadcast, 6–8; kinship loyalty and, 173–175; liminality and, 171; in Park Chung Hee era, 28, 155, 156, 182, 184n33; pre-Summit, 31n32; reunions and, 28; of Syngman Rhee, 51; U.S., regime, 51, 57, 62
aristocracy, 47–48
Armistice Agreement (1953), 1–2, 55, 78–79, 218, 222n2
armistice talks, 55, 76–79, 90n40
Armstrong, Charles K., 21, 40, 52, 63n8, 73, 159n16
Asian Financial Crisis, xix, 18–19, 101–105, 109; IMF bailout during, 102; Kim Dae-jung and, 102–103; neoliberal reforms after, 23, 103, 103–104; origin of, 101; public identity due to, xix; South Korean reaction to, 101–102,

103, 109, 133–135

background checks, 155–156, 169, 178–179
Bell, Catherine M., 106
Benjamin, Walter, 24
Berlant, Lauren, 198
Bhabha, Homi, 27
Bleiker, Roland, 79, 210
bloodlines. *See* nationalism, blood-based
Bodnar, John, 18
A Bold Family, 26
Bolshevik revolution, 46
borders and boundaries, 21, 72, 76, 121, 190, 208; characteristics of, 22, 72, 208, 218–219; of Chosŏn dynasty, 40; cosmopolitanism and, 189–190; crossing types with, 72–73, 75–76, 113–114; phenomena of, 76; reunions influence on, 208–209. *See also* Demilitarized Zone
Borneman, John, 191, 194
Bourdieu, Pierre, 104, 208
Boyer, Pascal, 130
Brilliant Legacy (Ch'allanhan Yusan), 5
Brown, Wendy, 114
Buddhism, 43
Butler, Judith, 165, 173

Cairo Declaration, 49
Cammack, Paul, 104

243

244   *Index*

Caprio, Mark, 58
Center for Deliberative Democracy,
    34n84–35n85
Ch'allanhan Yusan (Brilliant Legacy), 5
Chang, Kyung-Sup, 196
Cheju massacre, 69–71, 166–167, 172
Chen, Kuan-Hsing, 119
Chiang Kai-shek, 49
China: Chosŏn dynasty relationship with,
    40–42; in Korean War, 55, 56, 60–62;
    private reunions in, 84–85; as rival
    power, 39. *See also* People's Republic
    of China
Chinese Civil War, 52, 53, 59, 61
Chinese People's Volunteers (CPV), 55
Cho, Sungmi, xviii, 199–200
Cho, Uhn, 12
Cho Han, Hae-Joang, xviii, 174
Choi, In-hun, 100, 151
Ch'ŏn Yi-du, 25
Chosŏn dynasty, 40–42; agrarian society
    in, 44; boundaries of, 40; China's
    relation with, 40–42; foreign
    occupation of, 43–44; Japan's relation
    with, 41, 42–43; military preparedness
    of, 42; Sinocentric tributary system and,
    41–42
Christians, 51, 74
Chun Doo Hwan, 33n61
Churchill, Winston, 49
citizens: individuality of, xviii–xix; Joint
    Declaration distrust of, 97–98; Korean
    War displacement of, 13
COEX. *See* Convention and Exhibition
    Center
Cold War, xxiii, 1; Chinese Civil War and,
    59; consequences of, xxiv, 2, 204, 205;
    family separation in, 35n85; Korean
    War influenced by, 19–20, 53;
    marginalized families in, 27–28;
    persistence of, 16; reconciliation and
    ending, 17–18, 19; reunions during, 8;
    Sunshine Policy and, 8; transformation
    in, 81–82
colonial rule. *See* Japanese colonial rule
comfort women, 14–15, 32n44, 48
commemorations: 50th and 60th,
    comparison, 215, 216–217; public
    memory and, 18; 60th year significance

of, 215–216, 222n2. *See also* anti-
    commemorations
Committee for Assisting the Return of
    Displaced Civilians, 78
communism, 183n10; Kim Il-sung and, 57;
    North Korean attack and, 56–57; Stalin
    expanding, 56, 59; U.S. "rollback" of,
    55. *See also* anticommunism; Cold War
communists: discrimination against
    families of known or suspected,
    xxiv–xxv, 79–80, 154–157, 164–168;
    early North Korean, 52; foreign aid to
    Korean, 59; government-created, 167;
    POW negotiations with, 77–79
Comaroff, Jean, 204
Comaroff, John, 204
Confucianism: familial values in, 196;
    family separation and, 169–170;
    historical elites and, 41, 42; influence
    of, 47–48, 174, 182n2; nationalism and,
    48; patriarchal family in, 126, 169;
    theories of Korean, 63n12; Tonghak
    and, 43
Connerton, Paul, 18
Convention and Exhibition Center
    (COEX), 113, 115–117, 119, 137n3
Coronil, Fernando, 39
cosmopolitanism, 189–192
CPV. *See* Chinese People's Volunteers
Crapanzano, Vincent, 221
cultural policy, 45–46
Cumings, Bruce, 43–44, 49; on Korean
    War origins, 95; on pro-Japanese
    elements, 66n75; on U.S. remilitarizing
    Japan, 60

Dae Jang Geum (Jewel in the Palace), 5
Das, Veena, 18
Dayan, Daniel, 30n8, 106
dead, presumed: bad or good death for,
    165–166; death report filing for, 28,
    165–166, 169, 200–201; exilic diaspora
    and, 150–151, 153; family response to,
    161–164; guilt with, 13, 169; reunion
    consequences with, 4–5; TV dramas
    with theme of, 5
deaths: with bad or good designation,
    165–166; in Cheju massacre, 70; in
    Korean War, 67, 88n2, 88n9, 181,

219–221; NGL, 167–168, 172, 183n16; of reunion candidates, 222n7; war-dead reclamation and, 4, 13
deaths, social, 20–21, 150, 165, 218–219
The Deaths of Others (Tirman), 67, 88n2
De Ceuster, Koen, 9
Delissen, Alain, 9
Demilitarized Zone (DMZ), 55; flying around, 113–114; invasion along, 19, 53, 95; North compared to South crossings of, 73–75; politics of crossing, 73; post-Liberation crossings of, 73–74, 159n16; POWs crossing, 75–76; pro-reconciliation commercial at, 98; totality of, 79
Democratic People's Republic of Korea (DPRK): armistice talks with, 55; beginning of, 19, 52–53; discrimination in, 80–81; UN joining of, 85
democratization: civic organizations with, xix; elections and, 33n61; historical memory with, 16
diaspora, exilic, 150–153, 159n5, 159n15
discrimination: against communists, xxiv–xxv, 28, 79–80, 154–157, 164–168; in DPRK, 80–81, 130; of *Wŏlbukcha* families, 80, 154–157, 178–180. *See also* stigmatization and marginalization
Divided Families Information Center, 30n6
division literature, 35n86
DMZ. *See* Demilitarized Zone
DMZ Crossing: Performing Emotional Citizenship Along the Korean Border (Kim, Suk-Young), 73, 211n3
Douglas, Mary, 121
DPRK. *See* Democratic People's Republic of Korea
Dulles, John Foster, 58
Durkheim, 107, 121

economic cooperation, 8, 11, 87, 102, 106, 135, 192, 195, 197, 208, 209, 210
elections, 10, 192, 217; democratization and, 33n61; of Kim Dae-jung, 18, 33n61, 86, 102; national division and, 9, 20, 52, 70
Elise, Prébin, 30n8
emotional transparency, 132–135

Eng, David L., 25, 223n12
Epstein, Stephen, 207
ethnic nationalism. *See* blood-based nationalism
exchange visits. *See* reunions

family: in Confucianism, 126, 138, 169, 196; corporations as, xix; dissolution of, 181; predominance of, 3. *See also* kinship; patriarchal family; uterine family
family separation, xviii; anticommunism and, 79–80, 121, 154–157, 164–168, 171–175, 182, 183n21–183n22; categories of, 73, 74–75, 79–80, 138n19, 198; causes of, 2, 13; in Cold War, 35n88; communist ideology and, xxv; Confucianism and, 169–170; as cultural metaphor, 13; exilic diaspora and, 150–153; in films and TV, 5, 26–27, 182n1–182n2, 187–189, 188; sense of helplessness and indifference toward, xxiv; as humanitarian issue, 108–109; Kim Dae-jung policy on, 86, 87–88; liminality and, 21, 39, 122, 135, 168–182; long-term, consequences, 20–21, 175, 221; media influence on, 132, 138, 146, 205; for mothers and women, 80, 162–164; national division and, 17, 29n2; in 1950 to 1951, 151; reasons for, 13, 74–75, 188, 188–189; response to presumed dead in, 161–164; social isolation with, 171; statistics of, xxviin8, 30n6; stigmatization in, 28, 80–81, 121–122, 164–167, 181–182, 195, 200–201, 212n33; temporality of, 145–146. *See also* dead, presumed; kinship; reunions; *Wŏlbukcha* families; *Wŏllammin* families
family state, 196–198, 212n22
Feldman, Allen, 17
feminism, 15
fieldwork: liminality in, xx; locations of, xvii; methodology xvii–xviii; at Red Cross, xvii, xxi; at reunions, 116–117; sources of, xvii–xviii; taboo subjects in, xxv, 143–144, 200; vernacular used in, xx

films and TV, xvii; DMZ location for, 98; family separation themes in, 5, 26–27, 182n1–182n2, 187–189, 188; Northerners portrayal in, 131, 189, 207, 211n3; reconciliation themes in, 26–27, 98–100; Samsung scandal and "Another Family," xix. *See also* Korean Broadcasting System
financial crisis. *See* Asian Financial Crisis
"Finding Dispersed Families," 5–8, 7
Foley, James, 75, 82–83, 129
Foucault, Michel, 174–175
Freud, Sigmund, 24–25

Geertz, Clifford, 107
Gelézeau, Valérie, 9
Geneva Conference, 1
geography. *See* Korean peninsula
Ghosts of War in Vietnam (Kwon, H.), 191
globalization, 105, 115, 152, 189–190, 196
Gluckman, Max, 22
The Graves of Tarim (Ho, E.), 152
The Grey Man (Choi, I.), 151
Grinker, Roy Richard: on family state, 196, 197; on liminal stage of Korea, 26; on mourning and melancholia, 23–24, 25; on unification support, 34n84

han, 25
Hanley, Charles, 14
Hein, Laura, 15
Hideoyoshi Toyotomi, 41, 63n7
Hirohito, 32n42
Ho, Enseng, 152
Hoare, James, 79
Hodge, John, 51
Hoon, John, 26
Hwang, Kyung Moon, 198
Hwang, Su-kyoung, 70–71, 71

IAEA. *See* International Atomic Energy Agency
Imaginative Horizons (Crapanzano), 221
IMF, 86, 102
Imjin War, 40–41, 41
imperialism, 31n35, 62
independence, national, 49–50
intellectuals, xx, 41, 73–74, 124, 154, 159n16

inter-Korean reconciliation: and Kim Dae-jung, 10, 18, 182, 197–199; and Kim Jong-il, 11; and Kim Young-sam, 86; film and TV themes of, 26–27, 98–100; impact of, 11; June Summit breakthrough for, 86–87; under Kim Dae-jung, 10, 18, 182, 197–199; under Kim Jong-il in the North, 11; under Kim Young-sam, 86; liminality and, 22–23; material culture of, 98–101; under Park Chung Hee, 82; passing of the Cold War and, 17; reunions and, 3, 11, 18, 23, 119–121, 135, 195, 196–197, 206–207, 219; under Roh Moo-hyun, 11; support for, 10; reversal of U.S. support for, 192–193; war blame and, 19–20, 31n35, 95
inter-Korean relations: economic cooperation in, 135, 192, 195, 197, 208, 209, 210; Kim Jong-il and, 8, 9; of Lee Myung-bak, 9; after military crisis (2010), 9–10; post-9/11, 193–194, 217; Red Cross as contact for, 147; Sunshine Policy and, 8; transformation of, 81
inter-Korean summit (June 2000): anticommunism before, 31n34; conservatives reaction to, 197; date significance of, 96–97; Kim Jong-il in, 8, 9, 86–87, 96; mood in South after, 12–13, 98–101; reconciliation breakthrough of, 86–87; reunions agreement reached at, 193; symbol of, 31n19; *Wŏlbukcha* families and, 79–80, 121, 138, 198
International Atomic Energy Agency (IAEA), 85
isan'gajok: as cipher of anticommunism, xxiv; interpretations of, xviii, 27. *See also* family separation
Itō Hirobumi, 158

Jackson, Jean E., 122, 138n11
Jager, Sheila Miyoshi, 61, 109
Japan, 40, 52, 66n75; atrocities in World War II by, 14–15; Chosŏn dynasty relations with, 41, 42–43; colonial settlers of, 34n75, 34n83; as rival power, 39; taboo in criticism of, 32n42; U.S. policy with, 58–59; U.S.

rearmament of, 58–59, 59–60, 61, 62.
    See also Russo–Japanese War;
    Sino–Japanese Wars
Japanese colonial rule, 16; blood-based
    nationalism response to, 48; comfort
    women and, 14–15, 32n44, 48;
    influence after World War II, 52; legal
    norms under, 63n17; liberation from,
    48–51; Namsan and, 157, 160n22;
    national division after, 19–20, 48–49;
    nationalism rising under, 45–46, 46–47;
    political engagement and protest after,
    49; social division under, 43–44;
    violent legacy of, 71–72. *See also*
    foreign occupation
Jeon Seung-Hee, 16
Jervis, Robert, 57
Jewel in the Palace (Dae Jang Geum), 5
Jews, 151–152
Joint Declaration (June 15th): citizens'
    doubts concerning, 97–98; date
    confusion regarding, 96–97; details of,
    87; Kim Jong-il and, 8; reunions
    outlined in, 8, 11
Joint Security Area, 98, 207
Joint Security Area (film), 207
June Summit. *See* inter-Korean summit
    (June 2000)
Jun Uchida, 34n83

Kaesong Industrial Complex (KIC), 192
Kanghwa Treaty, 42, 44
Kang Jegyu, 187
Kang Tek-koo (Hoon), 26
Karim, Lamia, 180
Katz, Elihu, 106
Kazanjian, David, 24–25, 25, 223n11
KBS. *See* Korean Broadcasting System
KCIA. *See* Korea Central Intelligence
    Agency
KIC. *See* Kaesong Industrial Complex
Kim, Dong-Choon, 69, 71, 72; on
    massacres, 168; on pre-invasion
    tensions, 95; on *Wangdda*, 176
Kim, Gwi-Ok, 75, 151
Kim, Jae-yong, 80
Kim, Jiyul, 109
Kim, Seong-nae, 166–167
Kim, Suk-young, 26, 73, 211n3

Kim, Suzy, 52
Kim, Yong-sŏp, 44, 63n15
Kim Dae-jung, 96, 158; election of, 18,
    33n61, 86, 102; family separation
    policy of, 86, 87–88; financial crisis
    and, 102–103; neoliberalism under,
    203–204; "cash-for-summit" scandal,
    133–135; reconciliation under, 10, 18,
    182, 197–199; reunions under,
    108–109, 196; Sunshine Policy and, 8,
    9, 86–87, 105–106
Kim Dong-won, 131
Kim Il-sung, 9, 86, 130; communism and,
    57; DPRK beginning with, 52–53;
    Korean War beginning and, 20, 59;
    sentiments for, 129; title of, 110n7;
    unification policy of, 56, 82
Kim Jong-il, 129; inter-Korean summits
    with, 8, 9, 86–87, 96; Joint Declaration
    and, 8; reconciliation efforts under, 11;
    title of, 110n7
Kim Young-sam, 86
kin-based punishment, 154–157, 164
Kingsley, J. Donald, 68
kinship, 171–173, 184n29; consequences
    of, 180–181; terminology, xix–xx
kinship loyalty: anticommunism and,
    173–175; in Korean War, 176–178,
    188; of *Wŏlbukcha* families, 176–178
*Korea and Its Futures: Unification and the
    Unfinished War* (Grinker), 23, 26
Korea Central Intelligence Agency
    (KCIA), 158, 168
Korean Broadcasting System (KBS):
    anticommunist position of, 8;
    "Mother's Tears" documentary on,
    124–125; reunion candidate broadcast,
    145; reunion telethon in 1983, 5–8, 7,
    30n8, 83; unification support study of,
    34n84
Korean history. *See* Chosŏn dynasty;
    Japanese colonial rule
"Korean My Lai". *See* No Gun Ri
    massacre
Korean National Police, 71
Korean peninsula, 54; geographical
    significance of, 62, 63n8; strategic
    importance of, 61, 62, 65n58;
    vulnerability of, 40, 62

Korean People's Army (KPA), 53; armistice talks with, 55; 1950 attack by, 60; UN assault on, 55
Korean Provisional Government (KPG), 52
Korean War: anti-commemorations of, 97, 110; apathy in U.S. toward, 68; armistice talks during, 55; atrocities in, 16, 68–72; blame for, 19–20, 31n35, 95; Chinese intervention in, 55, 60–62; citizens displaced by, 13; Cold War context of, 19–20, 53; commemorations of, 215–217; consequences of, 6; deaths in, 17, 67, 88n2, 88n9, 181, 219; destruction in, 68; factors escalating, 19–20, 56–57; foreign power involvement in, 56, 56–57; interpretations of, 16; Kim Il-sung and, 20, 59; loyalty to state and kin in, 176–178, 188; Mao Zedong in, 60–61; motives for, 62; national division and, 20, 43–44, 53; nationalism and, 56; non-resolution of, 1–2, 17; interpretations surrounding date of outbreak, 95–96; reunions acknowledging, 17, 23, 29, 206; Seoul during, 13, 53, 55; Soviet Union and, 20, 57, 60–62, 68; stages of, 53–55, 54; Stalin at start of, 49, 60, 61; unification and, 56, 59; U.S. in, 20, 57; U.S.–Soviet relations in, 20, 57; War for Rollback in, 55; War for the South in, 53. *See also* memory, war
Korean War Memorial, 95–96
The Koreas (Armstrong), 63n8–63n9
Korea's Divided Families (Foley), 75
KPA. *See* Korean People's Army
KPG. *See* Korean Provisional Government
Kwak, Tae-yang, 82
Kwon, Heonik, 17, 173, 190–191
Kwon, Tai Hwan, 73

landlord system, 44, 51, 63n15
Lankov, Andrei, 81
Lee, Ho-Chul, 75–76
Lee, Kwang-Kyu, 126
Lee, Ryong-kyong, 168
Lee, Soo-Jung, xviii, 116, 184n29; on family separation, 74–75, 121, 195; on

KBS telethon impact, 8, 35n88, 83
Lee Myung-bak, 9
Liberation Day, 29n5, 43
Liénard, Pierre, 130
Lim, Dong-won, 8
liminality, 185n42; anticommunism and, 171; family separation and, 21, 39, 122, 135, 168–182; in fieldwork, xx; during foreign occupation, 34n83; history of Korea's geopolitical, 39–40, 45; national division and, 25–26, 219–222; nationalism and geopolitical, 56; nation-space and, 27; origins of, theory, 22; political ritual and, 106–107; reconciliation and, 22–23; reunions illuminating, 27; stigmatization and, 122, 138n11; TRC and, 105; war memory and, 27
Location of Culture (Bhabha), 27
Lone, Stewart, 53
Loss: The Politics of Mourning (Eng and Kazanjian), 25
loyalty: conflicts with state and kin, 171–175, 176–178; in North Korea, 130–131. *See also* kinship loyalty
Lukes, Steven, 107

MacArthur, Douglas, 55, 58, 61
Manchus, 41, 42, 63n7
Mao Zedong, 57, 59, 60–61
March First Movement (1919), 45, 46, 46–47
marginalization. *See* stigmatization and marginalization
massacres: blood-based nationalism and, 72; categories of, 69; in Cheju, 69–71, 166–167, 172; media silence on, 14; Nanjing, 14; NGL, 167–168, 172, 183n16; No Gun Ri, 14, 16; phenomenon of, 68
McCormack, Gavan, 53
McCune-Reischauer system, xviii
MDL. *See* Military Demarcation Line
media: family separation and, 132, 138, 146, 205; of Pyongyang reunions, 138–123; of Seoul reunions, 3, 5–8, 7, 27–28, 31n29, 114, 116, 117, 118–121, 119, 120, 124–125, 145–146, 205, 207, 209; silence on massacre, 14

Meeting Once More: The Korean Side of Transnational Adoption (Prébin), 30n8, 35n90

melancholia: lack of resolution and, 25, 164; mourning compared to, 24–25, 223n11

memorials, 95–96, 135–137, 138n19, 148

memory, cultural: commemoration and, 18; political influence of, 17; reunions mobilizing, 18, 218–219

memory, war, 32n49; liminality and, 27; in North Korea, 31n35; reframing of, 23; revival of, 14, 16; state-allowed, 16; taboos with expressing, 14, 17; of World War II, 14, 16

Mendoza, Martha, 14

Meray, Tibor, 68

Merrill, John, 72, 95

military: of Chosŏn dynasty, 42; U.S., aid, 82; U.S., exercises, 84, 216–217

military crisis (2010), 9–10

Military Demarcation Line (MDL), 55, 76

missing persons. *See* dead, presumed; family separation

Morris, Rosalind, 133

mothers, 159n4; devotion and waiting of, 162–164, 182n1–182n2; imagery of, 120, 138n19; KBS documentary on, 124–125; power of, 124–128; reunions with sons and, 120, 124–128

Mother's Tears, 124–125

Mount Kŭmgang Resort, 192, 211n13, 216

mourning: lost relatives, 35n90; melancholia compared to, 24–25, 223n11; national division inhibiting, 23, 219–222, 220

"Mourning and Melancholia" (Freud), 24–25

Namsan, Seoul, 157–158, 160n22

Nanjing Massacre, 14

napalm, 68, 88n9

national division, 35n86; after colonial rule, 19–20, 48–49; elections and, 9, 20, 52, 70; family separation and, 17, 29n2; Korean War and, 20, 43–44, 53; legal prohibitions of, 21; liminality and, 25–26, 219–222; disrupted or impossible mourning due to, 23,

219–222, 220; severity of, 21; theories on, 209; U.S. and Soviet involvement in, 50–53; after World War II, 40

National Guidance League (NGL), 167–168, 172, 183n14, 183n16

national reconciliation. *See* inter-Korean reconciliation

National Security Council (NSC), 57–58

National Security Law, 34n68, 70–71, 84, 100

nationalism, 213n39; under colonial rule, 45–46, 46–47; Confucianism and, 48; cultural compared to radical, 46–47; generation gap and divided, 46–47; geopolitical liminality and, 56; Korean War and, 56; socialism influencing, 46–47. *See also* nationalism, blood-based

nationalism, blood-based, 72; massacres and, 72; as response to colonization, 48; reunions and, 109–110; rise of, 47–48

Negara (Geertz), 107

neoliberalism: Asian Financial Crisis and, 103–104; contradictions within, 203–205, 212n33; under democratic state, 203–204; implications of, 103–105; shallow versus deep forms of, 104; in South Korea, 103

New Deal, 58

NGL. *See* National Guidance League

9/11 terror attacks, 193–194, 217

No Gun Ri massacre, 14, 16

"Northern Policy," 84

North Korea, 56; agriculture reform in, 44; border "non-crossing" by, 113–114; diplomatic ties of, 30n18; early communists in, 52; economic standings of, 82, 84, 110n10; film and TV representation of, 131, 189, 207, 211n3; flood aid offer by, 83; intellectuals' migration to, 73–74, 124, 159n16; leadership change in, 9; migrating or fleeing from, 73–74; NPT withdrawal of, 85; nuclear weapon rumor and, 74; reunions humanizing, 131; reunions in, 11, 87, 128–132; self-isolation of, 80–81; social purging in, 52; social ranking in, 130; Southerners distrust of, 97–98; Soviet Union and, 51–52, 85;

Stalin's support of, 57, 66n79; state
    loyalty in, 130–131; travel to, 34n69;
    U.S. mediations with, 85–86; war
    blame and, 19–20, 31n35, 95; war
    memory in, 31n35. *See also* Democratic
    People's Republic of Korea
North–South Joint Declaration. *See* Joint
    Declaration (June 15th)
North–South Korean border. *See*
    Demilitarized Zone
North to South crossing. *See* Wŏllammin
    families
NPT. *See* Nuclear Non-Proliferation Treaty
NSC. *See* National Security Council
Nuclear Non-Proliferation Treaty (NPT),
    85
nuclear weapons, 74, 85, 85–86

occupation, foreign: and agrarian society,
    44; during Chosŏn dynasty, 43–44;
    liminality during, 34n83
Oh, Yeon-Ho, 14
Ong, Aihwa, 103, 152
Oppenheim, Robert, 174
The Other Cold War (Kwon, H.), 173

Paik, Nak-chung, 209
Pandolfo, Stefania, 153, 159n15
Pares, Susan, 79
Park, Christian, 193
Park, Hyun-ok, 203–204
Park, Myung-Lim, 20, 56
Park, Wan-Suh, 183n14
Park Chung Hee era, 16; anticommunism
    in, 28, 155, 172, 182, 184n33; loyalty
    and, 174; inter-Korean reconciliation
    in, 82; U.S. withdrawal of aid in, 82
patriarchal family, 3, 125–126, 169
peasants, 49, 51
People's Liberation Army (PLA), 53
People's Republic of China, 57, 82
PLA. *See* People's Liberation Army
Politburo, 57, 61
Political Crime and the Memory of Loss
    (Borneman), 191
political ritual, 106–107, 109, 119–121,
    138, 209–211
popular culture, 27, 98–100, 99
post-Washington Consensus, 103–104

POWs: armistice talks about, 76–79,
    90n40; border crossing of, 75–76;
    communist negotiations with, 77–79;
    number of, 77–78; release and
    repatriation of, 77–79, 90n39
Prébin, Elise, 30n8, 35n87
*Precarious Life: The Powers of Mourning
    and Violence* (Butler), 165
Prisoners of War Convention (1929), 77
protests: in Cheju, 69–70; after colonial
    rule, 49; during colonial rule, 45–46
publicity. *See* media
Purity and Danger (Douglas), 121–122
Pyongyang, North Korea: June Summit in,
    8; reunions in, 3, 128–132, 138–124

Red Cross, 158; fieldwork at, xvii, xxi; as
    inter-Korean contact, 147; reunion
    organization of, 4, 30n14, 146,
    147–150, 149, 158n2; reunion
    participation of, 116, 117; reunion talks,
    82–83, 85
Red Peasant Union, 49
religion, 42–43, 52, 74
Repatriation, 131
Republic of Korea (ROK): beginning of,
    20, 52; negotiations and, 65n57; UN
    joining of, 85; wartime defenses of, 53
research participants, xviii; name
    transliteration of, xviii; naming
    convention with, xx; openness of, xxi;
    pseudonyms for, xxvi, 212n32;
    selection of, 4; suspicions of U.S. in,
    xxiii
reunification. *See* unification
reunion candidates: age and death statistics
    of, 222n7; applicants for, 136, 149–150;
    identifying, 114; KBS broadcast of,
    145; selection of, 123–124, 147–149,
    158n2; vilified to sympathized with,
    121–122, 138, 181
reunions, 29n5, 138n19; ambulance, 127,
    128; anticommunism and, 28; blood-
    based nationalism and, 109–110; border
    integrity and, 208–209, 213n48; citizen
    support for, xxviin8, 83; Cold War, 8;
    contact prior to, 21; contradictions with,
    208–209; criticism of, 202–203;
    cultural memory mobilized by, 18,

218–219; differences in, 129; economic importance of, 107–109; emotionality of, 117–118, 119, 120, 132–135; fieldwork at, 116–117; grief with, 127–128; Joint Declaration outlining, 8, 11; June Summit arrangement for, 193; KBS live telethon for, 5–8, 7, 30n8, 83; under Kim Dae-jung, 108–109, 196; legal prohibitions and, 21; liminality illuminated by, 27; media coverage of, 3, 5–8, 7, 27–28, 31n29, 114, 116, 117, 118–121, 119, 120, 124–125, 138–123, 145–147, 205, 207, 209; mother-son, 120, 124–128; mural of names at, 135–137; national intimacy and, 198–199; national reconciliation and, 3, 11, 18, 23, 119–121, 135, 195, 196–197, 206–207, 219; non inter-Korean, 6–8; North compared to South, 128–130; North Koreans humanized by, 131; permanent site for, 192; political ritual of, 106, 119–121, 138, 209–211; post-9/11, 193–194, 217; post-2000, 192–195, 216–218; pre-2000, 8, 31n28, 83–84, 212n16; and return of the presumed dead, 4–5; private and unofficial, 34n68, 84–85, 91n54; in Pyongyang, 3, 128–132, 138–124; Red Cross involvement in, 4, 30n14, 82–83, 85, 116, 117, 146, 147–150, 149, 158n2; security at, 115, 116–117; site exclusivity for, 113, 115, 137n3–137n4, 183n18; U.S. relations influence on, 84, 192–193, 216–217; war legacy recognized by, 17, 23, 29, 206. *See also* family separation

The Rites of Passage (Van Gennep), 22
ritual. *See* political ritual
Robinson, Kenneth R., 41–42
Robinson, Michael, 46
Roh Moo-hyun: neoliberalism under, 203–204; Peace and Prosperity Policy of, 9; reconciliation under, 11
Roh Tae-woo, 33n61, 84
ROK. *See* Republic of Korea
Roosevelt, Franklin D., 49
Russia. *See* Soviet Union
Russo–Japanese War, 43
Ryang, Sonia, 181

Ryukyu, 41

Salmon, Andrew, 88n9
Samsung, xviii
Second Battle of Seoul, 13
Self-Defense Forces, 58–59
Seoul, South Korea: COEX in, 113, 115–117, 119; fieldwork in, xvii; in Korean War, 13, 53, 55. *See also* reunions
SEZs. *See* Special Economic Zones
Sherman, Daniel, 136
Shin, Gi-Wook, 12–13; on blood-based nationalism, 47; on colonial protests, 49
Shin, Michael, 44
Shiri, 207
Sigal, Leon, 85
Sin Ch'ae-ho, 48
Sinocentric tributary system: Chosŏn dynasty and, 41–42; collapse of, 43
Sino–Japanese Wars, 43, 48
SNCC. *See* South–North Coordinating Committee
social capital, 104–105
socialism, 46–47
social outcast. *See* Wangdda
Southerners, Northerners (Lee, H.), 75–76
South Korea: agriculture reform in, 44; citizens joining KPA, 74; cosmopolitanism in, 189–192; distrust of Northerners, 97–98; economic status of, 101–102, 110n10; elections in, 9, 10, 18, 33n61, 86, 102, 217; financial crisis reaction of, 101–102, 133; fleeing, reasons, 74; flood aid acceptance by, 83; neoliberal economics in, 103; presidential campaign (2012), 10; social development in, 10; transparency in, 132–135; U.S. economic aid to, 110n10. *See also* Republic of Korea
South–North Coordinating Committee (SNCC), 82
South to North crossing. *See* Wŏlbukcha families
Soviet Union, 40; Korean War and, 20, 57, 60–62, 68; national division and, 50–53; NPT withdrawal and, 85; occupation of North approach by,

51–52; as rival power, 39; sovereignty
  dismissal by, 50. See also U.S.–Soviet
  relations
Special Economic Zones (SEZs), 192
Stalin: communist expansion and, 56, 59;
  and Korean War onset, 49, 60, 61;
  North Korean support of, 57, 66n79;
  pro-Japanese elements and, 52
statistics, 29n3, 30n6, 222n7
stigmatization and marginalization: in
  family separation, 28, 80–81, 121–122,
  164–167, 181–182, 195, 200–201,
  212n33; liminality and, 122, 138n11
Sullivan, Walter, 68
Sunshine Policy: Cold War and, 8;
  consequences of, 9; criticism of, 10,
  105–106; goal of, 8; Kim Dae-jung and,
  8, 9, 86–87, 105–106; support for, 11,
  131
Syngman Rhee, 20, 51, 61; anticommunist
  campaign of, 70; policies of, 52, 70,
  155; unification by force and, 56,
  65n56–65n57

taboos: subject, in fieldwork, xxv,
  143–144, 200; with vernacular, xxvin5;
  war memory, 14, 17; Wŏlbukcha
  families and, 143–144
Tae GukGi: The Brotherhood of War,
  187–189
Taoism, 43
Tarlo, Emma, 18
tenant unions, 49
territorialization, 39–40
Theses on the Philosophy of History
  (Benjamin), 25
38th parallel. See Demilitarized Zone
Tikhonov, Vladimir, 41
Tirman, John, 67, 88n2
Tonghak Movement, 42–43
Truth and Reconciliation Commission
  (TRC), 68–69, 105
Turner, Victor, 22, 106, 121, 208

UN. See United Nations
UNC: bombings by, 68; POW exchange
  negotiation by, 78–79; POWs held by,
  77

The Unending Korean War (Kim, Dong-
  Choon), 69
unification: ambivalence to, 26–27; first
  statement on, 82; Kim Il-sung policy
  on, 56, 82; Korean War and drive
  toward, 56, 59; Korea's history and, 40;
  in popular culture, 27; Syngman
  Rhee's, by force, 56, 65n56–65n57
United Nations (UN), 55, 85
United Nations Korean Reconstruction
  Agency, 68
United States (U.S.), 40; anticommunist
  regime of, 51, 55, 57, 62; armistice
  talks and, 90n40; Chinese Revolution
  response of, 58; imperialism of, 31n35;
  Japan's rearmament by, 58–59, 59–60,
  61, 62; Korean War and, 20, 57; Korean
  War apathy in, 68; military and
  economic aid from, 82, 110n10;
  military exercises with, 84, 216–217;
  national division and, 50–53; North
  Korea mediations with, 85–86;
  occupation in South, 69; policies with
  Japan, 58–59; reconciliation support
  reversal by, 192–193; research
  participant suspicion of, xxii–xxiii;
  reunions influenced by, 84, 192–193,
  216–217; as rival power, 39;
  sovereignty dismissal by, 50. See also
  U.S.–Soviet relations
USAMGIK. See U.S. Military Government
  in Korea
U.S.–DPRK Nuclear Framework
  Agreement, 85–86
The Use of Pleasure (Foucault), 174–175
U.S. Military Government in Korea
  (USAMGIK), 51, 69, 71
U.S.–Soviet relations: deterioration of, 52,
  57; in Korean War beginning, 20, 57;
  national division as result of, 50–53
uterine family, 126

Van Gennep, Arnold, 22, 121, 208
vernacular: in fieldwork, xx; kinship
  terminology in, xix–xx; taboos with,
  xxvin5; for women, xx
Vietnam, 67, 68, 82

Wangdda, 175–178

war survivors: memories of, 14, 16, 17;
missing family trauma of, 21; as
refugees, 79
Watts, Michael, 104
Who Ate Up All the Shinga? (Park, W.),
183n14
Wilson, Richard, 105
Wisebook.com, 98–100, 99
Wŏlbukcha families, 74–75; background
checks of, 155–156, 169, 178–179;
discrimination and surveillance of,
154–157, 178–180; kin-based
punishment and, 157; loyalty to state or
kin of, 176–178; post-Summit view of,
121, 138, 198; pre-Summit view of,
79–80; taboo of, 143–144
Wolf, Margery, 126

Wŏllammin families, 73, 74–75, 121, 198
women, 15, 182n2; enslavement by
Japanese, 14–15; family separation for,
80, 162–164; vernacular for, xx. *See
also* comfort women; mothers
World Bank, 104–105
World War II: colonization influence after,
52; independence after, 49–50;
Japanese atrocities in, 14–15; memories
of, 14, 16; national division after, 40

Yoneyuki Sugita, 58
Yoshida, 58

Zamindar, Vazira Fazila-Yacoobali, 29n2
Žižek, Slavoj, 203–204

About the Author

Nan Kim is associate professor in the Department of History at the University of Wisconsin–Milwaukee. Trained as a cultural anthropologist, she has pursued research at the intersection of memory studies, contemporary history, and the anthropology of politics. A native of New York City, she earned her bachelor's degree in English language and literature from Princeton University and her doctoral degree in sociocultural anthropology from the University of California–Berkeley. Her work has appeared in the *Journal of Asian Studies* and the *Routledge Handbook of Memory and Reconciliation in East Asia* (2015), and she is a regional editor of the *Asian Journal of Peacebuilding*.